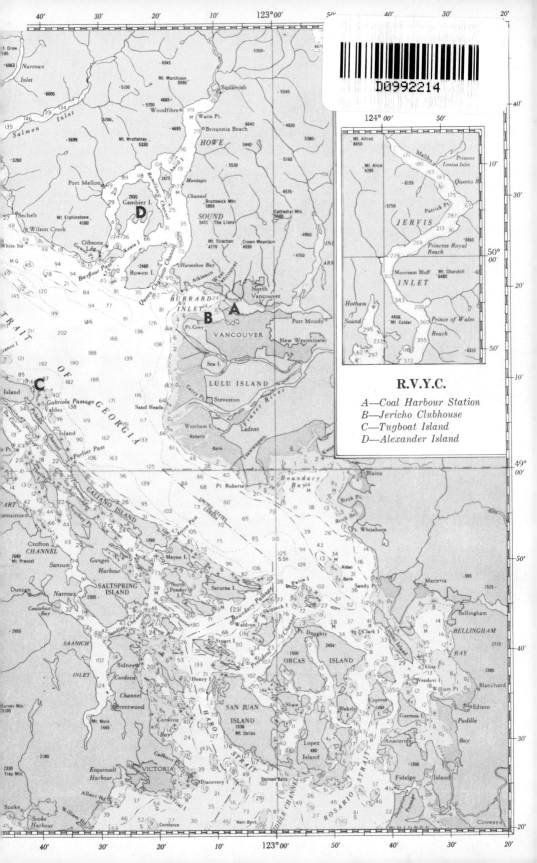

R.V.Y.C.

A—Coal Harbour Station
B—Jericho Clubhouse
C—Tugboat Island
D—Alexander Island

Annals of the Royal Vancouver Yacht Club
1903-1965

Annals
of the
Royal Vancouver Yacht Club
1903-1965

History of the Club's founding
Granting of the Royal Charter
Prominent early yachtsmen
Racing contests and trophies

Officers of the Club and a general review of sail and power boat activity for sixty-two years in the waters of Burrard Inlet and English Bay, Vancouver, B.C. and Gulf of Georgia, British Columbia, Canada

Condensed and rewritten from records of G. B. Warren, first Historian of the Club, and the personal recollections of the members of the History Committee, R.V.Y.C.
by
NORMAN HACKING

Compiled, Arranged and Edited
by
GEORGE A. CRAN

Published under the supervision of the History Committee
of the Royal Vancouver Yacht Club

Evergreen Press, Vancouver, B.C.

Copyright, 1965, R.V.Y.C.

Second Edition Copyright, 1971, R.V.Y.C.

Contents

Foreword

Acknowledgement

Frontispiece

Foreword

This is a record of events, ships and individuals who have contributed much to the advancement of organized sailing and cruising in the area covering many hundred square miles of sheltered waters at the front door of Canada's western metropolis — VANCOUVER, realistically termed "a yachting paradise".

Perhaps many notable events and persons have not been recorded — due to lost or destroyed records, but it is an effort to set forth the Royal Vancouver Yacht Club's contribution to the sport of boating and the development of vigorous, healthy and happy Canadians.

GEORGE A. CRAN,
Editor.

Acknowledgement

The History Committee acknowledges with grateful thanks the loan of many private scrap-books and snap-shot albums from senior club members. These have materially assisted in the preparation of this work, supplementing original records compiled by the late Gordon B. Warren, and it is hoped that pictures and references from these will be donated to the Club as a permanent historical exhibit in the Jericho Club-house. Unfortunately many interesting pictures were too faded to reproduce here.

The Editor has also received invaluable assistance from many members, notably Miss Patricia Maitland, Mrs. Temple H. Wright, Mr. Eric Marsden, Mr. E. S. Earle and Mr. A. H. Jefferd.

MEMBERS OF THE

History Committee

ROYAL VANCOUVER YACHT CLUB

1962-1965

HARRY J. BIRD, *Chairman*
Hon. Treasurer 1950-51

W. G. BREEZE
Vice-Commodore 1914-15, Rear Commodore 1912-13,
Hon. Secretary 1924, 1946-49, Hon. Treasurer 1909, 1919

GEORGE A. CRAN, *Editor*
Hon. Secretary 1952-57

W. H. DAY
P.I.Y.A. Hon. Secretary 1945-56, P.C.Y.C. Hon. Secretary 1950-52

COL. C. C. FERRIE
Rear Commodore 1939, Staff Captain 1936-38

A. H. JEFFERD
Hon. Hydrographer 1940 continuously for twenty-one years till 1960

CAPT. B. L. JOHNSON, c.b.e., d.s.o., r.c.n.
Commodore 1929, 1930, 1936, 1950, Vice-Commodore 1925, 1926, 1928, 1931,
Rear Commodore 1921, 1923

E. D. STONE, *Photo Editor*
Rear Commodore 1951, 1952

R.V.Y.C. — THEN — 1903

First Clubhouse, foot of Bute St., Coal Harbour.
Vancouver City Archives.

Early yachts racing on Burrard Inlet. Old C.P.R. coal hulk, ROBERT KERR at extreme right.
Vancouver City Archives.

R.V.Y.C. — NOW — 1965

Coal Harbour Station and moorings Stanley Park, Vancouver.

Chisholm Photo.   *Jericho Clubhouse on English Bay, Vancouver.*

R.V.Y.C. Clubhouse, Stanley Park, 1912. This building still stands west of our present Station. It was sold to the Dominion Government in 1930 for R.C.N.V.R. use before H.M.C.S. Discovery was established on Deadman's Island shown with its squatter shacks in the background beyond part of our Coal Harbour moorings.

CHAPTER 1

Founding of Yachting

BURRARD INLET, ENGLISH BAY
AND THE GULF OF GEORGIA

FROM THE EARLIEST DAYS of human habitation on Burrard Inlet the most practical means of transport was by water. The Indian tribesmen who were settled on both sides of the inlet travelled everywhere in their dugout canoes, and sometimes hoisted a crude blanket sail to ease the labour of paddling. Later, after the coming of the white man the native population utilized discarded flour sacks fashioning very acceptable and useful sails.

The first European visitors to sight Burrard Inlet came by sail on July 5th, 1791, when Don Jose Maria Narvaez and the crew of the 36 foot schooner *Santa Saturina* from Spain sailed into the outer waters of our present day magnificent harbour.

The first yachtsman may be said to have arrived a year later, when Captain George Vancouver R.N. and members of his crew surveyed the upper reaches of the inlet as far as present day Port Moody. His Majesty's ships *Discovery* and *Chatham* were not employed for this purpose. They were too large and unwieldy to navigate the narrow inlet waters and were anchored at Birch Bay. Vancouver used instead two small tenders, a yawl and a launch, which operated under both sail and oar power.

On the first memorable voyage into Burrard Inlet beyond the First Narrows, Captain Vancouver commanded the yawl and Lieut. Peter Puget the launch. They apparently passed through the First Narrows under sail, for Vancouver relates that after being greeted by about fifty Indians, "For the sake of the company of our new friends, we stood on under easy sail, which encouraged them to attend us some little distance up the arm."

The English sailors spent the night of June 13th 1792 at Port Moody, most of them sleeping in their boats. Some of the crew preferred to sleep ashore, as many a yachtsman has done since. However they didn't take into account the rising tide, and were rudely awakened when nearly afloat. As Vancouver wrote: "One of them slept so sound, that I believe

1

he might have been conveyed to some distance, had he not been awakened by his companions".

For seventy years after the visit of Captain Vancouver, Burrard Inlet remained almost in its primeval state. In 1858 H.M.S. *Plumper* made a new survey of the inlet, and a trail to Port Moody from New Westminster was completed in 1859, but it was not until 1863 that the first sawmill was built on the North Shore, later to be known as Moody-ville. Four years later the first mill on the south shore of the inlet began operations, Hastings Mill, at the foot of Dunlevy Avenue.

The mills brought a steady influx of deepsea sailing ships, and also created a resident population. There was little recreation beyond boozing in the numerous saloons of Gastown, as the future city of Vancouver was known.

The sailing ships were often in port for months at a time, and many seamen deserted for the Cariboo gold mines. The officers remained, however, and to relieve the tedium during the summer months, frequent races were held in the harbour in the longboats and whalers belonging to the deepsea vessels.

Permanent residents, approximately 1000 around 1885, also built their own sloops and cutters, both for normal transport and for pleasure. A primitive steam ferry ran across the inlet in these early days, but it was more reliable to use sails or oars. Some of the young men of the two sawmill villages built their own sloops, and this resulted in the first organized racing on the inlet, usually on Dominion Day or on the Queen's Birthday.

R. H. Alexander, manager of Hastings Mill, was an enthusiastic yachtsman, and so were his three sons, Dick, Harry and Fred. He organized annual races off the mill docks, and competitors came from New Westminster, Nanaimo, Bellingham and Victoria. The open sailboats were tied to a line stretched between the wharves until the signal was given to start.

With the arrival of the first C.P.R. transcontinental train at Port Moody in 1885, Burrard Inlet suddenly became a hive of activity, as thousands poured in to make their fortunes in the new city of promise, which was to be incorporated as Vancouver next year.

Sailing quickly became the most popular outdoor pastime in the young community. Roads were few and far between and the hinterland was undeveloped, so the young men naturally took to the sea. Many built their own open deck or half deck sloops, for materials were cheap. Others rented boats, which were available from Andy Linton's wharf at the foot of Carrall Street. There were three pioneer boat builders in the city, all of whom turned out fast and sturdy craft. Andy Linton's

May was described as the fastest boat on the inlet, while her rivals were Capt. Billy Watts' *Siren* and Haydon's *C.P.R.*

On May 24th 1886, when Vancouver had been only incorporated for a month, the harbour was alive with sailing craft for the holiday. Soon match races were being arranged by eager young yachtsmen, and sizable wagers were changing hands. On June 6th the new yacht *Senor* outdistanced the sloop *Marcia*, owned by Calvert Simson of Hastings Mill store. On July 25th Alderman Cordiner's new *Effie* outstripped them all in a high wind. The *Senor* gave up and the *Marcia* came third. Other boats racing that memorable first season included Art Sullivan's *Adele*, and the *Galatea, Puritan, Priscilla* and *Addie*.

Next season many new boats were added to the local yachting fleet, and plans got under way soon for the first yacht club on the inlet. On May 27th it was announced that the Burrard Inlet Sailing Club had been formed, with Henry Bell-Irving as Chairman and E. E. Rand as Secretary. There were 16 charter members enrolled. It was planned to build a slip, a floating wharf and a boathouse at once.

The city's first regatta was held on July 1st 1887, in honour of the Queen's Jubilee. R. H. Alexander and W. E. Graveley were the judges, and $325 was donated as prize money. The course was from the City Wharf at the foot of Carrall to a flag boat near Moodyville, then to a flag boat off Deadman's Island and back to the wharf. There were two races . . . one for half-decked boats under 30 feet, and one for undecked boats under 22 feet.

In the years that followed, yachting became one of the city's most widely popular sports, and races were held every July 1st. In 1888 handicapping was introduced under American Yacht Racing Association rules. At the Dominion Day Regatta the first prize for a boat over 20 feet and under 30 feet was $100, and the second prize was $25. For boats under 20 feet, the prizes were $25 and $10. Boats racing that day in the first class included the *Mayflower, Annie, Laura, Rob Roy, Thistle* and *Loran*.

But for some reason organized yacht clubs didn't seem to flourish in early Vancouver. The Burrard Inlet Sailing Club languished and died, and was succeeded in 1891 by the B.C. Yacht Racing Association, with Walter Graveley as President and George Cassady as Vice President.

Then came the economic slump of 1894, Vancouver fell on hard times, and the association died. There was another attempt at revival in 1897 when the first Vancouver Yacht Club was formed. R. Y. Ellis was Commodore, C. Gardner Johnson, Vice-Commodore and Walter Graveley, Fleet Captain. Clubrooms were secured in the Whetham Block at the northeast corner of Cordova and Cambie, and sailing headquarters were Andy Linton's float at the foot of Carrall.

This venture also languished and died, but after the turn of the century Vancouver began to boom again, and yachting once more became a popular sport. By 1902 there were more than a dozen yachts competing in organized racing on Burrard Inlet, although no yacht club existed. Some of the crack sloops of that day were Alex Grant's *Glendochart*, 16 feet at the waterline, built in 1897; Andy Linton's *May*, Hayden's *Triton*, and C. S. V. Branch's *Orphan*. Alex Grant also raced the *Siren*, built by Capt. Billy Watts, a five-tonner, 30 feet overall and carrying 1200 sq. ft. of sail. Unlimited sail spread and sandbag ballast were much in vogue in those days.

A big event of the 1902 season was a race around Bowen Island between V. M. Dafoe's 30 foot sloop *Halcyon*, which he had built in 1897, and the Columbia River class centreboard sloop *Pirate*, 27 feet at the waterline, owned by Springer Brothers. There was a good wind and *Pirate*, being a heavy weather boat, left *Halcyon* far behind. *Pirate* crossed the line at English Bay in a very fresh westerly and there being no time to reduce the press of sail, she headed for the beach, and with her centreboard hauled up, she ran high and dry up on the sand. *Halcyon* came boiling along about six miles behind out of sight and seeing no sign of her rival standing by nor heading for First Narrows, concluded she had dropped out, and proceeded to celebrate winning the race, after crossing the line. They never dreamt that *Pirate* was "on the beach"— no place for such a ship—and it was a discomfited crew that learned after returning to moorings, that their celebration was premature.

There was also a big increase in yachting interest at Seattle in 1902, in which year an English firm offered the Mackie Trophy, a goat's head snuff moll, for international competition on the north Pacific Coast. Although there had been international competition in previous years, it was obvious that a strong new yacht club was necessary in Vancouver if it was to be revived. The Seattle Times took upon itself to light the spark, and started a vigorous newspaper campaign to re-establish a yacht club in Vancouver. The newspaper sent a representative to Vancouver who interviewed many prospective members.

The most enthusiastic of these was Walter Graveley, a real estate dealer, who had been closely identified with all the other efforts to form a yacht club. He had sailed in the Canadian challenger for the America's Cup, the *Countess of Dufferin*, in 1876, and was particularly qualified as a yachting authority. He was already called "Commodore" in Vancouver yachting circles, and was described by the Seattle Times as "The daddy of them all in the Vancouver yachting world".

As a result of this impetus, it was announced in late 1902 that a new yacht club would soon be organized, and on February 5th 1903 a meeting was called at Hope, Graveley & Co's. real estate office on Cambie Street. In almost no time flat, the new Vancouver Yacht Club was organized, with Walter E. Graveley elected Commodore; William Hodson, Vice-Commodore; C. S. V. Branch, Captain; O. L. Spencer, Secretary-Treasurer. The management committee comprised J. H. Senkler, K.C., A. G. Thynne and Austin French. The committee was authorized to choose colours and draft by-laws.

Others attending this memorable meeting were Capt. P. N. Thompson, Hilton Keith, Paddy Cambie, Oswald Moseley, Albert Hancock, C. H. Usborne, W. H. Billings, A. C. Burdick, A. E. Bull, K.C., and Bert Austin. Two of this original group who met over sixty years ago, still survive—Oswald Moseley living in Victoria, and Bert Austin in San Diego, California.

Arrangements were soon made to rent the club's first headquarters, a small dinghy house, from the Vancouver Rowing Club, which at that time had its floats immediately west of the C.P.R. wharf, at the foot of Thurlow Street, in Coal Harbour. The original club flag was a Cambridge blue burgee, with a black diamond in the centre.

It was not long before the burgee was flying over the boathouse, and it was announced that there were 18 yachts in the club's fleet. The roster was as follows:

Commodore Graveley's *Margot*, a 20 foot keel cabin sloop.
P. N. Thompson's *Bertha*, a 35 foot aux. cruising yawl.
Oswald Moseley's *Thelma*, a 25 foot waterline, keel cabin sloop.
E. W. Stark's sloop *Alpha*.
A. J. Hancock's sloop *Petrel*, 25½ foot waterline.
A. G. Thynne's *Golliwog*, a 35 foot yawl.
Austin French's *Trixie*, a 33 foot cabin yawl.
Alexander Grant's *Siren*, a 30 foot half-deck clinker built sloop.
Mr. Hooper's *Norma*.
William McDougall's *Rob Roy*, a centreboard sloop.
H. W. Robertson's *Rip Rip*, a centreboard sloop 19 foot waterline.
Rev. John Antle's *Laverock*, a sloop.
William Hodson's *Frolic*, an open deck yawl.
Paddy Cambie's *Pirate*, a Columbia River centreboard sloop 27 ft. waterline.
Hilton Keith's *Maple Leaf*, a half-deck sloop 20 feet overall.
Gorden Legg's *Waterwag*, a lugger.
Albert Austin's *Addie*, an open cat-boat 19 feet waterline.
Alexander Grant's *Glendochart*, a flush deck sloop 16 feet waterline.

Although these may be considered the nucleus of the fleet, as it existed in May 1903, there were many additions as the season progressed. By August the following were flying the club's burgee:

W. H. Billings' *Mischief*, a Columbia River sloop, 27 ft. waterline.
C. S. V. Branch's *Nancy*, a yawl 31 ft. overall.

William Hodson's *Jabberwock,* a sloop 25 ft. waterline.

Robert Cassady's *Banshee,* a sloop known as "Irish" Banshee, 19 ft. waterline.

Austin French's *Banshee,* a yawl known as "French" Banshee, 19 ft. waterline.

E. W. Stark's *Edna Meryl,* a sloop 17 ft. waterline.

A. D. Hossak's *Irish,* a sloop 13 ft. waterline.

Fred Lucas' *Blue Grouse,* a sloop 13 ft. waterline.

F. W. Fisher's *Hiawatha,* a sloop 13 ft. waterline.

P. W. Charleson's *Halcyon,* a sloop 30 ft. overall.

The first organized race by the new club was held in August over the English Bay course for the Hodson Cup, presented by Vice-Commodore William Hodson. The race turned out to be a bit of a fiasco, due to the failure of the marker buoys to remain in their allotted positions. Seventeen yachts took place in the race, which was on a triangular course from English Bay Beach to a buoy off Great Northern Cannery to a buoy off Spanish Bank.

As the leading yachts approached the place where the first buoy ought to have been, they were surprised to find it was not in sight. The yachts flitted around a bit until Commodore Graveley, sailing *Golliwog,* spied it—turned turtle and the fishes playing with the flag. Those that could manage it rounded the buoy and headed across the bay to the south shore. Here the buoy was sighted well up on the shore near the English Bay Cannery, foot of Bayswater Street, so the idea of rounding it had to be abandoned. The survivors of the race headed for the finish line anyhow, with Robert Cassady's little "Irish" *Banshee* getting across the line first.

The first Hodson Cup contest was raced again the following Saturday. Twenty boats were entered, including two important new additions to the club fleet. These were R. H. Alexander's big 46 foot yawl *Claymore* and William Hodson's 32 foot speedy sloop *Wideawake.* The *Claymore* had formerly been the pilot boat at the Skunk Cove pilot station (Caufield's) and was soon re-named *Slani.* The *Wideawake* came from Victoria, and soon made a reputation as the fastest yacht in the Vancouver fleet, particularly under the ownership and handling of E. B. "Jimmy" Deane, who acquired her in 1905.

Of the early trophies, the most keenly contested for a number of years was the Graveley Cup, presented in 1903 by Commodore Graveley for yachts under twenty feet load waterline. The course for the Graveley trophy ran from Deadman's Island to a buoy off Moodyville to a buoy off the Indian Mission. The Cup had to be won three times before becoming the property of any yachtsman. The winner of the first race for the Graveley trophy was the little *Blue Grouse,* sailed by Fred Lucas,

Sloop MARGOT, 1903, flagship of first Commodore, W. E. Graveley.

Sloop THELMA, 1903, owned by Oswald Moseley.

Aux. ketch MAPLE LEAF, 1905, built and owned by Alexander Maclaren of Barnet Sawmill.

later Mr. Justice Lucas. The cup was finally won in 1912 by Horace Stone in the fast *Adanac,* which he built himself.

After a successful first season, the club members decided that they needed a clubhouse and permanent headquarters. H. O. Alexander proposed that the club rooms and yacht moorings should be at Jericho in English Bay, several miles from the city. He argued "the anchorage is fine and the position sheltered and far from the turmoil of city life". But it was considered much too far from city life for the majority of members, and it was not until 1927 that the Jericho Clubhouse was officially opened close to the location favoured by Mr. Alexander.

The chosen new location was a leased waterfront lot just west of the foot of Bute Street. A floating clubhouse was built, 30 by 60 feet, two stories in height. The lower part was used for storage while quarters for members were fitted on the upper floor. A long landing float ran out from the clubhouse to deep water.

Today, 1963, this structure is still in use as the spar house at the Coal Harbour Station, it having been floated over in 1905 from its original location and some years later set on piles on the Stanley Park foreshore.

In order to finance the clubhouse, members subscribed $800. Fourteen members bought life memberships for $50, a bargain that they never regretted. The original 14 Life Members were as follows:

C. S. V. Branch	Alexander Grant	
George G. Bushby	William Hodson	J. H. Senkler, K.C.
E. B. Deane	M. H. Leggatt	Arthur G. Thynne
Austin French	Oswald Moseley	P. N. Thompson
Walter E. Graveley	C. C. McCaul, K.C.	W. E. Thompson

Of these, Oswald Moseley is still a member 60 years after, and living in retirement in Victoria. He is still actively interested in yacht club affairs.

At the end of the first season it was reported that the Vancouver Yacht Club had 100 active members and a fleet of 25 vessels. Walter Graveley was re-elected Commodore, William Hodson Vice-Commodore, and the executive committee members were R. H. Alexander, C. S. V. Branch and Oswald Moseley. O. L. Spencer was re-elected Secretary-treasurer.

By 1904 the Vancouver Yacht Club was a lively and integral part of Vancouver's sporting and social life. Many important additions were made to the fleet that year, including the first power launches, of which the most notable was B. T. Rogers' *Mow Ping,* a teak hulled steam powered vessel which he had built at Hong Kong in 1901 and shipped to Vancouver on the deck of one of the C.P.R. Empress liners.

Walter Graveley built the 33 foot cruising yawl *Eileen,* which had a long career in the club under various owners. Other additions included C. B. Wainwright's sloop *Narbethong;* the cruising yawl *Yuno,* owned by Frank Wright, father of the future Commodore Temple H. Wright; the former Nanaimo pilot boat *Dawendeena,* a sloop purchased by Oswald Moseley; the big aux. schooner *Maple Leaf,* owned by Alex. Maclaren; C. O. Julian's sloop *Delores;* the 36 foot centreboard sloop *Britannia,* a sandbagger owned by F. G. N. Seaton; Albert Austin's *Madeline* from Seattle; and J. C. Cripps' sloop *Titania.*

"Barney" Johnson began his association with the yacht club in 1904 when he acquired the speedy *Siren* from Alex. Grant, his future father-in-law. Sixty years later 'Barney" is still racing regularly in the inlet and English Bay.

Of the smaller racing craft, the most notable additions in 1904 were the *Cheemaun, Tillicum* and *Redskin. Tillicum* and *Redskin* were sister ships, formerly owned in Victoria and designed by C. D. Mower, the noted New York designer of the day. Two others of 'the same design, the *Aloha* and *Marietta,* subsequently joined the fleet, so that for the first time in its history, the yacht club had a uniform class for racing.

The *Tillicum* was 24 feet overall by 6.6 feet beam by 4½ feet draught. She was 16 feet at the waterline and carried 1000 pounds of lead keel. "Jimmy" Deane was the first local owner of *Tillicum* and Harry Frith brought in the *Redskin.* These two began their long rivalry on July 8th 1904, competing for the Graveley Cup at the club's first annual regatta. On the Burrard Inlet course to Moodyville, the *Tillicum* came in the winner by 42 seconds over *Redskin,* followed by *Cheemaun* and "Irish" *Banshee.* At the same regatta the first international race for the Mackie Trophy was held, the prize going to *Gwendolyn* of Seattle, with Hodson's *Wideawake* a close second.

The club had hardly been established for a year in their new clubhouse at the foot of Bute Street before it was apparent that another move was necessary. The club was growing so fast, the quarters were already inadequate, while the increasing value of foreshore property also indicated a move was needed.

Lease of a site on the Coal Harbour shore of Stanley Park was secured from the park commissioners, and early in 1905 the floating clubhouse was towed across to the new site, lying in the shelter of Deadman's Island. By this time the club had 187 members and 43 craft flew its burgee, including four power boats.

Coincident with the move to the new location, application was made through the Governor-General for a royal charter, which would give the club the right to use the prefix "Royal", and for members to fly the blue ensign under warrant.

Announcement of the arrival of the Royal Warrant was made by Commodore Graveley at the annual meeting on February 1st 1906. The

Aux. Cutter LAVITA, 1909, owner
E. W. McLean, Skipper C. O. Julian.

H. F. Burton-Brooke 1909,
for many years Hon. Secretary.

Sloop REDSKIN, 1912—a Half Rater, 24 ft., Mower design.

first blue ensigns were then presented to the owners of yachts that were qualified to wear them. These were as follows:

R. H. Alexander, sloop *Slani*.
Rev. John Antle, schooner *Columbia*. ✓
Albert Austin, sloop *Madeline*.
Dr. Duncan Bell-Irving, schooner *Agnes*.
P. W. Charleson, sloop *Halcyon*.
Alexander Grant, sloop *Irene*.
Alexander Maclaren, schooner *Maple Leaf*. ✓
C. B. MacNeill, yawl *Golliwog*.
Oswald Moseley, yawl *Nancy*.
William McDougall, sloop *Rob Roy*.
B. T. Rogers, steam yacht *Mow Ping*. ✓
F. T. Schooley, schooner *Dawendeena*.

It is told that there was some consternation when it was discovered that B. T. Rogers was not entitled to fly the blue ensign on the *Mow Ping* because he was an American citizen. He quickly remedied this oversight by applying for and receiving British citizenship.

At this time R. G. Macpherson, then Federal M.P. for Vancouver, was made an Honorary Life Member of the club, the first to be so honoured, for his assistance in forwarding the application for the Royal Warrant. A new club burgee was designed also, to include the royal crown.

Walter Graveley took this opportunity to step down as Commodore, after three years' stint in which he had brought the infant club to a flourishing state. He was elected Honorary Life Commodore. R. H. Alexander was elected the new Commodore, with A. G. Thynne as Vice-Commodore. C. O. Julian succeeded the late O. Leigh Spencer as Secretary.

And so the Royal Vancouver Yacht Club was launched, and plans were promptly put under way for erection of a new clubhouse at the Stanley Park site, with provision for a large assembly hall, numerous smaller rooms, and wide verandahs encircling the whole building.

One of the two surviving charter members, Albert Austin of San Diego, California, the other being Oswald Moseley, Victoria, tells of the personalities and yachts that were active during the first years of the Club.

"I well remember the birth of the Vancouver Yacht Club, as it was then called. Eighteen of us met on Feb. 5, 1903 at Hope, Graveley and Co's. real estate office. I was a member of the Vancouver Rowing Club committee at the time, so I was asked by the new club to see if we could put a small float alongside the Rowing Club, which was at the foot of Bute Street at that time.

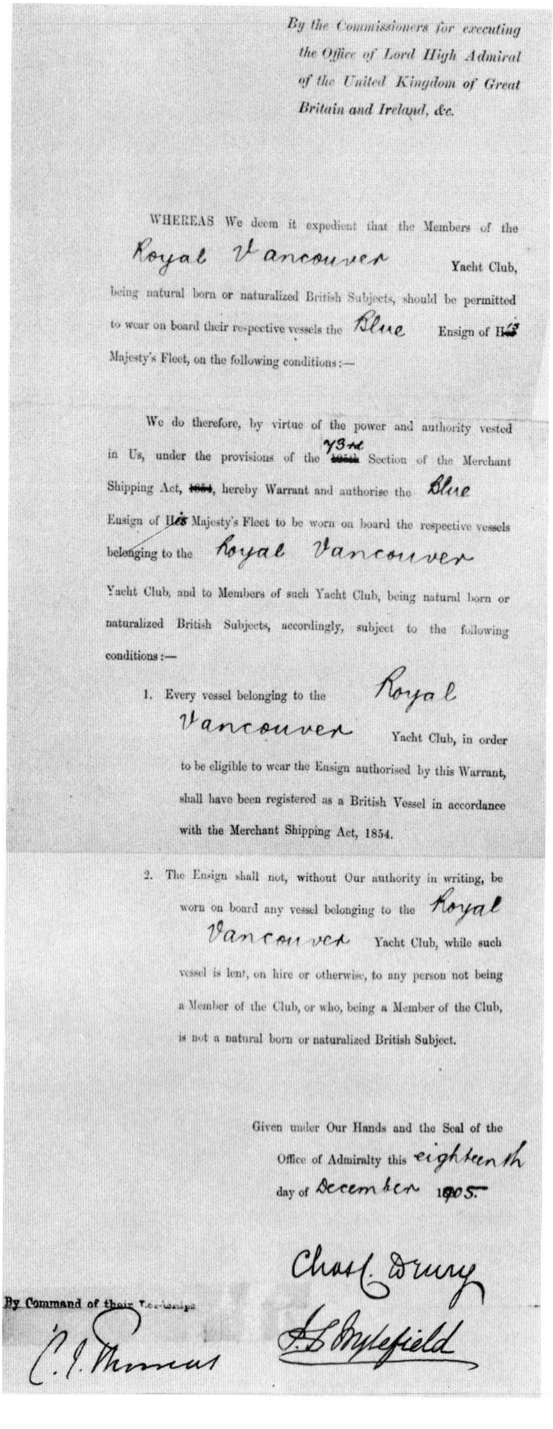

By the Commissioners for executing
the Office of Lord High Admiral
of the United Kingdom of Great
Britain and Ireland, &c.

WHEREAS We deem it expedient that the Members of the *Royal Vancouver* Yacht Club, being natural born or naturalized British Subjects, should be permitted to wear on board their respective vessels the *Blue* Ensign of His Majesty's Fleet, on the following conditions:—

We do therefore, by virtue of the power and authority vested in Us, under the provisions of the *73rd* Section of the Merchant Shipping Act, 1854, hereby Warrant and authorise the *Blue* Ensign of His Majesty's Fleet to be worn on board the respective vessels belonging to the *Royal Vancouver* Yacht Club, and to Members of such Yacht Club, being natural born or naturalized British Subjects, accordingly, subject to the following conditions:—

1. Every vessel belonging to the *Royal Vancouver* Yacht Club, in order to be eligible to wear the Ensign authorised by this Warrant, shall have been registered as a British Vessel in accordance with the Merchant Shipping Act, 1854.

2. The Ensign shall not, without Our authority in writing, be worn on board any vessel belonging to the *Royal Vancouver* Yacht Club, while such vessel is lent, on hire or otherwise, to any person not being a Member of the Club, or who, being a Member of the Club, is not a natural born or naturalized British Subject.

Given under Our Hands and the Seal of the Office of Admiralty this *eighteenth* day of *December* 1905.

Chas. Drury

By Command of their Lordships

C. I. Thomas   *F. L. Brydefield*

*Royal Warrant to
fly the Blue Ensign.*

"Our first regatta was in the first week of July, and many yachts towed over from Victoria where the international regatta had taken place a few days before.

"The Johnson boys from Seattle in *Gwendolyn* won the Class A and *Madeline* won Class B, beating the A class, although starting ten minutes or so behind them. Ted Geary of Seattle won the Class C with *Empress*, a 26 foot length overall sloop built much like the flatties he later designed. At this regatta Ted Geary was in knee pants, and had with him as crew Jim Griffiths.

"Next spring I bought *Madeline* and brought her to Vancouver. We raced the *Britannia* and beat her handily. In the fall of 1904 I sailed *Madeline* down to Seattle and raced the *Gwendolyn* for the Mackie Trophy. It was on a Sunday afternoon in Elliott Bay, and we were beaten 14 seconds by *Gwendolyn*, after breaking down several minutes on the windward leg.

"That fall the *Wideawake* was brought from Victoria by William Hodson, who operated the Metropole Hotel at that time. The Lucas boys had a small sloop, the *Blue Grouse*, a one design built by Vic Dafoe, a really good builder, though at that time we thought he was high priced.

"He also built the *Golliwog* for A. G. Thynne, I believe, and the small yawl *Vera*, owned by Owen Sawyer. Austin French built a sloop called *La Hirondelle*, and Jimmy Cripps brought the sloop *Titania* over from Victoria, a bit over 30 feet. I beat her badly with *Madeline*.

"Then the Cao boys built a centreboard sloop from "Rudder" plans. They named her *Swipe* because they got every piece of timber from the keel to the foredeck from Stanley Park one night. That same year, 1906, Spec Jewitt built a 36 foot sloop called *Intrepid* after a design by Bert Griffiths, who had designed and built *Madeline*. However *Madeline* cleaned her, too.

"At the big regatta in Vancouver in 1905 I started late in Class B and was beaten by Harry Abbott in the Seattle yacht *Ariadne*, a fast centreboarder. We almost nipped her at the finish. At that time Vancouver Shipyard built *Gazeka*, a 40 foot yawl, built on the same lines as *Lila*, winner of the second Bermuda race. Later she was raced by Ron Maitland, who first owned *Dione*, which came from Victoria. "Mike" Cassidy, the lawyer, had a small sloop, the *Banshee*, and she was fast, too.

"We had several of the Half Rater 24 foot Mower designs, such as *Marietta*, *Redskin* and *Aloha*. They were one of the first one design classes on the coast.

"I remember a chap named C. B. Wainwright had a patent centre-board, and he built a nice sloop called *Narbethong*, and used to race her against *Madeline*. Then there were many fine weekend trips we made to Skunk Cove and Bowen Island and Indian Arm. The Cao boys and Wainwright and several others, including Charlie Julian and his old sloop *Delores*, used to have some fine Saturday nights singing and keeping the natives awake until early morning.

"Among other sloops at the time the club was formed were the *Triton*, owned by Ham Hayden who ran a boathouse near the foot of Abbott Street, and the *Spray*, owned by Billy Findlay. Phil Thompson had a long double ended centreboard yawl called the *Bertha*, a nice comfy boat. Phil was a crack trapshooter, and used her for duck hunting.

"Vic Dafoe had a small cutter-rigged boat called *Halcyon*. About 1904 there was a match race around Bowen Island from a start at English Bay between *Halcyon* and a Columbia River fishing type boat called *Pirate*, and *Pirate* won easily.

"Billy Stark, who was one of the original 18, had a topsail sloop called *Alpha*. We spent the 24th of May 1903 at Nanaimo and won our first sailing race in *Alpha*. I remember we had a hectic trip home, with head winds and seas, and much to our surprise the Vancouver boys met in Howe Sound next morn just before noon. Billy Stark later sold his sloop *Alpha* and bought a small schooner, the *Yuno*, afterwards a yawl. One of the early boats was the yawl *Nancy*, owned by Oswald Moseley, who later sold her, and had the schooner *Tenderfoot*. The latter was a fine sea boat, and is now a modern looking sloop lying at the Seattle Yacht Club. Another fine old sloop at the turn of the century was the fast *May*, owned by Andy Linton, the boat builder. The Lucas brothers, Fred and Eddie, had a small sloop called *Chemaun*, one of the one design centreboarders.

"After Charlie Julian sold *Delores* he built the 33 foot sloop *Verona* from a "Rudder" design. Billy McDougall, the boat builder, brought a small centreboarder down from the Arrow Lakes called *Rob Roy* and cleaned up all the small centreboarders. In 1905 he built a nice 30 footer called *Onaway*. She cleaned up the C Class, and was later sold to Okanagan Lake.

"I well remember the regatta at Bellingham in 1906. It was one of the best wins I ever had in yachting circles. *Madeline* won by 23 minutes and almost beat *Gwendolyn* for the Key City Trophy, which was for the fastest time over the course. I was also a member of Victoria Yacht Club, and since the Vancouver gang would not race, I sailed under Victoria colours. I still have the B Class trophy.

"One of the great old-timers in the club was Billy Templeton, who had the 40 foot sloop *Imp*, later the *Amorita*, and in 1921 built the yawl *Tamahnowus* to Small Bros. design. Billy, otherwise known as "Goney", was one of our basketball boys, and a great rugby and lacrosse player.

In an exhibition game in San Francisco against the famous New Zealand All-Blacks he got the ball and ran through most of the New Zealand team and scored, the second time their goal had been crossed in all their world tour.

"Billy had a superstition about drinking out of a tin cup. One time Ted Willis tricked him into drinking out of one. When told about it the next morning, Bill packed his bag and left the ship and cruise.

"The first Secretary of the club was O. L. Spencer, whose son O. Leigh Spencer was the first Junior member, later Publisher of the Vancouver Province newspaper during 1945 and 1946, now retired and living on Salt Spring Island near Ganges Harbour. His father, our first Secretary, was a jolly old chap and I felt the club lost a great member when he passed on. He was a great storyteller, and we used to have some wonderful week-ends at Bedwell Bay and other favourite spots. We had no motors then, and when the tide went up the harbour, we went that way, or out if the tide was ebbing.

"My first boat at the turn of the century was a 16 foot sloop called *Flora*, which I bought from a chap called Jack Thurston. I sailed her several years before having the 27 foot catboat *Addie* built. It was the first boat built at the new Vancouver Shipyard, which was started by Billy Watts, who had come from Lake Superior.

"When the club moved to its original clubhouse at the foot of Bute Street it issued some life memberships at $50, but I was hard up for cash at the time and did not know enough to buy one. But that was a long time ago and the club has since made me an Honorary Life Member.

"The only other surviving original member is Oswald Moseley, now living in Victoria. Moseley was one of the fortunate investors in the $50 life memberships which he certainly has never regretted. He owned and sailed a variety of yachts, the last being *Ashigamik*, a 36 foot schooner built in Seattle."

Signal Cannon Presented

A link with the old days is the Signal Cannon which points over our Jericho moorings from the front lawn of the clubhouse. This venerable piece was presented to the club July 1st 1906 by our member J. E. Macrae, who was the owner and skipper of the 36 foot yawl *Four Winds*.

Diligent search of newspaper files of that period fails to reveal any trace of the origin of this piece. Our current gun or ordnance expert, D. C. McPherson, reputedly an ex-navy armourer, has microscopically examined the relic and reports that it is of Government origin since he has uncovered traces of a Crown on it—but no serial numbers. So we, who relax on our front verandah of a summer's afternoon, idly watching the strenuous efforts of younger sailors to match past racing and "luffing-match" glories, can blythely speculate that here indeed is a contact with the grand old days of fire-belching muzzle-loaders—and in our mind's eye we are again raking the Spaniards or the blood-thirsty pirates as our fore-fathers did under the White Ensign, in the days of yore.

Figurehead from M.V. SYRENE presented 1927 by Rev. John Antle installed at Jericho Clubhouse, English Bay.

Signal Cannon presented by J. E. Macrae 1906.

CHAPTER 2

Early Commodores

ROYAL VANCOUVER YACHT CLUB 1903-1918

W. E. GRAVELEY
Commodore 1903 - 1905

CHAIRMAN OF THE FOUNDING COMMITTEE of enthusiastic yachtsmen who met on February 5th, 1903 in Hope, Graveley & Co. office on Cambie Street to form the Vancouver Yacht Club, was elected the first Commodore. He hoisted his pennant on the sloop *Margot* for the first official cruise in May, 1903 to Bedwell Bay, North Arm, Burrard Inlet where fourteen yachts anchored. For many years previous, Mr. Graveley had been an active yachtsman having been a member of the Royal Canadian Yacht Club, Toronto, winning the Prince of Wales Cup in his cutter *Gorilla* on Lake Ontario in 1871.

He was also a founder of the two local yacht clubs, predecessors that were not successful in weathering formative years — The B.C. Yacht Racing Association in 1891, of which he was President, and The Vancouver Yacht Club in 1897. He held the position of Captain in the latter. Largely through his efforts the Club received the Warrant to fly the Blue Ensign of His Majesty's Fleet with the right to prefix the word Royal to the name of the Club.

In 1876 Mr. Graveley sailed as one of the crew of the America Cup challenger *Countess of Dufferin* in the fourth attempt to lift this notable trophy defended by the schooner *Madeleine*.

He had the 33 ft. yawl *Eileen* built from designs by Mower in 1904 and in 1908 was one of the four joint owners of *Minerva*, brought to this coast from Kowloon, China, where it was built in 1906.

The Graveley Cup was presented by him in 1903, the three time winner and permanent owner of the trophy in 1912 being Horace Stone's *Adanac*. On completing his term of office in 1906 Mr. Graveley was elected Honorary Life Commodore.

Yawl MINERVA in 1907.

R. H. ALEXANDER
Commodore 1906 - 1907

A LEADING PIONEER BUSINESS MAN, head of the famous Hastings Mills, R. H. Alexander was the Club's second Commodore. He had organized yacht races on Burrard Inlet and, in the early days, with W. E. Graveley, was judge at the City's first Regatta held July 1st, 1887 in honor of Queen Victoria's Jubilee. The picturesque four masted 'windjammers' from Australia, Orient and United Kingdom tied up at Hastings Mills for their lumber cargoes as late as 1910 and gave a fitting background to the Club's early Harbour races. Mr. Alexander and his three sons were keen sailors and it was during his terms that the first International Races for the Alexandra Cup were held.

He presented the beautiful Beaver Perpetual Challenge Trophy — miniature capstan made from the oak of the wrecked *Beaver*, first steam vessel to ply the Pacific Ocean. His flagship was the yawl *Slani*, 46 ft., originally the pilot boat *Claymore*. In 1913 he had the all teak yawl, *Uwhilna*, built in Shanghai and with it that year won the Beaver Trophy after seven years effort to annex the cruising championship of the Club Fleet. His sons were also active in the Club executive, H. O. Alexander being Commodore in 1911 and R. H. H. Alexander Vice-Commodore in 1908.

Under Mr. R. H. Alexander's Commodoreship the Club membership and Fleet made substantial growth, necessitating larger quarters which were later erected in Stanley Park.

Yawl UWHILNA cruising on Howe Sound.

A. G. THYNNE
Commodore 1908

A CHARTER MEMBER of the Club, Mr. Thynne was a member of the original management committee and with J. H. Senkler and Austin French formed the committee authorized to draft the By-Laws and choose colours. The original club flag selected was a Cambridge blue burgee with a black diamond in the centre. His original yacht in the Club was *Golliwog*, 36 ft. yawl built for him by V. M. Dafoe in 1903. He was one of the fourteen original members who purchased Life Memberships assisting the Club to build the first clubhouse, the two storey float house anchored on a water lot leased from the C.P.R. at the foot of Bute Street, which was subsequently towed over to Stanley Park foreshore. Later it was set on piles and is the spar house in use today. In 1906 he built the 40 ft. yawl *Gazeka*, twice winning the Beaver Cup in her.

During Mr. Thynne's term of office the first permanent clubhouse was built on the shores of Stanley Park, the club having obtained a lease to the water lot adjacent to Deadman's Island for the nominal rent of $1.00 annually from the Department of Marine & Fisheries, Ottawa.

He presented the Thynne Cup to the Club for the race around Texada Island for cruisers. The first race in 1908 was won by Curtis Davidson's *Elsa May* which made the round trip from English Bay and back in about 24 hours, May 23rd—the only boat to complete the course. He hugged the north shore while the fleet worked the Point Grey side, missed an easterly breeze that carried *Elsa May* right up to the head of Texada Island when a westerly roared in that made such heavy weather for the other boats that they all gave up the race.

In 1908 the Pacific International Power Boat Association race from Seattle finished at Vancouver, won by *Traveller* of Seattle, R. P. McLennan's *Allanbee* being second and Mr. Bell-Irving's *Beatrice* third out of an entry of 17. It was this year that Capt. E. B. Deane in the *Alexandra* won the Alexandra Cup for the Club, beating *Spirit I.* of Seattle 2 out of 3 races in English Bay at the P.I.Y.A. Regatta held in July.

Aux. yawl GAZEKA, 1908.

C. B. MACNEILL
Commodore 1909 - 1910

FOURTH COMMODORE, MR. MACNEILL served two terms and sailed *Gazeka* as his flagship. He presented the Macneill Cup for international racing in the 18 ft. class of the international rule, but the 18 ft. *Adanac,* designed and built by 17 year old Horace Stone to defend this trophy, was the only boat ever built to this class and was never challenged.

It was at 7 a.m. on December 20th 1909 that the new clubhouse in Stanley Park was completely destroyed by fire. It had been occupied for two years and was insured for $4500.00. The loss was placed at $5979.35, which seems little enough today, but in 1909 it was a very sizable sum. The loss of the clubhouse was not greatly mourned for it was said at the time that the arrangements of the building were not of the best. H. F. Burton Brooke, the Secretary, who lived on the premises, had a narrow escape from the blaze, managing to save only the Minute Book on which he had been working. All other records and a number of trophies were lost, including the "famous" Goat's Head Snuff Moll (International Trophy) which truth to tell was not too much bemoaned as it had become somewhat mangy with age. With the $4500 insurance and another $2000 raised, new premises were erected on the same site and the building still stands, being sold in 1930 to the Dominion Government for R.C.N.V.R. and used as Naval Officers' Mess during second world war and subsequently taken over by the Parks Board and used to make and store scenery used by Theatre Under the Stars.

It was during Mr. Macneill's first term that the third international race for the Alexandra Trophy was held at Seattle. This was the occasion on which the measurement of *Spirit II* was questioned. On refusal of Commodore Macneill's proposal to sail the race under protest and refer the whole matter to a full executive meeting of the North West International Yacht Racing Association, he withdrew *Alexandra* from competing in the third race and ordered all Club vessels to return to Vancouver.

He was elected Honorary Life Member in 1938.

Rebuilt after 1909 fire, Clubhouse, Coal Harbour looking west, 1910.

View of moorings looking east, sloop TILLICUM in foreground.

H. O. ALEXANDER
Commodore 1911

FIFTH COMMODORE OF THE CLUB, Mr. H. O. Alexander was one of the sons of second Commodore H. R. Alexander, the other, R. H. H. Alexander, being Vice-Commodore in 1908. Keen sailors on Burrard Inlet since boyhood, both brothers took an active part in the affairs of the Club. It was in 1904 that H. O Alexander first suggested the establishment of moorage and a clubhouse at Jericho and he continued to agitate for "outside" moorings during his tenure of office. As a result of his farsightedness, the following year Commodore B. T. Rogers was empowered to interview the Jericho Country Club for a potential site on or near their property—Jericho Golf and Country Club, now Dept. of National Defence property. It was during 1911 that the spar house (original clubhouse) was set up on piles. This year the Royal Victoria Yacht Club received its Royal Charter and Warrant to fly the Blue Ensign, and the Club tendered a letter of congratulations to the Victoria Club. Horace Stone's *Adanac* won the Graveley Cup. *Gazeka* won in A Class at the May 24th Regatta, *Britannia* won in B Class, *Eileen* in C Class and *Asthore* in D Class. In the White Rocks race *Golliwog* was first in yawls, *Amorita* in A sloops, *Astore* in B sloops and Knox Walkem's *Half Moon* won the Power Boat race. The Beaver Cup was won by *Minerva*, Julian Cup won by Miss Sophie Deane in *Wideawake*. The Buscombe Cup was won by *Spirit I.*, sailed by the Cao brothers.

M.V. PHROSO, Commodore H. O. Alexander.

Square Rigger's loading lumber at Hastings Saw Mill—1911.
Vancouver City Archives.

B. T. ROGERS
Commodore 1912 - 1918

MR. B. T. ROGERS, sixth Commodore, led the Club for seven years, the longest period in office of any Commodore. It was an important span in the life of the Club. The boom years were fading into the crash of real estate values in 1912 and 1913, followed by the strenuous war years 1914-1918. In his first years of office, Commodore Rogers developed and led the many Club cruises with port to port races and did much to enhance the standards of both racing and cruising. A man of great wealth, he never stinted himself on behalf of the Club. He was the owner of the ocean going steam yacht *Aquilo*, the largest vessel ever to fly the Club's burgee. He endeavored to cultivate a spirit in keeping with the standing of a royal yacht club, and many a careless skipper was checked up for not saluting the Commodore's flag. While essentially a "power boat man", Commodore Rogers was very interested in sailing and his sons, Blythe, Ernest, Phillip and Forrest, were sailing skippers par excellence. Commodore Rogers built the R Class *Turenga* in 1914 as a challenger for the Lipton Cup and placed it in the hands of the Club to find a skipper and crew. The Rogers family owned and sailed many fine yachts whose records are enumerated elsewhere in the History. When war broke out in 1914 he placed *Aquilo* at the disposal of the Naval Authorities at Esquimalt, and for a short time she was accommodation ship for the crews of Canadian submarines on the Pacific Coast. During the war years when Club activities were at a low ebb, Commodore Rogers acted Host at a series of memorable dinners he gave for Club members and those returning from overseas. He died suddenly in 1918.

Few families have had longer associations with yachting in Vancouver and with the Royal Vancouver Yacht Club than that of the late B. T. Rogers, Club Commodore from 1912 to 1918, and his sons Ernest, Forrest, Blythe and Philip.

As early as 1901 B. T. Rogers brought out from Hong Kong aboard one of the Empress liners the steam yacht *Mow Ping*, which had been built to his orders. The name meant "Foreign Devil", or more literally, "Without a Pigtail". From early photographs she had a reverse slope to her bow, like the old-fashioned battleships, but later her hull was lengthened and her bow changed to the clipper type, which greatly improved her appearance.

She was sold by Mr. Rogers to C. B. Macneill, Club Commodore in 1909-10, and eventually ended her days as a towboat.

In her place, Mr. Rogers acquired the magnificent steam yacht *Aquilo* on the east coast of the United States and a professional crew brought her to Vancouver in the winter of 1911-12. This meant coming around Cape Horn, and as she was a coal burner at that time, extra bunkers had to be built on her decks. At that time her helm was fully exposed to the deck above the dining saloon, so the helmsman must have had some uncomfortable moments.

Later she was converted to oil burning and a pilot house and chart room built, which not only improved her appearance but made life more comfortable for the man at the wheel.

Aquilo was probably the first yacht in Vancouver to have two-way wireless installed. Blythe Rogers was keenly interested in wireless and operated the set before the 1914-18 war.

In the early months of that war *Aquilo* proudly flew the white ensign on loan to the Royal Canadian Navy. She acted as mother ship to the Canadian submarines at Esquimalt, and later patrolled outside the Strait of Juan de Fuca.

The "R" class sloop *Turenga* was ordered by B. T. Rogers in 1914 as a Lipton Cup contender. She competed many times but was never successful. Originally she was gaff rigged, but in the early twenties she was changed to Marconi rig, and some of the lead removed from her keel was placed in the bilge for ballast.

This made her very tender, and during the Lipton Cup races off Royal Roads in 1925 *Turenga* heeled over until her rudder was planing on the water. Then she would round up into the wind, only to repeat the process.

Ernest Rogers sailed *Turenga* until 1926, and Philip Rogers took over until 1929. She was then sailed by Forrest Rogers until 1934. He completely re-rigged the boat, stepping the mast further aft, but this did not solve the problem of her weather helm. He sold her to Frank Duff-Stuart, under whose ownership she was rammed and sunk in English Bay by the S.S. *Lady Pam* in 1939.

The 49 foot yawl *Andi Lailey* was built in New York in 1917 by James Lawley and Sons as the *Dawn*. She came to Victoria for the 1926 P.I.Y.A. Regatta via the Panama Canal, being brought around by a professional crew. Ernest Rogers purchased her in Victoria and renamed her *Andi Lailey*. The word "Andi" is Fijian for Princess, while Lailey is the nickname for Ernest's eldest daughter.

Ernest Rogers raced and cruised in *Andi Lailey* from 1926 to 1932, when Philip Rogers purchased her. Forrest Rogers bought her in 1935 and sold her in 1941 to a Tacoma yachtsman.

Other yachts owned by the Rogers family included the power boat *Saltpetre* (now *Hope Point III*), used by Ernest to commute to Cowan's Point; the *Kagome*, a former rum runner converted into a yacht in 1934 by Philip Rogers and used during the war by the R.C.A.F.; and the *Brenhines*, at present owned by Forrest Rogers.

Commodore B. T. Rogers flagship AQUILA.

CHAPTER 3

Prominent Early Yachtsmen

E. B. 'JIMMY' DEANE, owner and skipper of *Alexandra* in the Alexandra Cup races, was one of the most active of the racing skippers in the early days of the club. He held the Graveley Cup for two years with the sloop *Tillicum* in the 21 foot class, and he challenged for the international Mackie Trophy with his sloop *Wideawake*. He also owned the B class sloop *Titania* and the 73 foot power cruiser *Davy Jones*. His two daughters, Mrs. Harold A. Jones and Mrs. Percy Sills, were for many years among the most active of lady yachting enthusiasts; both won the Julian Trophy for lady skippers, Mrs. Jones nee Miss Louise Deane in 1913 and again in 1935 and 1946, and Mrs. Sills nee Miss Sophie Deane in 1911 and later in 1930.

The three CAO BROTHERS, whose *Spirit I* was the great rival of the *Alexandra*, were dedicated yachtsmen for many years, and with Cliff Cao at the tiller and Reek and Chris Cao at the sheets, they were a hard trio to beat. Their first yacht was the sloop *Swipe*, which they built themselves in 1906. She was so named because they swiped the lumber from Hastings Mill and the accessories wherever they could. In 1908 they built and raced the centreboard sloop *Iola*, 33 feet overall, which they raced in the international regatta of 1908. Cliff Cao was skipper of the unsuccessful challenger *Turenga* in the R class races of 1920, which went to Seattle's *Sir Tom*. The brothers owned the *Spirit I* from 1913 to 1924, when she was sold to Ernie Woodward, but Cliff continued to skipper her until she was lost by fire on Indian Arm in 1931.

TOM and VINCENT RAMSAY were another pair of brothers who were keen racing skippers. Vincent gave his life in World War One. He won the Rand Trophy Series in the *Redskin* in 1913 and this Trophy was later donated to the club in his memory as the Redskin Trophy by his mother. Tom is now an Honorary Life member of the club. He raced the *Tillicum* for the Graveley Cup before the first war, and in 1927 headed the syndicate which built the *Lady Van* to compete for the Lipton Cup. He was her skipper in 1928 when she lost to *Sir Tom* in a very close contest. Later he raced the well-known yawl *Ailsa I*, and was the original winner of the famous Bird Rock Trophy in 1932 for the doubtful achievement of driving *Ailsa I* hard and fast on Bird Rock in Active

31

Pass. For his pains he was presented with a battered mug by the late Col. Rooke and the Hon. Ian MacKenzie, and he in turn presented the "trophy" to the custody of the club to be awarded annually to the most worthy successor committing the "faux-pas" of the year in yacht handling. In 1935 Tom had the fine yacht *Armida* built by Don Sinclair at Coal Harbour Shipyards from designs by Tom Halliday, who was one of Camper and Nicholson's top men. This graceful 36 ft. yawl with Mr. Ramsay at the helm was a consistent winner during her nine year life in the club—in 1939 *Armida*, skippered by Tom, was the record winner of all eight races she entered that year. He was elected to Honorary Life Membership in 1958.

The three THICKE BROTHERS, Walter, Claude and Harold, were another fraternal team that loomed large in the early annals of the club. Walter was made an Honorary Life member in 1959—he passed on recently. Claude is also an Honorary Life member; he still survives. They were keen competitors for the Graveley Cup in the 24 foot class when they owned the sloop *Redskin*. Later they acquired the American-built sloop *Madeline* from Bert Austin and raced her in the 29 foot class. They then built the 44 foot schooner *Adelphi* from a design by E. B. Schock. In the 1920's Walter raced the fast sloop *Ardrie*. Claude still skippers the 38 ft. power cruiser *Ubique I*, which he acquired in 1937.

The THOMPSON BROTHERS, Phil and W. E., were two of the original members of the club when they owned the 35 foot auxiliary yawl *Bertha*, a centreboard craft built for duck shooting on the Fraser. About 1906 Capt. Phil Thompson acquired an interest in the famous yawl *Minerva*, which he sailed many years with the team of Walter Graveley, Jack Scott and F. M. Chaldecott, until she was sold to Hubert Wallace in 1927. In 1914 the *Minerva*, crewed by Phil Thompson, Walter Graveley and Jack Scott, whose combined ages were then 186, won the A class trophy for large yawls at the Seattle Potlatch Regatta.

One of the fine old-time sailors was C. A. GODSON, a crusty character, who did much to improve the standards of racing in the club. He would stand no nonsense and drove his crews like a Bluenose bucko mate. He built the sloop *Ivanhoe* in 1906 at the Cedar Cove yard of Johnson and Walker, and won the Beaver Cup with her in 1908. *Ivanhoe* was well and truly built, for she is still winning races under yawl rig for the West Vancouver Yacht Club.

Another famous team of brothers were FRED and EDDIE LUCAS, two of the brightest spirits ever to belong to the club. Fred started racing in the little sloop *Blue Grouse* in 1903, and later he and Eddie raced in the centreboard sloop *Cheemaun*, a strong Graveley Cup competitor. Later they bought the heavy weather pilot cutter *Kelpie* in Seattle, in which they made many merry and rather riotous cruises.

Fred Lucas had a theory that if you anchored, you should do it properly, and the anchoring of the *Kelpie* became a legend. This resulted in a scrap of impromptu verse from Ronald Kenvyn, one of the crew and long time Marine Editor of the Vancouver Province, which ran as follows:

> "Our owner, Mr. Lucas, is a bully sort of skipper,
>   But 'e's fussy with 'is anchor
>   And 'e fairly busts my nerve,
> For it's 'ALL 'ands man the windlass,
>   'Eave 'er short, awash and trip 'er.'
>
> "If the Kelpie gets to dragging
>   Or she takes a little swerve
> 'E's a good old sort, is Freddy
>   But I'll quit and dare his frown,
> For 'e's always 'eaving of 'er up
>   Or 'eaving of 'er down."

For many years one of the most colourful members of the club was c. OTIS JULIAN, better known as 'Charlie' Julian, who after a long residence abroad is once again a welcome guest in the clubhouse. He became a member in 1904 with the sloop *Delores*, which he brought from Victoria. He was the second Honorary Secretary of the Club, being elected to that post on the passing of Mr. O. L. Spencer, in 1906. That year, a vintage year for the R.V.Y.C., he built the 27 foot sloop *Verona*, which had a long career under club colours. Later he was skipper of the big black cutter *Lavita*, which was brought up from Puget Sound in 1909.

Mr. Julian was the donor of the C. O. Julian Trophy in 1906 for lady skippers, one of the most keenly contested of the club's perpetual trophies, and which he presents annually to the winning skipper.

In the days before the first world war, when there were no loud-hailer systems, the voice of Charlie Julian was legendary for its long distance booming quality. No megaphones were needed when he was starting a race, although he did carry a little brass cannon.

H. F. BURTON BROOKE, known as 'Brookie,' was for many years Secretary of the R.V.Y.C. and was often the whole works: starter, timekeeper and judge of local races. He was living on the premises at Stanley Park in 1909 when the building went up in flames, from which he had an exceeding narrow escape. For twenty years he ably guided the club's activities and in 1928 was made an Honorary Life member. For many years thereafter he took a keen interest in starting and judging races along with another faithful worker, Frank Wilgress—they were practically fixtures on the starting tower until Art Jefferd took over in 1940. 'Brookie' also served as Honorary Secretary intermittently till 1942.

BILL MCDOUGALL, who was a partner of Billy Watts in the Vancouver Shipyards, was an enthusiastic yachtsman as well as a fine boatbuilder. He won the Mackie Trophy in international competition with the sloop *Onaway*, and later built the 32 foot sloop *Asthore*, painted sea green.

She was later owned by Reg Purves, W. Oliphant Bell, and others before going to Victoria in 1926.

w. g. 'billy' breeze, who passed on last year, was until recently a long time active member of the club, having joined in 1905. His racing experience on Burrard Inlet went back to 1896. He was Rear Commodore in 1912 and 1913 and Vice Commodore in 1914. He was also active for many years as Treasurer, Hon. Secretary or on the Executive Committee. He sailed in *Verona* and later built the 25 foot yawl *Tamerlane,* to the same design as Fleming Day's *Seabird,* which crossed from New York to Rome. He also raced a good deal in the sloop *Ivanhoe* and sailed in various club cruisers. He was elected Honorary Life Member in 1948.

Another of the popular old timers was alex marshall, Rear Commodore in 1911 and Vice Commodore in 1919 and 1927, Fleet Captain 1933-34, Hon. Treasurer 1914, Hon Meas 1916-17-18. He raced the sloop *Marietta* in the old 21 foot class, and at various times owned the yawl *Elmarsh,* sloop *Hazel,* and the 38 foot yawl *Nelmar,* which was winner in her class in the international regatta at Victoria in 1930, won the White Rocks Race in 1936, and the Ballenas Island B class race in 1938.

He took an active part in promoting the building of the *Alexandra* and some of the later R class challengers. He also fathered the 15 foot Kitten Class centreboard sailing dinghies, which were long popular. He was the donor of the Harry A. Marshall Trophy for the White Rocks Race in memory of his son Harry. He was elected an Honorary Life Member in 1938.

fred mills is another old-time member, now retired at Victoria, whose membership goes back to 1910. He first owned the sloop *Intrepid* in 1910, originally built by Louis 'Speck' Jewitt in 1906. In 1913 he bought the 33 foot schooner *Tenderfoot,* a beautifully built ship of the sealing schooner type and designed for ocean cruising. The builder of that vessel, Harry Bird of Victoria, cruised to San Francisco and returned in her before Fred bought her. In 1933 Fred Mills bought the *Uwhilna* from Seattle and in her, circumnavigated Vancouver Island—the first R.V.Y.C. ship to do so. He won the Beaver Cup in *Uwhilna* in 1938. He was the first Fleet Captain of the club when that post was created in 1921 and in 1955 he presented a fine library of yachting volumes to the club. He was elected an Honorary Life Member in 1964.

phil whitehead, Fleet Captain in 1923 and 1927, owned the American built sloop *Glendolyn* from 1919 to 1924, winning with her in the heavy sloop class of over 23 foot waterline in the 1922 international regatta in Seattle. He also crewed in the *Lady Pat* in the international R class and in many other craft of the R.V.Y.C. fleet. He met a tragic death by drowning off the North Vancouver Ferry wharf.

W. H. 'BILLY' FINDLAY joined the club in 1905. He was for many years Sports Editor of the Vancouver World and later transferred to the Vancouver Sun. He was very active in club sailing affairs and was a member of the sailing Committee from 1907 for a decade or more. He sailed the centreboard cruising sloop *Silver Spray*, picking up a few wins in the process, and was for years judge or timekeeper at most of the early international regattas. To distinguish him from another Billy Findlay who came on the Sun sports staff from Winnipeg, W. H. was later known as 'Vancouver' Billy, the Prairie arrival being known as 'Winnipeg' Bill. Our member, 'Vancouver' Billy Findlay, was a very keen yachtsman and in his capacity as Sports Editor of the two leading newspapers did much to develop the sport of yachting with his very complete reports, which dominated the sports pages of the day.

GORDON B. WARREN, another newspaper man, joined the club in 1908 and for 25 years was an active sailor, acquiring *Spraydrift ex Spindrift*, a 30 foot centreboard sloop built in 1912, and sailing her until the early 1930's. He faithfully recorded much of the early history of the club and it is from his detailed records that much of this work has been compiled —all records and minute books having been destroyed in the 1909 Stanley Park clubhouse fire. Later records up to 1953 were stored in the basement of the Jericho Clubhouse in 'McGee's Locker', which, like its namesake, held a little of everything—including some old netting—and it is presumed that spontaneous combustion set off that blaze. There is no truth to the rumour that 'incriminatory' or 'hot' records exploded by themselves. At any rate, Gordon's labours of several hundred bound sheets of closely typed material covering activities up to 1930 were saved and the club is indeed indebted to him for dedicated labours over many years.

The ROGERS BROTHERS, Ernest, Philip and Forrest, sons of B. T. Rogers, commodore from 1912 to 1918, took an active part in international regattas, racing the R class sloop *Turenga* in the Lipton Cup contests at Victoria, Seattle and Vancouver, each having a turn in her. In 1925 Ernest Rogers brought out the fine 49 foot yawl *Dawn* from Chicago, which he later named the *Andi Lailey*. She won the Beaver Cup with an all-time record of 11½ hours in 1926 and won again in 1929. He was drowned in 1939 when he dived overboard from the *Andi Lailey* in an heroic attempt to rescue his daughter, who had been knocked overboard by the boom. His daughter was saved but Ernest presumably suffered a heart attack in the chilly up-coast water because after surfacing he disappeared and was lost.

OSWALD 'SKIPPER' MOSELEY was a charter member of the club, a Life Member, and although now living in Victoria, still keeps an active interest in things nautical. Among his early yachts were the *Thelma*, a 33 foot sloop built for him by Billy Watts, and the 37 foot sloop *Dawendeena*, former Nanaimo pilot boat. Later he owned the 31 foot cruising yawl *Nancy* and the 32 foot sloop *Nancy M.* In 1923 he purchased the 36 foot trading schooner *Ashigamik,* built in Seattle in 1894, in which he cruised the coast for many years in fine seamanlike fashion.

Another of the early members was BILL TEMPLETON, who acquired the A class sloop *Imp* from Puget Sound and re-named her *Amorita,* racing her with success for several years. Later he sailed the red hulled *Tamahnowus,* 29 foot at the waterline, with a great deal of success, capturing the Beaver Cup with her in 1923 and 1928. Bill was a man of little patience, and Art Jefferd recalls one occasion in which Bill could not start the little auxiliary engine of the *Amorita.* Eventually, with a mighty heave and a mighty oath, he manhandled it over the side into Coal Harbour, and there it lies today in the mud.

In the early days of the club history, some of the stalwart young bloods, who included 'BARNEY' JOHNSON, BILL TEMPLETON, SPECK JEWITT, CHARLIE JULIAN, and others, formed a select section and took vows never to luff nor reef. They called themselves the Never Luff Club, and a meeting was held each Saturday night aboard a selected boat during the season and in the club's quarters in Stanley Park during the winter.

To gain the proper atmosphere drinks were confined to overproof rum, the smokes, to thick black pipe twist, and the conversation to ships. The club slogan, which was usually bellowed when lying safely at anchor, or in an armchair in front of the clubhouse fire, went as follows:

> *"Luff! luff! never luff!*
> *Reef! reef! never reef!*
> *Keep her full, keep her full,*
> *Give the blooming sheets a pull,*
> *And NEVER, NEVER, LUFF her."*

It was before the days of cars and motorboats, and the return journey was across Coal Harbour by dinghy from Thompson's Boathouse at the foot of Denman Street. The last departures . . . both men and dinghies . . . were generally overladen. On a certain dark night the last dinghy shoved off. She was a four man boat but had eight aboard, and in mid-channel gently slid from under the crowd. Four swam back to the clubhouse and four to the Georgia Street boathouse. Each contingent arrived safely, counted heads, wept bitter tears over the supposed loss of their shipmates, gave the alarm, commandeered other dinghies to search for the 'bodies' . . . and met each other in mid-channel.

That broke up the Never Luff Club, for when the story reached the ears of the Commodore, he decreed that "enough is enough", and pronounced the end of the "Never Luff".

Another of the pre-1914 era who is still very active in club activities is A. H. 'ART' JEFFERD, Honorary Life member, who joined the club in

1909, but first crewed in 1907. He owned the speedy red-hulled 21 foot sloop *Redskin* for several years, racing against the *Tillicum* and *Adanac*. He acquired the *Redskin* at the height of the Vancouver real estate boom, by swapping a lot out in the wilds of Fraser Road for her. Art was Hon. Hydrographer for 21 years, 1940 to 1960—by far the longest period of service by any club member. His late wife (nee Ernestine Smith) was the first and only woman to be accorded the honour of Honorary Life Membership in the Royal Vancouver Yacht Club. An ardent yachtswoman, she at one time owned the 40 foot sloop *Elsa May*. In her memory, Art has presented the beautiful Ernestine Jefferd Memorial Perpetual Trophy for Star Boat Racing to the club.

In 1938 while Art Jefferd was at the tiller of Fred Mills' yawl *Uwhilna*, Mrs. Jefferd was swept overboard by the boom, just west of the First Narrows. Without knowing who had fallen overboard, Art promptly jumped over the side. Since neither he nor his wife could swim a stroke, there could well have been a double tragedy. But they kept their heads and managed to keep afloat for half an hour until rescued.

CEDRIC and NORMAN GYLES, sons of G. F. Gyles, served a very useful initiation to yacht racing in the Kitten Class sailing dinghies at the time when this class was active with some of the best skippers in the club competing. Later they raced the sloop *Elsa May* in cruiser races and also had considerable experience on the crews of R class challengers *Patricia* and *Riowna*. Cedric skippered *Riowna* in the Lipton Cup contest at Seattle in 1926 and again in 1927 at Vancouver (see Lipton Cup Racing). He served as Fleet Captain in 1938 and in 1955 imported the Fife designed 8 metre sloop *Concerto* from the Clyde. He also served the club as Hon. Treasurer from 1952 to 1956 and was elected an Honorary Life Member in 1962.

W. G. (BILL) MCKENZIE owned and raced the sloop *Dionne* in 1924 and in 1930 owned the power cruiser *Macard*. He raced with Ron Maitland on the *Patricia* and *Riowna* in international contests for the Lipton Cup and was also one of the *Lady Pat's* crew when Mr. Maitland took her down to race at Los Angeles in 1928.

E. F. (JACK) CRIBB, famous in R.V.Y.C. annals as the *Lady Van* skipper who brought the Lipton Cup to Vancouver in 1929 by defeating the perennial victor *Sir Tom* of Seattle, had long association with the sea as a ship builder and salvage expert before he joined the club in 1926. He was an active sailor in the heyday of the R class and was one of the syndicate that built the *Lady Van*. His naval dockyard experience in England during the first world war was put to good use in the Second World War when he superintended construction of fifty-two 10,000 tonners at the False Creek yards of West Coast Shipyards and he designed a special landing barge for naval use, producing 75 of the craft in addition to hundreds of a reversible Cribb designed plywood life-raft.

Some time after the war he created some consternation among our "hardy" sailors by plowing up to the Jericho landing wharf at an English Bay regatta in one of his landing barges converted into a really palatial travelling house-boat. Leisurely power house-boating however was not for Jack because after one season so equipped, he designed and built the fine motor-sailer *Shirley Jane* which after some years he sold to J. W. (Ace) Lindsay who re-named her *Staghound*. Jack Cribb was elected on Honorary Life Member in 1954.

GEORGE ASKEW was another old time yachtsman who was also a builder of well known successful R.V.Y.C. yachts. He constructed the yawls *Westward Ho, Hereandthere* and *Nelmar,* the sloops *Gamine* and *Ardrie* and the cutter *Cresset.* He crewed with Jack Cribb when the *Lady Van* won the Lipton Cup, and he won the 1924 sailing dinghy championship with his *Native Daughter.* Another activity of George Askew and Jack Cribb together, was the building and re-assembling of stern wheelers for northern B.C. and Yukon rivers, including river boats used on the Fraser River by Foley, Welsh and Stewart, original builders of the Pacific Great Eastern Railroad. George Askew was elected on Honorary Life Member in 1948.

H. A. (HUBIE) WALLACE, Fleet Captain in 1929, 1930, 1931 and Rear Commodore in 1932, owner of the yawl *Minerva* from 1927 on, was very active in all club sailing events and regattas, winning the Beaver Cup 1934, 1935 and 1936. He and the club suffered a great loss when the beautiful *Minerva* was accidentally beached and burned to the waterline at Ganges Harbour, June 28th 1936. Confusion of shore lights with wharf lights caused *Minerva* to run aground to port of the Ganges wharf. A leak developed in cracked piping connections and the plumber obtained from Ganges accidentally set fire to the vessel with his torch and she was quickly consumed by flames. In 1948 he acquired *Buccaneer III,* 47 foot A class sloop imported from Nova Scotia by Jim McPherson in 1946 and sailed her in international regattas and in the Swiftsure Lightship Classic until sold to Russell K. Baker in 1956.

The Honorable IAN MCKENZIE, M.P., one time Minister of National Defence, Ottawa, was an active sailing member of the club during the 1920's. He won the Beaver Cup with the cruising sloop *Onoma,* later changed her to yawl rig. He took a leading part in the club "stag" and other gatherings, booming out sea chanties and reciting hilarious verse much to the enjoyment, if not the edification, of assembled yachtsmen. (See reference to famous match race betwen *Alexandra* and *Onoma* in chapter on Beaver Cup Races.)

J. EDWARD BIRD and his sons Harry and Ted were active sailors in the early 1920's in the 10 ton yawl *Nymph,* a heavy weather ship of 50 feet by 12 foot beam. Harry relates the fine training he received from his father in heavy weather sailing, born of the latter's experience on Lake Simcoe in the 1890's where he learned to race and cruise. Harry recalls the very rough Gulf crossing to attend the first Pacific International Regatta held after the First World War in 1920 at Victoria, and a memorable later occasion sailing up the Gulf past Cowan's Point in a heavy southeaster when *Nymph's* mast and rigging gave way, cleats pulled right out of the deck, backstays gone and the ship drove right through the wreckage.

It was probably heavy weather experiences like those.that prompted Harry, some years later in his *Penguin,* to start out on the White Rocks Race ALONE when his crew failed to show up at starting time. *Penguin* was a 33 foot racing sloop—certainly no ship to sail single-handed in an overnight race, yet Harry performed this feat which has never been equalled—George Askew tried it once alone, but gave up and returned long before he reached the White Rocks.

About this epic voyage and his acquiring of *Penguin,* Harry has this to say . . . "The good ship *Penguin* was a fast racing sloop of 33 feet with a fixed keel, having been converted from a centreboard sloop. All fittings were solid brass or bronze, lignum vitae blocks. The deck was teak with solid. mahogany king planks etc. She just looked like a little grand piano when scraped and painted for the season's racing and cruising.

"The gear and spars were lying up in the sail loft at Wallace's Shipyard in 1924 when a syndicate of 'wealthy' yachtsmen and I put up $50 each—$250 in all. And we had a hard time finding that $50 each, I assure you. Included in the deal was a one-lunger 2 cycle aux. engine which nobody could get to run. We tried to get Mr. Wallace to take back the engine for some refund—but he said he was more interested in bigger engines, so we later heaved the thing overboard and it now lies up Indian Arm at the bottom of the sea.

"However, we never regretted our purchase for we won many races with her and I still have 8 trophies at home which my wife has been hiding for years because they take a lot of polishing.

"Having bought out my partners I had a hard time finding a crew—what with girl trouble, financial embarrassment, etc., etc. it was quite a job to keep a crew together.

"One Saturday I set out for Jericho under power, ready for the White Rocks Race. I was at the starting line—the gun went off, and there I was waiting for my crew to show up. No show—so I crossed the line alone, with one box of sandwiches, a copy of Reader's Digest and an old teapot which I used to balance the tiller when I was in the cabin.

"It was a lovely day, and a nice race; we did short tacks up the southwest shore of Bowen Island and past Gower Point and then ran out of wind. However, the wind came up later and I remember waking up in the middle of the night going at a fast clip the wrong way. I had rounded White Islets off Sechelt at about 22:00 hours and it was now about 02:00 hours in the morning and I was back at White Islets where I had been 4 hours ago. Well I came about, headed for the finish line and I remember getting up the spinnaker by myself for the long run home.

"As I crossed the finish line I was surprised to see a number of other ships at anchor waiting for me to finish. It took 3 men to take off the spinnaker—it was so tangled up. I had a good time and suffered no hardship whatsoever but after a session at the clubhouse I didn't remember much for the next 24 hours. That old teapot stayed with me for many years—better than these new-fangled gadgets any day."

Later, Harry acquired the 35 foot sloop *Dolphin II*, sailing it for some years.

Harry Bird served as Honorary Treasurer two years, 1950 and 1951, and with Commodore Capt. B. L. Johnson went personal guarantee for a club loan at the bank in 1951 to enable the raising of $15,000 for the creation of Junior quarters on the wharf at Jericho. He was elected an Honorary Life Member in 1964.

JOHN WINSLOW was one of the early active skippers whose name appears on many club trophies. He was the designer of the Kitten class sailing dinghies in which he made a name in local and international races, sailing the *Black Cat* which was one of the team that won the Gale Trophy from the Seattle dinghy team in 1922. He served as Honorary Measurer in 1920 and 1921, before moving to Seattle.

HENRY BELL-IRVING, eldest son of H. O. Bell-Irving, was another of the prominent skippers in the old Kitten class. He also raced the *Dione* and other yachts in the fleet and over the years owned several power vessels.

L. T. ALDEN, brother of the famous yacht designer, John Alden, was another well known yachtsman who served the club as Honorary Measurer from 1927 to 1931. He raced the sloop *Gamine*, built from his brother's designs, with a great deal of success, winning a large number of trophies.

H. C. ELLIOTT, his son Clint, and Ben, his cousin, must be included in the list of early active yachtsmen. In their large cruising yawl *Anywhere*, which they had built themselves, selecting the "sticks" from standing timber near Deep Cove, Indian Arm, they won the Beaver Cup two years in a row—1931 and 1932. Clint still sails the fine yacht after 35 years, not racing now but cruising Howe Sound and Gulf waters. Ben Elliott won the international Kitten class contest at the 1928 P.I.Y.A., the last international event in this class.

ROY GINN's service to the club must not be forgotten. He was Rear-Commodore 1928 to 1931 and Vice Commodore 1932 to 1934. He sailed the yacht *Truant*, a yawl, with much success, finally turning to power craft when he acquired the fine estate at Lamalchi Point, Kuper Island. He served many years as Justice of the Peace among the Gulf Islands and was affectionately known to all cruising yachtsmen as the "Laird of Lamalchi". He contributed a great deal to the revision of the club by-laws about the time that we were incorporated under the Friendly Societies Act. His eloquence at annual meetings was relished and will be long remembered.

Another legal "light" who was a most enthusiastic yachtsman was the late Justice of the Admiralty Court, the Hon. Mr. Justice SIDNEY SMITH. He and other lawyers like the late Mr. Knox Walkem were a "tower of strength" when it came to annual meetings where the question of by-laws were concerned. The masterpieces of rhetoric and "legal mumbo-jumbo" that these gentlemen hurled forth did much to enliven the somewhat "stodgy" business meetings. Mr. Justice Sidney Smith served as Vice-Commodore in 1939 and 1940 as well as many terms on the Executive Committee. Previous to taking up law, Sidney served his apprenticeship in sail and was a "Cape-Horner". Well remembered is the Annual Meeting of 1940 when the Honorable Justice, concluding in a burst of oratory, completely "boxed" the compass and received a standing ovation from the envious amateurs present, many of whom had difficulty in even remembering the principal points of the compass in their proper sequence.

KNOX WALKEM was primarily a power boat man, but he was a very capable navigator and engineer. His *Half Moon* won the international power boat classic in 1910, and again he carried off the honours in 1912 with his fine new *Full Moon* (see reference in Early Power Boats).

He was also a capable trumpeter and enlivened the arrivals and departures from anchorages at many of the early cruises with his spirited rendering of "Hail, Hail, the Gang's All Here" and "Aloha" or "Auld Lang Syne". His last ship, *Sal Lal*, a 44 foot power cruiser, regularly attended all club functions and regattas with Skipper Walkem at the helm.

Another well known father and son team in the 1920's was WALTER CLINE and his son DR. HAROLD M. CLINE. For them, in 1927, George Askew built the 54 foot yawl *Whitewings II*, which was traded three years later with "Barney" Johnson's *Alexandra*. They actively sailed this fine historic yacht for several years before selling her to Temple H. Wright. Capt. B. L. Johnson re-christened *Whitewings II*, naming her *Westward Ho.*

W. A. "BILL" ROEDDE, well within the memory of today's vigorous sailors, was also a "great" among the old-timers of the club. He joined the club as a Junior in 1905 and but for his four years service overseas in the First World War, was a continuous and active participant in all club races, fixtures and gatherings. Bill was a natural sailor—he not only knew how to sail a boat, but he knew how to design and build one. He was the moving spirit in the keen group of Star Boat sailors who wanted to graduate to a larger type of vessel giving some protection from the elements and providing accommodation for cruising. This was in the "hungry thirties" and a low cost ship was imperative. Accordingly Bill and pals got together and designed the original *Roedde* with the help of Tom Halliday, naval architect. (See chapter on Star and Roedde classes.) Again in 1949, Bill Roedde, Bert Tupper and Jack Williamson got together and produced an improvement on the original design and the first of six or seven of the new type off Tom Taylor's ways was christened *Carita II*. Bill captured many club trophies with his *Carita* and *Carita II* in addition to being very active in club management. He was Honorary Hydrographer in 1934-35-36, Fleet Captain in 1941-42-43 and Rear Commodore in 1945. Few men were more active than Bill in club affairs or did more for the development and advancement of yachting in local waters. In later years he was wont to head off for some fishing and probably the most satisfying picture of sailing contentment is that of "Old Bill" heading into the sunset for the Gulf Islands, alone in *Carita II*, but astutely trailing his dinghy on a long, long line behind him. He was elected an Honorary Life Member in 1945.

HARRY E. (SKIPPER) WYLIE joined the club in 1919 and was one of the founders of the English Bay Star Fleet in 1923. He had sailed as a boy in Ireland, learning how to handle small boats in Belfast Bay, and was one of the most capable skippers ever to hold a tiller in local waters. He had an uncanny knack of keeping a ship moving in practically a dead calm—and when the first little puff came along—he was away. His original Star was Number 118, *Astrea*. In 1923 he came second in the International Star Class Championship races held in Long Island Sound, and he also competed in the 1932 Olympics at Los Angeles. Sailing *Windor*, which was shipped down, he tied for third place after being fouled in the first race. He skippered the *Lady Van* during the years she was owned by Commodore, the Hon. E. W. Hamber, winning the R class Club Championship Series in 1936.

Although he had owned several Star Boats he built a new Star, *Talisman,* when he was approaching seventy years of age. He served the club as Hon. Hydrographer in 1924 and in 1947 was elected an Honorary Life Member.

Another pair of brothers who have given sterling service to the club, with a fine reputation as sailors, are the URRY BROTHERS, Doug. P. and F. Wavell. They designed, owned and sailed the cutter *Cresset,* which was built at George Askew's yard in 1929. Winner of the Julian Cup in 1931, sailed by Mrs. F. Wavell Urry, *Cresset* also won the Fraser River Lightship Race for the Minerva Trophy in 1937 and was twice winner of the Beaver Cup, in 1940 and 1946.

Doug served as Hon. Measurer in 1932-33-34 and was Rear Commodore in 1935-36-37-38. He is best remembered, however, as the designer and builder of "Urry Maru" our famous starting tower which lies off Jericho in the summer months and languishes in the back reaches of our Coal Harbour station in the winter months. Doug and Wavell, both professional engineers, have given unstintingly of their advice and services in the construction and development of our floats and mooring facilities at both stations and in recent years Wavell made a very extensive survey of potential developments to extend facilities at Stanley Park.

In 1953, while on a visit to the United Kingdom, Doug, Wavell and Mrs. Victoria M. Urry bought the 12 metre *Jenetta,* 71.5 ft. overall, designed by Alfred Mylne for Sir William Burton in 1938 and built by the Bute Slip Dock Company, Isle of Bute, Scotland. She had been raced by Sir William in the 1939 season when the American twelve metre *Vim* visited British waters, was laid up during the war and was converted to a cruiser by an Ipswich yard in 1946. After acquiring *Jenetta* in 1953 the Urrys raced it successfully in the Clyde Fortnight of that year and immediately afterwards designed a conversion to ketch rig in consultation with Robert Clark. Subsequently, after cruising Scottish waters, *Jenetta* was shipped to Vancouver, arriving in February 1954. Doug P. Urry was elected to Honorary Life membership in 1956.

J. Edward Bird's NYMPH, 1920.

Sloop ALEXANDRA (old rig).

Sloop SPIRIT II (old rig).

CHAPTER 4

Early Yachts

IN THE R.V.Y.C.

FROM 1903 TO ABOUT 1933

THE FOLLOWING LIST of the first sail yachts in the Club cannot be said to be complete, nevertheless it provides a record of the better known vessels and was compiled from newspaper files of The Province, News-Advertiser, The World and The Sun during the first three decades of the Club activities. Vancouver newspapers gave very complete coverage of sailing events in that period when yacht racing commanded wide public interest.

ABEGWEIT—32 ft. aux. Columbia River centerboard cruising sloop built at Steveston in 1912 for H. C. Shaw, who joined the Club in 1911.

ADANAC—18 ft. sloop designed and built by Horace Stone in 1910.

ADDIE—27 ft. open catboat sloop built in 1902 for Bert Austin at Vancouver Shipyard by William Watt, the first yacht constructed at the yard. Addie was in the original R.V.Y.C. fleet.

ADELPHI—44 ft. schooner designed by E. B. Schock for Thicke brothers. Built 1912, sailed by the Thicke brothers till 1919 when sold to Bert Austin, who sold it in 1922 to Seattle.

AILSA I—28.5 ft. D class aux. yawl, Mower design. Built 1907 by Bob Granger, originally named Ta-Meri. Subsequent owners included Ron Maitland, Tom Ramsay, Alan Leckie, Bill Ball and N. S. McDonald.

AILSA II—22.5 ft. D class aux. yawl built 1911 by Bob Granger. Owners included J. H. Willard and Joe Wilkinson.

ALEXANDRA—45 ft. sloop designed for R.V.Y.C. syndicate by William Fyfe of Fairlie, Scotland and built 1907 by Wm. Watts of Vancouver Shipyard. Won on raffle by A. J. Kapelle and purchased from him by E. B. Deane who raced her keenly for years against Spirit I and Spirit II. During First World War her lead keel was commandeered and she was beached. Capt. B. L. Johnson and two other returned naval officers, R. Rowe Holland and Fred G. T. Lucas re-conditioned her. Subsequently Capt. Johnson was sole owner and he later traded her to Walter Cline, who sailed her for some years. In 1938 she was practically completely rebuilt by Don Sinclair at Coal Harbour Shipyards for Temple H. Wright who sailed her in active competition till the war years and again till 1951 when she was sold to Seattle. The original tiller of Alexandra was donated to the Club as a perpetual trophy for Frostbite Dinghy competition by Temple H. Wright in 1955.

ALOHA—B class sloop brought from Victoria in 1906 by W. E. and C. L. Norris. Both were drowned off the yacht near Deep Cove, North Arm, Burrard Inlet. The yacht was found drifting and it was presumed that either both brothers were knocked overboard or that one fell overboard and the other jumped in to help, and that the ship sailed on. The bodies were never found. Aloha was owned in 1908 by Bill Templeton and was destroyed in the fire which razed the Stanley Park Clubhouse, December, 1909.

AMORITA ex **IMP**—A class sloop built by Johnson Bros., Seattle. Brought to Vancouver by George Beveridge in 1910. In 1912 she was owned by Bill Templeton who sailed her with some success till he built the Tamahnowus in 1921. Amorita was sold to Seattle.

ANDI LAILEY ex **DAWN**—49 ft. yawl built 1917 at New York. Brought from Chicago to Victoria 1925 and purchased 1926 by E. T. Rogers, who, in 1927, re-named her Andi Lailey. Sold to Tacoma in 1941.

ANYWHERE—45 ft. yawl built 1929 by H. C. Elliott and his sons Clint and Harry at the foot of Angus on North Arm, Fraser River, to design by Gerald Seaton. "Sticks" of yellow cedar were selected, cut and trimmed from standing timber at Deep Cove, North Arm, Burrard Inlet by the Elliotts. Clint Elliott still sails Anywhere after 35 years in commission—an outstanding record locally.

ARDRIE—B class sloop built at Prince Rupert in 1915 by George Askew. Owned by Harry Marshall in 1921 and by Walter Thicke 1923-26.

ARMIDA—36 ft. yawl designed by Halliday, built by Don Sinclair at Coal Harbour Shipyards for Tom Ramsay in 1935. Was record winner of all eight races entered in 1939. Sold 1944 to Seattle and later to California.

ASTHORE—32 ft. B class sloop built 1913 at Vancouver Shipyard for Wm. McDougal who raced her for some years. Other owners were Oliphant Bell and Reg Purves. Sold 1926 to Victoria.

ASHIGAMIK—36 ft. schooner built 1894 at Seattle. Purchased 1923 by Oswald Moseley who sailed her till the early forties.

ATLANTA—26 ft. cutter built in U.K. Owned by W. L. (Bill) Hunt from about 1926 to 1961.

BANSHEE—Known as "French" Banshee, sloop in the original fleet 1903 owned by Albert French, in 1905-6 by Norman Sawers.

BANSHEE—Known as "Irish" Banshee, sloop also in the first fleet, owned 1903-06 by Robert and George Cassidy, K.C. The latter became Justice of the Admiralty Court, Supreme Court of Canada.

BELLA E—29 ft. yawl, raised deck cruiser. Built 1921 at Beach Avenue Shipyard, foot of Burrard St., by H. C. and Clint Elliott to design by Gerald Seaton. Owned 1949 by E. B. Shearman who re-named her Free Lance.

BERTHA—34 ft. aux. centreboard yawl was in the original fleet. Reputed to be the first yacht in the Club to have an aux. gasoline engine. Owners included P. N. Thompson, C. S. V. Branch, W. A. Bauer, and A. E. White. Was originally designed for duck shooting on the Fraser River.

BLUE GROUSE—Sloop owned by Fred Lucas in 1903. Was first winner of the Graveley Cup.

BLUE MIST—46 ft. cruising cutter built 1932 by C. G. Crebbin.

BOSUN—Aux. sloop owned 1904-05 by George Bushby.

BRITANNIA—36 ft. centreboard sloop, was a "sandbagger". Owners included F. G. N. Seaton and Fred Sterling, in 1905 and 1906. In 1913 S. R. Smith and in 1919 R. A. Bindley.

CANUCK—32 ft. C class sloop built 1913 by R. K. Scarlett to give competition to Ted Geary's "Empress" sloops from Seattle.

CHEEMAUN—Centreboard sloop owned 1904-06 by Fred G. T. Lucas.

CHINOOK—Aux. schooner built in 1900. Owned in 1906 by Max Macgowan and in 1913 by Capt. A. W. Davidson.

COLUMBIA—Aux. schooner owned 1904 by Rev. John Antle. It became a British Columbia Coast Mission vessel.

COOLBAWN—Columbia River sloop owned 1904-06 by D. Cambie.

COPPER QUEEN—Centreboard sloop from Crofton, V.I., owned in 1906 by James Sterling and later by Ron Maitland.

CRESSET—40 ft. cutter, designed and owned by Douglas P. and F. Wavell Urry, built by George Askew and launched from his False Creek Yard near Burrard Bridge in June, 1929. Originally rigged as a gaff head club topsail, three headsail cutter, she passed through the usual stages of rig modernization. Carrying a crew of 15, she won her first English Bay Regatta in the year of her launching. She was sold to H. St. Claire Jellett in 1953 and in 1958 to her present owner, Gerry Palmer.

DAWENDENNA—37 ft. former Nanaimo pilot cutter. Purchased by Oswald Moseley 1903 and in the first fleet. Owned by Fred Schooley in 1905.

DAWN—See Andi Lailey.

DELORES—Sloop from Victoria, owned 1904 by C. O. Julian.

DIONE—26 ft. B class sloop from Victoria. Won Graveley Cup in 1907. Owners included Henry Bell-Irving, W. G. McKenzie, Fred Foster, Ron Maitland, Bob Marshall, Allan Leckie.

DOLPHIN—Schooner owned in 1905 by William Stark.

DORIS—32 ft. aux. centreboard sloop built in 1924 by George Askew.

EALASAID—32 ft. B class cruising sloop designed by Tom Halliday, built by Ken MacKenzie and launched 1930. Owned and sailed in active competition by Mr. Mackenzie for thirty-five years, Ealasaid has a unique record of racing victories. In 1952 she won the coveted Lipton Cup in International competition at Cowichan Bay, a frequent winner at English Bay Regattas, and has won the Ballenas Island and Fraser Lightship Races. Originally a gaff-rigged sloop she was changed to Marconi rig in 1936 and had a new mast and modern mast-headed rig fitted in 1955. Still winning races with Ken at the tiller, this trim sloop is one of the best maintained vessels and is a credit to the fleet.

EILEEN—33 ft. yawl built 1904 for Commodore W. E. Graveley. Later owners included Phil Whitehead, Reg Purves, Bill Roedde, H. St. Claire Jellett, Tom Halliday.

ELMARSH—Yawl owned 1912 by Alex Marshall, sold 1923 to Victoria.

ELSA MAY—40 ft. aux. sloop built at Johnson & Walkers Shipyard in 1907 for Curtis Davidson. Later owners included Ernestine Smith (Mrs. A. H. Jefferd), Commodore G. F. Gyles, Noel Jones. Her name is engraved on many Club Trophies for the early day long distance races. Wrecked May, 1931, at North Entrance to Silva Bay, Flat Top Islands.

FOUR WINDS—36 ft. yawl, double-ender, built 1906 for J. E. Macrae who that year, when the Club became "Royal", presented the signal cannon which graces the front lawn of Jericho Clubhouse. Sold to Victoria. As recent as 1959 Art Jefferd saw Four Winds up coast, in commission and in apparent good shape.

FREE LANCE—See Bella E.

FROLIC—Open yawl. Was in original fleet 1903, owned by Wm. Hodson.

GAMINE—Sloop built 1925 by George Askew to John Alden design for L. T. Alden. Later owned by H. T. (Freddie) Frederickson. Sold to the U.S.

GAZEKA—40 ft. aux. yawl built for A. G. Thynne in 1906. Owners included Commodore C. B. Macneill, Ron Maitland, Walter Cline, F. Griffiths. Sold in 1926 to Seattle.

GLENDOCHERT—30 ft. flush deck sloop built 1897 to design by J. H. McNab. Was in the original fleet, owned by Alex Grant.

GOLDEN ROD—B class centreboard sloop owned 1905-06 by H. C. Clarke.

GOLLIWOG—36 ft. yawl built by V. M. Dafoe. Was in the first fleet, owned by A. G. Thynne. Other owners were C. B. Macneill and Tom Pattison.

GLENDOLYN—Sloop purchased in 1913 in Puget Sound. Was built by L. & D. Johnson, Seattle, as a trial horse for Spirit I. Owned here by Tom Pattison, Phil Whitehead, R. Rowe Holland. Sold 1924 to Seattle.

HAIDEE—40 ft. centreboard yawl built at Vancouver Shipyards. Owned by W. A. Bauer in 1906, later by C. B. Stahlschmidt in 1926-31.

HALCYON—30 ft. sloop built 1897 by V. M. Dafoe. Owned 1905 by Percy Charleson, in 1923 by Dr. Ernest Gillies and in 1925 by Claude Effinger. She was re-named Patteran in 1936.

HAZEL—32 ft. aux. sloop owned 1922-26 by Alex Marshall. Re-named Madeline.

HEREANDTHERE—40 ft. yawl built 1930 by George Askew. Sister ship to Nelmar. Sold to C. W. Clarke in 1953, who sold her to J. Boyd Gordon of Campbell River in 1963.

HIAWATHA—Sloop in first fleet, owned in 1903 by F. W. Fisher and in 1904-06 by Erl Macgowan.

IMP—See Amorita.

INTREPID—C class aux. sloop built in 1906 by Louis (Speck) Jewitt. Later owned by Ron Maitland. Sold to Seattle in 1921.

IOLA ex **SWIPE**—33 ft. centreboard sloop built 1906 from lumber and fittings "acquired" by the Cao brothers. Later fitted with keel. Owned 1912 by Dave Manley and later by R. Rowe Holland and A. Buckerfield.

IVANHOE—39 ft. sloop built 1906 by Johnson & Walker, Cedar Cove, for C. A. Godson. This sturdy vessel is now yawl rigged and is still in commission sailing out of West Vancouver Yacht Club, owned by Ralph Vittery.

JABBERWOCK—25 ft. sloop in the original fleet, owned 1903 by Wm. Hodson. Was owned 1904 by C. B. Macneill.

KELPIE—38 ft. heavy weather cruising cutter, built 1893 at Port Blakeley, Wash., as a pilot cutter. Owned by the Lucas brothers. In 1913 re-named Kyrielle.

KYRIELLE—See Kelpie.

LADY PAT—38 ft. R class sloop, John Alden design, built 1927 at North Vancouver for Ron Maitland—see chapter on Lipton Cup R Class Racing. Sold to Seattle.

LADY VAN—39 ft. R class sloop, 23 ft. waterline, C. E. Nicholson design. Built 1928 at North Vancouver for R.V.Y.C. syndicate headed by Tom Ramsay—see chapter on Lipton Cup R Class Racing. Owned 1931-34 by Commodore Hon. E. W. Hamber. Sold to Seattle. Still in commission and was at the 1964 P.I.Y.A. Regatta in English Bay.

LAVEROCK—Sloop owned in 1903 by Rev. John Antle, was in first fleet.

LAVITA—Aux. cutter built in Puget Sound. Purchased 1909 by E. W. Maclean. Later owners were C. O. Julian, Ron Maitland.

MABEL DELL—See Naden.

MADELINE—29 ft. B class sloop from Puget Sound. Owned in 1905-06 by Bert Austin, later owners were A. H. Smythe, J. Green, W. J. Thicke.

MADELINE—32 ft. aux. sloop, former Hazel (see Hazel).

MAPLE LEAF—Aux. ketch built and owned by Alex MacLaren, Barnet Saw-Mills.

MARATEA—40 ft. aux. yawl built 1927 at Linton's Yard for W. Oliphant Bell. Owned later by Commodore J. A. Longley. Now in W.V.Y.C. fleet.

MARGOT—20 ft. keel sloop owned 1903 by Commodore W. E. Graveley. Was the first flagship of the fleet. Owned in 1904 by C. O. Julian.

MARIETTA—B class sloop purchased in 1906 by Alex Marshall from Victoria. Owned in 1908 by Gordon Willis who sold her later to Bill Templeton.

MARLOU—26 ft. C Class sloop built 1935 at Stanley Park Shipyards for Temple H. Wright. Sold 1937 to Pat Field, who sold her in 1939 to H. J. Knight.

MINERVA—46 ft. yawl built at Kowloon Dockyard, Hong Kong, for James Adamson, chief engineer of the C.P.R. trans-Pacific liner Empress of India. Purchased 1908 by W. E. Graveley, P. N. Thompson, F. M. Chaldecott and Jack Scott, owned later by P. N. Thompson and sold 1927 to H. A. (Hubie) Wallace. This beautiful yacht had a very active racing and cruising career— see chapter on Beaver Cup and Other Races—coming to an untimely end with its accidental destruction by fire at Ganges Harbour in 1936.

NADEN—100 ft. aux. schooner built by Wallace Shipyard for the Dominion Government. Purchased in 1924 by Sir Joe W. Hobbs and re-named Mabel Dell. Was later sold to California.

NAIVETTE—26 ft. yawl built 1927 at Vancouver for C. G. Crebbin.

NANCY—31 ft. yawl built in Victoria 1900 and acquired in 1903 by C. S. V. Branch. Owned in 1905 by Oswald Moseley and in 1906 by A. T. Paddon.

NANCY M—32 ft. sloop owned 1914 by Oswald Moseley.

NARBETHONG—B class centreboard sloop owned 1904-05 by C. B. Wainwright. She was later sold to Prince Rupert.

NELMAR—38 ft. aux. yawl built for Alex Marshall by George Askew in 1930—see Beaver Cup Races. Mr. Marshall actively cruised Coast waters in Nelmar for over 10 years when she was sold to Vans MacDonald, who sold her in 1946 to the O'Hanlan brothers and sailed to Newport Beach, Calif.

NYMPH—50 ft. yawl built in Puget Sound. Brought to Vancouver by J. Edward Bird in 1920. Actively sailed by Mr. Bird and his son Harry J. Bird till sold in 1924 to movie actor Ken Maynard in Los Angeles.

ONAWAY—Sloop built 1905 by William McDougall. She won the Mackie Trophy in 1906 or 1907, the symbol at that time of International Championship.

ONOMA—40 ft. sloop built at Boston, Mass. Purchased in 1913 by a syndicate of J. P. Fell, John Nichol, Bill Billings, and the Hon. Ian McKenzie, M.P. Converted to yawl rig in 1930. Sold 1932 to Tom Usborne.

ORPHAN—Sloop owned in 1903 by C. S. V. Branch. There is some doubt if she was an original member of the fleet, but it is known that Mr. Branch owned the 31 ft. yawl Nancy in August of 1903.

PATHFINDER—25 ft. cruising yawl built from designs by Thomas Fleming Day, a "Seabird" similar to Tamerlane. Dr. Day was the Editor of "Rudder" and made the west to east crossing of the Atlantic on a ship of this design. Pathfinder was purchased from Victoria by Gordon Stuart.

PATRICIA—36 ft. R Class sloop, Nicholson design, built 1921 by R.V.Y.C. syndicate headed by Ron Maitland. First yacht in fleet with Marconi rig (see R Class Racing Chapter). Sold 1923 to Pierpoint Davis of Los Angeles.

PATTERAN—See Halcyon.

PENGUIN—33 ft. sloop built 1907 by Wallace Shipyard for Gordon Legg. Owned 1920-24 by Clarence Wallace, in 1924-28 by Harry J. Bird and in 1928-31 by Harry Eakins. Burned off Spanish Banks in 1931.

PETREL—25½ ft. sloop owned by Albert Hancock, in original fleet 1903.

PIRATE—27 ft. Columbia River sloop, also an original, owned 1903 by D. Cambie. Was owned by the Springer brothers in 1904.

QUEENIE—25 ft. centreboard sloop owned in 1906 by Ron Maitland.

REDSKIN—B class sloop, C. D. Mower design. Owned 1905-06 by Harry Frith. Thicke brothers won the Graveley Cup with her in 1906. Owned by George Beveridge in 1908 and Art Jefferd in 1912. Sold to Vince Ramsay who won the Rand Series and possession of the Rand Cup in 1913. Some years later, Mrs. Ramsay, mother of Vincent, donated the Cup to the Club in his memory—he was killed on active service in the First World War—and the cup is now known as the Redskin Trophy. Redskin sank in Howe Sound.

RIOWNA—R class sloop from the Great Lakes, designed by George Owen of Boston, Mass. Purchased by R.V.Y.C. syndicate 1925 to contest the Lipton Cup—see chapter on R Class Racing. Later purchased and sailed by Commodore G. F. Gyles and son Cedric. Sold to Seattle and renamed Svea.

ROB ROY—Centreboard sloop built for Wm. McDougall in 1902. Was in original fleet.

SALLY LUNN—40 ft. cruising yawl, purchased 1924 by Ernest Woodward from The Lake of the Woods. Wrecked at Kitsilano Beach 1924.

SILVER SPRAY—B class centreboard cruising sloop, owned and sailed by W. F. (Billy) Findlay 1906 to 1913.

SIREN—30 ft. half-deck clinker built sloop from Vancouver Shipyard. In the original fleet, owned by Alex Grant. Was owned in 1905-06 by Capt. B. L. Johnson. It was a "sandbagger". Her bowsprit extended 6 feet over straight stem and main boom 6 feet over stern.

SLANI—46 ft., originally the pilot sloop Claymore. Converted to yawl rig in 1904 by R. H. Alexander and later converted to ketch rig.

SNOOKY—Sloop owned in 1924-26 by Stuart Dollar.

SPENDRIFT—See Spraydrift.

SPIRIT I—42 ft. sloop designed and built by E. L. "Ted" Geary in Seattle, 1906. (See chapter on Early International Races.) Purchased in 1913 by the Cao brothers and by E. A. Woodward in 1924. It was burned on Indian Arm in 1931.

SPIRIT II—48 ft. sloop also designed and built by Ted Geary, Seattle, in 1909. Owned in 1913 by Archie Selwood. (See Early Int. Races.) R. A. Bindley owned her in 1921-23 when she was acquired by Harold A. Jones who rebuilt and actively sailed this champion ship until 1947 when he built the new 66 ft. Spirit. Spirit II was sold to Jay Augustine in Seattle, 1947.

SPRAYDRIFT ex **SPENDRIFT**—30 ft. centreboard sloop built in 1912. Owned and sailed until the early thirties by Gordon B. Warren.

SWIPE—See Iola.

TAMAHNOWUS—34 ft. yawl built 1921 by Bill Templeton. Her distinctive red hull was a familiar sight on English Bay and long distance races for over two decades, winning the Beaver Cup in 1923 and twice winning the Julian Cup with lady skippers Mrs. E. W. Templeton in 1925 and Miss B. Pedlow in 1937. She was sold to Seattle.

TAMERLANE—25 ft. aux. yawl, a "Seabird" designed by T. F. Day, built 1910 at North Vancouver for W. G. (Billy) Breeze, who sailed her for several years before selling to C. W. Lauback.

TA-MERI—See Ailsa I.

TENDERFOOT—33 ft. schooner built 1910 by Harry Bird, boatbuilder, Victoria. Sailed by him and a crew of three to San Francisco and return in 1912. Bought 1913 by Fred O. Mills and sailed actively by him for twenty years. Sold to Seattle in 1933. Harry Bird took three years to build her and she was reputed to be one of the finest built yachts afloat—not a butt in any plank.

THELMA—28 ft. sloop built Vancouver Shipyard 1902. One of original fleet and owned 1903 by Oswald Moseley, in 1904-05 by J. P. Roberts, and in 1906 by J. Padden.

TILLICUM—B class sloop, C. D. Mower design, sister ship to Redskin, Aloha and Marietta. Owned 1904-07 by E. B. Deane, and won the Graveley Cup in 1904 and 1905. Owned by Fred Lucas in 1908 and by Tom Ramsay in 1912. Owned by Capt. A. C. Crawford in 1931.

TITANIA—B class sloop owned by E. B. Deane in 1904 and by V. L. Venable in 1906.

TRUANT—38 ft. yawl built 1908 at Victoria for Walter E. Adams, later Commodore of Royal Victoria and Admiral of P.I.Y.A. in 1927. Was owned 1929-32 by Roy Ginn.

TURENGA—R class racing sloop built by Commodore B. T. Rogers to compete in first Lipton Cup race for this class. She was defeated by Sir Tom, Seattle (see chapter R Class Lipton Cup Racing). Subsequently sailed by E. T. Rogers, P. T. Rogers and F. Rogers. Sold to Frank Duff Stuart in 1935. Sank in collision with Steamship Lady Pam off Port Atkinson 1939.

UWHILNA—48 ft. all teak yawl built in Shanghai for R. H. Alexander in 1913, winning the Beaver Cup that year. Sold to Puget Sound in 1920 and brought back to the Club by Fred Mills in 1934. He sailed it actively in competition, winning the Beaver Cup in 1938 and was awarded the "Bird Rock Trophy" in 1941. Uwhilna, sailed by Fred Mills, was the first Club yacht to circumnavigate Vancouver Island. Sold in 1944 to Seattle, where she still sails.

VALKYRIE II ex **WANDERING LASSIE**—Schooner purchased from Victoria 1930 by S. R. Smith.

VAMPIRE—B class sloop brought from Halifax 1905 by W. B. Ferrie. Owners included R. W. Holland in 1909, Vincent Ramsay 1912, D. F. Morrison 1913, E. Shear 1919.

VERADA—40 ft. yawl built 1910 at Seattle. Sold 1926 to A. E. White.

VERONA—B class aux. sloop built 1906 for C. O. Julian. Owners were Ron Maitland, G. C. Van Horne, S. P. Judge and C. Smalley.

VOLAGE—Yawl built at Victoria in 1890's for H. F. Kirk. In R.V.Y.C. fleet 1907.

WESTWARD HO ex **WHITE WINGS II**—54 ft. yawl built 1927 by George Askew for Walter Cline who traded her to Capt. B. L. Johnson for Alexandra in 1930. Capt. Johnson fitted her with the first Genoa sail in local waters and sailed her very actively for over a decade, winning the Beaver Cup in 1930, 1937 and 1939, the Swiftsure Classic in 1931, and acquired the Bird Rock Trophy in 1936. (See chapters on Swiftsure Races, P.I.Y.A. Regattas.) Later became a missionary vessel in the South Seas.

WIDEAWAKE—32 ft. sloop purchased from Victoria 1904 by William Hodson. Owned in 1906 by E. B. Deane.

WINONA—27 ft. sloop designed and built by Ted Geary, Seattle, in 1910. Was a "trial-horse" for Spirit I. Purchased in 1913 by Ron Maitland. Owned in 1922 by Allan Leckie and in 1926 by G. M. Harris. Returned to Puget Sound.

YELLOW KID—18 ft. yawl, owned 1906 by W. G. (Billy) Breeze.

YUNO—Aux. cruising ketch acquired 1904 by E. W. Stark and Frank Wright, father of Temple H., later Commodore Wright.

Schooner ADELPHI, 1912.

Sloop AMORITA ex IMP, 1912.

CHAPTER 5

Early International Races

SAIL AND POWER

A S FAR AS THE RECORDS GO, the first international race in which a Vancouver yacht took part was in Bellingham Bay, at Fairhaven, on July 4th, 1891. The local contender was the *Siren*, a five-ton cutter, 30 feet overall, with 1200 square feet of sail area.

She was specifically designed and built by Capt. Billy Watts, founder of Vancouver Shipyard, to outrace all comers. She had her workout in Burrard Inlet on Dominion Day 1891, when Watts outsailed Andy Linton's famous speed queen *May,* which was skippered by the old maestro, Walter Graveley.

So Watts sailed to Bellingham with a crew consisting of J. W. McFie, Dr. Bob Mathison, D. S. McKenzie, Dr. C. H. Gatewood and Jim McKay. At Fairhaven he picked up a local man who knew the tides. The six competing boats included the *Ariadne* of Herreshoff design, considered the queen of Puget Sound waters.

The race started at 10 a.m., with a nice westerly breeze of about ten knots. The first leg, six miles, was sailed with a started sheet. *Siren* jockeyed herself into the windward berth and boomed off with mainsail, two jibs and a club topsail.

"After getting in the lead in the first half mile," Captain Watts recalled many years after, "the lug of the mast band at the shrouds pulled out, so I took in the kites. J. W. McFie, carrying a marlinspike and a piece of new one inch manila, went up that shroud like a cat and had the shroud fastened in less than five minutes. Even with this delay, we were first round the stake boat. The wind was freshening and the next leg was a thrash to windward. That was where we put it to the Herreshoff boat, which was our next astern.

"The wind had freshened to fifteen knots and we stormed along under mainsail and jib. This leg was about eight miles out to Lummi Island. On rounding the second stake boat, we broke out a big spinnaker, sent up the topsail and we came down that stretch at ten to twelve knots, winning by more than half an hour."

Captain Watts recalled that the committee presented him with a purse of gold to the amount of $80, but as a new hotel was being opened that day, the Vancouver contingent left the purse in American waters . . . for value received!

The *Ariadne* got her chance to revenge her defeat several years later, when she came up to Vancouver for the 1896 Dominion Day regatta. That race is vividly recalled by veteran R.V.Y.C. member Billy Breeze, who helped crew *Ariadne* on that occasion.

Here is how Mr. Breeze recalls that memorable race:

"In 1896 a carnival was arranged to celebrate the tenth birthday of Vancouver. A yacht race, open to all comers, was widely advertised, and entries were received from the *Wideawake* of Victoria, the *Ariadne* of Bellingham, the *Copper Queen* from Crofton, and a new boat from Nanaimo called the *Whisk*.

"There were, of course, as entries from Vancouver, Andy Linton's *May*, Billy Watts' *Siren*, and Hayden's *Triton*, so there was quite a showing when they all jockeyed up to the line.

"The race was sailed on a typical summer day, and the prize of $200 cash was won by *Ariadne* of Bellingham.

"The *Ariadne* was owned and sailed by W. E. Abbott, an old friend of.my dad's, and my brother and I were invited to crew on˙ *Ariadne*, which like most of the rest of the fleet was a shallow beamy centre-boarder.

"The course sailed was the old Burrard Inlet course, the starting line was off Deadman's Island, with the first leg of the course to a buoy off Moodyville, then westward down the North Vancouver shore to a buoy off the Indian Mission, and thence to the starting line.

"The wind was a nice summer westerly, and good tactics took us right out to the flood tide, and with spinnakers set we were all pretty well bunched at the first buoy off Moodyville. This was where the real race started, a beat along the north shore. There were no big wharves or grain elevators, no shipbuilding yards to steer clear up or to break up the wind.

"Port tack into the beach as close as you dared, then starboard tack out into the comparatively dead water until you struck the edge of the incoming tide and then back in again to shore. We beat right on past the mission buoy because we had to get as far to windward as we could in order to lose as little as possible crossing the tide.

"Our skipper was wise and kept right on until we were off the mouth of Mosquito Creek and were leading the fleet.

"The little craft was sent into the tide a rap full and we got out of the heavy current just nicely clear of the Burnaby Shoal. The distance from there to the finish line was soon covered and we got the winning gun with a comfortable lead over the nearest competition."

The *Ariadne* prize money was not spent in the same manner as the *Siren's*. "The next time I saw *Ariadne*," Billy Breeze recalls, "she was sporting a nice new suit of sails paid for by the City of Vancouver's tenth birthday yachting regatta."

After the formation of the Vancouver Yacht Club in 1903, the Mackie Trophy was put up for international competition between B.C. and Puget Sound yachts. *Gwendolyn,* owned by Lloyd Johnson of Seattle, held this for several years, although E. B. Deane's *Wideawake* of Vancouver gave her some anxious moments in the defence, especially on Bellingham Bay. William McDougall's sloop *Onaway,* built in 1905, finally brought it to Vancouver. The goat's head trophy was getting a bit mangy, and no one mourned its loss when it was destroyed in the fire that burned the clubhouse in 1909.

Vancouver yachts came close to making a clean sweep at the international regatta held at Bellingham on July 3rd and 4th, 1906. In the Mackie Trophy race, E. B. Deane's *Wideawake* finished nearly a mile ahead of the *Gwendolyn* of Seattle, but owing to the distance not being accomplished in the time limit of five hours, it was deemed no contest. However Vancouver yachts won seven of the twelve prizes, the successful boats being Louis Jewitt's sloop *Intrepid,* winner of Class B; Cliff Cao's sloop *Swipe,* second in Class B; Bill McDougall's *Onaway,* winner of Class D; Walter Thicke's *Redskin,* second in Class D; James Adamson's yawl *Minerva,* second in Class A; C. O. Julian's *Verona,* winner of Class B cruisers; and J. E. Macrae's yawl *Four Winds,* second in Class B cruisers. *Four Winds* was still in commission at Prince Rupert in 1959 and no doubt is still there. *Verona* was active locally in recent years.

In 1906 a delegation from the R.V.Y.C. approached Hon. James Dunsmuir, then Lieutenant-Governor of B.C., with a suggestion that he put up a cup for international competition in the 29 foot class of the international rule.

He provided the magnificent Alexandra Cup, named in honor of the queen. The R.V.Y.C. was made the defending club, and William Fyfe of Fairlie was commissioned to design the fastest boat he could under that measurement.

The Seattle Yacht Club pinned its faith on E. L. "Ted" Geary, a local yachtsman who had turned out several successful racers on the Sound.

The Vancouver defender was built by Capt. Billy Watts at Vancouver Shipyard, and was launched as the *Alexandra,* one of the most notable sloops ever to fly the R.V.Y.C. burgee. The veteran Walter Graveley was chosen to be her skipper, with a crew consisting of P. N. Thompson, R. A. Corbett, William McDougall, Claude Thicke, Owen Power and Gordon Willis.

Her length overall was 45 feet, load waterline 29.1 feet, beam 8.3 feet and draft 6.2 feet, with original sail area of 1348 square feet. The Seattle challenger, the *Spirit,* was 42 feet long overall, load waterline

26.6 feet, beam 8.6 feet, and draft 5.8 feet, with original sail area of 1085 square feet.

The Northwest International Yacht Racing Association had awarded the international regatta in 1907 to Seattle, so the contest for the Alexandra Cup was held there early in July.

Spirit was sailed by Ted Geary, her designer. Light summer breezes prevailed on the first day's race, and approaching the finish line *Spirit* had pulled out a long lead when the wind dropped and left her practically becalmed. *Alexandra* in the meantime had felt a freshening air, and came sweeping along bringing the wind with her. *Spirit* drifted slowly on towards the line only a few feet away, with her rival fast coming up. *Alexandra* went under *Spirit's* lee, and by so doing allowed *Spirit* to catch a puff of air that just put her across the line with a five seconds lead. The next race was won by *Alexandra* in another good contest, but *Spirit* carried off the third race and the cup.

It is hard to believe the enthusiasm and excitement caused by these races in both Vancouver and Seattle. Both cities were young and booming, yet small enough to be full of local pride. Newspapers gave extensive front page coverage, and without the benefit of radio or television, citizens waited for the breathless despatches that came every few minutes on the telegraph line.

In 1908 the Alexandra Cup races were held at Vancouver over the English Bay course, a twelve mile triangle. In the meantime *Alexandra* had been raffled and purchased by E. B. Deane, for many years one of the keenest sportsmen in the club. Ted Geary was once more at the tiller of *Spirit* and the two met for the first race on July 1st in view of the largest gathering of yachts ever seen on English Bay. *Alexandra* led the *Spirit* home, winning the first race. The next race was under conditions threatening rain, with a fresh easterly wind, and when two thirds of the way round the course *Spirit* was seen to run aground on Spanish Bank. The crew immediately got to work with the spinnaker pole, and aided by the fresh breeze heeling the yacht, worked her into deep water, and she continued the race.

Meanwhile "Jimmy" Deane, in the *Alexandra*, had gone to leeward to turn around and go to the assistance of *Spirit*. That was fatal, for while he was turning around the *Spirit* got off the bank and romped ahead, crossing the finish line with a lead of several hundred feet. The third day's race was won easily by *Alexandra* with a lead of more than twenty minutes, so the cup came to Vancouver.

After these races *Spirit* was sold to Victoria owners and the Seattle Yacht Club made preparations to meet the Canadians in 1909 with a new boat. This was *Spirit II*, also designed by Ted Geary. When subsequently measured in Vancouver, she was 48 feet overall, load waterline 30.33 feet, beam 8.33 feet, and original sail area 1276 feet.

The 1909 international races were a sad disappointment. In the

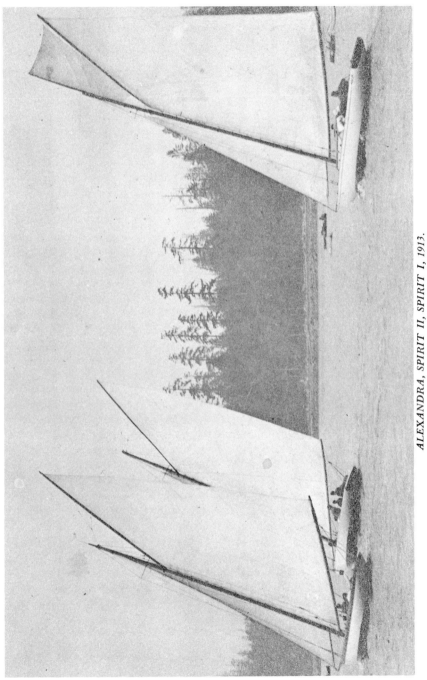

ALEXANDRA, SPIRIT II, SPIRIT I, 1913.

first race at Seattle, *Spirit II*, sailed by Ted Geary, won over *Alexandra*, sailed by Jimmy Deane, in light conditions. Then it was revealed to the Canadians that *Spirit II* had been improperly measured, and that she exceeded the prescribed 29 feet at the waterline. C. B. Macneill, then commodore of the Royal Vancouver Yacht Club, offered to sail the races under protest to be referred to a full executive meeting of the North West International Yacht Racing Association, and when this was refused he ordered all the Canadian vessels to return home. This they did, and the Alexandra Cup was never contested again. It has been in custody of the Royal Vancouver Yacht Club ever since.

However many years of keen racing lay ahead for the *Alexandra*, *Spirit I* and *Spirit II*, for all three were eventually owned in Vancouver. In 1909, after the Seattle fiasco, E. B. Deane took the *Alexandra* to Victoria and defeated *Spirit I*, thus annexing a cup put up in Victoria.

In 1910 *Spirit I* was brought to Vancouver and the rivals met again, *Alexandra* granting a time allowance. In the first race *Spirit* was skippered by the Thicke brothers, and won by one minute and eight seconds over the English Bay course, although *Alexandra's* actual time lead was five seconds. In a second race the *Spirit* was skippered by Cliff Cao. She won by one minute 44 seconds corrected time, and was only 16 seconds behind in actual time.

In 1911 *Alexandra* was not in commission, but in 1912 she had plenty of competition with *Spirit I*, which had been purchased by the Cao brothers, Cliff, Chris and Reek, who for many years were among the finest sailors in the R.V.Y.C. fleet. The boats raced on even terms that year, and *Spirit I* won three out of four contests. Meanwhile *Spirit II* had been purchased by Archie Selwood from her Seattle owners, and 1913 became a vintage year, with *Alexandra* winning four races and *Spirit II* two. However there was no more international racing until the 1914 season, when the keenly fought Lipton Cup series for R class yachts commenced.

Archie Selwood, who owned and sailed *Spirit II* from 1913 to 1916, gives the following interesting reminiscences:

"There was no cabin on *Spirit II* when I bought her in 1913 from a Seattle syndicate. I put the cabin on according to the plans of Ted Geary, the designer. I also lowered the keel a foot and inserted heavy timber, properly shaped, between the keel and the original timber.

"Jimmy Deane always claimed that he could have beaten any boat on the coast with *Spirit II*. He was a very competent skipper, and almost uncanny in finding a breeze to help him, if and when he got behind in a race. An old Australian, George Ellis, was Jimmy Deane's guide and mentor. Deane's *Alexandra* was canvassed for British conditions, and Ellis lengthened her mast, increased her sail area and strengthened her gear.

"For her size, the smaller *Spirit I* was the best boat in the fleet.

She could be handled with a little finger on the tiller. Both the *Alexandra* and *Spirit II* were oversize for their class, *Spirit II* on account of my lowering her keel, and the *Alexandra* on account of her lengthened mast and extra canvas, but we raced as "special sloops", rather than as a measured class.

"The Little *Winona*, which later came to Vancouver, walloped the *Alexandra* off Victoria when Jimmy Deane tried to lug too much canvas on. *Winona* became a sort of legend, but she never did anything in Vancouver. She could take it in a blow, and got her opportunity in Victoria.

"I bought the *Spirit II* shortly after she came up from Seattle on a cruise to Long Bay. She had hatches but no cabin and was a big empty basket inside. When a few R.V.Y.C. members became over exuberant they were given enough to put them to sleep and were then stored like freight under the hatches in *Spirit II*.

"Later she was forbidden to moor in the club anchorage on account of the alleged deplorable behaviour of the Seattle crew, who, in fact, were quite innocent. By some mistake, I was regarded as a sober law-abiding member, so *Spirit II* under my ownership was accepted into the club.

"The *Rival* was built by a group at Everett to race against the two *Spirits* and the *Alexandra*. She turned out to be a flop and was torn apart and rebuilt into *Genevieve*, oversize for the 29 foot class, very powerful in moderate to heavy winds. Her skipper was an uncouth monster who liked to eat with bare hands rather than use a knife and fork.

"*Genevieve* had two match races with *Spirit II* for $500 a side. In both cases *Genevieve* got her fresh breeze at the start of the race but ran into soft breezes later in each race. *Spirit II* won both races after being apparently well beaten.

"They tried to raffle *Genevieve* and sold tickets around our club. You took a chance, one cent up to $10. Can I ever forget? I took three chances, and drew $9.96, $9.73 and $1.50. Tickets did not sell very well and the raffle was called off.

"In one great race at Cowichan, *Alexandra*, *Genevieve* and *Spirit II* competed. There was a little too much wind for *Spirit II*, but it just suited *Genevieve*. The *Alexandra* sailed a beautiful race and *Spirit II* was in the race all the way. *Genevieve* pulled out a short lead on the first leg, a close haul. The flag on the windward buoy had blown away, though the barrel and flag stick were there.

"With her usual bad luck *Genevieve* sailed by the outer mark and kept on going after *Alexandra* and *Spirit II* had turned the buoy and were heading home. Her skipper thought we were giving up. We were anchored near the starting buoy when *Genevieve* finally came in. Her skipper wanted to know what was going on, and when informed he had oversailed the outer buoy he entertained the Cowichan spectators with a flow of profanity I have never heard equalled.

"Both the *Alexandra* and *Spirit II* were better off the wind than the *Genevieve* and it is doubtful if she could have held her lead on the run home, even if she had rounded the buoy. Foxy Jimmy Deane in the *Alexandra* quite possibly could have cut off *Genevieve's* wind, and as *Spirit II* was just a shade faster than either, I might have pulled ahead while the other two were jockeying with each other. I was not far behind the *Alexandra*.

"Horace Stone, whose father was responsible for building our Art Gallery, was in my *Spirit II* crew at times before the First War, in which he was killed. On one club race and cruise to Clam Bay it was blowing pretty hard and Horace was trying to get the dinghy aboard when he fell overboard, but managed to grab the main sheet. We were running free and too close to shore in the pass to round up. I was afraid to jibe for fear of shaking Horace loose from his grip.

"Old Benny Rogers, the commodore, and his guests were gazing at us over the rail of his flagship, the *Aquilo*, which was just overtaking us to starboard, 20 yards away. It was blowing hard but Horace managed to inch his way along the main sheet to near our cockpit and it took four of my crew to drag him in. In the meantime the dinghy was half inboard and half in the water.

"After the fleet reached Clam Bay the commodore received all skippers aboard the flagship. I, as skipper of *Spirit II*, slicked up a little, and went aboard the *Aquilo* and had a couple of rums, being the centre of interest on account of Horace Stone's narrow escape, for the Stones and Rogers were great friends.

"Just when all the formalities were being rigidly observed on the deck of *Aquilo*, to my horror alongside came my dinghy bearing six disreputable, soggy, so-called yachtsmen. They got aboard anyhow, and Horace Stone saved the day by being welcomed personally by Benny Rogers himself. The other five were given a drink and taken below to look at the engines.

"The Bird Rock Trophy, put up each year for the yachtsman making the gravest error in seamanship, went one year to *Chinook*, who caused more trouble to the fleet than anyone else ever managed to do. Our club fleet were on their way to Bellingham, many of them sailing. As usual, we intended to keep well outside the Sandheads lightship. *Chinook* was a schooner, and she had started early and had run aground on the sandheads. Many of the other boats, thinking *Chinook* was the lightship, got caught and ran ashore also. She was then owned by Erl Macgowan.

"I sold *Spirit II* while I was away in the First World War. Two more owners had her before Harold Jones bought her about 1923."

CHAPTER 6

Beaver Cup

AND OTHER EARLY RACES

IN 1906 COMMODORE R. H. ALEXANDER put up the Beaver Challenge Cup, which has become emblematic of the cruiser championship of the R.V.Y.C. It was first put up for a cruiser race from English Bay to Entrance Island, off Nanaimo, and return. In the first race in 1907 C. A. Godson's 40 foot cruising sloop *Ivanhoe* finished ahead, but she was protested for carrying sandbag ballast. The race was ordered re-sailed and was won by Charlie Julian's sloop *Verona* on time allowance. In 1908 Godson's *Ivanhoe* won without protest, and in 1909 the course was changed from English Bay to White Islets to the Ballenas Islands and return, leaving all the marks to port. It has since become the club's most popular Gulf cruising classic.

The first winner over the Ballenas course was Graveley and Thompson's 46 foot yawl *Minerva*, which was followed in 1909 to the finish line by the sloop *Ivanhoe*, sloop *Elsa May*, yawl *Gazeka*, yawl *Haidee*, yawl *Elmarsh* and sloop *Lavita*.

The famous *Minerva* led the pack again in 1910 and 1911, but in 1912 there was no contest. The 1913 race was won by R. H. Alexander's Shanghai-built *Uwhilna*, a 48 foot yawl, with the schooner *Adelphi* second, followed by *Gazeka* and *Minerva*. R. M. Maitland's *Gazeka* led the field against *Minerva* and *Uwhilna* in 1914, and she repeated in 1915 against the Thicke brothers' schooner *Adelphi*.

Ballenas Island races were resumed in 1920 after the First World War and *Minerva* again recaptured the trophy, ahead of *Adelphi*, *Elsa May* and *Onoma*. Next year in 1921 the 40 foot sloop *Onoma*, then owned by W. H. Billings, showed her prowess by beating *Minerva* and *Adelphi*. *Minerva* was back again in the lead in 1922, ahead of Bill Templeton's *Tamahnowus*, repeating in 1923 ahead of *Onoma*, *Minerva* and *Elsa May*.

In 1924 G. F. Gyles' 40 foot sloop *Elsa May* was the winner against *Tamahnowus* and *Minerva*, but the latter made a comeback in 1925 when she led *Elsa May* and *Verada* to the finish line. The fastest race ever recorded over the course occurred in 1926, when the trophy went to Ernest Rogers' 48 foot yawl *Dawn*, later renamed *Andi Lailey*.

A full report of this memorable race was given at the time in The Province, and it is well-remembered by many old timers. The *Dawn*, which Rogers had recently brought out from Chicago, finished course in the all-time record time of 11½ hours for 82 nautical miles, followed only a minute behind by *Minerva*.

According to the private records of Capt. B. L. Johnson, *Minerva* once made this course in exactly 11 hours, followed by *Andi Lailey* in 11 hours 20 minutes and *Alexandra* in 11 hours 40 minutes, but this could not have been for the Beaver Cup Trophy, as it is not in any official record. Many races over the Ballenas Island course were held, generally in April or early May when strong winds could be expected.

In the great 1926 race the *Dawn* started the race at 10 a.m. on June 26, and completed the course at 9:30 p.m. With Rogers as crew were Hubert Wallace and four others. The *Minerva* was skippered by Walter Graveley, with Phil Thompson, F. M. Chaldecott and Jack Scott, whose ages averaged well over 70. *Minerva*, the defender of the trophy, was barely a minute behind *Dawn*, with Bill Templeton's yawl *Tamahnowus* third, with a 12 hour run, followed closely by Ian Mackenzie's sloop *Onoma*, and C. H. Elliott's yawl *Bella E.* about an hour and a half behind.

The special race sailed over the same course by yachts that could not qualify as cruisers under the Beaver Cup rules was won by Barney Johnson's 29-rater sloop *Alexandra*, which had been altered to a short cruising rig of about 650 square feet of working sail. L. T. Alden's sloop *Gamine*, a 32 footer designed by his brother, John Alden, came in about an hour later, followed by the R-class *Turenga*. It was the first and only Ballenas Island race that was sailed entirely in daylight hours.

Both classes were started at the same time, with *Alexandra* crossing the starting line 10 seconds after the gun. The yachts set balloon jibs and some carried spinnakers also. They were soon making a speed of more than seven knots as they ran up the Gulf to White Islets.

Minerva ran into the lead soon after the start, but was passed at Gower Point by *Dawn*, and these two yawls had a very keen contest right to the finish, while the sloop *Alexandra* stayed close to them most of the way around. *Dawn* rounded White Islets at about 12:37 with *Minerva* three minutes behind, while *Alexandra* followed a few hundred yards behind her. *Tamahnowus* and *Onoma* were several miles behind the leaders at this point, and the rest still further away.

The wind continued to freshen until it was blowing about 25 miles an hour and the boats were making splendid time with balloon jibs carried to starboard. *Minerva's* balloon would not stand the strain and split, after which a reaching jib was set in its place, then the topsail halyard carried away, and the topsail had to be taken in, but *Minerva* still pressed hard after *Dawn* in the strong wind.

Dawn rounded the Ballenas Islands at 3:31 p.m., five minutes ahead of *Minerva* and 20 minutes ahead of *Alexandra,* with the rest still a long way astern. There was a good strong breeze, though not quite so strong as the easterly had been at times. The boats carried it right to the finish, though it lightened up a lot at the last. *Dawn* continued to hold her lead though the crew of *Minerva* did everything possible to make up for the loss of their topsail by setting water sails under the bow, and other rags, but every time they thought of something fresh, the *Dawn* followed suit until they had everything drawing but the dish towel.

Next year, in 1927, Ian Mackenzie's 40 foot sloop *Onoma* was the Beaver Cup winner, with Oliphant Bell's new 40 foot yawl *Maratea* second, followed by *Andi Lailey,* ex *Dawn, Tamahnowus, Minerva, Bella E.* and *Elsa May.* The 1928 race was won by *Tamahnowus,* with *Minerva,* now owned by Hubert Wallace, second. *Minerva* was back in her old form in 1929, when she led *Andi Lailey,* Walter Cline's new 54 foot yawl *White Wings II* and *Maratea. White Wings II,* one of the largest vessels in the R.V.Y.C., was built by George Askew, and later had a distinguished career under the name *Westward Ho* with Barney Johnson at the helm, who traded in *Alexandra* as part payment.

The 1930 Beaver Cup race was won by Barney Johnson with his new *Westward Ho,* which led at White Islets and Ballenas, followed by Clint Elliott's new 45 foot yawl *Anywhere, Minerva, Andi Lailey* and Alex Marshall's new 38 foot yawl *Nelmar,* built by George Askew. She put up a very good performance for a big boat in light and baffling winds, finishing at 2:55:13, well ahead of *Anywhere* at 3:44:15.

In the years that followed Barney Johnson won the Beaver Cup again in 1937 and 1939 with *Westward Ho,* while the gallant *Minerva* copped the trophy for the three years 1934-36, with Hubert Wallace at the tiller, making a total of 11 Beaver Cup wins during her long career, which ended on 28th June 1936, when she was burned to the water's edge at Ganges Harbour, through the carelessness of a plumber who was working inside her with a blow torch. Barney Johnson sold *Westward Ho* in 1939 to the United States, and she is now a Roman Catholic mission ship in the South Sea Islands, fitted up with a chapel amidships. Some years after the Second Warld War she won the race from Hawaii to Fiji and return. *Elsa May,* another prominent Beaver Cup contender, and winner in 1924, was wrecked in May 1931 in Porlier Pass, while owned by Noel Jones.

In 1931 Clint Elliott's *Anywhere* was the Beaver Cup winner, with L. C. Alden's *Gamine* only six minutes behind, and Doug Urry's new 40 foot cutter *Cresset* third. *Anywhere* repeated her win in 1932, but in 1933 the prize went to Oliphant Bell's *Maratea. Uwhilna,* which had been owned in Seattle for some years, was brought back to Canada in 1938 by Fred Mills, and she proved herself by winning the Beaver Cup that year for the second time, the previous win being under R. H. Alexander's ownership in 1913.

Gallant *Cresset* showed her form in 1940 when Doug Urry sailed her to victory to win the last of the Beaver Cup races until 1946, when he again took the coveted trophy. Harold Jones' new *Spirit* led the field in 1947, and since then winners have included the Scottish-built *Gometra,* the big A-class sloop *Oho,* owned by P. R. Burr, and Bill Morrow's Roedde class *Elusive.* In 1938 the Vice-Commodore's Cup was offered for competition by B class vessels in the Ballenas Island race, and winners have included Alex Marshall's *Nelmar,* Tom Ramsay's *Armida,* Ken McKenzie's *Ealasaid,* Bill Morrow's *Elusive* and Ken McRae's *Barracouta.*

At one time a cup was put up by A. G. Thynne for a race around Texada Island. This cup was won in 1908 by Curtis Davidson's new 40 foot sloop *Elsa May* which made the round trip in only 24 hours, carrying a fair wind all the way. She was the only one of the fleet to complete the course. At the start of the race most of the fleet worked the Point Grey shore, while *Elsa May* stood over to Point Atkinson where she picked up an easterly breeze that the others missed, and this wind carried her right up to the head of Texada Island, where the wind obligingly changed to westward, and *Elsa May* came racing home before a gale that made such heavy weather for the other boats beating against it that they gave up the race.

Next year's race round Texada Island was heavy weather all the way, with Phil Thompson's *Minerva* an easy first over the big Seattle yawl *Gwendolyn II* by two hours, after a gruelling three day ordeal in late May. When there was wind there was plenty of it, but it was always a head wind and the crews had no rest, for short tacks were the rule and each watch saw some strenuous work. The yachts had a lee rail breeze most of the time, for although the winds were baffling and delayed progress, there was always a strong breeze. The course around Texada on straight legs is about 190 miles, but the competing yachts easily covered 300 miles in their hard windward fight, and sailed the whole distance close-hauled. One of the six entrants in this race was E. W. McLean's big black cutter *Lavita,* and two of her crew are still around to tell the tale 54 years later, Oswald Mosley and Charlie Julian. Other notables in the *Lavita* crew were the Lucas brothers, Fred and Ed, Dick Holland, Ron Kenvyn and Roxy Rochester. C. A. Godson's *Ivanhoe* finished third to *Gwendolyn II,* a big yawl which had sailed in the San Francisco-Honolulu race the previous year, and which sailed under R.V.Y.C. colours from 1913 to 1924.

Yawl ANDI LAILEY, 1927.

Sloop ONOMA, 1914.

Another Texada race was held in 1929, when the yachts were allowed to use both power and sail, being allotted a certain quantity of gasoline. They got a premium for the number of gallons unused at the end of the race, and were penalized for anything used over the allotted quantity.

Walter Cline's *White Wings II* won on corrected time from Hubert Wallace's yawl *Minerva*. The boats started at 2:13 p.m. Saturday and *Minerva* got back at 5:37 p.m. Sunday.

In addition to cruiser races over the Ballenas Islands course there were some special sloop races concurrently in the 1920's, which were keenly contested. In the 1925 race Ernie Woodward's *Spirit I* won from Barney Johnson's *Alexandra,* both having short cruising rigs. *Spirit I* gained an hour on *Alexandra* at the start, where a strong tide and very light wind delayed a number of the boats in crossing the starting line. *Spirit* still held this hour's lead at White Islets and increased it to about two hours beating up to the Ballenas Islands against a strong Qualicum. The yachts carried this heavy breeze back nearly to Point Grey, then finished with light airs, *Spirit I* about two hours in the lead. In 1928 Harold Jones' *Spirit II* won by a minute and 40 seconds over Barney Johnson's *Alexandra,* with Philip Rogers' *Turenga* half an hour later.

One of the notable nights in R.V.Y.C. annals was during the 24th of May weekend in 1913. The fleet had gone on a cruise to Nanaimo, where they were caught in a howling southeaster. Twenty sailing craft were anchored in the harbour, with a piping strong wind from the southeast which showed every indication of continuing. Some began to drag anchor and decided to risk crossing the gulf. The first of the sailing fleet to leave was Gordon Warren's *Spindrift*. With a reef tucked in, this handy little cruiser got away an hour before the next boat to start. This was the cutter *Kelpie,* owned by the Lucas brothers, and as it turned out, she got the worst ducking of the fleet. R. H. Alexander's yawl *Uwhilna* went out, followed by the Thicke brothers' schooner *Adelphi,* and Cliff Cao in *Spirit I,* made a bid for cruising fame by going out with the big fellows. The little racer was tucked down to nothing. Mainsail and jib were double-reefed, and under this small area of canvas she was able to thrash to windward. Seas continually swept over her and once she was pooped, Cliff Cao sitting up to his waist in water as he steered. The pump was choked, so *Spirit I* had a really heavy weather trip. But she got to Bowen Island on one leg, and then the worst was over.

The *Kelpie* had the time of her life. She got under way under plain sail with no reefs, and would have made the beat to windward without much trouble under ordinary circumstances. When she got clear of Entrance Island, she was close-hauled on the starboard tack, bowling merrily along with her lee rail buried and making good weather of it. Further out in the gulf she ran into short steep seas, and she took a header into one which filled the jib and ripped the sail right up. The cutter was put about and got back under the lee of the land. It was decided to carry on. The only headsail now available was a small jib topsail, and to balance the craft a reef was put in the mainsail. Under this rig the big cutter was again put into it, and for a couple of hours she did very well.

However as she got out into the gulf it was seen she was not going to windward as she should. Instead of laying up for Bowen Island, she was falling gradually off, until she was almost bearing for Sechelt, and furthermore she took the seas over her, and for the first time in her history she shipped water below. It was decided to come about and take another tack offshore, but the small headsail proved faulty, and gave signs of carrying away. It was impossible to go to windward, so the cutter had to run for shelter. Trail Islands were handiest, and the cutter logged off great speed as she squared before the breeze. When an anchorage was reached all hands got to work cleaning up the sodden cabin, and a big fire was built on the beach to dry clothes and blankets. Numerous fishermen had also sought shelter. One of these was a Japanese sailmaker who patched up the big jib in a few hours work. A start home was made the next morning and some good sailing made the end of the cruise pleasant.

The Keyes Trophy, presented in memory of Commander Adrian Keyes in 1929, was originally intended for 9-metre yachts racing over a course from Jericho to the Fraser lightship and return. It is now contested by B class yachts. The first winner of this event was Barney Johnson in *Alexandra* in 1929, and for several years it was contested keenly by *Alexandra* and her great rival *Spirit II,* owned by Harold Jones, with *Spirit II* winning five times to *Alexandra's* two wins. Harry Wylie sailed *Lady Van* to victory in this race in 1938, and Barney Johnson won again in 1949 and 1954 with his Evergreen class sloop *Winston.*

The Minerva Trophy was put up in 1935 for a Fraser River lightship race between A and B class yachts, and this event has often been keenly contested. Among the big fellows which have lifted this trophy were Harold Jones' *Spirit* in 1947, P. R. Burr's *Oho,* E. J. Palmer's *Gometra,* Doug Urry's *Jenetta* and Ken McRae's *Mary Bower.*

In the years between the wars some of the keenest racing was between the three yachts of the 29 rater class then owned in Vancouver, the *Alexandra, Spirit I,* and *Spirit II. Alexandra* had fallen on evil days during the First World War, and even her keel had been melted down. After the war she was bought by a syndicate of former naval officers, of whom the leading lights were B. L. Johnson and Adrian Keyes. Eventually she was solely owned by Barney Johnson. Walter Cline then had her for several years, and in 1938 she was completely rebuilt by

Don Sinclair, Coal Harbour Shipyard, for Temple Wright, and emerged like a new ship. She was subsequently sold to American owners.

After the old 29 raters had been altered in various ways and given marconi rigs, they were called the nine-metre class. *Spirit I*, which was raced by Cliff Cao for many years, was purchased by Ernie Woodward in 1924. She won the special sloop class racing against *Alexandra* and *Spirit II* at the P.I.Y.A. regatta at Victoria in 1925, and continued to win many races with Geoff Woodward at the helm until she was burned in 1931 in the North Arm. *Spirit II* was acquired by Harold Jones in 1923, and for many years he raced her enthusiastically at every possible opportunity. In 1947 he replaced her with the queenly A class *Spirit* and *Spirit II* was sold back to the United States.

For several years there was keen rivalry between Barney Johnson's *Alexandra* and Ian Mackenzie's 40 foot centreboard sloop *Onoma*, and this culminated in a famous match race to the White Rocks and return in late September 1926. Each skipper wagered $100, a large sum in those days, with the winner to provide a dinner for both crews at the Jericho Country Club. The race was memorable, and even more so, was the dinner that followed.

The yachts were started in a moderate westerly breeze from Jericho. *Alexandra* made a long tack to Caulfeild, while *Onoma* worked up the Point Grey shore. When they crossed tacks about an hour later, *Alexandra*, which had the right of way, forced *Onoma* to go about, and from then on *Alexandra* gradually drew ahead, holding to the Bowen Island shore. *Onoma* abandoned the favorable set of the ebb tide out of Howe Sound and stood out into the Gulf looking for better wind. She lost so much by this that *Alexandra* soon sailed her out of sight and reached White Rocks with the last of the sea breeze, which died away about 20 minutes later. *Onoma* managed to round the rocks more than eight hours later. On the homeward run *Alexandra* first drifted with light head winds, but picked up a Squamish out of Howe Sound and soon foamed along with lee decks awash. *Onoma* was less lucky and arrived back in the anchorage in the slow time of 28 hours.

Sailing *Alexandra* were B. L. Johnson, Philip Whitehead, Reg Purves and Tommy Ramsay, while in the *Onoma* were Ian Mackenzie, A. G. Thynne, Jim Hutchinson, Jack Paterson and Jack Newell. At the subsequent victory dinner Barney Johnson felt assured that his $100 prize money would be plenty to meet all expenses, despite Ian Mackenzie's bottomless capacity for Scotch whisky. However when Ian decided to end the evening with a highland toast, in which all the glasses were cast into the fireplace, Barney saw the last of his prize money, and then some, go up in flames.

CHAPTER 7

Early Julian Cup Races

ONE OF THE MOST keenly contested trophies over the years has been the Julian Cup for lady skippers, first presented by C. O. Julian in 1906, and which he presented to the winner as recently as two years ago. His perpetual challenge cup is competed for by yachts to be steered by ladies alone, although men are allowed to hoist the sails and sit around where their weight might be useful as ballast, and also give advice. But if a man dares to touch the helm, the yacht is disqualified. There has always been keen interest in the Julian Cup races for they are often the best contested races of the season. The yachts are handicapped on past performance and all classes of yachts in the fleet can enter with reasonable chance of success, except for the smaller classes, for which separate prizes are now awarded.

The first winner of the trophy was Fred Lucas' little skimming-dish centreboard sloop *Cheemaun,* sailed by Miss Jessie McGeachie. A yellowed newspaper clipping saved by Mr. Julian recalls this memorable race of August 1906, which was held over a triangular Burrard Inlet course.

"The starting line was due north and south from the Robert Kerr buoy off Deadman's Island, and when the starting gun was fired the yachts all got away well together. The run to the buoy off Evans Coleman and Evans was very close. All the yachts had spinnakers set, and all sails were drawing to perfection. The *Intrepid,* sailed by Miss Olive Jewett, crept away from the rest and rounded the buoy first, with the *Winnie,* sailed by Miss Winnie Wainewright, a close second. The *Onaway* and *Swipe* came together for a friendly little chat and allowed the *Cheemaun* to get around third. The course from this buoy was a close beat into the wind to the spar buoy on Burnaby Shoal. On this leg the *Wideawake,* sailed by Miss Sophie Deane, stepped into the lead and was not again headed throughout the race. From this buoy to the starting buoy was another beat, necessitating a double tack.

"Around the starting buoy all yachts set spinnakers again for the second run to the first buoy, and by this time the fleet was beginning to stretch out again, beating out the Burnaby Shoal buoy. All yachts made well around it and headed for home. The *Wideawake,* which had sailed a beautiful race, crossed the line first, with *Intrepid* three minutes and 22 seconds after her, and *Onaway,* sailed by Miss Ollie McLennan, third. While all this was going on, Miss Jessie McGeachie was sailing the *Cheemaun* a straight and true course to a winning. All buoys had been rounded sharply and although the larger yachts had crossed the finish line before her, the *Cheemaun* bore down on the buoy, and rounding it, got the gun, giving her the race by 17 seconds, corrected time. After the race the lady skippers were entertained aboard Mr. Julian's new sloop *Verona*."

One of the amusing Julian Cup races was held the next year, when E. S. "Bun" Deane, the good-looking son of E. S. Deane, entered the ladies' race with the *Dione,* disguised is Miss Teria, a visiting yachtswoman from the east. It is recalled by old timers that Charlie Julian was so impressed by the stunning stranger that he made a special effort to make "her" acquaintance. However Miss Teria failed to win the ladies' cup that year, which went to "her" sister, Miss Sophie Deane, who skippered her father's speedy *Wideawake*. As late as 1930 Miss Deane (now Mrs. Percy Sills) was again winning the Julian Cup at the tiller of *Alexandra*.

The most exciting of all Julian Cup races must have been that sailed on July 14, 1913, which was marked by violent squalls and a series of accidents. The winner on this occasion was Miss Louise Deane (later Mrs. Harold A. Jones) at the helm of the famous racing sloop *Alexandra*. The notable 1913 race was reported by the The Province as follows:

"Under the most boisterous conditions ever experienced in a yacht race on Burrard Inlet, Miss Louise Deane sailed the racing sloop *Alexandra* first across the finish line of a fleet of 12 yachts, winning the Julian Cup. Miss Deane in this race established a record for the fastest time over the Inlet course, making the two rounds in 49 minutes and 30 seconds. Mrs. Ron Maitland, sailing *Winona,* came a close second on time allowance and *Spirit,* sailed by Mrs. Reek Cao, won third place. In several cases yachts became unmanageable in a heavy squall through the press of sail they were carrying, and the girls, not having strength to hold the laboring yachts, the men had to take charge, and they dropped out of the race. In the case of the sloop *Britannia,* Miss DeBeck, having done her utmost to hold the yacht on her course before a violent squall with the balloon jib dragging over the bow full of water, gave up the helm to the men to try and avert a wreck. Three of them threw their weight on the tiller in an effort to wear her, and failing in that tried too late to luff up, but with the drag of the headsail in the water she refused to answer quickly and at the high speed they were travelling piled up on the boom of logs at Hastings Mill, riding up on the boom sticks more than a third of her length till checked by the deep fin keel. As she struck the mast went by the board. The intricate network of rigging and wide spread of sail collapsed like the bursting of a bubble, going over the bow in a tangled mass of wreckage, but without hurting a soul, though some of the crew were thrown down by the impact of the collision. 'Anyway we're safe on land' chorused the crew as they scrambled out on the logs of the boom pending investigation of the yacht to see if she would still float. Finding the hull practically undamaged, the crew gathered up the wreckage and were shortly after towed home by the committee boat.

"The wind had been blowing fresh from the westerly all Saturday morning, but just previous to the start of the race it softened considerably, and a number of yachts that had been prepared to go out with reefs decided to carry full sail, *Spirit II* and *Britannia* being the only exceptions. While the boats jockeyed for the start off the entrance to Coal Harbour at 2:30 the wind commenced to freshen again and dark threatening clouds were seen filling all the western sky. There was then undoubtedly too much wind for full sail, but the first leg was a run to a buoy near Hastings Mill, so with a young gale astern the yachts got away at the starting gun, the crews crowding light sail on the already hard driven craft. The spirit of the 'Never Luffers' still seems to pervade the fleets of the Royal Vancouver Yacht Club, so when it comes to carrying on sail in a breeze, little short of running the boat under will induce these yachtsmen to shorten down. *Alexandra* and *Adanac* were first away, with the rest of the fleet romping after them. Troubles early began to develop in the hard-driven craft. The men on the judges' boat nearly got nervous prostration as they watched the little *Tillicum* careering down the course with her boom soaring skyward and threatening to jibe and take the mast out of her. *Chinook* with the light sail crew forward struggling with the spinnaker, was burying by the head in a way that threatened a somersault, a performance supposed to be habitual with catboats when over-driven. The crew succeeded in getting some of the canvas off and regained control. Then just as the fleet approached the buoy off Hastings Mill the wildest squall struck them.

"The waves were scattered in dusty spray as the yachts tore on with creaming ridges of foam sheering away in long diverging lines from their path. Here and there one was seen to yaw, wildly fighting to come into the wind, while spinnakers fought like sea-birds to be free. *Spirit, Spindrift,* and some others came about rather than risk a jibe at the buoy, the boats in some cases refusing to wear away for a jibe and had to be luffed, as the only alternative was the Hastings Mill boom where *Britannia* came to grief.

"On the beat up to the buoy off Brockton Point all the yachts had trouble carrying full sail, and *Spirit II*, with a reef in, seemed to be having more than she wanted. One or two boats luffed up and put in a tuck, but as the wind seemed to be lightening somewhat, most of them preferred to try and carry full sail. *Alexandra* was flying along in the lead with *Spirit I* hard in chase. The third leg, to the starting point, was another beat. Then the yachts went on around the course a second time. In this round *Alexandra* carried away her port spreader, but with this handicap still managed to maintain her lead, winning by a little over a minute from *Winona*, which was receiving time allowance, and made a remarkably good showing in spite of a couple of jibes that nearly wrecked her spars, and in one of which the fastening of one of the peak halyard blocks came adrift from the bridle of the gaff. She finished the race with the peak depending on a single part of the halyard leading through the masthead block.

"Nine of the 12 yachts completed the course. *Britannia* was dismasted and two others were forced to drop out. *Intrepid,* which came through the race safely, had the misfortune in reaching her mooring in Coal Harbour to be dismasted through getting her halyards foul of the spreaders of the yacht *Madeline,* anchored close by. *Intrepid* had already picked up her buoy, but was sheering around with sail still up."

And so ended a day to be remembered in the annals of the Julian Cup!

In the years between the wars, interest continued to grow in the ladies' day of racing, and in addition to the Julian Cup for lady skippers in all handicap classes, additional prizes were awarded for "A" and "B" class sloops, cruisers, and star class. With such fine boats as the two *Spirits, Alexandra, Riowna, Lady Pat* and *Lady Van* in the running, there was rarely a lack of excitement. In 1928 no less than 35 yachts came out with lady skippers. On that occasion Mrs. Hubert Wallace won the Julian Cup for the cruising yawl *Minerva.* In the "R" class, Mrs. Tom Ramsay sailed the new *Lady Van* to victory, and in the 9 metre class, Mrs. Harold Jones (nee Louise Deane), at the tiller of *Spirit II,* won by a minute over *Spirit I,* skippered by Miss Shirley Woodward. In the star class race, Mrs. Reg Purvis sailed the *Stella Maris* to victory over Miss Dorothy Wylie in *Astrea.*

With a fresh southerly wind, *Westward Ho,* steered by two girls, won by one length. There were 19 people on deck, of which 14 were girls and the usual crew of seven men. *Spirit II* was runner up, barely one length behind.

Veteran yachtsmen reminisce to Editor G. A. Cran, W. G. Breeze, C. O. Julian, A. H. Jefferd, 1963.

CHAPTER 8

Lipton Cup

AND "R" CLASS RACING

THE RACING OF "R" CLASS universal rule boats got its start when Sir Thomas Lipton, on a visit to Seattle in 1912, presented the handsome trophy known as the Lipton Cup to the Seattle Yacht Club, which invited delegates from other clubs to discuss the question of which class to put it up for. Ron Maitland, Reg Purves and E. B. Schock represented Vancouver. It was decided to encourage "R" class boats, and the Seattle Yacht Club built a defender, the famous *Sir Tom*, from designs by L. E. "Ted" Geary. She was 40 ft. overall, 7.4 ft. beam at waterline, and 5.4 ft. draft.

B. T. Rogers, who was then commodore of the Royal Vancouver Yacht Club, built as a challenger the *Turenga*, from designs by E. B. Schock, and launched at Menchions' Shipyard in Coal Harbour. She was 21 feet at the waterline, 7 foot beam, and 36 feet overall. The first Lipton Cup series was held at the Seattle International Regatta of July 1914. *Turenga* was sailed by Ron Maitland, with Owen Power, Curly Ellis and Ernest Rogers as crew. Ted Geary sailed *Sir Tom*, winning two straight races, and demonstrating pretty definitely that she was the better boat, though *Turenga* was at a disadvantage in one race through having to reef just before the start on account of a defect in the rigging. *Sir Tom* won the first race by 12 minutes and 39 seconds and the second by one minute and 53 seconds.

In 1920 the Royal Vancouver Yacht Club again challenged for the Lipton Cup with *Turenga*, which was sailed by Cliff Cao, the races being held at Cowichan Bay and Victoria. *Sir Tom*, with Geary at the helm, again won two straight races, demonstrating that on the average, she was about four or five minutes faster than *Turenga* over the 12 mile triangular course.

The failure of *Turenga* to lift the cup induced the R.V.Y.C. to build a new boat, and they were ready in 1921 with the Marconi-rigged *Patricia*, built from C. E. Nicholson's design, launched at Hoffar's yard in Coal Harbour, with Miss Patsy Maitland the sponsor. *Patricia* was the first Marconi-rigged sloop to be seen on Burrard Inlet. R. M.

Maitland was selected as skipper of the challenger and again the races were sailed at Cowichan Bay and Victoria. Particulars: 36.7 ft. overall, 24.4 ft. at waterline, 7.1 ft. beam at waterline, and 5.7 ft. draft.

Again *Sir Tom*, sailed by Ted Geary, won two straight races, though she had her old gaff rig and the same set of sails as in 1914. The finishes, however, were close, two minutes separating the boats in one race and two and a half minutes in the other. In September the two sloops met again in Vancouver for the international Isherwood Trophy, but although the series of five races was not completed owing to a couple of days of light wind, *Sir Tom* was defeated for the first time in one of the races. In a fresh easterly wind *Patricia* won the first race by six minutes and three seconds, but she lost the next two in close racing with her rival.

The contests were resumed in 1922 on Lake Washington, with Ron Maitland again at the helm of *Patricia*. The winds were very light, and *Sir Tom*, again skippered by Geary, and with a new Marconi rig, found the conditions very much to her taste and won two straight races. In the fall of that year both these yachts took part in the Southern California Yachting Association regatta at Newport Beach, where the Isherwood Cup was up for competition. *Sir Tom*, sailed by Ted Geary, won it under light weather conditions, with *Patricia* sailed by Ron Maitland second in the series, in which they met the best of the California "R" class.

In 1923, the P.I.Y.A. regatta was held in Vancouver, and again *Sir Tom* and *Patricia* raced for the Lipton and Isherwood trophies, with the yacht *Angela* of Los Angeles also competing. With Geary and Maitland still in the contest, *Sir Tom* won two straight races and *Patricia* came second.

There was no Lipton Cup race in 1924, but in 1925 a syndicate of Vancouver yachtsmen picked on the *Riowna* as a likely challenger. She was a heavy-weather "R" boat from the Great Lakes designed by George Owen of Boston, and winner of the George Cup on Lake Ontario. A boat of this type had been chosen because the 1925 regatta was slated for Victoria, where hard breezes are the rule. The *Patricia* meanwhile had been sold to a California yachtsman by Ron Maitland.

Again Ron Maitland was chosen to skipper the new challenger, while *Turenga* also re-entered the fray, with Ernest Rogers at the helm. The San Francisco sloop *Lady V*, sailed by John Winslow of Vancouver, was also entered, with, of course, the defending *Sir Tom*, again under the sure touch of Ted Geary. The first day's race off Royal Roads was sailed in a breeze of eight to ten knots with the usual tendency to be lighter at the start and finish point off the entrance to Esquimalt. *Sir Tom* covered the 12-mile triangular course in a little over two hours and 12 minutes, finishing ahead of *Turenga*, which had a new marconi rig, by about 4½ minutes and about 6¼ minutes ahead of *Riowna*, while *Lady V* was 12 minutes behind the leader.

Next day the wind was harder and showed velocities of 19 to 21 knots, but while the strength of the breeze was felt at the outer mark, it softened to about 8 knots at the inner mark, and *Sir Tom* won by 27 seconds from *Riowna* with *Lady V* third and *Turenga* fourth. As the Isherwood trophy rules called for three races, the yachts met again the following day. At last *Riowna* got the breeze she needed. With an average of 32 miles an hour *Riowna* made wonderful weather of it with a single reef, while *Sir Tom* seemed overpowered with two reefs in her mainsail. *Lady V* was disabled through a spreader giving away, though she was in third place when she had to give up. The result was that *Riowna* won by a five minute margin with *Sir Tom* second and *Turenga* third. However, *Sir Tom* retained both Lipton and Isherwood Cups.

The *Riowna* was then acquired by G. F. Gyles, and in 1926 she met *Sir Tom* at Seattle, with Cedric Gyles at the helm. *Sir Tom* on this occasion was skippered by Jack Graham, and *Turenga* was sailed by Philip Rogers. *Riowna's* crew was Cedric Gyles, Norman Gyles, Murray Rowan and Harry Jones, While *Turenga's* crew was Philip Rogers, Pat Burns, Temple McMullen and Gardner Boultbee. Again *Sir Tom* proved her superiority and held on to the Lipton trophy.

With *Riowna* hopelessly outclassed except in half a gale, the Vancouver yachtsmen began to think of a new challenger, and a syndicate was formed which secured designs from John Alden. This was the *Lady Pat,* built by Vancouver Drydock and Salvage Co. at North Vancouver. The 1927 international regatta was held in Vancouver and the new challenger was skippered by Ron Maitland, with a crew consisting of Phil Whitehead, Tom Ramsay and W. G. Mackenzie. Geary was again at the tiller of *Sir Tom* and Cedric Gyles handled *Riowna*. The first day's race was won by *Lady Pat* handily with a lead of one minute 58 seconds due largely to an error by Geary who apparently lost count of the rounds, and thought he had finished at the end of the second, where he was in the lead. He took up the race again but was unable to overtake *Lady Pat* although he passed *Riowna*. The boats had a westerly breeze of 7 to 9 knots.

Next day *Sir Tom* won by about six minutes in a light wind. On the third day, after the preliminary gun had been fired and the race was officially on, *Sir Tom's* main halyard carried away and the mainsail came down on deck. In the interests of good sport, Maitland and Gyles asked the judges to postpone the contest until Geary could get his repairs completed. After half an hour's postponement the race got away with Cedric Gyles sailing *Riowna* in the windward berth and *Lady Pat* under her lee but slightly ahead, and *Sir Tom* further to leeward. The race was sailed in a fresh easterly breeze, *Sir Tom* winning by about a minute from *Lady Pat,* and beating *Riowna* by about four minutes. So the Seattle boat once again captured the series and retained the Lipton Cup. *Riowna* was crewed in this race by Cedric Gyles, H. A. Jones, G. F. Gyles and Art Jefferd.

In 1928 another syndicate built an "R" boat and entered the lists under R.V.Y.C. colours to race against *Sir Tom*. This was the famous

Lady Van, designed by C. E. Nicholson. She was in many respects similar to the Nicholson-designed *Patricia,* but with specifications to suit the light weather conditions expected on English Bay. She was launched by Vancouver Drydock Co.

She measures 39 feet overall, 23 feet at the waterline, and seven feet one inch beam at the waterline. Her measurements were the closest to *Sir Tom* of any boat racing for the Lipton Cup, the American yacht being 40 feet overall, 22.7 feet at the waterline and 7.4 feet beam.

Lady Van was double planked with red cedar. There was very keen tuning up for the international regatta, with skipper Tom Ramsay having as his crew Art Jefferd, Bob Rowan and W. H. Savage. Ron Maitland's crew in *Lady Pat* consisted of Jack McDougall, Dean Johnson and W. G. Mackenzie, while G. F. Gyles in the *Riowna* had in his crew Cedric and Norman Gyles, Harry Jones and Francis Akhurst.

When the yachts met in the Lipton Cup contest at Vancouver in July 1928, *Sir Tom* won three straight races in light to moderate easterly winds, but it was no easy contest, and in the first race she did not get the lead until well along in the race. The margin between *Sir Tom* and the second boat ranged from two minutes and 20 seconds in the first race to nearly three minutes in the third. The finishes might have been closer and not so favorable to *Sir Tom* if it had not been for the keen rivalry between *Lady Pat* and *Lady Van*. *Lady Pat* got second place in the first two races and *Lady Van* was second in the third race, the points for the series being: *Sir Tom,* 12; *Lady Pat,* 8; *Lady Van,* 7; and *Riowna,* 3. *Riowna* was well sailed but had no chance with the others in the prevailing light weather.

By 1929 *Lady Van* had been purchased by E. F. "Jack" Cribb. Ted Geary again came up with *Sir Tom,* Ron Maitland was at the tiller of *Lady Pat,* and G. F. Gyles and his sons sailed the *Riowna*. At last the tide of victory turned in favor of Vancouver after 15 years of effort. The first race of the Lipton Cup series was sailed over a triangular course on English Bay in a light westerly breeze and was won by Ron Maitland's *Lady Pat,* which finished 13 minutes within the four hour time limit for the 12 mile course, leading *Sir Tom* by a whole leg. *Lady Van* was 25 minutes behind *Sir Tom* and *Riowna* was unable to finish.

Lady Pat's crew was Ron Maitland, W. G. Mackenzie, Aeneas Bell-Irving and Dean Johnson. *Lady Van* was sailed by Jack Cribb, Tom Pattison, George Askew and Harry Jones; while *Riowna's* crew was George, Norman and Cedric Gyles, F. Akhurst and Murray Rowan. In the second day's racing, success again rested with the Royal Vancouver Yacht Club, but it was Jack Cribb's *Lady Van* which carried the day. She took the lead when she passed to windward of *Sir Tom* a few seconds after the start in a strong easterly breeze, and soon drew away from them all. Heavy puffs were blowing over 20 knots, and all boats were carrying full sail. *Lady Pat* lost one of her weather shrouds and the mast followed, breaking off about a third of the way from the deck.

At the finish line of a grand race *Lady Van* was the winner 31 seconds ahead of *Sir Tom* and one minute and 45 seconds ahead of *Riowna*. On the third day of the race, Norman Gyles sailed in *Lady Van* in place of Tom Pattison, and she registered her second victory in a moderate westerly breeze, after a close contest with *Lady Pat*, which had procured a new mast. *Lady Van* was a minute ahead of *Lady Pat*, and 7½ minutes ahead of *Sir Tom*, while *Riowna* brought up the rear in a failing breeze. *Lady Van* got 12 points for the series, *Lady Pat* eight points, and *Sir Tom* eight points, thus after 15 years of failure by previous challengers, *Turenga, Patricia, Riowna* and *Lady Pat*, the *Lady Van* won the Lipton Cup for Vancouver.

The 1930 international regatta was held at Victoria over a new course off Cadboro Bay, and once again the Lipton Cup returned to Seattle. *Lady Van*, skippered by Jack Cribb, won the first race in a heavy easterly, with squalls of 30 miles or better. *Lady Van* finished 18 seconds ahead of *Lady Pat;* three minutes and two seconds ahead of *Sir Tom;* three minutes and 41 seconds ahead of *Riowna,* and 10 minutes and eight seconds ahead of *Turenga*, skippered by Forrest Rogers. The second race was sailed in a very light easterly. *Lady Van* was knocked out when she fouled a mark, and this put off *Lady Pat* from rounding smartly, so *Sir Tom* won with the safe lead of three minutes, 17 seconds.

So *Sir Tom* got the cup back, winning the third race in a light breeze with *Lady Pat* one and a half minutes behind. *Sir Tom* got 18 points for the series, *Lady Pat* 11, *Lady Van* 9, *Riowna* 6, and *Turenga* 5.

But the long supremacy of Seattle in the "R" class contests was on the wane, and in 1931 international regatta at Bellingham, Jack Cribb sailed *Lady Pat* to a decisive victory over the ageing *Sir Tom*. In the first race in light variable winds *Lady Pat* came across the line first with a lead of eight minutes 10 seconds. The second race, in a fresh northerly breeze, was won by *Sir Tom* with a lead of one minute and 10 seconds. The third race, which was won by *Lady Pat*, was declared no contest, because one of her crew members, Harry Jones, fell over board, and *Sir Tom*, again skippered by Ted Geary, stopped to pick him up. This led to a re-sailing of the race on August 15, with *Lady Pat* crossing the finish line 32 seconds ahead of *Sir Tom* in one of the closest and most thrilling races ever held in the series. *Lady Pat's* time over the 12 mile course was two hours, 15 minutes, 57 seconds.

In 1932 the *Lady Pat*, again with Jack Cribb at the helm, retained her possession of the Lipton Cup at the P.I.Y.A. regatta at Port Townsend. Her junior crew included Doug Maitland, 16-year-old son of the owner. *Lady Van* was also entered with Cedric Gyles at the helm, and of course Ted Geary had the perennial *Sir Tom*. *Lady Van* was now owned by E. W. Hamber.

In the first race *Sir Tom* came in first with a comfortable lead of three minutes 44 seconds over *Lady Pat*, with *Lady Van* close behind. However, Jack Cribb out-manoeuvered the old maestro Ted Geary in both the second and third races of the series and retained the cup. The final score was *Lady Pat* 8 points, *Sir Tom* 6 and *Lady Van* 4.

The 1933 international regatta was held in Vancouver, and was notable for the fact that both the "R" class contendors had junior crews. *Lady Pat* represented the R.V.Y.C., having eliminated the *Lady Van*, skippered by Ken Glass. *Lady Pat* was handled by Doug Maitland, with Bunny Whitcroft, Spud Akhurst and Jack Lindsay in his crew. For the first time in the Lipton Cup series *Sir Tom* didn't have the veteran Ted Geary at the stick, being handled by Arthur Ayres. In the first race *Lady Pat* lost her jibstay, but Ayres showed his sportsmanship by refusing to continue and the race was called off.

The next two races were a draw, with *Lady Pat* and *Sir Tom* each winning in the same day's racing. In the first race, in a nine knot breeze, *Lady Pat* won handily over her rival, finishing with a lead of 11 minutes and 7 seconds, for a time of three hours, 10 minutes, nine seconds. In the second race of the day *Lady Pat* got off to a poor start, losing about four minutes getting over the line. However, she managed to catch up to her rival in a seven knot breeze, but *Sir Tom* managed to slip over the finish line with a lead of 22 seconds. The third race was won by *Lady Pat* after a close battle, retaining both the Lipton and Isherwood trophies for the R.V.Y.C.

At the 1934 P.I.Y.A. regatta, also held at Vancouver, *Lady Van* showed her capabilities by winning the Lipton and Isherwood trophies in two straight wins. In the first race of the series, *Lady Pat,* skippered by Doug Maitland, was first to cross the line, but she was disqualified for fouling *Sir Tom* while rounding the first buoy, and *Lady Van,* which crossed the finish line several lengths behind, was acclaimed the winner. In the second day's racing, *Lady Van,* skippered by Harry Wylie, led all the way, beating *Lady Pat* by a bare minute. The Seattle entry, *Sir Tom,* under Arthur Ayres, grounded off the Point Grey bell buoy for 15 minutes and never regained the loss. A third race, required under the Isherwood Cup rules, was also won by *Lady Van* in very light winds, 12 minutes and 23 seconds ahead of *Lady Pat* and 38 minutes and 28 seconds ahead of *Sir Tom.*

In 1935 the veteran Ted Geary returned to the fray at the P.I.Y.A. regatta at Bellingham to puck up the Isherwood Trophy again with the new Seattle entry *Live Yankee,* which had been shipped round from the east coast the year before, and was owned by C. W. "Cully" Stimson of Seattle. The Lipton Cup was withdrawn from competition for technical reasons in 1935 and 1936. *Lady Pat,* under Doug Maitland, had a tough run of luck. Caught in a heavy blow in Bellingham Bay, she lost her mast, but borrowed another stick from *Turenga,* only to lose her starboard shroud in the first race, forcing her to put about. *Sir Tom* was also forced out with a broken shroud. Cedric Gyles in *Riowna* sailed a fine race, coming second to *Live Yankee,* with Harry Wylie bringing in *Lady Van* third.

Sloop LADY VAN, 1928.

LADY VAN'S first racing crew L. to R., Commander Savage, Bob Rowan, Skipper T. M. Ramsay, A. H. Jefferd.

The second race provided an easy win for Ted Geary, but the third race of the series proved a surprise. Breezes were light, and *Live Yankee*, a heavy weather boat, could get nowhere, coming in a poor fourth, crossing the line in a dead heat with *Riowna*. *Lady Van*, skippered by Harry Wylie came in first, making the score 12½ points for *Live Yankee* and 12 for *Lady Van*.

During the next five years of "R" class international racing, *Lady Van* consistently showed her superiority over all rivals. In Isherwood Cup racing at Victoria in 1936, *Lady Van* was skippered by Harry Wylie, *Sir Tom* by Arthur Ayres, *Lady Pat* by Doug Maitland, *Live Yankee* by Jack Graham and *Riowna* by Norman Gyles, with *Lady Van* leading the field in three straight wins: The international regatta in 1937 was at Port Townsend, with *Lady Van, Lady Pat, Sir Tom* and *Live Yankee* competing. *Lady Pat* was now under American colors, having been sold to Manson Backus of Seattle. The first race was won by Jack Graham in *Live Yankee*, then acknowledged U.S. Atlantic and Pacific champion in her class but *Lady Van* had no trouble romping home in the next two tests to cinch the Lipton Cup again. For the first time in international "R" class racing, *Lady Van* had a lady at the helm, Miss Dorothy Wylie, who showed that she possessed all the skill of her father, H. E. Wylie. Her crew for the series was Peter Winckler, Colin Campbell and Ron Roberts.

The 1938 P.I.Y.A. regatta was held in Vancouver, and Harry Wylie was again at the helm of Eric Hamber's *Lady Van*, holding both the Lipton and Isherwood trophies with five straight wins over *Sir Tom* and *Lady Pat*, the two cups being raced for in separate series instead of concurrently as in the past. In 1939 at Bellingham the *Lady Van* under Harry Wylie again cinched the Lipton and Isherwood trophies with six straight wins over *Lady Pat, Sir Tom* and *Riowna*. In the Lipton series, *Sir Tom* lost her mast in the second race and *Riowna* her mainsail in a 30 knot breeze in the third race, so *Lady Pat* was the only one to finish the course against *Lady Van*. Harry Wylie repeated again at the Cowichan Bay P.I.Y.A. in 1940, with six straight wins over *Sir Tom* and *Riowna*, skippered by Cedric Gyles.

That year marked the end of international "R" class racing in Pacific coast water, with *Lady Van* the acknowledged speed queen, after a generation of keen competition. Canada was now deeply embroiled in war, most of the younger yachtsmen were joining the colours, and defence regulations required all Vancouver yachts to stay east of Jericho. Consequently racing ceased completely from 1941 to 1944. *Lady Van* and *Riowna* were sold to Seattle owners, and *Turenga*, then owned by Frank Stuart, was sunk in collision with a coastal steamer off Point Atkinson, so for the first time in 27 years the R.V.Y.C. was non-competitive in "R" class. The Isherwood trophy is dormant, and the Lipton trophy was offered for six-metre competition after the war.

CHAPTER 9

Early Power Boating

IN THE EARLY DAYS of yachting in Vancouver, sail predominated almost entirely, for few could afford to operate one of the expensive steam yachts of the period. However, with the development of the gas engine, and later of the diesel, the once-despised power cruiser became an important feature in club activities. The adoption of small auxiliary engines in sail craft also became almost universal, at least in the larger classes.

The first private steam yacht to appear on Burrard Inlet is believed to be the *Nagasaki*, which was built in Japan, and brought to Vancouver on the deck of a steamer before 1890. She was of teak, copper fastened, with upholstered interior, and been built to the order of A. G. Ferguson, a C.P.R. official. She passed through several ownerships in the early days of Vancouver, but does not appear to have ever been on the club roster, for by 1904 she had become a tugboat, and finally ended her days in the fish business.

Somewhat similar to the *Nagasaki* was the *Mow Ping*, a fine teak-hulled steam launch imported from China by B. T. Rogers, and the first power boat in the fleet to fly the blue ensign—had a Scotch Marine Boiler and 2 cylinder compound steam engine. She had a gleaming brass funnel and was kept with all the pomp and splendor of a naval pinnace. She ended her days ingloriously on the west coast of Vancouver Island towing fish scows. Mr. Rogers followed the *Mow Ping* with the huge steam yacht *Aquilo*, the largest vessel ever to fly the R.V.Y.C. burgee. After his death, she was sold to Seattle owners.

The first gas engines to be imported and sold in Vancouver were brought out by a club member of many year's standing, A. W. LePage, who for many years owned the fine power cruiser *Tusitala*. By 1905, the club's fleet list shows 19 gasoline powered vessels on the roster, including Rev. John Antle's first Columbia Coast Mission boat, the *Columbia*.

The Rev. John deserves a special place in the club history, yachts and the sea were the great loves in the life of this doughty Newfoundlander. He will go down in B.C. history as the founder of the Columbia

Coast Mission, which brought medical care and religous consolation to many remote spots on the B.C. coast.

He first cruised the coast in 1903 in the open-deck sloop *Laverock,* and the experience persuaded him of the need for a coast marine mission, which he started in 1905. In 1933 he purchased in Europe the magnificent 75 foot yacht *Syrene,* later renamed *John Antle,* which he sailed out to this coast from Falmouth, England, for use as a hospital ship. Her figurehead was a bare-bosomed siren, which Mr. Antle thought rather unsuitable for a mission boat, so he donated it in 1936 to the Royal Vancouver Yacht Club, where it is a handsome ornament on the balcony of the Jericho station. The clipper-bowed yacht is now owned by the B.C. Forest Service.

When he was nearly 75, John Antle went to England and purchased the 48 foot yawl *Reverie,* which had been built of teak in Assam, India, in 1933. In the summer of 1940 he sailed her to Vancouver with only a Portuguese boy as crew. As soon as the war was over he set out again for a cruise to the West Indies with two young girls as crew members. Now over 80 years of age, the voyage proved too much for his health, and for the first time in his life John Antle admitted defeat and decided to return home from Panama. The R.V.Y.C. sent one of their members to California to help him sail the last lap home. The old sea dog continued to live aboard his yacht at the Coal Harbour station of the R.V.Y.C. until his death in 1949 at 84.

Power boating really came to the fore in the club in the boom years between 1910 and 1913, with the appearance of such vessels as F. L. Hutchins' *Ysidro,* E. B. Deane's *Emoh,* W. A. Bauer's *Wyrril,* R. P. McLennan's *Lo'Olbee,* E. J. McFeely's *Jolly Mac,* F. L. Buckley's *Epauline,* and Knox Walkem's *Half Moon* and *Full Moon.*

In the years just prior to World War I, a thriving business developed in importing teak-built yachts from Hong Kong, which were brought out on the decks of freighters. Notable among the Hong Kong yachts were Stuart Cameron's *Gleniffer,* W. F. Brougham's *Daphrona,* William Farrell's *Sheileena,* C. R. Gordon's *Walrondo,* the *Iphis,* later Newton Burdick's *Helena B.,* and the *Sutil,* later the *Athero.*

The early days of power boat cruising in the club are graphically recalled by Colin Ferrie, who before the war owned the *Colifer,* and since 1923 has owned the *Rhinegold.* Modern members haven't an idea of the difficulties power boat owners had in the early days, he recalls.

A popular early engine was the heavy duty Buffalo, which had a five inch bore and six inch stroke, and had to be started with a heavy bar. The bigger ships had Frisco Standard gas engines. The first semi-diesel in the club was in the *Sheileena,* which had to be started with a blow torch. Self starters first appeared about 1923. Every man had to be his own mechanic, for the power boats were inclined to break down any time and anywhere with little provocation. However there was a great spirit of camaraderie among club members who owned power boats, and they always rallied around to help those in distress. This often entailed towing a fellow member for a considerable distance. Often search parties were organized to look for yachts which failed to return from cruises on time.

International power boat races were very popular in the years 1907 to 1914, and many R.V.Y.C. yachtsmen were also affiliated with the Pacific International Power Boat Association, of which R. P. McLennan was commodore in 1909-10 and Knox Walkem in 1911-12.

Three Vancouver power boats were entered in the third annual long distance cruising race in 1910, between Tacoma and Victoria, which was won by Knox Walkem's new *Half Moon*, 42.2 feet long overall, by 10 feet in extreme beam, and powered by an 18 h.p. Eastern Standard gas engine. She was built and designed by Capt. Billy Watts of Vancouver Shipyards. Other Vancouver entries were the *Konomic*, a 58 footer built by Easthope Brothers specifically to enter the Puget Sound and Alaska long distance races, and the *Limit* of 1908, which had already won the Alaska race with E. B. Deane as skipper. In the 1910 race *Konomic* was skippered by Ernest Easthope and *Limit* by A. W. LePage. There were seven American entries.

Under the measurement handicap rules then applied, *Half Moon* was first and *Limit* second. *Konomic's* new engine gave her trouble and she rated seventh. Elapsed time of the *Half Moon* from Tacoma to Victoria was 23 hours, 52 minutes and 19 seconds. The course was a triangular one, and entailed the rounding of a stake boat in English Bay before the boats could proceed through Active Pass.

In the 1911 international race Walkem's *Half Moon* came second to the Tacoma yacht *Corsair*, so he decided on a new entry for the 1912 race. The result was the *Full Moon*, designed by the famous E. B. Schock, and built by J. R. Van Dyke and Sons at Vancouver. She was 56 feet long overall by 11 feet beam, powered by a 25 h.p. Eastern Standard. She easily triumphed over *Corsair*, winning the race with an elapsed time of 23 hours and 31 minutes. Other R.V.Y.C. entries were W. A. Bauer's *Wyrill*, which came in second, and F. L. Hutchins' *Ysidro*. The course was from Vancouver to Tacoma, via a stake boat at Port Angeles.

In 1912 there was sufficient interest in power boat racing in the R.V.Y.C. for Commodore B. T. Rogers to offer the Commodore's Cup.

There was a two day race, the first day from Vancouver to Nanaimo, and the second day from Nanaimo to Buccaneer Bay. Ten power boats started and the winner was W. A. Bauer's *Wyrill*, with S. J. Castleman's *Naturitch* second and Knox Walkem's *Full Moon* third. In 1913 the international race was between Olympia and Victoria. The Commodore's Cup was won by J. Emerson's *Arranmore*, with H. M. Burrit's *Elgomar* second and *Vaquero* third. In 1914 the Commodore's Cup race was from English Bay to Porlier Pass, and won by C. Wakeley's *Gene*. Alex Marshall's *Vireve* was the power boat race winner in 1915, but until the war was over racing of any nature at the club was non-existent.

One of the finest power yachts to join the R.V.Y.C. fleet in the prosperous pre-war years was the 60 foot teak-hulled *Walrondo*, built in Hong Kong in 1912 for C. R. Gordon. She was named after the two sons of the family, Wallin and Ron, and the family dog Do-do. The *Walrondo* has a claim to fame in club annals, for she is believed to be the only vessel in the R.V.Y.C. club ever to be captured by pirates, and spirited away from the Coal Harbour floats.

The *Walrondo* had been brought out from Hong Kong by a Seattle man named Jerry Woods, who did a thriving business ordering and supervising the building of yachts in the Orient for owners in the Pacific northwest. When the *Walrondo* arrived, she did not come up to Mr. Gordon's specifications in some respect, so there was a dispute over the final payment.

One dark night in December 1912, Mr. and Mrs. Woods climbed aboard the *Walrondo* at her Coal Harbour berth, managed to start the engine unobserved, and stole away out of the harbour to a remote cove near Seattle.

Several days went by before the *Walrondo's* owner was able to discover the whereabouts of his ship. Taking an engineer with him, Mr. Gordon sped away to Seattle, where he recruited the services of a lawyer and two deputy sheriffs. In the dark of the night the foursome crept up on the *Walrondo* at her berth, where they were greeted by Mrs. Woods with a shotgun and dire threats of violence if they attempted to come aboard.

The deputy sheriff read a writ of attachment; there was a scuffle with Mrs. Woods over possession of the shotgun, and finally the rightful owner again took possession. The Woods family were put on the shore with their baggage, and told where they could go.

Subsequently Mrs. Woods was forced to return to Vancouver to meet another charge against her, so she was also charged with theft and piracy for good measure.

The case was heard before the late Judge Billy McInnes, who happened to be a friend of the complainant. Early in 1913 Mrs. Woods was convicted of grand larceny, for stealing the *Walrondo's* engine . . . there was some legal doubt about the title to the ship . . . and was sentenced to a stiff jail term.

During the first Great War, the *Walrondo* was sold to the federal department of fisheries for use as a patrol boat, and she is now owned by the federal department of public works, used as an inspection boat, to carry engineers to remote spots on the coast. Her teak hull is said to be still as sound as when she was captured by the pirates from the R.V.Y.C. floats more than half a century ago.

International power boat racing was revived after the war, and in

C. R. Gordon's WALRONDO, 1912.

E. B. Deane's DAVY JONES, 1910.

Col. C. C. Ferrie's RHINEGOLD. Built 1911, still going strong. Opening Day, 1965.

1922 the Pacific Motor Boat race from Vancouver to Seattle attracted some interest, with W. P. Deewees' big *Reindeer,* a former U.S. Navy submarine chaser, coming in second. She also won the Rudder Cup race that season on Lake Washington. In 1923 the winner of the Pacific International Motor Boat Cup, for a race between Seattle and Vancouver, was won by Capt. James Griffiths' *Sueja* of Seattle. The White Rocks power boat race was won by *Reindeer,* and the Flat Tops race by W. J. Butt's *Jolly Mac.*

Between the wars many other large power boats were added to the fleet. In 1922 the 122 foot diesel yacht *Norsal* was completed, and has proudly flown the R.V.Y.C. burgee ever since. She was built for N. R. Lang of the Powell River Co. and was built at Menchions' yard in Coal Harbor. She was subsequently owned by W. P. Dewees and is now beautifully maintained by Clarke Gibson and his brothers, serving as commodore's flagship in 1952. Mr. Dewees was one of the most enthusiastic of power boat yachtsmen and his ships included the converted U.S. submarine chaser *Reindeer,* which he acquired in 1921, and later the famous *Moonlight Maid,* which was once the commodore's ship of the New York Yacht Club, and whose career is worthy of special notice.

She was originally the *Columbia,* built at Philadelphia of iron in 1898 to replace a yacht of the same time which had been sold to the U.S. Navy. The *Columbia* was purchased by the Royal Canadian Navy about 1915 for patrol duties on the Atlantic coast under the name of H.M.C.S. *Stadacona.* She later became an accommodation ship at Halifax, and gave her name to the naval shore establishment there. She also served at Esquimalt for a short time. After her war services, she was purchased by Capt. Joe Hobbs of Vancouver, who operated her for a time as a rum-runner under the unlikely name of *Kyukuzmt.* He subsequently converted her back to a luxurious yacht under the name of *Lady Stimson.* Mr. Dewees renamed her in turn, *Moonlight Maid,* and this fine clipper-bowed ship was long one of the outstanding power yachts in the club. She was sold during the second World War to become a tug operating between Seattle and Alaska, a rather sad end to a notable career. It has often been said that she also served in the Spanish American War as USS *Wasp,* and took part in the capture of Manilla, but it was an older, but similar sister, also called *Columbia,* that had this honor.

In 1925 Mr. Dewees offered a cup for a gulf power boat race, which was won by *Jolly Mac.* The Dewees Cup is still in active competition among club members. Races in the 1920's were under Rudder Club rules, which had some resemblance to the predicted log races of today. Each owner estimated the time his boat would take to cover the distance at a fixed number of engine revolutions, penalties being imposed for any engine adjustments after a five minute period at the start.

R. M. Maitland, commodore in 1924, was an enthusiast both in sail and power boating, and among the power cruisers he owned at various times were the *Yrrebeinna, Ysidro, Gleniffer, Heather M.,* and *Belmont.*

A. Melville Dollar, commodore in 1925 and 1926, was also an enthusiastic power boat cruising man, and his *Rio Bonita,* a 95 foot former sub chaser which he acquired in 1922, took part in many notable long coastal cruises. He was always a great booster for the beauties of Princess Louisa Inlet, and in 1924 the *Rio Bonita* took part with many other outstanding coast yachts in a cruise to that beauty spot. In those days organized club cruises were much more popular than they are now, and it was not unusual for 20 or 30 power boats to set off at one time for a long weekend up the coast.

The fleet cruise to Princess Louisa Inlet in July, 1924 was a memorable one. Taking part in the week long trip were 11 power yachts and seven sailing craft. They make an interesting list, for many well-known old-timers, their families and friends, were represented. Leading the flotilla was Commodore R. M. Maitland in the power cruiser *Ysidro;* Vice Commodore A. M. Dollar in the *Rio Bonita;* and Rear Commodore W. J. Butt in the *Jolly Mac.* Other power cruisers were W. P. Deewees' *Reindeer,* A. L. Bell's *Arrawac,* S. N. D. Robertson's *Iola,* C. C. Ferrie's *Rhinegold,* George Beeching's *Mandalay,* and the famous *Sueja,* flagship of Capt. James Griffiths, commodore of Seattle Yacht Club, and also a longtime member of the R.V.Y.C. Two power cruisers from Tacoma also joined the flotilla.

Sailing yachts taking part were Bill Templeton's yawl *Tamahnowus,* A. E. White's yawl *Verada,* Ernest Woodward's yawl *Sally Lunn,* J. Wilkinson's yawl *Ailsa II,* G. F. Gyles' sloop *Elsa May,* Harold Jones' sloop *Spirit II* and Stuart Dollar's sloop *Snookie.*

The 30 foot power cruiser *Iola* was an interesting addition to the fleet, for she had recently been shipped out from Scotland, where she had cruised extensively. Colin Ferrie's 35 foot *Rhinegold,* which he had recently acquired, had been built as long ago as 1911, but this fine little 35 footer has always been treated with loving care, and she is still Col. Ferrie's pride and joy and a credit to the power boat fleet.

One of the club's enthusiasts in the 1920's was Capt. (later Sir) Joe Hobbs who owned several famous yachts. He was one of the most famous of the rum running entrepreneurs of the period, so he was not averse to using his vessels for a little legal liquor running on the side. The first of his yachts was the 100 foot luxury schooner *Naden,* built at Wallace's shipyard as a government surveying vessel, and seconded to the Royal Canadian Navy during World War One. She became a depot ship at Esquimalt, and her name is immortalized in HMCS *Naden,* the Esquimalt naval establishment. Captain Hobbs purchased her from the navy in 1924 and later renamed her *Mabel Dell* in 1926. She was subsequently sold to California. Hobbs also acquired the famous *Stadacona* from the navy, so that by a strange coincidence, he owned the vessels that gave their names to both the Halifax and Esquimalt naval bases. He operated the *Stadacona* as the yacht *Lady Stimson* before selling her to Mr. Dewees. Captain Hobbs also brought out from England the 150 foot clipper-bowed steam yacht *Vencedor*, originally the training ship *Exmouth II*. She was later acquired by Hon. E. W. Hamber, and from 1931 to 1935 proudly flew the commodore's burgee.

A notable addition to the power fleet was made in 1939, when the 100 foot *Fifer* was completed at Burrard Dry Dock for the late Capt. W. M. Crawford. No expense was spared in her construction, for her owner hoped to use her for world cruising. However the outbreak of war made this impossible, and Captain Crawford died before he could enjoy his magnificent vessel. After the war she had numerous owners, and now flies the flag of Hon. Clarence Wallace.

M.V. CLEODOXA, built 1913, owned in recent years by Stan. Morton. Still sound.

M.V. EPAULINE, built 1911, renamed WALITHY, owned for many years by Hon. Clarence Wallace and recently by Mr. & Mrs. Les. Simmers.

CHAPTER 10

Early Power Vessels

IN THE R.V.Y.C.

FROM 1903 TO ABOUT 1935

ADORIAM—30 ft., built 1910, owner G. A. Roedde. Raised deck cabin cruiser.

AGNELLY—29.6 ft., built 1915, owner J. H. Willard.

ALICE HASTINGS—38.7 ft., built 1909, owner J. Hastings. Originally named Beulah, built by Matsumoto at Steveston. Powered with a 4 cyl. "Giant" truck engine, with engine room control, complete with bell system. Re-named Margaree and was owned 1936 by Wm. (Bill) Morrow. Owned 1941 to 1951 by F. Bryson Smith.

ANDANTE—31.6 ft., built 1911, owner Alex Marshall.

AQUILO—168 ft., built 1906 on east coast U.S. Brought to Vancouver 1912 via Cape Horn by Commodore B. T. Rogers. Originally coal burner, was converted to oil. Steam powered.

ARIEL—37.2 ft., built 1905, owner G. E. Bower.

ARIEL III—27.8 ft., built 1923, owner J. F. Malkin.

ARRANMORE—36.7 ft., built 1912, owner J. Emerson.

ARRAWAC ex **SUSIE W**—46 ft., built 1910, owner A. L. Bell.

ARTFUL DODGER—26 ft., built 1920, owner Harold A. Jones, later owned by W. H. Cotter.

ATHERO ex **SUTIL**—30.9 ft., built in Hong Kong 1912. Owned by J. H. Willard.

ATLINTOO—36.1 ft., built 1906, owner J. J. Deeks.

ATSILAC ex **SEA OTTER**—47.8 ft., built 1917, owner T. Yates.

BEATRICE—44.8 ft., built 1907, owner H. B. Bell-Irving.

BEATRICE R.—33 ft., built 1913, owner G. E. Gudewill.

BELMONT—64 ft., built 1917, owner R. M. Maitland.

BILJON—Built 1928, owner W. G. Ferguson.

BOLD MARY—44.5 ft., built 1911, owner J. A. Johnston.

CANCOLIM—71 ft., built 1928, owner Ray Phelps.

CATHRINE I.—33.5 ft., built 1922, re-built to 37.1 ft. in 1932, owned by T. E. (Tommy) Leigh.

CATHERINE II—Owned 1926 by H. E. Stafford.

CAWARRA—35.7 ft., built 1912, owned by A. L. Bell, later by E. C. B. Thompson.

CHARMAIN—Owned in 1926 by Carl Bingham.

CHICORA—30 ft., built 1921, owner J. S. Halse.

CHLORIS II—38.8 ft., built 1917, owner R. J. Sprott.

CLEODOXA ex **CORA MARIE** ex **YRREBEINNA**—49 ft., built 1913, re-built 1924. Owners included R. M. Maitland, W. C. Shelly, R. J. Sprott, Bruce Arundel and Stan Morton, who still maintains her in commission.

COLIFER—27.2 ft., built 1913, owner Colin C. Ferrie.

CORA MARIE—105 ft., built 1930, owner W. C. Shelly.

CORA MAY re-named **WANDERER**—56 ft., built 1926 by T. E. Leigh. Owned in 1961-62 by Commodore Temple H. Wright and J. D. Maitland who re-named the vessel Wanderer.

CORESEUS ex **REINDEER** re-named **EVELINA M., XANADU**—94.5 ft., built 1917. A United States sub-chaser brought to the Club by W. P. Dewees and subsequently owned by H. Haskamp, F. D. Lundy, Doan M. Hartnell.

CORSAIR I.—32 ft., built 1929, owner Ken Sulley.

DAPHRONA—57.3 ft., built in Hong Kong 1912 for W. F. Brougham, later owned by Roy W. Ginn.

DAVY JONES—73 ft., built 1907 in Seattle. Imported 1910 by E. B. Deane. Re-named Neydla by B. Arundel.

DEERLEAP re-named **FIFER, KITTEN F.**—67.8 ft., built 1928, owners included A. W. McLimont and Col. Victor Spencer.

DORSAL—Owned by B. P. Weston in 1926.

EILEEN—23.1 ft., built 1904, owned by H. D. Hulme.

ELGOMAR—38 ft., built 1912, owned by H. M. Burrit.

ELANE—Owned by E. A. Sherman in 1931.

ELAOITE—31.7 ft., built 1908, owners W. Collister, F. H. Mountain.

ELECTRA—36 ft., built 1905, owned by R. H. Sperling.

ELVIRA—Owned by the Most Reverend A. U. dePencier.

EMOH—44 ft., built 1912, owners R. W. Holland, H. O. Bell-Irving.

EPAULINE re-named **SEWICKLEY, WALITHY**—69 ft., built 1911, owners F. L. Buckley, W. C. Shelly, S. L. Howe, Mrs. K. A. Easton, The Hon. Clarence Wallace, Les Simmers, who still maintains her in commission.

ETHELDA—35.4 ft., built 1908, owned by W. J. Taafe.

EVELYN I—44.3 ft., built 1910, owned by S. C. Mortimer.

EVELINA M.—See Coreseus.

FIFER (original)—See Deerleap.

FORBES W. F.—Owned by I. A. Shaw.

FOXHOUND II—Owned by Hon. E. W. Hamber.

FULL MOON—48 ft., built 1912 by Knox Walkem.

FUSILIER ex **JEANEVA M.**—46 ft., built in Vancouver by Lind & Co.

in 1929 for Mr. Philip White. Sold in 1936 to Col. K. A. McLennan. Re-built and re-named Fusilier, sold to joint owners F. H. Clendenning, William Crawford, E. F. Riddell and Col. K. A. McLennan. In 1941 sold to R. J. Dawson and on loan to R.C.A.F. during the war, stationed at Victoria and Patricia Bay. In 1945 purchased by Dr. R. G. Large of Prince Rupert. Bought by Empire Shipping Co. Ltd. in 1948 and sold to F. S. Clendenning in 1953 who is the present owner.

GENE—40 ft., built 1912, owned by C. Wakeley.

GLENIFFER—40 ft., built in Hong Kong 1912 for Stuart Cameron, later owners were R. M. Maitland, J. C. McPherson and Ken F. Mair, who still maintains her in commission. ✓

GOGLU—24.3 ft., built by Hoffar Beeching Ltd. in 1928 for Mrs. C. E. Swift.

GOLLIWOG—Owned 1926 by Capt. A. Millman.

GRETA M. re-named THOMAS CROSBY IV.—61.5 ft., built 1922 for ✓ S. D. Brooks. Later owned by A. E. McMaster.

HAIDA PRINCESS ex CEDOLL—30 ft., built 1925, owned by E. D. Judson.

HALF MOON—38.6 ft., built 1909 by Knox Walkem.

HAZEL—29 ft., built 1906, owned by W. S. Wilband.

HELENA B. ex IHPIS—Originally owned by Mr. Norman Lang. Owned in 1926 by W. C. Ditmars. Name changed by N. T. Burdick, later owned by George Lindsay.

HERMIT—42.9 ft., built 1927 for George Kidd. Owned 1938 by P. Locke.

HOO HOO—28.5 ft., built 1909 by B. W. Sinclair.

I'LLAWAY—37 ft., built 1911 for W. A. Akhurst.

INOMAR I.—37.2 ft., built 1922 by Henry Hoffar.

INOMAR II.—37.4 ft., built 1924 by Henry Hoffar, subsequently owned by J. P. D. Malkin, Mrs. E. H. Moore.

INOMAR III—48 ft., built 1925 by Henry Hoffar, J. P. D. Malkin and owned later by Wes. Higbie.

IOLA—32 ft., built in Great Britain 1908. Brought out by F. N. D. Robertson.

IPHIS—See Helena B.

JOLLY MAC—53.2 ft., built 1911 for E. J. McFeely. Later owned by ✓ W. J. Butt. Owned in 1938 by A. J. Knowland.

KATHLEEN II—Owned by G. E. Williamson.

KENNET II.—38 ft., built 1927 for E. D. Clarke. Subsequent owners were Jack Newell, Commodore G. F. Gyles, Temple H. (later Commodore) Wright, Miss Ruth Jones. ✓

KIM—See Truant.

KIORA—37 ft., built 1906 for W. S. Chambers.

KITTEN F. ex FIFER ex DEERLEAP (see).

KONOMIC–57 ft., built 1910 for F. T. (later Commodore) Schooley.

KAGOME–Former rum-runner converted to yacht by Philip Rogers in 1934. Was taken over by R.C.A.F. during the war.

LANGARA–56 ft., built for J. L. Northey. She ended up 38 years later as a chicken house on Lulu Island.

LAMALCHI–35 ft., owned by Roy W. Ginn in late thirties.

LEOLA V.–39 ft., built 1928 by Will Vivian.

LIMIT–46 ft., built 1908 by A. W. LePage, later owned by E. S. Deane, W. J. Massey.

LITTLE JEAN–Owned by C. H. Corkum.

LOAFER–Owned by J. J. Banfield in 1906.

LO'OLBEE–64 ft., built 1911 by R. P. McLennan, later re-named Palmarsyl.

MACCARD ex **LEILA R.**–49.3 ft., built 1913 by W. C. MacKenzie.

MACUMBA–Built in 1930 for R. M. Maitland.

MAGNET V.–21.7 ft., built 1924, owned by W. E. Shannon.

MAKEHEWI ex **CHARLOTTE S.**–35.1 ft., built in 1910. Owned by W. Sulley and sold 1917 to Coast Missions.

MAULADAY–Owned in 1926 by H. Holt.

MAMITA–48.2 ft. Owners include Frank Wilkinson, P. A. Woodward and Dr. R. E. (Bob) McKechnie, who still maintains this fine vessel in commission with an enviable record of wins in Predicted Log Racing.

MANANA–34.6 ft., built 1926 by R. H. Spurrier.

MARGAREE ex **ALICE HASTINGS** (see).

MEANDER–60.5 ft., built 1934 for George Kidd.

MERRY MEADE–36 ft., built 1922 for Jack Newell.

MANDALAY B–46.8 ft., built 1923 for G. Beeching, later owned by G. Harris, L. F. Worsley.

MARDONBILL re-named **ACRASIA**–44.8 ft., built 1927. Owners included R. Arbuthnot, T. W. (later Commodore) Ayres, R. W. R. Day.

MI-PAL–40 ft., built 1922 for Robert Cran.

MOONLIGHT MAID ex **LADY STIMSON** ex **STADACONA** ex **COLUMBIA**–168 ft., built 1898 at Philadelphia to be flagship for the Commodore of New York Yacht Club. Sold to Royal Canadian Navy and became accommodation ship at Halifax in World War I. Purchased by Capt. Joe Hobbs and operated as liquor supply vessel off the U.S. Pacific Coast. Purchased by W. P. Dewees and operated by him as a luxurious cruising yacht for many years. Was ultimately sold during World War II to become a tug between Seattle and Alaska.

MOW PING–90 ft., built at Hong Kong in 1901 for B. T. (later Commodore) Rogers. She was a steam yacht. Was later lengthened and given a clipper bow. Sold to Commodore C. B. Macneill in 1912. Many years later she ended her days as a tug on the Alberni Canal.

NATURICH—38.5 ft., built 1910 for S. J. Castleman.

NEYDLA ex **DAVY JONES** (see).

NORSAL—122.4 ft., built 1921 for Norman Lang of the Powell River Paper Company. Later owners, S. D. Brooks, W. P. Dewees and W. Clarke Gibson, who maintains her in excellent condition, generously making it available for Crippled Children's Day and for staff outings.

NORTHERN LIGHT—43 ft., built 1928 for W. S. (later Commodore) Day. Owned 1938 by C. P. Schwengers.

OLIVE W—Owned 1931 by E. P. McDermitt.

OSOYOOS re-named **ARIEL** (see).

PHROSO—41 ft., built 1913 for H. O. (ex-Commodore) Alexander.

PHRYNE—47.2 ft., built 1911 for J. B. Woodworth.

PRIVATEER—39.8 ft., built 1922 by Hoffar Motor Boat Co. Owners include: 1922, I. Claman; 1924, J. B. Hoffar; 1924, J. T. North; 1927, W. D. Grant; 1932, E. McL. Boyd; 1939-49, Frank Wilkinson; 1949-52, Joe Wilkinson; 1952, J. C. McPherson; 1952 to date, Graham R. Nightingale.

PUDDLE DUCK—42.5 ft., built 1910 for H. deW. King. Walter Sturdy later owned her.

RAMBLER II—30 ft., built 1914 for Robert Cran.

REINDEER—See Coreseus.

RHINEGOLD—36 ft., built 1911 at Vancouver Shipyard for T. M. Davies. Owned 1912 to 1919 by Dr. Ian Glen-Campbell, 1919 to 1923 by Allan D. DesBrisay, and from 1923 to date by Col. Colin C. Ferrie, who has consistently cruised in her every season with the exception of the war years. In this outstanding period of service, attending every Club function, Opening Days, Remembrance Days, as well as extensive Gulf of Georgia cruising, the original engine, a 25 H.P. Buffalo 5″ bore, 6″ stroke (hand started with bar), was only replaced in 1937 with a 75 H.P. Grey Marine "Lugger" which still gives efficient service with a cruising speed of 8½ knots at 2000 R.P.M.

ROAMER—Size unknown, owned by J. S. Gall.

ROANOKE—Size unknown, owned by N. G. Cull.

RIO BONITA—94.5 ft., built 1918, originally a sub-chaser, acquired in 1922 by A. Melville (later Commodore) Dollar.

ROMANE—45 ft., built about 1927 at New Westminster as a tow boat. Converted to yacht in 1930 at Vancouver Shipyard for Air Vice-Marshall K. G. Nairn. Had a Hall-Scott Marine Gasoline engine. In the club from 1931 to 1936. Sold to Mr. Cowdry who later sold her for up-coast Mission work.

ROSCRANNA—24.3 ft., built 1927 by C. G. Beeching.

SAL LAL—44 ft., built 1911. Owned later by Knox Walkem.

SALTPETRE re-named **HOPE POINT III**—29.4 ft., built 1930 for

Ernest Rogers. Later owned by W. G. Dolmage. Now owned by Bob Fraser.

SEA BEE—34.4 ft., built 1911 for A. C. Brydone-Jack.

SEA DREAM—44 ft., built 1929. Owned by F. J. Whitcroft, Mrs. J. C. Abramson. Now owned by D. C. McPherson.

SEA OTTER—Later re-named Atsilac (see).

SEA SNIPE—Size unknown, owned by George Buscombe.

SEAL COVE—Owned 1926 by J. Emerson.

SERENA—40 ft., built 1926 for C. R. Sneyd.

SHEILEENA later **HEATHER M.**, then **PRIDE OF THE WEST**—52.8 ft., built at Hong Kong in 1911. Owners included Wm. Farrell, R. M. Maitland, L. A. Lewis.

SHELMERDENE—24.3 ft., built 1927 for H. McD. Ridley.

SILVER HEELS—34 ft., built 1922 for R. H. Merrick.

SINBAD—Size unknown, owned by R. A. Buchannan.

SNEDDENS—32 ft., built 1932 for Jack Storey.

SONGEE—49.6 ft., built 1911 for R. W. Holland.

SPARTAN—45 ft., built 1926 for Frank Barnes.

SUEJA III—117 ft., built 1926 in Seattle for Jas. Griffiths (U.S. Registry). but registered on Club roster.

SULHAMAR—35 ft., built 1924 at Benson's Shipyard for Art Benson. Later owned by J. B. Hoffar and by J. W. C. (Bud) Duck from 1945 to 1955. Now owned by L. L. Jamieson.

SUSIE W. re-named **ARRAWAC** (see).

SUTIL re-named **ATHERO** (see).

SWIFTSURE—35 ft., built 1905 for J. L. G. Abbott.

SYRENE—74.2 ft., built 1921 in Great Britain, brought out by Rev. John Antle. Bowsprit from Syrene, donated by Rev. Antle, graces our front balcony. The vessel is now in the B.C. Forest Service.

TACITA—34.6 ft., built 1921 for Andy Benyon.

TACONITE—116 ft., built 1930 for W. E. Boeing.

TETTA I—Owned 1906-1912 by Frank Parsons.

TETTA II—Owned 1912-1924 by Frank Parsons.

THETIS—Size unknown, owned by George Buscombe.

THETYS II—36.2 ft., built 1925 for Chas. Stringer. Re-built by R. A. Buchanan and re-named Mallard. Owned 1956 by B. Burnett. Still in Club.

THORA—33 ft., built 1925 for A. S. Bennett.

TICOMA—29.3 ft., built 1922 for A. E. Cox.

TILLY—Size unknown, registered in the Club 1906. Owner, G. A. Roedde.

TIMREH—28.8 ft., built 1929 for R. H. Tupper.

TRUANT ex **KIM**—30 ft. Columbia troller hull built 1929 at foot of Cardero Street. Owned by Dr. Scott Baxter, Doug McPherson, and now by R. H. (Robbie) Brown, 1965 Commodore of West Vancouver Yacht Club and is his flagship.

TUSCAN—Owned 1926 by George Kidd.

TUSITALA ex **BARNIBEE**, ex **ELIZABETH**—53.6 ft., built 1908 for Fred Buscombe. Subsequently owned by A. W. LePage.

UBIQUE I—38 ft., built 1929 at Bidwell Boat Works for Capt. Gray. Owned 1936 by C. P. Schwengers and in 1937 by W. S. Day. Since 1937 she has been owned by Claude S. Thicke, who still operates her.

URSILLA—Owned 1926 by T. R. Nickson.

VAQUERO—31.8 ft., built 1910. In club, but no record of owner.

VENCEDOR—146.3 ft., built 1913 in Great Britain. Originally the training ship Exmouth II. Brought to the Pacific Coast by Capt. Joe Hobbs, who sold to Commodore The Hon. E. W. Hamber whose flagship it was during his term 1931 to 1935.

VIREVE—31.7 ft., built 1913 for Alex Marshall.

VOYAGEUR III—Owned by P. N. Pretty.

WALITHY I—62.8 ft., built at Wallace Shipyard for C. Wallace, later The Hon. Clarence Wallace, Lieut.-Governor of B.C. ....-.........

WALRONDO—60 ft., built at Hong Kong in 1912 for C. R. Gordon.

WALRONDO II—34.3 ft., built by C. R. Gordon.

WHIPPETT, MISS—Owned 1931 by J. G. MacClay.

WHISTLE WING—39.3 ft., built 1907 for F. W. Foster.

WHITE IRIS—30.4 ft., built 1911 for John Ashby.

WILLENA F.—35.5 ft., built 1925 for Gordon Farrell.

WILLOWBEE G., later **AILEEN**—48.2 ft., built for G. E. Gudewill in 1927.

WYRILL—48.8 ft., built 1911 for W. A. Bauer.

WYRILL—62 ft., built 1931 for Pacific Mills Ltd. Owned 1950 to 1960 by Lol Killam.

XANADU—See Coreseus.

YSIDRO—39 ft., built 1910 for R. F. Marpole. Later owned by F. L. Hutching, Ron Maitland.

YOLANDA—31.5 ft., built 1914 for Bruce Arundel.

Knox Walkem's FULL MOON, 1912.

World War I Honour Roll.

CHAPTER 11

R. V. Y. C.

IN WORLD WAR I

AT THE ENTRANCE of the Royal Vancouver Yacht Club at Jericho are two bronze plaques, of which members are very proud. These are the rolls of honour of those who served in both World Wars. They are names of men who gave of their best to their country in both war and peace.

In the first World War, out of a membership of about 200, a total of 87 served in the armed forces, of whom a high percentage of 16 gave their lives. At first there was little opportunity for yachtsmen in naval service, except for members of the R.N.R., who were very quickly called up. These included Barney Johnson and Fred Crickard, both of whom served in the two ex-Chilean submarines which were purchased in Seattle in August of 1914 by the British Columbia government. However the majority of young yachtsmen enlisted in the Canadian Expeditionary Force, serving through the muddy slaughter of Flanders.

Those who were more patient got their chance in 1916, when a representative of the British Admiralty came to Vancouver to recruit volunteers for a motor patrol service. Men who were needed would be able to take charge of the swift motor launches that Great Britain was then turning out in great numbers. At a meeting of the yacht club, Commodore B. T. Rogers introduced Commander Armstrong, the naval representative to the members. The commander explained that he was looking for young men who had made a hobby of the sea, and had acquired some familiarity with the handling of small craft. They would receive a simple course in navigation sufficient for the requirements of the service. The age limits were 20 to 35. After a month's course in navigation at Greenwich, the recruits were to go to a depot ship at Southampton for six weeks, which would be followed by a month of gunnery at Whale Island.

The response from Vancouver was immediate, and 57 young men went to England in August 1916 for their initial training as sublieutenants. Those from the Royal Vancouver Yacht Club included Fred and Rowe Holland, and Curtis A. Davidson, Owen Power, Claude Thicke, Fred Mills, G. C. Van Horne, J. A. Leckie, W. L. Collister, Johnnie Green, Gordon Warren and Clair Jellett.

Others who saw service in the Royal Navy and Royal Canadian Navy included Charlie Julian, Lieut. R.C.N.V.R., Lieut. Henry B. Bell-Irving, R.N.V.R., C. W. Crofts, R.C.N.V.R., and G. H. Wailes, Lieutenant R.N. W. S. Earle was a lieutenant in the Royal Naval Air Service. Among those who took to the air in the Royal Flying Corps, ancestor of the Royal Air Force, were Harry Marshall, H. B. Branton, M. L. Gordon, C. Clement, Irwin Davis, and Harry Bird.

The great majority however joined the army, serving with distinction in all ranks, from Brigadier General R. G. Edwards Leckie to humble Private Clarence Wallace of the 5th Battalion, now Col. the Hon. Clarence Wallace, C.M.G. Tom Ramsay also went with the 5th. Bill Roedde served as a gunner in the Artillery and Vincent Ramsay was killed in action as a sergeant in the 16th Battalion. Lieut.-Col. H. G. Hulme commanded the 62nd Battalion, for which members of R.V.Y.C. raised the cost of a machine gun.

Captain Barney Johnson, who got his first glimpse of a submarine at Esquimalt in August 1914, was subsequently to make a great name for himself as a submarine commander in the Royal Navy, for which he received the Distinguished Service Order. An account of the feat which won him this honour was described by the late Commander W. G. Carr, R.C.N.R., in his account of the submarine service in World War One, called "By Guess and by God".

"To a Canadian," he wrote, "Lieut.-Commander B. L. Johnson, R.N.R. must go the credit for one of the finest feats performed in the annals of submarines. The extraordinary thing is that this officer was not a highly trained submarine officer with years of peace time training. He was in the merchant service before the war, and was appointed to bring the H8 over from Halifax. She was one of the boats constructed on that side of the Atlantic. He made her way across the Atlantic Ocean long before the world went mad about the feat performed by the *Deutschland*. Commander Johnson was submarine-minded. He loved them. He trained a crew consisting of nearly all reserve ratings like himself until they were the equal of any crew in the service. They were nearly all Canadians or Scotch. So well did this crew perform when they arrived at Harwich with their boat that Johnson was allowed to retain his command and take her out on active service. He was the first officer of the Royal Naval Reserve to command a submarine. Several more were given this honour before the war ended. With less than four years' experience they proved themselves qualified, and the confidence placed in them was never regretted. Many more reserve officers were serving as first lieutenants of submarines when hostilities ended. They knew nothing of engines and machinery when the war broke out. They joined submarines as navigating officers and for watch-keeping duties, but quickly mastered the most complicated work in the service. Submarine

H8 was patrolling off Ameland Gat on March 22nd 1916, when those inside her heard a slight scraping noise forward. They were down at 60 feet at the time, and hardly had they heard the weird sound than the boat rocked under the influence of a terrific explosion. The submarine sank by the bows and hit bottom at an angle of between 20 and 30 degrees in 85 feet of water. She had struck a mine, and when it exploded against the starboard forward hydroplane both forward hydroplanes were blown off, the bow caps protecting the torpedo tubes blown off, the torpedo tubes themselves wrecked, and the hull was badly damaged. No. 1 tank was ripped open to the sea.

"If it were not for the fact that her crew returned to Harwich and brought their crippled boat back with them, this story would never have been written. Johnson's report of the affair was, as might be expected, exceedingly brief: 'The forward bulkhead though leaking happened to hold. The watertight doors were closed. The motors were put astern, and No. 2 and No. 3 ballast tanks were blown. No. 1 tank was found to be open to the sea. The submarine then came to the surface. After blowing some fuel and making some temporary repairs, course was shaped for Terschelling and then Harwich. The flotilla captain of HMS *Maidstone* wrote, reporting on the matter: 'The captain (Johnson) reports that although it seemed obvious to all that the boat was lost, the officers and entire crew proceeded to their stations without any sign of excitement and all orders were carried out promptly and correctly. I would submit that such conduct in the face of apparent certain death, is an example of which the whole service may be proud.' "

Recalling this "incident" recently, Capt. Johnson said that after surfacing he slid down the jumping wire to the bow, noted the complete loss of bow caps thus leaving the four armed torpedos acting as cutwater; the sea was breaking over the bow and the torpedo pistols could not be removed so he went back to the conning tower and kept silent on that detail until arrival at Harwich 28 hours later when prompt action removed the pistols.

H8 was sent to the Greenwich Naval Shipyards and a complete new fore end fitted returning her to active service; Capt. Johnson was promoted to a larger submarine.

Many of the yachtsmen in the naval service served in M.L.'s in the zone around the British Isles where the German submarine campaign was mainly concentrated and where German mine fields were laid at every opportunity. Torpedoed merchant ships were a familiar sight, and occasionally the motor launches got a shot at a submarine or dropped depth charges. Others hunted for Austrian submarines in the Mediterranean and Adriatic. At times they engaged in the unhealthy service of minesweeping, and even after peace was declared the sea was still full of German and British mines that had to be swept up.

There was a great club re-union held at the Hotel Vancouver on
Nov. 21st 1919, by which time most of the members who had gone out
to serve in the various naval and military forces of the Empire had
returned and were welcomed back. There were still a few absent on
active service, Owen Power, lieutenant R.N.V.R. being reported sweeping
up mines off the Norwegian coast, while Lieut. Harry Marshall was
reported on the way home, having been engaged on the Russian front
fighting in the R.A.F.

Commodore Schooley opened with an address welcoming back
the returned men, followed by Magistrate Shaw who referred to the
club's Honour Roll and those who had given their lives in the service.
Then various branches of the navy and army were heard from: Commander Reed, R.N.R., described the work done by the "mystery ships"
or "Q" boats; Lieut.-Colonel Tait gave some accounts of the 29th
Battalion on the Somme in 1916; Lieut. Charles O. Julian was heard
on the doings of the R.C.N.V.R.; while Blythe D. Rogers also gave some
interesting experiences. Commander "Barney" Johnson got an enthusiastic
reception and outlined some highlights of his service in submarines;
Lieut. H. B. Bell-Irving told of the Dover Patrol with which he and a
number of other R.V.Y.C. members had been connected.

W. J. Butt's JOLLY MAC, built 1911.

CHAPTER 12

Commodores between the Wars

R.V.Y.C., 1919 - 1945

F. T. SCHOOLEY
Commodore 1919

A LIFE MEMBER of the Club who joined in 1904, Mr. F. T. Schooley was a prominent member of Vancouver's early business community, being manager of the pioneer Royal Crown Soap Works. In the early days of the Club he sailed the former pilot cutter *Dawendenna,* which he acquired from Oswald Moseley in 1905. His flagship was the power cruiser *Konomic,* 57 ft., which he had built in 1910. There had been very limited racing activity during 1917 and 1918 as many owners and crews were away on active service, but with members returning during 1919, three regattas were held in May, July and August. In the May regatta, R. A. Bindley's *Britannia* won in the A class sloops and F. Foster's *Dione* in the B class. The July regatta was really historic in that all yachts with the exception of J. Green's *Madeline* went the wrong course . . . . In the August regatta J. P. Fell's *Onoma* took the A class and Reg. Purves' *Asthore* the B.

A highlight of Commodore Schooley's year was the great re-union held at the Hotel Vancouver on November 21st, 1919—the largest gathering the Club had ever held—at which he welcomed returning members (see chapter R.V.Y.C. in World War I). It was also this year that plans were made to build a class of 15 ft. sailing dinghies designed by John Winslow to cost $200 each. Seven members agreed to purchase and fifteen were ordered. Cat rigged, they carried 185 sq. ft. sail, had steel centreboards and beam of 5 ft. 4 inches. The class was owned by: No. 1, F. Akhurst; No. 2, Joe Malkin; No. 4, E. T. Rogers; No. 5, T.

Pattison; No. 6, H. Bell-Irving; No. 7, Cedric and Norman Gyles; No. 8, H. H. Simmonds; No. 10, G. Hazen Phillips and Ron. Kerr; No. 11, W. Chambers; No. 13, J. Winslow; and No. 15, Harry Marshall. Among the owners of unnumbered dinghies were F. W. Crickard, B. C. Stephenson, W. C. Nichol, Geo. Wadds and the next Commodore, H. O. Bell-Irving. He was elected Honorary Life Member in 1937.

M.V. KONOMIC, 1910.

H. O. BELL-IRVING
Commodore 1920-1921

FOR OVER THREE DECADES the eighth Commodore of the Club, Mr. Henry O. Bell-Irving, had been very active in Vancouver yachting affairs, having been one of the founders of the first organized yacht club, formed only a year after the incorporation of the City. In 1887 he was elected Chairman of the new Burrard Inlet Sailing Club, with E. E. Rand as Secretary and 16 charter members enrolled. He became a member of the Vancouver Yacht Club in 1904.

By 1920 racing was in full swing again and the international contests were revived with the formation of the Pacific International Yachting Association at a meeting held May 15, 1920 in Victoria, B.C. As our representative on P.I.Y.A., Commodore Bell-Irving was elected Vice-Admiral of the new body, the Admiral being Mr. James Griffiths of the Seattle Yacht Club. *Turenga* was defeated by *Sir Tom* in Cowichan Bay and Victoria for the Lipton Cup and at a special General Meeting of the Club held August 31st, 1920 the decision was made to build a new challenger. Mr. A. M. Dollar put up $1000 and Ron. Maitland $500 towards the Nicholson design R boat which was named *Patricia* after the daughter of Mr. Maitland, Patsey, who christened the boat that her father was named to Skipper. With the re-election of Commodore Bell-Irving in 1921 a new post was added to the Executive, that of Fleet Captain, and Mr. Fred O. Mills was the first Fleet Captain elected. His yacht at that time was the 33 ft. schooner *Tenderfoot*. Commodore Bell-Irving's flagship was the power cruiser *Emoh*, and he did much to develop cruising to up-coast and Gulf Island points by leading many successful Club cruises. His summer home on Paisley Island was a favorite rendezvous for our sail and power fleets. At the P.I.Y.A. 1921 regatta, again held at Cowichan Bay, the *Patricia* was defeated by *Sir Tom* in the Lipton Cup series.

M.V. EMOH, 1912.

G. F. GYLES
Commodore 1922-23,
1927-1928, 1940-1941

NINTH COMMODORE, MR. G. F. GYLES, was elected for six terms to lead the activities of the Club, and in 1922 he was also elected Vice-Admiral of P.I.Y.A. In 1930 he was elected Admiral of that international body. Commodore Gyles was a very keen yachtsman and with his sons, Cedric and Norman, and daughter Gwynneth, took an active part in the cruising and racing over three decades, flying his flag on the cruising sloop *Elsa May* during his first term. Following our defeat by Seattle in the 1921 P.I.Y.A. regatta at Cowichan, a determined effort was made in 1922 at the P.I.Y.A. event in Seattle, but again *Patricia,* skippered by Ron Maitland, lost two straight races. In the class races, however, the Vancouver boats did better, collecting thirteen trophies. The Vancouver team of kitten class dinghies won the Gale Cup and John Winslow's *Black Cat* won the free-for-all coast dinghy championship. Our yachts also swept the boards in Special Sloops, Heavy Sloops, Yawls; schooners being won by Victoria. Public interest in the international competitions ran high in Vancouver and the newspapers posted bulletins in their front windows—radio being "non-est" then. In August, 1922 Ron Maitland took *Patricia* down to Newport, California and Ted Geary took *Sir Tom* from Seattle to compete in the Isherwood Series. *Sir Tom* took the Trophy but *Patricia* came second in a large fleet of California yachts.

It was during Commodore Gyles' first term that Star Boat racing started on English Bay with the formation of the English Bay Star

Fleet (see chapter on Stars), and Harry E. Wylie, the "daddy" of Star Boat men (later an Honorary Life Member of our Club) represented Canada at the International Star Class Regatta on Long Island Sound in 1923, capturing second place.

In the 1923 P.I.Y.A. held at Vancouver our *Patricia* again failed to beat *Sir Tom*, although she came in second, beating Ben Weston's *Angela*, a California entry. Pacific Coast Star Class championship went to *Maia* from Southern California, Harry Wylie's *Astrea* gaining second in a fleet of 14 stars. The Pacific Coast Championship in the Kitten class went to C. P. Leckie's *Meow*, R.V.Y.C.

In addition to the activity in sailing, at this time there was a large addition of power cruisers to the R.V.Y.C. fleet, including Norman Lang's 135 ft. cruiser *Norsal*, equipped with twin 200 h.p. Fairbanks-Morse semi-diesel engines; A. M. Dollar's 110 ft. *Rio Bonita;* W. P. Dewees' *Reindeer; Privateer;* and Tommy Leigh's *Catherine I.*

In the interim between his first and second terms, Mr. Gyles headed the syndicate that purchased the R class sloop *Riowna* from the Great Lakes to challenge *Sir Tom* for the Lipton Cup in 1925. *Riowna* lost to *Sir Tom*, and again, in 1926, skippered by Cedric Gyles, she took second place to the Seattle defender, although she came in ahead of *Turenga*, sailed by Phillip Rogers.

Early in Commodore Gyles' second term, as *Riowna* proved to be a heavy weather boat, a syndicate was formed to build a challenger from designs by John Alden, the *Lady Pat*. Following the formal opening of the new clubhouse at Jericho in June, 1927, the P.I.Y.A. regatta highlight was the contest between *Lady Pat*, sailed by Ron Maitland, *Riowna* by Cedric Gyles and Lipton Cup defender *Sir Tom*, skippered by Ted Geary, Seattle. It was the old story, *Sir Tom* 9 pts., *Lady Pat* 6 pts., *Riowna* 3 pts.

That fall (1927) Tom Ramsay promoted a new R class syndicate to build the *Lady Van* from designs by C. E. Nicholson, but at the 1928 P.I.Y.A., also held at Vancouver, *Sir Tom* again carried the day, *Lady Pat* second, *Lady Van* with Tom Ramsay at the helm third, and Commodore Gyles' *Riowna* fourth. Also, in March 1928, Ron Maitland's *Lady Pat* sailed to second place in the Lee Trophy Series held off San Pedro, California, the winner being Mr. Welch's *Live Yankee* from Boston. Mr. Maitland had with him as crew W. Merrick, W. G. Mackenzie and Geoffrey Woodward.

Mr. Gyles again held the post of Commodore in 1940 and 1941, flying his flag on the power cruiser *Kennet II* and guiding the Club's destinies during the early war years.

At a later date Mr. Gyles donated the Gyles Trophy for 6 Metre yacht perpetual competition, further evidence of his continuing interest in promoting the sailing game. He was one of the "greats" in the Royal Vancouver Yacht Club, and was elected Honorary Life Member in 1953.

Aux. sloop ELSA MAY, 1922.

R Class sloop RIOWNA, 1925.

R. M. MAITLAND
Commodore 1924

TENTH COMMODORE, RON MAITLAND was also one of the "greats" in the R.V.Y.C. history. His enthusiasm extended to racing, cruising, power boating, and as a boat swapper he had few equals. During his term the Club first applied for the lease of the Jericho property, and he led a memorable fleet cruise to Princess Louisa Inlet, the most ambitious that had been attempted up to that time. During his term as Commodore, R. M. Maitland flew his flag in the power cruiser *Ysidro*. That year Reg Purves represented the Star fleet in the International Star Class Regatta on Long Island Sound, getting seventh place.

The P.I.Y.A. regatta was held in Tacoma in 1924 and the Vancouver sailing craft did not attend. There was no Lipton Cup contest that year.

During the visit of the Special Services Squadron of the Royal Navy to Vancouver in 1924, officers of H.M.S. *Hood,* H.M.S. *Repulse* and H.M.S. *Adelaide* were given an opportunity to show their skill in yacht racing. A special regatta was held on English Bay in their honour. Teams of two Star boats each were manned by officers of the *Hood, Repulse* and *Adelaide* respectively while others sailed yachts of the sloop and cruiser classes. The Hood team, sailing the *Stella Maris* and *Astrea,* won in the Stars. In the light sloop class Adelaide won in *Turenga* and in the cruiser class Repulse won in *Tamahnowus.* There was a 10 to 15 knot breeze.

Ron Maitland was such a factor in Pacific Coast yachting that the brief resume of his year as Commodore does not begin to do justice to his yachting career and the efforts he was continually putting forth in the interests of his favourite sport. Recognition was fittingly given in an article published in the October 1929 issue of Pacific Motor Boat, the well known yachting magazine, which is reprinted herewith.

RON MAITLAND—A REAL YACHTSMAN

"R. M. Maitland of the Royal Vancouver Yacht Club is probably best known for his persistence in racing against Ted Geary of the Seattle Yacht Club for the possession of the R Class Lipton Cup, this little argument having extended over 15 years. He has also made occasional excursions to California waters with his R Class yachts, and on two occasions won second place in a series of races with the pick of California yachts, besides craft from farther afield.

"Ron Maitland has had a wide personal experience with various types of yachts in the 25 years that he has been connected with the Royal Vancouver Yacht Club, having in this period been the owner and skipper of a total of 16 power yachts, auxiliary cruisers and racing craft, besides being chosen to represent the R.V.Y.C. as skipper of various syndicate owned challengers and other international racing craft.

"He has also enjoyed the confidence of his fellow yachtsmen in the highest offices in the gift of Pacific Coast yacht clubs. Besides being an ex-commodore of the Royal Vancouver Yacht Club, he served a term as Admiral of the Pacific International Yachting Association, and also a season as Admiral of the Pacific Coast Yachting Association.

"His first venture in yachting was with the 16 ft. *Spray*, a boat which Ron and some boy friends rescued from a rubbish pile which workmen were about to burn up. Having got permission to carry off this prize, a group of kids was rounded up to carry it to the Seaton boys' back yard where they put some new planks in the bottom and fitted it with a mast and sail.

"In 1904 Maitland joined the Vancouver Yacht Club, which afterwards became the Royal Vancouver Yacht Club. He was 16 years old, and about this time owned the 23 ft. sloop *Queenie*, a centreboard boat. A few years later he bought the 27 ft. sloop *Dione* in Victoria and sailed her up to Vancouver. With her he won the Graveley Challenge Cup, and also won the Key City Trophy in a race at Seattle in the 26 ft. class.

"A great boat trader, Ron has nearly always exhibited excellent judgment in recognizing the good points of a yacht, and one after another he became owner of such well known craft as the aux. sloop *Intrepid,* the aux. sloop *Verona,* the aux. yawl *Ailsa I,* the aux. yawl *Gazeka,* the 30 ft. power cruiser *Macumba,* the sloop *Winona,* the aux. sloop *Lavita,* 41 ft. power cruiser *Trreheinna,* 40 ft. power cruiser *Ysidro,* 40 ft. power cruiser *Gleniffer,* 60 ft. power cruiser *Heather M,* and the R Class yachts *Patricia* and *Lady Pat.*

"Maitland has managed to get good speed out of most of his sailing craft. With the yawl *Ailsa I* he rarely lost a race, and with the yawl

Gazeka twice won the Beaver Cup, symbol of the cruiser championship of the Club, in the Ballenas Islands race, while his record in racing against California R Class yachts with *Patricia* and *Lady Pat* is high.

"Cruising is his favorite recreation, especially if there is some shooting and fishing thrown in, but since 1914 when Sir Thomas Lipton presented a cup for R Class competition to the Seattle Yacht Club, Ron has undertaken, as a sort of duty, to get this cup for Vancouver.

"He sailed Commodore B. T. Rogers' *Turenga* in the first Lipton Cup race against *Sir Tom*, and has sailed a challenging yacht in all except two of the subsequent contests. He was a member of the syndicate that brought the R Class yacht *Riowna* from the Great Lakes, and though he missed his best chance to win the Lipton Cup in 1929 when the mast of *Lady Pat* carried away, he had the satisfaction of tieing *Sir Tom* while *Lady Van* finally won for Vancouver the coveted trophy. His son Douglas is a chip off the old block, having won the International Flattie Championship in 1928 when 12 years old. Daughter Patsy also won the ladies' event in flatties that year."

M.V. YSIDRO, 1924.

R Class sloop PATRICIA, 1921.

R Class sloop TURENGA, 1915.

A. M. DOLLAR
Commodore 1925-1926

ELEVENTH COMMODORE A. MELVILLE DOLLAR flew his flag in the 110 ft. converted sub. chaser *Rio Bonita*. It was during his first year term that the first favourable report was made on progress towards securing a club site and anchorage at Jericho. Later that year at a special meeting October 28, Commodore Dollar announced securing a 21 year lease of 1½ acres eastward of the Point Grey Tennis Club.

As the *Patricia* had been sold to California, a syndicate was organized to purchase *Riowna* from the Great Lakes, and at the P.I.Y.A. regatta held at Victoria, sailed by Ron Maitland, she won the first race of the series for the Lipton Cup in a forty mile gale. However in the lighter winds that followed she came second and third, placing second to *Sir Tom* in the series.

That fall Commodore Dollar arranged with Captain J. R. Stewart to conduct navigation classes every second Thursday evening during the winter months, and these classes were very well attended.

New building plans presented by a committee headed by Mr. George F. Gyles were approved and the Committee authorized to proceed, provided they could raise $20,000 from Club membership. This was accomplished by the sale of debentures to members.

In June, 1926, following approval by the general membership, Commodore Dollar announced that all members in good standing were declared elected in the Royal Vancouver Yacht Club, now incorporated under the Friendly Societies Act.

In the P.I.Y.A. regatta held at Seattle, *Sir Tom*, sailed by Jack Graham, retained the Lipton Cup; *Riowna*, sailed by Cedric Gyles coming second, and Phillip Rogers in *Turenga* third.

This year (1925) G. Hazen Phillips, representing the club in the International Star Class championship races on Long Island Sound, won second place in the series and also was awarded the distant fleet trophy.

M.V. RIO BONITA, 1925.

CAPTAIN B. L. JOHNSON,
C.B.E., D.S.O., R.C.N.
Commodore 1929-1930,
1936, 1950

ANOTHER "GREAT", and probably the "greatest" of them all, is our Twelfth Commodore, Captain B. L. Johnson, C.B.E., D.S.O., R.C.N.—a born leader of men, who not only has been active in Club affairs since joining in 1904, but was three times Commodore. First, for two terms 1929 and 1930, again in 1936, and after strenuous service in World War II, again led the Club in 1950. And this amazing gentleman still takes part in Club racing events in his trim sloop *Cavalier* and in which he regularly observes the Opening Day Ceremony and takes practically daily jaunts up and down the harbour during the summer months. What a record of devotion to the sea! And what a record of performance ON the sea!

Apprenticed to sail when only 15 years old in 1893, he served in five different sailing ships under different skippers, learning something of the sea and its ways from all, he recalls. He is a "Cape Horner", having rounded that turbulent point three times in "square-riggers", also has rounded the Cape of Good Hope twice.

After five years, in 1898, he realized there was no future in sail (except rheumatism) and transferred to steam, where with his background in sail he quickly qualified for a unlimited Certificate to command any kind of ship to any part of the Seven Seas.

Captain Johnson's seafaring exploits would fill volumes, a few are recorded in other chapters, but space here permits only brief reference to his service as Commodore of the R.V.Y.C. for four terms. At heart a man of sail, he recently philosophized, "Seafaring in the ships of sixty-seventy years ago was really a fight for survival . . . in sail it is man against the sea and the sea generally wins, but the man learns the value of teamwork, survival, economy, 'make do', and brotherhood. From another viewpoint, sailing in a good yacht in a moderate wind is soothing and interesting and gives one the satisfaction of having harnessed natural forces. One day," he speculates, "I may need the comfort of a 'summer cottage'. (his term for power boats) to enjoy the peace and comfort of a family ship almost the year round" —but at 87 years of age he still SAILS!

When Captain Johnson joined the Club in 1904 he acquired the speedy 30 ft. sloop *Siren* from Alex. Grant. In succeeding years he has owned and sailed *Alexandra, Westward Ho, Winston,* and since 1955, *Cavalier,* a 29 ft. sloop designed by Roger de Quincy and built at St. George Yard, Walberswick, England.

Captain Johnson first flew his Commodore's flag on the *Alexandra,* which he sailed in the racing fixtures during 1929. It was an active year for sailors, distinguished by the Club finally capturing the Lipton Cup after fifteen years of effort.

E. F. (Jack) Cribb, sailing *Lady Van,* defeated *Sir Tom* two out of three races at the P.I.Y.A. regatta in English Bay. *Lady Pat* tied with *Sir Tom* for second place after being dismasted in one race. In the 9 Metre class (formerly the 29 Raters) H. A. Jones' *Spirit II* took the series. Commodore Johnson's *Alexandra* second, E. A. Woodward's *Spirit I* third. In the Julian Cup race that year *Alexandra* won, sailed by Miss Isabel McKinnon. The Commodore's flagship also won the Ballenas Island race and also the Keyes Trophy in the Fraser River Lightship race.

In his second year as Commodore, Captain Johnson acquired the *White Wings II* from Walter Cline and re-named it *Westward Ho.* It therefore became the flagship of the fleet. He had a Genoa jib designed and completed by Alex. Vass, the first in the fleet. It was known as "Little Willie" and was 800 sq. ft. in area.

In the 1930 P.I.Y.A. Regatta held at Victoria, *Sir Tom* recaptured the Lipton Cup.

At that regatta, in the yawls and schooners over 30 ft., Ray Cook's *Claribel* of Seattle beat out *Westward Ho, Minerva* and *Andi-Lailey.* Alex. Marshall's *Nelmar* won over *Ailsa II, Gwendolyn* (Seattle), *Ailsa I.* and *Truant* in the yawls 30 ft. and under, while in the sloops, H. A. Jones' *Spirit II* led Doug. Urry's *Cresset.*

Commodore Johnson was one of the initiators of the Swiftsure Classic Race up and down the Straits of Juan de Fuca in the year 1930 (see chapter on Swiftsure Races), coming in second to the Seattle schooner *Claribel,* followed by *Cresset.* However, in 1931 the *Westward Ho* won the Swiftsure Classic, and carried off the trophy again in 1933.

Also in 1930, the Coal Harbour (Stanley Park) Clubhouse was sold to the Federal Government for use by the R.C.N.V.R.

Well known local businessman, P. D. Gordon, represented the R.V.Y.C. in New Orleans, La., at the International Star Class Championships, winning the distant fleet trophy.

Harry Bird recalls an occasion when *Westward Ho,* skippered by Capt. "Barney", lost her mast while sitting becalmed:

"It was indeed a privilege and an honour to sail on the good ship *Westward Ho,* skippered and owned by Captain B. L. "Barney" Johnson, D.S.O. As a young man I remember one Cowichan Regatta when we had entered the P.I.Y.A. Regatta held there about 1935 or 1936 and were leading our class when the wind failed and we decided to go swimming or just loafing about the deck. Captain Barney in those days was a pretty tough skipper and did not approve of such goings on, but there was absolutely no wind and we just sat there, not even drifting. We were caught with our backstays down, when a "gentle little zephyr" came along, and took our mast, rigging, light sails, etc., overboard before you could say "Jack Robinson" or whatever sailors say on such an occasion.

"I can remember Claire Jellett and I diving down the forard hatch just as the mainmast gave way about 8 feet from the deck. I used to work in a logging camp and all I could yell was 'TIMBER'. The mast was so big it looked like a tree falling down.

"In the true tradition of the navy, the skipper immediately ordered all hands to clear the wreckage and we finished the race. Even if we were last I will always remember that race, finishing with a jury rig and in very smart style. I was proud to be a member of the crew."

Commodore Johnson's exploits in submarine service in the Atlantic and North Sea during World Wars I and II are related in another chapter, also his founding of the Naval Training Section of R.V.Y.C. when N.O.I.C. Port of Vancouver in 1940.

It was during his term as Commodore in 1950 that Captain Johnson succeeded, after a stiff battle at the Annual Meeting of that year, in getting Club approval to construct Junior Quarters on the wharf at Jericho. There was resistance to expending the $15,000 required, as Club funds were at a low ebb and the money would have to be borrowed from the bank. Our banker took a very dim view of our financial position, and while members approved making the loan, the bank didn't. Finally, both Commodore Johnson and the Hon. Treasurer, Harry Bird, signed personal notes guaranteeing the obligation, thus the present accommodation for Juniors was provided which has enabled the Club in later years to launch the very successful Junior Training Programme. He presented the B. L. Johnson Perpetual Trophy for Junior achievement in 1954 and in 1960 gave the club a lease of Alexander Island, Centre Bay, Gambier Island, for a nominal $1.00 annually. (Alexander Island was purchased by the club in 1965.) Capt. Johnson was elected Honorary Life Member in 1951.

Yawl WESTWARD HO, 1930.

HON. E. W. HAMBER
Commodore 1931-1935

LEADING BUSINESSMAN, outstanding Canadian sportsman and Lieutenant-Governor of British Columbia from 1936 to 1941, Eric W. Hamber was the thirteenth commodore of the club, which he led with distinction in the difficult depression years when economic conditions retarded normal development. His flagship was the trim, stately *Vencedor*, 146.3 ft., built 1913 in Great Britain. Originally the training ship *Exmouth II*, she was brought to the Pacific Coast by J. H. Hobbs and sold to Mr. Hamber in 1930. Although few new yachts came into the club during Commodore Hamber's terms, sailing and power boat activity was well maintained and the membership total was fairly constant. The Julian Cup was won in 1931 by Mrs. F. Wavell Urry in the *Cresset*, in 1932 by Mrs. Isabelle Dickson sailing *Minerva*, in 1933 by Miss Gwynneth Gyles sailing *Riowna*, in 1934 by Miss E. Wylie sailing *Lady Van*, in 1935 by Mrs. H. A. Jones sailing *Spirit*. The Beaver Cup was won in 1931 and 1932 by C. H. Elliott in *Anywhere*, Mr. W. Oliphant Bell in 1933 sailing *Maratea*, and H. A. Wallace 1934 and 1935 sailing *Minerva*. Power boaters' records show that Colin Ferrie in *Rhinegold* won the Dewees Trophy in 1933, Jack Halse won it in *Saronia* 1934, and E. Keenlyside in *Avalon* 1935. The Harry Marshall Trophy was won in 1931 and 1932 and again in 1935 by W. O. Bell, in 1934 by Joe Wilkinson sailing *Ailsa II*, and by Alex Marshall in 1933. Phil and Sid Miller won the World's Flattie Championship at Seattle in *Silver Wings* in 1935.

Famous all across Canada for his prowess in outdoor sports, soccer, hockey and rowing, "Tammy" Hamber became President of B.C. Mills, Timber and Trading Company, operators of Hastings Mills, after a distinguished career as a banker, and had the honour in 1928 of preparing under his supervision a mast of B.C. spruce for King George's yacht *Britannia*. Produced by Mr. Hamber's company from the standing tree to the finished mast, the spar attracted wide attention among international yachtsmen for its excellence. He was elected to Honorary Life Membership in 1953.

VENCEDOR, 1931.

W. S. DAY
Commodore 1937-1938

FOURTEENTH COMMODORE, MR. W. S. DAY was an enthusiastic sail and power boat yachtsman and very capable executive who successfully handled the club financial affairs as Honorary Treasurer in 1933-34-35, and in 1936 held the post of Vice-Commodore. He presented the Catherine Day Trophy to encourage competition in the Snipe Class in 1935 when many of today's best skippers were juniors. Later, in 1955, this trophy became symbolic of Club Championship in the Davidson Frostbite Dinghy Class. He owned the power cruiser *Northern Light* from 1928 to 1936, and his flagship was the well known *Deirdre*. Following the successful raffle of the Roedde & Halliday designed original *Carita* in 1936, a syndicate of members built an additional five yachts of the same turtle deck design and amid great excitement these were raffled to members early in 1937 and the distinctive 30 ft. Spencer Class was formed. This impetus to medium sized design prompted the creation of another slightly smaller class of cruiser—a 26 footer—the Hi Ho Class, of which seven or eight were built, designed by Halliday and named after the original yacht *Hi Ho* built for G. A. Cran. Full schedules of racing were carried out both summers: Phil Miller and Jack Gillies won the World's Flattie Championship sailed here 1937 in *Blue Wings* and next year Sid Miller and his wife Janet became World's Flattie Champions in *Silver Wings*. The Julian Cup was won 1937 by Miss B. Pedlow in *Tamahnowus*, and in 1938 by Miss E. Wylie in *Lady Van*; the Beaver Cup was won by Capt. B. L. Johnson in *Westward*

Ho in 1937, and by F. O. Mills in 1938 sailing *Uwhilna;* The MacNeill Trophy won by W. A. Roedde in 1937 sailing *Carita,* and in 1938 by J. M. Lindsay in *Lady Luck;* the Keyes Trophy won by H. A. Jones sailing *Spirit II* in 1937, and in 1938 by H. E. Wylie in *Lady Van;* Dewees Trophy in 1937 by G. H. Rae in *Gerald C.* and in 1938 by K. A. (Bert) Cruise in *Caprice.* Past Commodore Day was elected to Honorary Life Membership in 1959.

M.V. NORTHERN LIGHT, 1937.

HAROLD A. JONES
Commodore 1939, 1944,
1945, 1946, 1947

FIFTEENTH COMMODORE, HAROLD A. JONES had a long and very active association with maritime affairs, being the founder and builder of one of the largest tug-boat operations on the British Columbia coast, The Vancouver Tug Boat Company Ltd., of which he was President. He knew and had personally visited practically every one of the myriad coves and inlets of our inland coastal waters in the pursuit of his business as a tow-boat man and as an enthusiastic yachtsman. He was forever lauding and promoting the unmatched attractions of our "Yachtsman's Paradise" and it goes without saying that he made an excellent and much respected Commodore. A capable, if exacting and dominant skipper, he sailed *Spirit II* to many victories, and his pride and joy was the beautiful present day *Spirit* which he built from Monk designs in 1946. He did much to encourage Junior member activities and was very generous in his donations and contributions to their welfare. Many of today's skippers have fond memories of the "luscious pies" handed out to them as hungry youngsters by Harold's tug-boat cooks, as they cadged a ride, hitched to log booms, when becalmed along the coast. A practical seaman, he inaugurated the fine marine railway haul-out which is a feature of our Coal Harbour Station, and in his terms our mooring facilities were greatly improved. He was elected to Honorary Life Membership in 1953.

It was during Commodore Jones' 1944 term that the Annual Children's Day and Family Weekend Cruise was inaugurated. This event grew out of the suggestion that in spite of wartime, the club should endeavour to hold a Family Cruise of all members, both sail and power, not too far from home base.

Vice Commodore O. H. Bell and a Committee arranged to utilize the old Castleman House on the former McLennan farm at Long Bay, Gambier Island, Howe Sound. However, landing facilities were not suitable, necessitating a change of locale for the 1945 event. Through his contact as Director and Property Manager of the Anglican Diocese of New Westminster camp facilities at Artaban on Long Bay, Gambier Island, Vice Commodore Bell was able to arrange for their use and our Children's Day and Family Weekend Cruise has been held there annually ever since.

The keen interest of club members and their families has enabled Artaban to extend its yearly period of utilization for the benefit of children within the Diocese irrespective of race or creed.

A feature of the Family Weekend Cruise is the Sunday morning religious service in the beautiful inspiring outdoor chapel which accommodates up to 250 persons. The R.V.Y.C. Padre, currently the Rev. Stanley Smith of Mission to Seamen, conducts the service and the current Commodore reads the lesson.

Prompted by Mrs. Bell and well known power boater Ed. Dueck, the R.V.Y.C. executive presented Artaban with a beautiful manual organ, cherished by the congregation of children and adults who attend or visit the summer camp.

Another innovation of Commodore Jones' regime was the framing and hanging of several dozen burgees of foreign yacht clubs presented to R.V.Y.C. in appreciation of the hospitality extended to visiting yachtsmen. Vice Commodore Bell, in charge of the Jericho Clubhouse, had uncovered these in basement storage, and realizing the historical and decorative value of these distinctive world wide yacht club symbols, arranged to have them all framed and appropriately hung on our Marine Room walls. Regretfully, the onrush of so-called "decor moderne" in recent years has brushed them aside, but salty yachtsmen patiently await a resurgence of the "old-time sailing spirit" to see them ensconced where they properly belong, giving a true nautical flavour to the atmosphere of our Jericho Clubhouse. (See list elsewhere in History.)

In the furtherance of his absorbing interest in yachting development, Commodore Jones presented two perpetual trophies, the Harold A. Jones Trophy for National Class sailing dinghies in 1937, and the Vice Commodore's Cup for B Class racing around Ballenas Island in 1938. He was elected to Honorary Life Membership in 1953.

Sloop SPIRIT II, 1939.

Sloop SPIRIT, 1946.

J. A. LONGLEY
Commodore 1942

SIXTEENTH COMMODORE, J. A. LONGLEY held Flag Office for five terms in addition to being a member of the Executive for a number of years. He was Fleet Captain in 1938 and again in 1947; Hon. Hydrographer in 1937; Hon. Measurer in 1939 and Rear Commodore in 1940-41. His flagship was the 40 ft. aux. yawl *Maratea*. At various times he owned and sailed a number of yachts, including *Ganessa* and the P.C. sloop *Serena*. As in the case of several Commodores during the war years, his tenure was largely one of caretaking, as sailing activities were at a minimum and power boating practically non-existent due to gasoline rationing. He took an active part in the formation of the Naval Training section of the club initiated in 1940 and after his term as Commodore, although a veteran of the First World War, he again served in an executive capacity with the air force till the end of hostilities. He joined the club in 1919 and was elected to Honorary Life Membership in 1958.

Yawl MARATEA, 1942.

J. S. HALSE
Commodore 1943

SEVENTEENTH COMMODORE, J. S. HALSE also had a caretaking tenure of office, but he was active in club management for quite a number of years. He was Staff Captain in 1935, Vice Commodore in 1942 and Hon. Secretary in 1938-41-58-59-60. His flagship was *Saronia,* and at various times has owned a number of power cruisers, including *Chicora* and *Saronia I.* He joined the club in 1925 and has always taken an active interest in power cruiser affairs. As with Past Commodore Longley and his successor Harold A. Jones, Commodore Halse performed his duties in exceedingly difficult times and, like them, deserves a great deal of credit for the successful operation of the club on skimpy budgets. All club services were maintained on a restricted basis, ready to resume full sailing and cruising activities on the return of our large quota of members from active service. He was elected to Honorary Life Membership in 1960.

M.V. SARONIA, 1943.

Stars line up for start, 1960.

Dr. Warren photo.

CHAPTER 13

Star Class

MAKES RECORDS

FOR MORE THAN FORTY YEARS the international Star Class has been the most popular small racing class for R.V.Y.C. members. It has consistently evoked some of the keenest competition, and has cradled some of the club's finest racing skippers.

Among those prominent in the Star Class over the years have been such keen sportsmen as Harry Wylie, W. P. Weston, Reg. Purves, G. Hazen Phillips, Ron Kerr, P. D. Gordon, Tom Pattison, W. H. Alcock, Bill Roedde, Cedric Dill, Percy Burr, George Parsons, E. D. (Doug) Stone, the Miller brothers Phil and Sid, the Day brothers Bob and Bud, Pat Leslie, Ches. Rickard, Ray Delaplace, and latterly George Mason, Maurice (Shorty) Hunt, the Kirkland brothers Ian and Ken, Bonar Davis, Bill Burgess, Dr. Tom Hope, Dave Miller, Steve Tupper, Carl Petersen, Paul. Sturdy, Bill West, Barney Perry and Alan Vittery.

The International Star Class is the oldest class of any of the one-design yachts in the world; it was started in 1911 with the formation of the first fleet on Long Island Sound, New York, and has never stopped growing. Today, there are over 5000 Star boats recorded in the official Star Log Book. International status was achieved in 1922 when the local English Bay Star Fleet applied for and received its Charter—the first fleet outside the United States to do so. Today, there are representatives of 30 countries throughout the world registered as members of the International Star Class.

The class was introduced at Vancouver in 1922 and quickly superseded in popularity the little "Kitten" Class, 15 foot dinghies designed by John Winslow, which produced some keen competition in the years immediately following World War One. The Star Class, however, proved much more to the taste of the small-boat sailors. As originally designed, these boats measured 22 feet, 8 inches overall; 5 feet, 8 inches beam; and 3 feet, 4 inches draft; carrying 282 square feet of sail in a gaff rig. They have a bulb fin keel. The Stars were the first marconi rigs to appear in the R.V.Y.C. fleet.

The original Stars were gaff rigged but by the time the class started here, the rig had been modernized to a "low" marconi rig. The designation "marconi" comes from the association of ideas between high masts and high radio towers then making their appearance following Marconi's invention of radio transmission; Senor G. Marconi had nothing to do with the development of the so-called "marconi rig" known on the eastern seaboard as "Bermuda Rig", probably because the style originated in Bermuda where small boat sailing is a way of life. The first marconi rigs were known as "low marconi's" but about 1932 the Star boom was shortened, and the mast height increased to provide greater efficiency with the same sail area—282 sq. feet. Nowadays, with their high marconi rigs, Stars are probably the fastest vessels under sail.

The first of the Stars were ordered by club members in the fall of 1922, so that there were five of them finished in time for the Victoria Day regatta the next spring. The originals in the fleet were the *Stella Maris*, sailed by Reg Purves, and built by Hoffar's Shipyard in Coal Harbour; three built by John Winslow's yard, the *Corona* for Tom Pattison, *Astrea* for Harry Wylie and H. H. Simmonds, and *Centaur* for W. H. Alcock. *Auriga* was built by Hazen Phillips and Ron Kerr. They were soon followed by A. N. Wolverton's *Mercury* and W. P. Weston's *Daphne*.

Winner of the first Star Class race in English Bay was Reg Purves' *Stella Maris* on May 24, 1923, who was also the winner of the Roedde Cup, put up that first year by G. A. Roedde Sr., father of Bill Roedde, as a perpetual Star Class challenge trophy.

The Macneill trophy, which was originally put up for competition in the old 18 foot class, was in 1923 changed to a perpetual challenge trophy for the coast championship in the Star Class. At the international regatta in Vancouver in 1923 the cup was won by Wylie and Simmonds' *Astrea*, although when it came to presenting it, the cup could not be found. The trophy then remained in abeyance until 1937 when it turned up again, and has since been the challenge trophy for Roedde Class sloops in the White Rocks race.

The first Roedde Cup competition resulted in a tie between Reg Purves' *Stella Maris* and Tom Pattison's *Corona*, with 27 points each, 24 points for *Astrea*, 23 for *Auriga*, 13 for *Centaur* and 8 for *Mercury*. The fate of the cup was settled in a race twice around a triangular course on English Bay between Purves and Pattison, with *Stella Maris* coming in ahead with a lead of 7 minutes 16 seconds.

So keen was the interest in the club in Star Class racing that in 1923 a challenge was forwarded to the International Star Class Association naming Harry Wylie as the Vancouver representative at the international Star Class races to be held on Long Island Sound in late August. His expenses were raised by subscription among club members. He took his own sails, but borrowed a boat. Mr. Wylie proved his fine qualities as a racing skipper by winning second place in the series of three races, as well as some special trophies.

Flushed with this success, the R.V.Y.C. decided to try again in 1924, when Fleet Captain Reg Purves was selected to represent the club at the Long Island regatta. He took with him as his crew Purves McLennan, and sailed a chartered yacht under his own name of *Stella Maris*. On this occasion, the Vancouver challenger came seventh out of ten contestants in five races. However Mr. Purves came second out of 20 Stars in the Knickerbocker Yacht Club general regatta and fourth out of 23 starters in the Larchmont Yacht Club general regatta.

In 1925 the R.V.Y.C. again entered a challenger in the Long Island Sound regatta, with Hazen Phillips representing the Star fleet. He won second place, and captured the distant fleet trophy from a score of entrants. By this time there were 38 organized fleets in the International Star Class Racing Association and 327 registered yachts.

The year 1926 was notable for the first long distance cruise undertaken by adventurous Star Class yachtsmen. Three of the class made a six day cruise to Vancouver Island and the Gulf Islands, cooking their meals on the beaches. Taking part in this midsummer safari were Harry Wylie and R. C. Mathieson in *Mercury*, Reg Purves and Bill Roedde in *Stella Maris* and Hazen Phillips and Ron Kerr in *Auriga*.

The next international Star Class series to be contested by the R.V.Y.C. was in 1928 at Newport Beach, California, over a ten mile course on the open sea. Racing for the world title were that year's Roedde Cup winners, Phillips and Kerr in the *Auriga*. Unfortunately they came in 13th out of 17 competitors, due entirely to their lack of experience in open ocean racing. Faced with a ground swell and light fitful breezes, they found that the successful competitors under difficult conditions had stepped their masts further aft than usual, and moved their iron keels a little forward, giving more weather helm.

The 1932 Olympic Games were held at Los Angeles, so, late in 1931 a new Star Class challenger, the famous *Windor*, was built at George Askew's False Creek yard with the express purpose of representing R.V.Y.C. in the Canadian elimination trials, which were to be held in Vancouver. *Windor* was beautifully built, and was given the new Star Class lofty rig. Harry Wylie was chosen to be her skipper at Los Angeles, with P. D. Gordon as crew. She made her debut on English Bay in June 1932, painted a light sea-green, and quickly proved herself faster than the old speed queens *Auriga* and *Astrea*. In the Olympics elimination trials she easily outsailed *Nomana*, skippered by Dick Leckie, which also had the new lofty rig.

The Olympic yacht races were held that summer off the San Pedro breakwater under wide open blustery conditions. Harry Wylie proved the new *Windor* was a worthy competitor, and that he had few equals as a skipper. He had the bad luck to be fouled in the first race, but despite this handicap he tied for third place on overall points.

The Star Class fleet had always had their headquarters in English Bay, off the old pier, from the time of their formation, and Star owners were among the most enthusiastic leaders of the move to build a new clubhouse on English Bay off Jericho Beach, and the actual move in 1927 was a great boon to the class. In 1934 the Kitsilano Yacht Club was formed, with a clubhouse off Kitsilano Beach. This resulted in some keen inter-club competition for Stars, Snipes, and other small racers.

Adding to the records achieved by our Star sailors in the "twenties", this class continues to bring honour and worldwide publicity to Vancouver and the Royal Vancouver Yacht Club.

The name and fame of our British Columbia "yachtsman's paradise" continues to be spread worldwide by their enthusiastic participation in the following important yachting fixtures:

WORLD INTERNATIONAL STAR CHAMPIONSHIPS

Held	Year	R.V.Y.C. Entry	Place
Long Island Sound, N.Y.	1923	H. E. Wylie and Purves McLennan in borrowed Star	2nd
Long Island Sound, N.Y.	1924	Reg. Purves and Purves McLennan in borrowed Star	8th
Long Island Sound, N.Y.	1925	G. Hazen Phillips in borrowed Star	2nd
Newport Beach, California	1928	Phillips and Kerr in *Auriga*	13th
San Diego, California	1938	R. W. R. Day in *Nomana*	17th
San Pedro, California	1947	Phil and Sid Miller in *Clear Sky*	13th
Chicago, Illinois	1950	George Parsons and George Forbes in *Windor*	26th
Newport Beach, California	1959	Ken Kirkland and Ian Kirkland in *Scram*	29th
San Diego, California	1961	Bonar Davis and Bill May in *Cetus*	12th
Lisbon, Portugal	1962	Bonar Davis and Ches. Rickard in *Simba*	36th
Chicago, Illinois	1963	Dave Miller and Bill West in *Glissen*	41st
Boston, Massachusetts	1964	Dave Miller and Bill West in *Simba*	Broke Mast, D.N.F.

INTERNATIONAL STAR CHAMPIONSHIP OF THE AMERICAS

Held	Year	R.V.Y.C. Entry	Place
San Francisco, California	1939	George Parsons and Sid Miller in *Windor*	13th

WORLD OLYMPIC GAMES – STAR CLASS CHAMPIONSHIP

Held	Year	R.V.Y.C. Entry	Place
San Pedro, California	1932	Harry Wylie and P. D. Gordon in *Windor*	3rd
Melbourne, Australia	1956	Eugene Pennell and George Parsons in *Manana*	10th
Naples, Italy	1960	Bill Burgess and Bill West in *Scram*	23rd
Tokyo, Japan	1964	Dave Miller and Bill West in *Glissen*	7th

NORTH AMERICAN STAR CHAMPIONSHIP

Held	Year	R.V.Y.C. Entry	Place
Seattle,		Dr. Cec. Helmer in *Totem*	7th
Washington	1948	Phil and Sid Miller in *Clear Sky*	8th
Toronto,			
Ontario	1961	Ian and Ken Kirkland in *Surf*	30th
Seattle,		George Mason in *No Mo*	6th
Washington	1962	Ian and Ken Kirkland in *Surf*	15th
Long Island			
Sound, N.Y.	1963	Dave Miller and Bill West in *Glissen*	6th

PAN AMERICAN GAMES, STAR CLASS CHAMPIONSHIP

Held	Year	R.V.Y.C. Entry	Place
Chicago,			
Illinois	1959	George Mason and Maurice Hunt in *Ghost*	5th

WINNERS IN 6th DISTRICT (BLUE STAR) CHAMPIONSHIP

Year	Star, Skipper	Year	Star, Skipper
1928	*Stella Maris*, Reg. Purves	1946	*Clear Sky*, Phil and Sid Miller
1929	*Astrea*, Harry E. Wylie	1948	*Clear Sky*, Phil and Sid Miller
1930	*Mercury*, C. P. Leckie	1950	*Clear Sky*, Phil and Sid Miller
1933	*Astrea*, Harry E. Wylie	1951	*Marina*, Eug. Pennell
1940	*Clear Sky*, Phil and Sid Miller	1958	*Sparkle*, George Mason
1944	*Clear Sky*, Phil and Sid Miller		

WINNERS IN 6th DISTRICT (GREEN STAR) CHAMPIONSHIP

Year	Star, Skipper	Year	Star, Skipper
1952	*Wisp*, George Mason	1963	*Susan II*, Carl Petersen
1962	*Windor*, Bill West	1964	*Spindrift*, Paul Sturdy

ENGLISH BAY STAR FLEET — FAUX PAS TROPHY WINNERS

1949	Pat Leslie	1958	Geo. Mason
1950	Geo. Forbes	1959	Dr. T. D. Hope
1951	Dr. C. Helmer	1960	Ann Helmer
1953	P. and S. Miller	1962	Geo. Mason
1954	Bill West	1964	Bill Burgess
1956	Herb. Wilson		

A. H. Jefferd and E. S. Earle are Honorary Life Members in the English Bay Star Fleet in appreciation of their services as Hon. Hydrographers to the fleet.

Trio of Race Judges — H. J. Bird, A. H. Jefferd, E. S. Earle.

Four of the original Star skippers continued in active competition up to the early "fifties"—Harry Wylie, Hazen Phillips, Ron Kerr and W. P. Weston—and while the following roll is by no means complete it records the Stars in the club with the names of their original owners and is taken from the English Bay Star Fleet lists and R.V.Y.C. year books for the years stated. Many changed names and hands several times.

1939	*Astrea*, H. E. Wylie	1949	*Black Fish*, Ches Rickard
	Aura, J. C. Barltrop		*Crusader*, N. S. White
	Auriga, Phillips and Kerr		*Night Mare*, White and Hargrave
	Ariki, Cedric Dill		*Polaris*, Pat Leslie
	Clear Sky, Phil and Sid Miller		*Reverie*, C. Bayne
	Daphne, W. P. Weston		*Whisp*, Geo. Mason
	Dipper, Stu Slade	1952	*Snowflake*, G. H. Robinson
	Maori, Capt. B. L. Johnson	1956	*Sparkle*, Geo. Mason
	Marina, Ditmars and Brooke		*Zephyr*, H. G. Henniker-Wilson
	Murralet, C. and T. Burke	1957	*Black Hawk*, Eric Marsden
	Nomana, Bob Day		*Duz*, Bonar Davis
	Pat, C. H. Foster		*King Billy II*, G. W. MacLaren
	Serenade, E. Doug Stone		*North Star*, R. Rayner
	Stella Maris, L. B. Culter	1958	*Libra*, J. Campbell
	Stormy, Bob Gale	1959	*Twinkle*, J. Bowron
	Tally Ho, Bill Hewlett	1961	*Cetus*, Bonar Davis
	Taseko, Bud Day		*Diggin*, Dr. Tom Hope
	Windor, Geo. Parsons		*Ghost*, Geo. Mason
	Stardust, F. J. (Bunny) Whitcroft	1962	*Scram*, Ian and Ken Kirkland
1941	*Mercury*, Percy Burr		*Surf*, Ian Kirkland
1942	*Twilight*, Terry Thompson		*Susan II*, Carl Petersen
1944	*Victory*, E. Doug Stone		*No Mo*, Geo. Mason
	Uranus, C. Bayne	1964	*Gypsy*, Ken Kirkland
1945	*Flying Cloud*, Stan Davies		*Glissen*, Dave Miller
1946	*Spitfire*, Geo. Parsons		*Scram II*, Bill Burgess
	Totem, Dr. C. Helmer		*Simba*, Bonar Davis
1947	*Havoc*, Ray Delaplace		*Spindrift*, Paul Sturdy
	Talisman, H. E. Wylie		*West Wynn*, Bill Burgess
1948	*Ghost*, Robbie Brown		
	Sapphire, Ron Kelly		

Dave Miller and Ken Baxter race Star DIGGIN.

Province photo.

CHAPTER 14

Flatties (Geary 18's)
Dragons and
Lightnings

ALTHOUGH NOT AS POPULAR with the younger members now as in the Thirties and Forties, the 18 foot centerboard Flattie designed by famed Ted Geary of Seattle in 1928 provides thrilling sailing sport and is the vehicle through which quite a few of our members have achieved Championship status. (Flattie Class recently renamed Geary 18's.)

Flatties appealed to junior members who were looking for a one-design centerboard sloop which could be easily made by amateurs at low cost, would be easily transported by car-trailer and at the same time would be a smart sailing craft. As designed by Geary, it is 18 ft. long, 5 ft. 3 inches beam, carries 157.5 square feet of sail and must weigh 525 pounds or more. Easy to build because of her flat bottom athwartships, she is also very fast, even planing beautifully on a run. She can be put on her beam ends and righted without filling because of her wide decks, and under no circumstances will she sink.

Twelve Flatties were built in 1928 for club members by Pacific Salvage Company, North Vancouver, at a cost of $200 each. Dean Johnson was the shipwright and our well-known racing skipper Jack Cribb, who was then Superintendent of the company, kept an eye on the construction.

At the P.I.Y.A. Regatta held in Vancouver that year a fleet of Flatties came up from Seattle and our R.V.Y.C. Flattie *Dynamite*, skippered by Doug Maitland with his sister Heather as crew, carried off the International Flattie Championship. Doug was then 12 years old—twenty-seven years later, to be our Commodore. He relates an interesting incident that took place in the local Flattie Series at that 1928 Regatta which was won by P. D. Gordon in *David* with Claude Thicke as crew, closely followed by *Goliath* skippered by Harry Rendell with Walter Thicke as crew.

There was a bet on between these two crews, the loser to pay for the others' boat. *Goliath* was well ahead in a fresh westerly when she "dumped" and the discomfitted, soaked Harry and Walter had to "fish-up" $200 for Pete and Claude's *David*—biblical history repeated!

Flatties were soon sailing in increasing numbers up and down the Pacific Coast, from Vancouver to Acapulco, Mexico. In 1935 the skippers at Vancouver took down three Flatties to Seattle for an International Championship Series which R.V.Y.C. won, and it was at that event held under N.A.Y.R.U. auspices that Phil and Sid Miller in *Silver Wings* copped their first World Championship.

This was to be only the first of a series of World Championship achievements for the talented sailing Miller family, Phil, Sid and his wife Janet and son David, as the following outstanding record shows—

INTERNATIONAL FLATTIE WORLD CHAMPIONSHIPS

1935 at Seattle *in Silver Wings*. Skipper, Phil Miller; Crew, Sid Miller.
1936 at Vancouver in *Blue Wings*. Skipper, Phil Miller; Crew, Jack Gillies.
1937 at Vancouver in *Blue Wings*. Skipper, Phil Miller; Crew, Jack Gillies.
1938 at Seattle in *Silver Wings*. Skipper, Sid Miller; Crew, Mrs. Janet Miller.
1960 at Vancouver in *Silver Wings*. Skipper, David Miller; Crew, Sid Miller.

The Miller brothers built their flatties themselves and also designed, cut and sewed their own sails and their oustanding ability in this regard is amply demonstrated by the fact that the same boat, *Silver Wings*, won the world's championship in 1938 and again twenty years later, in 1958. Also it should be noted that the Millers have turned their boyhood sport and hobby into their business careers, for in recent years they have built an international reputation and a flourishing business as fine sail-makers to particular and exacting yachtsmen.

The Sears Cup is emblematic of the Junior Sailing Championship of North America. Competition for the Cup is open to crews of three boys or girls who have not reached their eighteenth birthday by September first of the year in which they compete. Contenders or parents must be members of a recognized yacht club in North America.

Although Commodore Herbert M. Sears of the Eastern Yacht Club, Mass., placed the Sears Cup in competition first in 1921 for Massachusetts Yacht Clubs, competition was made national in scope when he deeded the cup on June 23rd, 1931, to the North American Yacht Racing Union and thereafter these contests have been held under the jurisdiction of the Union. In 1951 the Deed of Gift was changed to include Canada, thus making the Sears Cup international in scope.

Our club was signally honoured by being selected the host club for the Sears Cup Regatta August 24 to 28, 1958, the first time the event was held on the Pacific Coast in Canada and on this occasion, sailing in Flatties, after a heart-breaking inadvertent foul in the first race, our boat, skippered by David Miller with crew of Steven Tupper, Colin Park and (alternate) Paul Sturdy, finished second in the Series.

Due to the historic nature of this North American International Junior Sailing Championship event, a condensed version of the Official N.A.Y.R.U. Judges' report, signed by W. H. (Bud) Day, chairman, is reprinted—

The Race Committee, under chairman E. S. Earle, did an outstanding job of conducting the races and setting starting lines, and it was only necessary for the Race Committee to confer with the Judges on a few occasions . . .

Three protests were filed at the end of the second day, all of which were disallowed without the necessity of holding a hearing. None of these involved N.A.Y.R.U. racing rules fouls, or contact between boats. They involved interpretation of the race instructions. There was one incident involving contact between two boats, which occurred at the start of the first race. The Royal Vancouver Yacht Club Crew were in a windward position, and were unable to respond to a luff without swinging the transom of their boat into the leeward yacht. Skipper Miller, and his crew members, earned the high regard of all attending the Series for their fine display of sportsmanship in withdrawing from this race immediately. There were two other disqualifications in the Series. The Newport Harbour Yacht Club Crew hit a mark in the fourth race, and the Royal St. Lawrence Yacht Club Crew were over the starting line early in the last race, and did not hear the recall signal from the Race Committee.

There was one breakdown during the Series. This involved the Hull Yacht Club Crew, and the rudder on their boat jammed, resulting in a broken tiller. The start of several races was postponed by minor rigging difficulties, resulting from missing shackles, cotterpins, etc., and the Judges felt that more care could have been used by some Crews in leaving the boats properly and completely equipped. First prize in the shipshape inspections went to the Lake Geneva Yacht Club Crew for an outstanding job of attention to their boats. The second prize went to the Royal St. Lawrence Yacht Club Crew, and it was interesting to note that it was the first Crew in Sears Cup history skippered by a girl. One of the regular members of the Crew was also a girl, and their influence no doubt contributed greatly to their success in the shipshape competition . . .

FINAL STANDING, 1958 SEARS CUP CONTEST

Place	Skipper	Club	Points
1	Kevin Jaffe	Noroton	48¾
2	David Miller	Royal Vancouver	43¼
3	Wm. M. Hogan III	Hull	40½
4	John W. Jenning	St. Petersburg	35¼
5	Tom Gates	Newport Harbour	35¼

Sid Miller and son David (skipper) in champion Flattie, SILVER-WINGS.
Sun photo.

R.V.Y.C. DRAGONS
BRIGHTEN ENGLISH BAY!

WHILE THE R.V.Y.C. DRAGON FLEET is not a large one their racing events on English Bay provide a very arresting picture with beautiful vari-colored spinnakers billowing out over their trim hulls. Fortunate indeed to enjoy the picture are Vancouver residents overlooking English Bay in the summertime, when gentle westerlies puff out their spinnakers as yachts vie with each other on the downwind leg of the courses. With their colorful sails Dragons were the first of the local yachts to adopt the sleek Dacron sails now so popular in light airs with all classes, from Lightnings to the big racing cruisers.

First registered Dragon in Canada, the *Lady Nan*, was imported from Norway in 1951 by W. H. (Bud) Day, who fathered the class here. Soon there were five or six in commission and there have been as many as eleven in our club—today there are nine on the R.V.Y.C. register. The active participation of His Royal Highness the Duke of Edinburgh, sailing *Bluebottle* in Dragon races, and the fact that the Dragon has been regularly selected for the Olympics, has stimulated the class. In 1951, Bud Day won the Dragon series at the P.I.Y.A. Regatta in Victoria, beating two Dragons from Seattle and one each from San Francisco and Bellingham.

His Royal Highness the Duke of Edinburgh presented his trophy to the Canadian International Dragon Council in 1953, the Council consisting of Dragon sailors in Toronto, Montreal, Halifax, Ottawa, Kingston, Vancouver and Victoria. Dragon Class contests for this trophy are held on English Bay approximately every four years, and this year (1965) five U.S. Dragons from Puget Sound were included in the nine yachts contesting.

H.R.H. DUKE OF EDINBURGH TROPHY

	Dragon	Skipper	Club
1953	Dandilion	G. S. Hanna	Royal Canadian Yacht Club
1954	Flying Cloud	G. S. Hanna	Royal Canadian Yacht Club
1955	Okolina	R. K. MacDonals and Davidson Black	Royal Canadian Yacht Club
1956	Cam	J. P. Leslie	Royal Vancouver Yacht Club
1957	Puzzle II	Rycken Suydam, R. J. Wood, Alan Scott	Royal Canadian Yacht Club
1958	Argo II	Dr. Sam MacDonald	Royal St. Lawrence Yacht Club
1959	Happy Talk	L. H. Muir	Royal Canadian Yacht Club
1960	Cam	Jack Shepherd	Royal Vancouver Yacht Club
1961	Tip	W. Windeyer	Royal Canadian Yacht Club
1962	Joanna II	J. Letourneau	Royal St. Lawrence Yacht Club
1963	Swift	R. G. Townsend	Royal St. Lawrence Yacht Club
1964	Serendippity	E. J. Bottrell	Royal St. Lawrence Yacht Club
1965	Cam	Steven Tupper	Royal Vancouver Yacht Club

The Bluebottle Trophy was presented in 1959 by the Pacific Northwest Dragon Fleet in honour of the visit of H.R.H. The Duke of Edinburgh's Dragon, *Bluebottle,* sailed here on English Bay by Surgeon-Lt. Ross Coles in 1959. The trophy contests are open to Dragons from anywhere on the North American Continent (sailed on English Bay) and the winners have been:

	Dragon	*Skipper*	*Club*
1959	Bluebottle	Surg.-Lt. Ross Coles	Visitor, Royal Cowes Yacht Squadron
1960	Tjep	Bob Burgess	Royal Vancouver Yacht Club
1961	Tjep	Bob Burgess	Royal Vancouver Yacht Club
1962	Two Bits	Dr. T. V. Jones	Royal Vancouver Yacht Club
1963	Audax	Barry Clark	Royal Vancouver Yacht Club
1964	Kris	Butt, Downie & Skibbe	Royal Vancouver Yacht Club

Three club trophies are contested by the Dragon Class over English bay courses: the English Bay Trophy, Stromboli Trophy and Gyles Trophy, all Perpetual Trophies.

Steve Tupper sails AUDAX (foreground) in 1964 Olympic trials.

R.V.Y.C.
LIGHTNING ACTIVITIES

LIGHTNING CLASS ASSOCIATION No. 90 was granted in 1956 to a group of local Lightning enthusiasts, the majority of whom were R.V.Y.C. members; they were Don Black, Geoff Ince, Douglas Jewett, Dr. Eric Lehmann, Tom Sturgess, Adrian Thompson and Dr. Reid Townsley. The Association was formed in 1939 soon after Lightning No. 1 was launched at Lake Skaneateles, New York, built from Sparkman & Stevens designs in 1938. Small boat sailors headed by C. L. Nicholson II and John Barnes called for a comfortable 19 ft. day sailer, suitable for a family or a group of five or six people, and yet would be fast and sporty enough for racing. Soon after No. 1 was shown at the 1938 New York Boat Show there were 20 Lightnings in commission and by 1941 no less than 700 had been registered and 40-odd Fleets organized. By 1946 there were over 2100 registrations and 90 Fleets.

Hunter Vogel of Maple Bay and Haney built the first Lightning in British Columbia waters around 1945. In 1963 the class became International after receiving International Yacht Racing Union approval and at the end of 1964 there were over 9,000 registered boats in 368 chartered Fleets, and twelve in our club.

Local Lightnings turn out every week-end on English Bay and although they have little decking quite a few venture across the Gulf on week-end cruises through the Gulf Islands. With tarpaulin stretched over the boom and air mattresses to sleep on, hardy families enjoy the thrills and pleasures of yachting at minimum cost.

Four of our club trophies have been allotted to Lightning Class racing, and these are very actively contested. They are Redskin Trophy, Venture Trophy, Rogers Trophy and Port of Vancouver Trophy.

VANCOUVER LIGHTNING FLEET #90

Fleet Champion, Runner Up

1957	Adrian Thomson, Geoff Ince
1958	Geoff Ince, Adrian Thomson
1959	Adrian Thomson, Jim Weir
1960	Adrian Thomson, Darrell Jones
1961	Adrian Thomson, Geoff Ince
1962	Adrian Thomson, Peter Thomas
1963	Dr. D. G. Marshall, Geoff Ince
1964	Dr. D. G. Marshall, Geoff Ince

PACIFIC NORTHWEST DISTRICT-INTERNATIONAL LIGHTNING CLASS ASSOCIATION

Fleet Champion, Runner Up

1957	M. & M. Barber, Seattle; ....
1958	M. & M. Barber, Seattle; Bob Brown, Seattle
1959	Bob Brown, Seattle; A. Thomson, Vancouver
1960	Jack Gainer, Portland; Ty Campbell, Eugene
1961	Ken Bostram, Seattle; F. Taucher, Portland
1962	R. Sahlin, Bellingham; C. Clark, Seattle
1963	Don Clark, Seattle; Bob Clark, Seattle
1964	Don Clark, Seattle; Dick Blickle, Portland

CHAPTER 15

Spencer and Roedde Classes

URING THE MIDDLE 1930's racing was at a low ebb in the club because of the depression. Some of the members felt there was a need for a small one-design racing craft, a little bigger than the Stars, which could be built at relatively small cost, and could also be used for cruising. The promoters of this project were Roy Ginn, Reg Purves, Bill Roedde, Cedric Dill and Ron Jackson, and they spent many pleasant hours arguing over the ideal design. They eventually decided on a craft 30 feet overall by 6 feet 3 inches beam by 4 feet 4 inches depth. Armed with their plans they went to Tom Halliday, the marine architect, who gave his professional advice, and drew up the final blueprints. The sail area was 340 feet, and a 2½ h.p. auxiliary was provided. Bids were asked and it was found that the total amount for the complete boat would be $2315. The same vessel would cost $12,000 30 years later.

But no matter what the cost, none of the younger members had the money for any such expense in those hard times. Purves, Roedde and Dill formed a building committee, and in the early spring of 1936 organized a $5 raffle, selling $2500 worth of tickets.

It was a hectic night at the Jericho clubhouse in the spring of 1936 when over two hundred excited and tense yachtsmen awaited the drawing of the name of the lucky winner following a preliminary wrestling match at the club's annual "Smoker". To re-live that momentous evening at which quite a number of leading Vancouver businessmen "came close to being yachtsmen", here is the fast-running commentary published in the Vancouver Sun next morning by Hal Straight, Sports Editor, now a well known suburban newspaper owner:

> Run by "the building committee" through the co-operation of the Yacht Club, the long awaited draw for the 30 ft. racing-cruising sloop designed by Bill Roedde and Tom Halliday was a tense exciting event.
>
> Ticket-holders craning their necks, their hearts beating like breakers on a rocky shore, who just before ·had been telling what they would do with the boat when they won it, nervously awaited the draw to start.
>
> Due to formalities there was suspense. You could feel the air tingle. The boats in the pictures on the wall stopped, the water stopped, the clock

stopped. The stewards left their chores and waited. Secretary Allen rushed in.

This is a country for boats; they love boats here, and they all wanted this pretty little thing.

More suspense was felt when Commodore Johnson said they would draw 24 names, then 12, then 6, then 3, then 2, and the one left in the hat would be the new skipper.

There was some more dithering, and finally a committee of non-ticket-holders retired to choose the first 24.

They were gone for weeks. It was a tense period. In the room filled with nervous tobacco smoke again each ticket buyer was telling what he would do with the boat. Sid Bowman, Art Jefferd and Ken Davidson decided if they were drawn in the first 24 they would sell their ticket for $75, and save their health and nerves.

The committee came in. Through the loud speaker came the commodore's booming voice.

"Number so-and-so," he shouted, twenty-four times.

Each number was put on a blackboard, and each number brought groans and "My gosh, I was only one away . . . Look at that, how's that for close? . . . Oh, Herb Fullerton's got a ticket . . . George Cran has one . . . Just missed it—was darned near a yachtsman."

Then the committee went to work again to draw 12 from the 24. This time the names were called with the numbers.

"J. Simpson" was the first name. Much shouting. And more shouting with the names of Jack Storey, Capt. Harrison, P. Gordon, DuMoulin, E. S. Earle, O. B. Allan, R. H. Squire, John Dunsmuir, T. Perry, Mrs. Hughes, A. E. Jukes.

With these names drawn and the room just buzzing with excited conversation, six names were pulled: O. B. Allan, Jack Storey, Capt. Harrison, Mrs. Edith Hughes, John Dunsmuir and E. S. Earle.

More buzzing, sandwiches and coffee, and Nelson's blood had been brought in to give some of the men strength.

Then Jack Storey was called. Then O. B. Allan, and the last was E. S. Earle. One of these three was the winner. Who? The last one left in the big silver cup. Storey was offered $800 for his ticket.

With the first pull O. B. Allan came out of the cup and out of the competition. After the next pull they would know who won. They fussed around. They took a year, and the name was E. S. Earle. It was Jack Storey left and the winner . . . and did he go limp!

Immediately Storey jumped on to the platform and announced Bill Roedde his skipper, because Storey knows no more about sailing than we do about malted milk shakes. But he intends to learn.

The idea of this draw is to start a racing class of yachts with the vessels all uniform. The conditions of the draw last night were that the boat could not be changed. It is expected that other boats will be built of the same design as the one that went to Storey last night, and a special class of racing be established.

The vessel was christened *Carita* and was built at the Boeing Shipyard in Coal Harbour.

Thus was born the original of the "turtle-decked" Spencer Class, which was to prove so popular for several years. Jack Storey soon sold the *Carita* to Bill Roedde and Ron Jackson, and she sailed in P.I.Y.A. regatta at Victoria in 1936 with Bill Roedde and Reg Purves as crew. The *Carita* proved to be such a success, the building committee decided to build up a fleet of five more ships, and again recourse was made to holding a raffle to raise the funds. However it required a lot of selling to raise the funds for five boats at $2500 each, and the committee found hard sledding, for the depression was still being felt by members. Eventually four "angels" were approached, in the persons of Col. Victor

Spencer Class sloop ARIKI, 1938.

Roedde Class, opening day, 1959.

Spencer, Ken McLennan, Austin Taylor and Capt. Bill Crawford. All were wealthy men and they formed a group to guarantee payment to the shipyard, so that the fleet could be ready for the 1937 season. It was decided to christen the class the "Spencer" Class in honor of Col. Victor Spencer.

At the Club Annual Smoker May 28th, 1937, with over 300 enthusiastic sailors present, five sleek miniature models were auctioned in an exciting elimination system that kept interest at fever point. The successful "bidders" were Bob McAdam, Pat Taylor, R. E. Cromie, Captain Wm. Crawford, and T. O'Donnell.

The five Spencer boats proved extraordinarily successful during their brief careers with the R.V.Y.C., racing until 1942, when the war brought an end to such activities, and the entire class was sold to Seattle owners. Several trophies were put up for Spencer Class racing, which have since been raced by the Roedde Class. These included the Fraser River Lightship Trophy, the masthead light from the old *Empress of Japan,* won by Ced Dill's *Ariki* in 1939 and 1940; the Entrance Island Trophy, won by *Ariki* in 1938 and 1939, and by *Carita* in 1940; the English Bay Trophy, won by *Carita* in 1937, *Ariki* in 1938 and 1939, and Bert Tupper's *Vogad* in 1940.

After the war was over Bill Roedde had a dream of an improved Spencer type that would be more comfortable for cruising. With the assistance of naval architect Tom Halliday, the design was primarily the work of Bill Roedde, Bert Tupper and Jack Williamson. The Roedde Class are sloops 34 feet 4 inches overall, 25 feet on the waterline, with a beam of 8 feet and a draft of 5 feet 4 inches. They have lead keels of 4250 pounds and a sail area of 500 sq. feet. As originally designed they had the Spencer type turtle-deck, but that was later changed to conventional cabin top. The first of the Roedde Class was built at Taylor's Boat Works in 1949 for Bill Roedde, and was christened *Carita II.*

Other originals in the Roedde Class were Jack Williamson's *Fantasie,* Lorne Cutler's *Miss Lee,* Dr. Bob McCaffrey's *Hymac,* Tom Baird's *Tomboy* and Bill Morrow's *Elusive.* The latter sailed many times in the Swiftsure Classic finishing second (corrected time) on one occasion. Another keen sailor in the Roedde class is Len Murrell's *Treveda;* Len has sailed in eight consecutive Swiftsure races from 1957 on. He came first in the B Class 1960 Swiftsure and just lost out for first position in the B's in 1958 and in 1959, by handicap.

CHAPTER 16

Swiftsure Racing

F EW LONG DISTANCE RACES have proved more popular and enduring than the annual Swiftsure race, now known as the Swiftsure Classic, which was first promoted in 1930 by Captain B. L. Johnson and other R.V.Y.C. members. The original course was from Victoria to the Swiftsure Lightship, off the mouth of the Strait of Juan de Fuca, now replaced by a marker.

The race has always attracted a large number of American competitors, and now has the reputation of being one of the classic endurance races on the Pacific Coast. Organization of the classic is now chiefly handled by the Royal Victoria Yacht Club, which acts as host club to the visitors.

The object of the race is to encourage amongst the clubs of the Pacific International Yachting Association the racing of cruising yachts capable of an open sea venture in which winds of from fresh to half gale force may be expected. A shorter Juan de Fuca race has recently been added to the fixture to enable smaller yachts to finish in reasonable time. The races are sailed under the rules of the International Yacht Racing Union. Swiftsure race entries must have a rating between 15:0 and 21.9. The use of radar and automatic pilots is not permitted.

The distance of the Swiftsure race for time allowance purposes is 136.2 miles and the Juan de Fuca race 75.6 miles. The Swiftsure course is from the vicinity of Brotchie Ledge Beacon to the Swiftsure Mark and return. The Juan de Fuca race is from the starting line to Clallam Bay Mark and return. The time limit for both races is 50 hours.

In addition to the Swiftsure Trophy for the overall handicap winner, there are many other trophies for various classes, and the City of Victoria Trophy for the first boat to finish. The Juan de Fuca Trophy is awarded to the winner of the shorter race.

The first Swiftsure race was held in July 1930 at the conclusion of the P.I.Y.A. Regatta at Victoria. The race was sailed in light to moderate winds and was won by the Seattle schooner *Claribel*. Barney Johnson's 54 foot yawl *Westward Ho* was second and D. P. Urry's cutter *Cresset* came in third. None of the other entries finished within the time limit.

However Barney Johnson's *Westward Ho* showed her capabilities the following year when she won the Swiftsure handily with H. S. "Clair" Jellett at the helm. Her time was 44 hours, nine minutes and four seconds. None of the three other entries finished the course in the time limit.

Sailing conditions in the strait were very poor, particularly in the homeward reach, and it took *Westward Ho* more than five hours to reach the finishing line from Race Rocks. Other entries in this race were the *Minena* of Victoria and *Cresset* and *Minerva* of the Royal Vancouver club. *Westward Ho* again held the trophy in 1933, but in 1934 last out of *Circe* of Seattle, which covered the course in 52¾ hours. *Westward Ho*, skippered by Clair Jellett, took 61 hours, while *Minena*, owned by Harry Barnes of Victoria, and *White Cloud* of Tacoma came back under power.

The Swiftsure Classic has grown with the years, and instead of the modest four or five entries of 30 years ago, there were 88 starters in the 1963 race. In the post war years American boats have greatly outnumbered Canadian entries, and for many years consistently carried off the trophy. However in 1954 Bill Morrow's "Roedde" Class *Elusive* came second against a large fleet with a corrected time of 39:22:16, and that must have broken the long series of American victories. In 1961 Ches Rickard's "L-36" Class *Winsome III*, skippered by Bonar Davis, was declared the winner, and she repeated the feat in 1962. This was the first time the same vessel had won the Swiftsure twice in succession. *Winsome III* was again declared winner in 1963 after a protest had put Bob Reagan's Seattle-based 40 foot *Thetis* out of the race.

In 1956 the Vancouver yachts *Mary Bower* and *Gometra* competed in the Swiftsure; in 1958 Pat Leslie's *Tricia, Winsome III, Troubadour,* Ralph Farris' *Hawk* and Norman McCarvill's *Spirit*. In 1960 *Tricia* was winner in the BB Class and Bob Ross' *Concerto* the winner in the AA Class. *Hawk, Fulmar* and *Mary Bower* also competed. In 1961 Philip Graham's big *Troubadour* was the first home, the first Canadian racer to lead the van for many years.

SWIFTSURE CLASSES AND TROPHIES

Overall Handicap Winner of Swiftsure	*Swiftsure Trophy*
First Boat to Finish Swiftsure	*City of Victoria Trophy*
Class "AA" — Rating 39.0 and above	*B.C. Cement Company Trophy*
Class "A" — Rating 30.0 to 38.9	*T. Eaton Company Trophy*
Class "BB" — Rating 26.0 to 29.9	*Seattle Yacht Club Trophy*
Class "B" — Rating 22.0 to 25.9	*Royal Vancouver Yacht Club Trophy*
Class "C" — First Boat to Finish	*San Juan Trophy*
Class "C" — Rating 15.0 to 21.9 (Juan de Fuca Race)	*Juan de Fuca Trophy*

ROYAL VANCOUVER YACHT CLUB ENTRIES IN
SWIFTSURE CLASSIC 1952-1965

	Yacht	Skipper	Class, Position	Overall Position
1952	*Elusive*	W. R. Morrow	B — 3	16
	Hymac	Stan. Davies	B — DNF	DNF
	Tomboy II	H. B. Barkes	B — 2	15
1953	*Elusive*	W. R. Morrow	B — 1	5
	Gometra	K. G. Glass	A — DNF	DNF
	Hymac	Stan. Davies	B — DNF	DNF
1954	*Elusive*	W. R. Morrow	B — 1	2
	Gometra	K. G. Glass	A — 2	5
1955	*Elusive*	W. R. Morrow	B — DNF	DNF
	Gometra	E. J. Palmer	A — 5	12
1956	*Gometra*	E. J. Palmer	A — 4	9
	Mary Bower	K. J. McRae	A — 5	11
1957	*Delphin*	A. W. Way	BB — 6	23
	Gometra	E. J. Palmer	A — 7	22
	Mary Bower	K. J. McRae	A — 3	9
	Treveda	Len Murrell	B — 1	20
1958	*Cresset*	G. M. Palmer	BB — 4	12
	Gometra	E. J. Palmer	A — 6	14
1959	*Concerto*	R. D. Ross	AA — 2	10
	Coral Reef II	A. W. Way	A — 11	26
	Delphin	E. Chisholm	BB — 7	21
	Hawk	R. K. Farris	A — 7	19
	Mary Bower	K. J. McRae	A — 1	6
	Spirit	N. R. McCarvill	AA — 5	16
	Treveda	Len Murrell	B — DNF	DNF
	Tricia	J. P. Leslie	BB — 3	3
	Troubadour	P. D. Graham	AA — 8	25
1960	*Concerto*	R. D. Ross	A — 4	7
	Coral Reef II	A. W. Way	A — DNF	DNF
	Delphin	E. Chisholm	BB — 9	28
	Fulmar	L. E. Balmer	AA — 7	24
	Gabrielle II	P. R. Sandwell	A — DNF	DNF
	Hawk	R. K. Farris	A — 6	12
	Heather VI	J. G. Innes	BB — DNF	DNF
	Mary Bower	K. J. McRae	A — 5	8
	Spirit	N. R. McCarvill	AA — 4	21
	Toroa	A. J. Rees	B — DNF	DNF
	Treveda	Len Murrell	B — 4	35
	Tricia	J. P. Leslie	BB — 1	2
	Troubadour	P. D. Graham	AA — 3	20
	Winsome II	C. L. Rickard	BB — 6	14

ROYAL VANCOUVER YACHT CLUB ENTRIES IN
SWIFTSURE CLASSIC 1952-1965—Continued

	Yacht	Skipper	Class, Position	Overall Position
1961	Alcion	C. D. Campbell	A — 17	48
	Concerto	R. D. Ross	A — 19	52
	Coral Reef II	A. W. Way	A — 4	18
	Delphin	J. W. Chisholm	BB — 12	22
	Fulmar	J. E. Balmer	A — 18	51
	Gabrielle II	R. K. Baker	A — 5	23
	Hawk	R. K. Farris	A — 10	37
	Hazel Maid	R. H. Ellison	BB — 11	21
	Jester	S. B. Watts	BB — 7	9
	Maredea	R. G. Lundy	BB — 2	2
	Mary Bower	K. J. McRae	A — 8	26
	Nyon	D. G. Simpson	BB — 14	29
	Spirit	N. R. McCarvill	AA — 6	55
	Toroa	A. J. Rees	B — 11	34
	Treveda	Len Murrell	B — 14	40
	Tricia	J. P. Leslie	BB — 5	7
	Troubadour	P. Graham	AA — 5	54
	Velaris	L. H. Killam	A — 15	45
	Winsome III	Bonar Davis	BB — 1	1
1962	Alcion	C. D. Campbell	A — 10	29
	Coho	G. M. Palmer	B — 5	33
	Concerto	R. D. Ross	A — 20	54
	Coral Reef II	A. W. Way	A — 13	34
	Delphin	J. W. Chisholm	BB — 12	40
	Gabrielle II	R. K. Baker	A — 16	41
	Hawk	R. K. Farris	A — 7	20
	Jester	S. B. Watts	BB — 3 (Tied)	5
	Long Gone	J. Innes	BB — 9	26
	Maredea	B. Lundy	BB — DNF	DNF
	Mary Bower	K. J. McRae	A — 4	12
	Nyon	D. G. Simpson	BB — 13	45
	Pandora of Rhu	J. K. Sloan	A — 14	38
	Toroa	A. J. Rees	B — 13	55
	Treveda	Len Murrell	B — DNF	DNF
	Tricia	J. P. Leslie	BB — 3 (Tied)	5
	Troubadour	P. Graham	AA — 8	43
	Velaris	L. H. Killam	A — 2	10
	Winsome III	C. L. Rickard	BB — 1	1
1963	Alcion	C. D. Campbell	A — 13	34
	Benora II	R. A. Delaplace	BB — 6	18
	Coho	J. Brandlmayr	B — 5	40
	Fulmar	J. E. Balmer	A — 7	15
	Gabrielle II	P. R. Sandwell	A — 10	27
	Hawk	R. K. Farris	A — DNF	DNF
	Hazel Maid	R. H. Ellison	B — 12	56
	Jester	S. B. Watts	BB — 5	17
	Long Gone	J. Innes	BB — 4	16
	Maredea	R. G. Lundy	BB — 9	22
	Mary Bower	John Long	A — 16	43
	Nyon	D. G. Simpson	BB — 3	12
	Penelakut	R. D. Ross	A — 18	45
	Spirit	N. R. McCarvill	AA — 4	36
	Treveda	Len Murrell	B — DNF	DNF
	Tricia	J. P. Leslie	BB — 11	25
	Troubadour	P. Graham	AA — 7	50
	Velaris	L. H. Killam	A — 8	21
	Winsome III	C. Rickard	BB — 2	2

ROYAL VANCOUVER YACHT CLUB ENTRIES IN
SWIFTSURE CLASSIC 1952-1965—*Continued*

	Yacht	Skipper	Class, Position	Overall Position
1964	Alcion	C. D. Campbell	A — 13	28
	Fulmar	J. E. Balmer	A — 4	9
	Long Gone	J. Innes	BB — 8	16
	Maredea	A. W. Way	BB — 10	27
	Mary Bower	J. H. Long	A — 17	35
	Pandora of Rhu	J. K. Sloan	A — 8	14
	Sanderling	A. H. Meakin	BB — 6	11
	Tricia	J. P. Leslie	BB — 3	5
	Troubadour	P. Graham	AA — 3	23
	Velaris	L. H. Killam	A — 5	10
	Veleda	J. Grubbe	BB — 9	17
	Winsome III	C. L. Rickard	BB — 7	15
1965	Alcion	K. J. McRae	A — 12	21
	Benora	P. D. Graham	BB — 15	49
	Fulmar	J. E. Balmer	A — 2	4
	Gabrielle II	P. R. Sandwell	A — 16	47
	George Kitamike	H. Davidson	BB — 12	41
	Jester	S. B. Watts	BB — 7	25
	Jeunesse	P. T. Cote	B — 11	48
	Jolly Olly	V. Ruskin	B — 8	39
	Long Gone	J. Innes	BB — 8	26
	Maredea	A. W. Way	BB — 5	14
	Mary Bower	J. H. Long	A — 21	63
	Nyon	D. G. Simpson	BB — 11	36
	Pandora of Rhu	H. M. Ellis	A — 7	13
	Penelakut	R. D. Ross	A — 8	16
	Sanderling	A. H. Meakin	BB — 16	51
	Serapis	A. J. B. Forsyth	BB — 17	53
	Spirit	N. R. McCarvill	AA — 6	43
	Treveda	Len Murrell	B — 18	65
	Tricia	J. P. Leslie	BB — 2	2
	Velaris	L. H. Killam	A — 10	19
	Winsome III	C. L. Rickard	BB — 3	8

Typical start, Swiftsure Classic.

Ches L. Rickard's WINSOME III at start, 1960 Swiftsure Classic.
J. A. McVie photo.

Ken J. McRae's MARY BOWER drives home at maximum hull speed, 1962 Swiftsure.
J. A. McVie photo.

TROUBADOUR "roaring" down the Strait of Juan de Fuca!
J. A. McVie photo.

Minutes later "knock-down" HITS — and over she goes!!
J. A. McVie photo.

Phil Graham, skipper and owner of TROUBADOUR, relives the above "thriller" near the end of the 1962 Swiftsure Classic —

". . . we came boiling through Race Passage on a dead run with Spinnaker at the bursting point . . . once through the Passage sheets were trimmed and the yacht was brought around on to a reach, heading straight for the finish at Victoria . . . then the squall hit and over she went . . . life-lines and all under water. It was fun while it lasted . . . lines and nerves stretching to breaking point . . . a mad scramble to slacken off . . . and she eased back onto more or less of an even keel . . . Whew!! . . . No harm was done (except to nerves) . . . and the Suckling Pig never even fell out of the oven!"

World War II Honour Roll.

CHAPTER 17

R. V. Y. C.

IN WORLD WAR II

M ANY OF THOSE who fought in "The Kaiser's War", as Captain Barney Johnson still describes it, "the war that was to end war", were to fight again in "Hitler's War", which added many new names to the roll of honour of the R.V.Y.C. In 1939 Canada was quite as unprepared as she was in 1914. At first there was a call-up of reservists, but then came the dreary period known as the "phoney war", and many wondered if they would ever have a chance to see action. Those yachtsmen who wished to join the navy were particularly frustrated at first, for with few exceptions, their offers of service were turned down. The army and air force offered more scope, which was particularly galling to those who wanted action at sea. However, after the fruitless winter of 1939-40, the disasters of Narvik and Dunkirk brought a new sense of urgency, and a realization that only by an all-out national effort could Hitler's monstrous tyranny be overthrown. Early in 1940 the R.V.Y.C. organized from its members a naval training section, which trained at the old R.C.N.V.R. headquarters in Stanley Park, adjoining the club's Coal Harbour station. Here the yachtsmen trained regularly in the rudiments of navigation, seamanship, gunnery and signals. Soon many of the younger members were accepted for active naval service. With what they had learned about boats at the yacht club, all those who joined the navy found their new life right up their alley.

Since there was little room in the emerging Royal Canadian Navy in those days for new recruits, most of the early enlistees from the R.V.Y.C. embarked directly for England, and spent most of their sea-going time with the Royal Navy, often in command of M.L.'s, like their fathers before them. Among those accepted for active service in the summer of 1940 were Hazen Phillips, Dick Smith, Frank Stuart, Bill Dolmage, John Leckie, Temp Wright, John Calland, Bruce Allan, Ken Glass, Russ Baker, Owen Wright, Ted Le Page, and John Hockin. Six of these, sporting new uniforms and commissions, left for England in a group in September. They were followed by many many more, for at the end of the war more than 200 of the club's 600 male members had traded tillers for guns.

There were many who never returned. Lieut. Eric Ditmars was killed in action. Lieut. David Killam, D.S.C., was blown up with his MTB by German guns in the English Channel. Lieut. Stu Lane lost his life in Tobruk harbour, when Rommell's guns got his little ship. Lieut. Fred Whitehead was washed overboard from a destroyer. Bill Maitland and Blake Wallace, who chose the air force, died in action. Bill won the D.F.M. before being posted as missing in air operations over Germany. Casualties in the service of the army were Robert F. Hume and R. L. J. Rankin, and in the air force in addition to the above mentioned were G. V. Bartle, E. G. K. Bullen, Robert Johnston, Richard C. Sandes and G. R. A. Walkem.

Older warrior veterans of the First World War who climbed into uniform again have an enviable record of service in World War II: Commander B. L. Johnson started the war as N.O.I.C. (Naval Officer in Charge), Port of Vancouver, and emerged as Captain B. L. Johnson, C.B.E., D.S.O. Not one to be content with a shore appointment, "Barney" saw service afloat again in command of H.M.C.S. *Preserver*, a mother ship for Fairmiles in the Straits of Belle Isle patrol. T. M. (Tom) Ramsay served again in H.M.C.S. *Robert* in the Aleutian area and in North Pacific examination vessels. Fred W. Crickard, a veteran in the submarine service of the first war, served again in the merchant navy, as did that well known old time sailor H. St. Claire Jellett, while Colin C. Ferrie saw service again overseas as O.C. of the famous Seaforth Highlanders, returning as Colonel of the regiment. Both Past-Commodore J. A. Longley and Harry J. Bird gave service again in the air force, as did Air Vice-Marshal K. G. Nairn, C.B.

Among the famous of those who returned were the "Three Musketeers", Lieut.-Commander J. D. "Wimpy" Maitland, D.S.C. and Bar, and Croix de Guerre with Palm; Lieut.-Commander Cornelius "Corny" Burke, D.S.C. and Bar; and Lieut. Tommy Ladner, D.S.C. and Bar. These three R.V.Y.C. members attended school together, sailed boats together, enlisted in the navy independently. By coincidence they each made the choice of joining swift coastal craft and were slightly surprised when they found themselves in the same flotilla in England. However, coincidence didn't part company with them, and they came together again in the Mediterranean, assigned to the same flotilla. During the Sicilian and Italian campaigns they earned their decorations and several mentions in despatches with successful raids on enemy shipping and for bombarding shore batteries. Their raids were so numerous and successful that "Corny" Burke earned himself the title of "Robin Hood of the Adriatic", and the trio's exploits are the subject of the fascinating book, "Gunboat 658".

On his return to Canada, Doug Maitland was decorated with the Croix de Guerre with Palm for the assistance given French forces in the capture of the isle of Elba. When he wasn't ferrying French troops ashore he was busy keeping enemy warships at respectful distance with daring forays. Ladner was mentioned four times in despatches for attacking and sinking German E boats.

Ken Glass returned home as a Lieutenant-Commander after performing convoy work with M.T.B.'s for two years. Lieut.-Cmdr. John Leckie also served with M.T.B.'s in convoy work, and later patrolled off the Atlantic coast of North Africa. Bill Dolmage and Ted Le Page both won renown and were awarded the o.b.e. for their outstanding work as salvage experts. Bill also was awarded the U.S.N. Bronze Star. They served in both Iceland and the Mediterranean, and spent much of their time on the ocean bottom. Both were made lieutenant-commanders. Massey Goolden, serving in the naval service, was awarded the d.s.o., and W. G. Gooderham the d.s.c.

Ken C. McRae was wounded in the Mediterranean, and returned home to be appointed officer commanding H.M.C.S. *Discovery* at Stanley Park, with the rank of commander. He was awarded the o.b.e. Lieut. Frank Stuart had several strenuous years overseas in small boats in the North Sea before being invalided home. Temp Wright was serving aboard H.M.S. *Maori*, a Tribal Class destroyer, during the action in which the mighty *Bismarck* was sunk.

Dana Ramsay, in the Royal Navy with Combined Operations, commanded L.C.I. L115 all through the Mediterranean engagements and was torpedoed after the Oran landings, being picked up by a Norwegian destroyer and taken to Gibraltar. He took part in commando landings in Italy and North Africa and was with the Canadian landings at Dieppe and at Caen on D Day.

Don Brooke served on H.M.C.S. *Robert* in the Aleutian, Pacific and European areas and on Royal Navy frigates manned by Canadians, from Murmansk and Iceland to the North West African Coast.

Other R.V.Y.C. ex-juniors of the "thirties", whose names decorate many of our perpetual trophies, served with the naval forces in the various theatres of action, including Dave Fladgate, Jack Lewis, Dr. Gordon Baker, Geoff Tullidge, Stanley Burke Jr., H. W. Akhurst, J. D. Askew, J. Barltrop, Charley Drainey, Fred McMeans, Lorne Kyle, G. A. Roedde Jr., W. A. Roedde Jr., Robin Hurrell, J. A. and Ross McCutcheon, John Stacey, J. K. Sloan. Two lady members, Miss Ruth Tomlinson and Miss Pat. Wilgress also served, making a total of 110 members of the Royal Vancouver Yacht Club who saw service in the naval forces.

Fifty-four R.V.Y.C. members served in the army, two making the supreme sacrifice, Robert F. Hume and R. L. J. Rankin.

Details are not available, but two members were awarded the Military Cross, Kenneth Campbell and Barney Carswell, and John W. Toogood received the American Silver Star. In a unique action described in the press as "Tanks sink ships", Lieut.-Colonel J. W. Toogood commanded tanks of the British Columbia Regiment which engaged and sank three German gunboats supporting enemy ground forces on the estuary of the Island of Shower (near Bergen op Zoom, Holland). The ship's bell off one now decorates the Officers' Mess at the Beatty Street Drill Hall of the B.C. Regt. (D.C.O.R.).

In addition to Col. C. C. Ferrie already mentioned, the following well known ex-juniors also served in the army: Jack Lindsay, F. J. (Bunny) Whitcroft, G. T. Cruise, R. H. (Robbie) Brown, David Burr, Ray Delaplace, E. G. and T. K. Eakin, and others. One lady member Miss Janet Whitten, also served. (See Honour Roll.)

Fifty-three R.V.Y.C. members served in the air force, six of whom gave their lives as previously noted. Air Vice-Marshal K. G. Nairn, C.B., a veteran R.F.C. Lt.-Pilot 1916-19, saw service again in Great Britain, Africa, India, Burma, Italy, Malta, France, and was awarded the C.B.

R. W. R. (Bob) Day served with distinction as Squadron-Leader in the Burma Theatre and was awarded the D.F.C., as were L. G. D. Fraser and Roy Harrison. W. H. (Bud) Day served in the radar division in England, and other well known ex-juniors in the air force were Bill Cunningham, Phil and Sid Miller, Alex Forsyth, James and H. G. Eakins Jr., Peter Maitland, Sandy Martin, Douglas Sudbury, Ernest and Kenneth Thompson, Ralph Vittery, John Wallace, K. G. Watt and D. T. Woodley. Three lady members also saw service in the air forces, Miss Catherine Day, Miss Marion Downes and Miss K. Schwengers. (See Honour Roll.)

Eleven R.V.Y.C. members served in the merchant navy, the two veterans of the First War, Fred Crickard and H. St. C. Jellett, and nine others.

Two lady members of the club served with the Red Cross, Miss M. Coote and Mrs. M. Fernie.

The scope of operations in which R.V.Y.C. members served during World War Two covered every active field of operations. There were members at Dunkirk, in the Battle of Britain, in the landings at North Africa, Sicily and Anzio, and at Dieppe and D Day. Scores of former yachtsmen engaged in North Atlantic convoys, and several commanded corvettes and frigates. They were found on the Murmansk run, at the Normandy invasion, fighting guerrilla warfare in the Balkans, in Burma and the South Pacific; they bombed Germany from the air and Italy from the sea.

CHAPTER 18

R. V. Y. C.

LOCAL NAVAL TRAINING
AND VOLUNTEER YACHT
PATROL, 1940-1944

THE DRAMATIC EVACUATION at Dunkirk by a fleet of small-boat sailors early in the Second War emphasized the duties that amateur yachtsmen could perform in war emergencies while not being actual members of the official forces. Earlier reference has been made of the fine response by R.V.Y.C. members to the call in World War I, and although many members volunteered for active service early in World War II, it was not until late 1940 that their services were accepted.

Meanwhile, through the foresight of Commander B. L. Johnson, D.S.O., who had been appointed N.O.I.C., Port of Vancouver, a group of R.V.Y.C. ·members were receiving training in navigation, signalling and other basics to fit themselves to be of value to naval authorities should local emergency arise.

At a meeting of sundry members called by Fleet Captain C. J. Dill and Staff Captain Dr. J. A. Sampson in the Jericho Clubhouse July 27th 1940, it was moved by E. R. (Jack) Cribb, seconded by Rear Commodore J. A. Longley, "that we form ourselves into a unit.and request naval instruction to fit ourselves to be of value to the naval authorities".

Commander Johnson, addressing the group, stressed that no official naval standing could be given, and that in offering to provide qualified naval instructors on a voluntary basis he was doing so as a senior member of the R.V.Y.C. and not as a member of the naval service. He recommended that the group be limited to twenty-five members and that five suitable power cruisers be formed into half a flotilla, five men to a boat.

Commander Johnson arranged for a number of his officers to give the necessary instruction under the general direction of Lieut.-Commander McCulloch, and a semi-weekly series of lectures were commenced August 20th, 1940, with the full complement of twenty-five members attending.

Five members of the group, W. G. Dolmage, T. N. Le Page, G. H. Phillips, Owen Wright and Temple Wright were immediately accepted for active service and their places in the training group were quickly filled.

In September 1940 Lt.-Commander J. M. Smith, R.C.N., assumed direction of the training programme, which was stepped up three evenings weekly with manoeuvers, lamp and flag signal exercises between vessels on weekends. From August 1940 to April 1941 a total of 67 exercises, lectures and parades were held. On resumption of active training in September 1941 the Patrol carried out a survey of Sturgeon Bank and the mouths of the Fraser River at the suggestion of Commander Johnson. Soundings were taken and charts prepared by A. H. Jefferd, hydrographer for the patrol, the motor vessels taking part being *Tequila, Dorisar, Kennett II, Latona, Diana Joan* and *Coal Harbour.*

On the declaration of war between Japan and Canada December 8th 1941, the commanding officer of the Patrol, Dr. J. A. Sampson, received a call from N.O.I.C. Vancouver to hold the group in readiness for immediate duty to assist in immobilizing the local Japanese fishing fleet consisting of approximately 1000 fishing boats of all sizes in the Fraser River, Burrard Inlet and adjacent waters. On December 9th 1941 our six vessels (above) were ordered by N.O.I.C. to instruct all Japanese fishing boats to proceed to selected anchorages in the Fraser River and at Bedwell Bay, North Arm, Burrard Inlet. Assisting the local naval forces, approximately 1182 Japanese fishing boats were impounded in the Fraser River at Annacis Island (see illustration). Our half flotilla of six motor vessels ...... *Tequila,* Capt. J. A. Sampson; *Dorisar,* Capt. Basil Rae; *Latona,* Capt. O. H. Bell; *Diana Joan,* Capt. G. D. Wilson; *Coal Harbour,* Capt. C. J. Dill; *Kennett II,* Capt. C. H. Gyles, with four-man crews, assisted in this work under the direction of naval officers assigned by N.O.I.C. Vancouver, remaining on full-time duty from December 9th to December 22nd, 1941.

On the completion of this duty the following naval message and official letter from the Naval Secretary, Ottawa, was received:

NAVAL MESSAGE	
To:	From:

S. 1320d.
25M Pads of 200
2-40 (4103)
N.S. 815-9-1320d

NOI/C   VANCOUVER   COPC

YOUR 1929Z/24. PLEASE CONVEY MY PERSONAL APPRECIATION TO THE OWNERS

OF YACHTS FOR THE PROMPT PATRIOTIC MANNER IN WHICH THEIR VESSELS &

SERVICES WERE PLACED AT THE DISPOSAL OF THE NAVAL SERVICE.

(2) A REPORT WILL BE FORWARDED TO NSHQ.

0059Z/27

0132Z/27 JS AA

Japanese fishing fleet impounded 1941 at Annacis Island, Fraser River, B.C.

Reproduction of letter received by Volunteer Yacht Patrol.

On the establishment of blackout regulations throughout the Vancouver area in 1942, the Volunteer Patrol was requested by Lt.-Commander J. M. Smith, Naval Control Station, Vancouver, to assume the patrol of five designated zones in Burrard Inlet, and this work was carried out for the duration of the regulations until December .16th 1943.

Although actual patrol duties were limited to six vessels and thirty men at a time, a total of sixty-five club members are registered on the rolls of the Patrol from 1940 to 1944.

The following eighteen original members were quickly accepted into the forces and left for active service in 1940 and 1941:

Dr. Gordon Baker	Derry Dwyer	Phil Miller
W. G. (Bill) Dolmage	John Hockin	Sid Miller
Harry J. Bird	J. A. Longley	G. Hazen Phillips
Don Brooke	Ted LePage	Geoff Tullidge
Bill Cunningham	Jack Lewis	Owen Wright
Dave Fladgate	A. P. (Bert) Morrow	Temple H. Wright

Over the three year period, the following forty-seven members continued with training and duties assigned by N.O.I.C. Vancouver.

Alex Aitken	Les Golman	W. R. C. Patrick
Dr. Alan Anthony	Clarke Gibson	George Parsons
Harry Barrett	Claude Hill	Forrest Rogers
O. H. Bell	Norman Hanly	W. A. Roedde
Tom Baird	Jack Halse	B. H. Rae
J. M. Black	George Halse	Jack Skinner
K. A. (Bert) Cruise	Frank Insley	Dr. J. A. Sampson
G. A. Cran	Art Jefferd	Jack K. Storey
Dr. W. J. Currie	J. M. Kerr	Ed. Thompson
Jack Cranham	Stan Morton	Hugh Thomas
George Cutler	Oswald Moseley	Ed Towns
Cedric Dill	Ken McCandless	Doug. P. Urry
W. Fred Evans	T. McFeely	Gerry D. Wilson
Gordon Ferris	Gordon Oliver	Art Way
Les Grant	O. B. Omundsen	Jack Williamson
Cedric Gyles	R. B. Pinney	

For this contribution to the war effort the following letters of commendation were received, addressed to executives of the group because, under orders from N.O.I.C., all operation reports were made direct to naval authorities as laid down in King's Regulations and Admiralty Instructions, and the Royal Vancouver Yacht Club, as such, did not receive official recognition.

Reproduction of letter from Minister of National Defence.

CANADA

Department of National Defence
NAVAL SERVICE

IN REPLY PLEASE QUOTE
NO. PC 18-3-1

Pacific Coast Naval Hqs.,
Jericho Beach,
Vancouver, B.C.

25th February, 1944

Dear Sir:

    As the Defence Category for the West Coast
has now been greatly reduced, the likelihood of the
Volunteer Yacht Patrol being required in connection
with the Defence of the Port of Vancouver is considered to be very remote, and it has been decided
to discontinue the activities, the holding of lectures,
and the supply of gasoline, etc., in connection with
this organization.

    It has been noted that, since the inception of
this organization, the members of the patrol have carried out their duties in a keen and efficient manner,
and at all times have been available at short notice,
and I wish to express the appreciation and thanks of
the Naval Service for the valuable services performed
by your organization. It would be appreciated if you
would convey this message to the personnel under your
command.

    Should circumstances so arise in the future
it is most gratifying to know that such a co-operative
and efficient organization could again be formed.

    Copies of this and other correspondence concern-
ing the excellent work which your organization has done
are being sent to Naval Service Headquarters in Ottawa
for the attention of the Naval Board.

                  Very truly yours,

                  (V.G. BRODEUR)
                  REAR ADMIRAL, R.C.N.,
                  Commanding Officer,
                  Pacific Coast.

Dr. J.A. Sampson,
925 West Georgia Street,
Vancouver, B.C.

Reproduction of letter from Admiral Brodeur.

CANADA

Department of National Defence

Naval Service

IN REPLY PLEASE QUOTE

No. B. 15-71-2

Vancouver, B. C.
16th February, 194 4

Dear Sir,

Information has been received from the
Commanding Officer Pacific Coast that, in view of
the recent reduction in the Defence Category for
the West Coast, the likelihood that the Volunteer
Yacht Patrol would be required in connection with
the defences of the Port of Vancouver is now very
remote. It has therefore been decided to discontinue
the activities of your organization, and in accordance with Naval Regulations it is requested that
your files of correspondence, orders, etc., be
returned to this office.

It is fully realized that the time and
energy expended by the various members of the
Vancouver Volunteer Yacht Patrol, to say nothing
of the physical discomforts experienced, have been
a considerable imposition. The efforts of the Yacht
Patrol have measurably reduced the commitments of
the Royal Canadian Navy in this area during a period
in which it would have been difficult to maintain a
similar Naval Patrol, and it is a matter of deep
concern to me that there is no tangible recognition
of this fact. The knowledge that the Patrol's
activities have been of definite assistance to the
Navy will, however, give a feeling of satisfaction
to those who contributed so much to its undisputed
success.

At this time I would like to express my
personal appreciation for the keen and efficient
manner in which the Vancouver Volunteer Yacht Patrol
has carried out its duties, and the enthusiasm with
which the responsibilities placed upon it have been
received.

Yours very truly,

Jm Smith

A/Commander, R.C.N.(Temp.)
Naval Officer-in-Charge

FRM:jf

Mr. G.A. Cran,
Secretary,
Vancouver Volunteer Yacht Patrol,
1509 Dunbar Street,
Vancouver, B. C.

Reproduction of letter from Lt. Com. J. M. Smith.

CHAPTER 19

P.I.Y.A. Regattas

INTERNATIONAL YACHT RACING came to a halt during the war years 1914-1918, but after the many soldier and sailor yachtsmen returned from overseas, the subject of forming a new international yachting association on the Pacific coast came very much to the fore.

As a result a meeting was called at Victoria in May 1920, attended by representatives from the Victoria, Vancouver, Seattle, Everett and Tacoma yacht clubs, at which it was decided to form a new international yacht racing association, which was tentatively called the Northwest International Yachting Association. The name was subsequently changed to Pacific International Yachting Association. Capt. James Griffiths of the Seattle Yacht Club was named admiral, H. O. Bell-Irving of the R.V.Y.C. was vice-admiral, and the commodore of the Royal Victoria Yacht Club was rear-admiral.

The first post-war international regatta was held in July 1920 at Cowichan Bay and Victoria, and R.V.Y.C. yachts made a very good showing, although Seattle's *Sir Tom* held the Lipton Cup against *Turenga*. The Cowichan Bay Free-For-All Trophy was won by *Spirit I*, under the Cao brothers, and Ron Maitland's *Dione* took second prize. The international Kitten Class trophy went to H. B. Bell-Irving, with second to G. Hazen Phillips. The international trophy for yawls and schooners was won by Walter Graveley's *Minerva*, with Bert Austin's schooner *Adelphi* second. The trophy for sloops over 23 feet went to *Spirit I*, with J. P. Fell's *Onoma* second. In the race for sloops under 23 feet, Ron Maitland's *Dione* was winner, with E. W. Purves' *Asthore* second.

The international series was again held at Cowichan Bay in 1921, with the new Vancouver challenger for the Lipton Cup, the *Patricia*, losing to *Sir Tom* in two straight races. *Adelphi* won the trophy for cruising yawls and schooners, followed by *Minerva* and *Gazeka*.

The P.I.Y.A. regatta for 1922 was held in Seattle, where *Sir Tom* again held the Lipton Cup with two straight wins over *Patricia*. In the class races Vancouver boats collected 13 trophies.

The winners included Cao brothers' *Spirit I* in the special sloop class; Phil Whitehead's *Gwendolyn* in the heavy sloop class; and J. Wilkinson's *Ailsa II* in the small yawl class.

The 1923 P.I.Y.A. regatta was held in Vancouver, where Ted Geary in *Sir Tom* again triumphed over *Patricia* to hold both the Lipton and Isherwood Cups. The Macneill Cup, emblematic of Star Class championship in the northwest, was captured by Wylie and Simmonds in *Astrea*, while the Kitten Class championship cup went to C. P. Leckie's *Meow*. Other Vancouver winners were R. A. Bindley's *Spirit II* in the special sloop class; Jack Nichol's *Onoma* in sloops over 23 feet; Bob Marshall's *Dione* in sloops under 23 feet; and Bill Ball's *Ailsa I* for yawls under 30 feet.

The 1924 P.I.Y.A. regatta was held in Tacoma, but no Vancouver yachts were represented, However they were back in force again for the 1925 regatta at Victoria, when *Sir Tom* again proved unbeatable. Vancouver winners included Ernie Woodward's *Spirit I* in the special sloop class; Bill Templeton's *Tamahnowus* in the small cruiser class; Ian Mackenzie's *Onoma* for sloops over 25 feet; *Dione* for sloops under 25 feet, sailed by H. B. Bell-Irving; and Gwen Austin's *Kittiwake* won the Kitten Class trophy.

In 1926 the regatta was held in Seattle, and again *Sir Tom* held the Lipton Cup against *Riowna* and *Turenga*. Trophy winners from Vancouver included Bill Templeton's *Tamahnowus*, first in yawls under 30 feet; and L. T. Alden's *Gamine,* winner of the sloop class under 25 feet, with Harry Bird's *Penguin* second.

The P.I.Y.A. came to Vancouver in 1927, and again *Sir Tom* held on to the Lipton and Isherwood trophies against *Lady Pat* and *Riowna.* Local winners included Ernie Woodward's *Spirit I* in the special sloop class; Barney Johnson's *Alexandra* was winner for sloops over 25 feet; Fred Foster's *Dione* led sloops under 25 feet; and *Ailsa II* was the winner in yawls and schooners under 30 feet. Phillips and Kerr's *Auriga* won the Star Class trophy, while C. P. Leckie won the Kitten Class trophy.

The P.I.Y.A. regatta was again held in Vancouver in 1928, with *Sir Tom* winning the Lipton Cup in three straight races against *Lady Pat, Lady Van* and *Riowna.* Winners from Vancouver included Ernie Woodward's *Spirit I* in the nine metre class; L. T. Alden's *Gamine* for sloops under 25 feet; Oliphant Bell's *Maratea* for yawls under 30 feet; G. Hazen Phillips in the Star Class; Ben Elliott in the Kitten Class; and Doug Maitland in the Flattie Class.

The 1929 regatta, which was held in Vancouver for the third year in succession, was notable, for Jack Cribb's *Lady Van* at last succeeded in wresting the Lipton Cup from Ted Geary's *Sir Tom*. Other Vancouver winners were Harold Jones' *Spirit II* in the Nine Metre Class; D. P. Urry's *Cresset* in sloops over 25 feet; L. T. Alden's *Gamine* in sloops under 25 feet; and H. E. Wylie's *Astrea* in the Star Class.

Ted Geary got his revenge at the P.I.Y.A. regatta at Victoria in 1930, when *Sir Tom* recaptured the Lipton Cup. Trophy winners from the R.V.Y.C. included Harold Jones' *Spirit II,* Alex Marshall's *Nelmar* in yawls under 30 feet; and H. E. Wylie in the Star Class with *Mercury.*

The following year was a vintage one as far as the R.V.Y.C. was concerned, for Vancouver yachts swept up most of the trophies at the P.I.Y.A. regatta at Bellingham. *Lady Pat,* skippered by Jack Cribb, took the Lipton Trophy. Doug Urry's *Cresset* won the series for sloops more than 25 feet; Barney Johnson's *Westward Ho* won the large cruiser races; L. T. Alden's *Gamine* won for sloops under 25 feet; Ernie Woodward's *Spirit I* tied with Walter Cline's *Alexandra* in the Nine-metre series; while the Star Class was tied by *Mercury, Auriga* and *Daphne,* all of Vancouver.

Lady Pat retained the Lipton Trophy at the P.I.Y.A. regatta at Seattle in 1932. On their home courses, Seattle yachts carried off the other major trophies.

The 1933 P.I.Y.A. regatta was held at Vancouver and was notable for *Lady Pat* winning both the Lipton and Isherwood trophies with a junior crew, skippered by Doug Maitland. The 1934 regatta was also held at Vancouver, with *Lady Van,* skippered by Harry Wylie, picking up the coveted trophies in two straight races. At the regatta in Bellingham in 1935 Ted Geary picked up the Isherwood Trophy with *Live Yankee,* but it again fell·to *Lady Van,* skippered by Harry Wylie, at the 1936 regatta in Victoria. At this regatta Alex Marshall's *Nelmar* won the Lipton cruising trophy for the race from Victoria to Port Angeles and return, in a time of 7 hours, 41 minutes, with Tom Ramsey in the yawl *Armida* second with a time of 8 hours 3 minutes.

The 1937 regatta was held at Port Townsend and Tom Ramsey's *Armida* won all three races for Class B. An interesting feature of the 1938 regatta at Vancouver was the contest for special sloops between the old rivals, *Alexandra, Riowna, Spirit II* and *Turenga.* The *Alexandra,* which had been recently rebuilt by Temple Wright, ghosted in to defeat *Spirit II* for first place.

In B Class Gulf races, Alex Marshall's *Nelmar* was first, followed by Jim Longley's *Maratea.* Fred Mills' *Uwhilna* was the winner in A Class, while Bill Roedde's *Carita* took the Spencer Class.

In 1939 at Bellingham, Tom Ramsey took two firsts and one second with *Armida* in B Class, while George Cran's *Hi-Ho* was second in C Class.

The only P.I.Y.A. regatta to be held during wartime was the 1940 event at Cowichan Bay, at which Harold Jones' *Spirit II* distinguished herself by winning the Key City, Swiftsure and Spicer trophies. Sid Miller's *Clear Sky* won the Griffiths Trophy for Star boats in three straight races.

International racing was not to be resumed until after peace had been declared and conditions were back to normal.

Meanwhile, an example of the trials our ships and crews sometimes undergo in making the passage to or from Seattle to take part in these international races is given by the experiences of our "doughty sailor" Harry Bird, who relates:

"Our trip home from the Seattle P.I.Y.A. of 1926 nearly finished me. Five of us had taken the *Penguin* down without any particular incident. My crew consisted of Harold Jones, Frank Broadfoot, Frank Curry and a lady member (properly chaperoned, of course, by the four male members). Our only auxiliary power was an outboard in a dinghy lashed alongside, which worked very well in the calm southward trip.

"For some reason or other only one of the crew were willing to sail back to Vancouver with me. Harold motored back with his wife, and Frank Curry admitted he was just not up to the arduous trip home, so got a ride home with Harold. Frank Broadfoot and I sailed home and had a very uneventful trip up to Port Townsend, having made it to Edmonds the first afternoon.

"Our troubles started when we pulled out of Port Townsend, rounded Point Wilson and ran into a strong westerly blowing down the Straits of Juan de Fuca. We crossed Smith Island, leaving it to starboard, and then sailed along Admiralty Head until we came to Deception Pass. We had decided that we were going to lose our ship and dumped all our belongings into the dinghy, as we were on a lee shore with tremendous seas drifting us shoreward. Well, we got as far as Deception Pass, our main boom trailing in the water, sheets out as far as we could let them go (we could not reef our main because we tried and the reef points just pulled out.

"When we came to the pass a great rolling wave, just outside the entrance to the pass, hid our view and we just sailed over it like a roller coaster, not knowing where we were going. It was the result of an ebb tide and a strong westerly, and a fearsome thing to come upon. We got into a small harbour at Rosario Beach and I hauled on the tiller for dear life and we just kept spinning around until we lost way and stopped. We were soaked, shivering, but no harm done, just plain scared to pieces. Our mattress and gear were slopping around below and there was about 3 feet of water in the bilge. We had a bottle of rum aboard for just such an occasion, so we rowed ashore and slept on the beach. Dear God, it's wonderful to be young. That was 38 years ago. We arrived home safely and no worse for wear, either ship or crew.

"Another time we were on our way to Victoria and we put into Roche Harbour on San Juan Island. There was a Coast Guard cutter tied up to the wharf and we asked the skipper (a Chief Bosun's Mate in the U.S. Coast Guard) what they were doing there. He came aboard and told us they were watching for rum runners (that was in prohibition

Cutter CRESSET, 1958.

Tense Race Committee, 1958 P.I.Y.A. L. to R.: H. J. Bird, Commodore E. J. Palmer, Past Commodore K. G. Glass, Past. Hon. Secy., P.I.Y.A., W. H. Day, Past Commodore J. A. Longley, A. H. Jefferd, E. S. Earle.

days) and asked us if we had any liquor aboard. We were rather reluctant to admit that we had two bottles of Ne Plus Ultra stowed away in the bilge. The Coast Guard skipper seemed very pleased and asked us for a drink, saying that it was a cold night and they were going out on patrol in a couple of hours. After a suitable celebration cementing the bonds of international friendship, etc., etc., I was invited to go on patrol with the Coast Guard and promptly accepted. I hope I will not create any embarrassment on the diplomatic level by recalling that all we did was roar out into the middle of the Straits, turned off the engine, put one man on watch and all the rest of the crew turned in for some shut eye. I awoke in the middle of the night and heard a fast boat going by, but nobody else seemed to care so why should I worry?"

Sailors in Seattle and Vancouver were quick to reactivate international competition, as they organized an informal regatta July 1-4, 1945, at Sucia Islands, with about 20 boats taking part. A highlight was the prizes—the Americans bringing a good supply of bottles (full) which were rationed in Canada, and our boys matched this with hams and steaks which were rationed across the line. Over the years, since the first official post war P.I.Y.A. regatta in Vancouver in 1946, a number of changes have been introduced in both the regatta and the organization of the association, all in line with the changing times.

The "R" Class racing disappeared, although both *Lady Van* and *Riowna* (renamed *Svea*) were converted to cruising boats in Seattle and took part in many regattas under their new colours. The Sir Thomas Lipton Cup was put into competition for a large and active Six Metre Class fleet, with many of the world's leading ships of this class racing for the Seattle, Corinthian, Royal Victoria and Royal Vancouver clubs. The City of Vancouver presented a perpetual trophy

Panorama of arrivals for 1958 P.I.Y.A.

commemorating the 60th Jubilee of the city, in 1946, for an interclub race, and the competition for this trophy, together with international team races, are now one of the highlights of the regattas. The growth of a number of fine new racing and racing-cruising one design classes such as the Dragons, Evergreens, Thunderbirds, L 36's, Seafairs, Cubs, and others has also added colour and competition, as these boats are widely distributed amongst the clubs.

The regatta has been held at our club five times since the war, and each time the Kitsilano Yacht Club has assisted by holding the small class races on their course, and by sponsoring junior social activities at their clubhouse. In 1965 the West Vancouver Yacht Club, under Commodore Robbie Brown, sponsored the regatta in Howe Sound, using their fine new clubhouse as headquarters.

The host club's commodore is also elected Commodore of the P.I.Y.A., and the following R.V.Y.C. members held both offices during the years the regatta was at our club:

1946 Harold A. Jones
1950 Capt. B. L. Johnson, C.B.E., D.S.O.
1953 Kenneth G. Glass
1958 Elmer J. Palmer
1963 Kenneth J. McRae

Past Commodore and Honorary Life Member Bill Day was elected Secretary-treasurer of the Association in 1939 and served until 1945, to be followed by his son "Bud" who carried on the office until 1956. Many other club members have held other offices and committee appointments in the Association and have made an important contribution to its progress.

Prize giving, 1958 P.I.Y.A. L. to R.: Gerry Palmer, Commodore E. J. Palmer, W. H. Day, G. L. Cran.

Ches L. Rickard's 6 Metre ALANA, 1955.

CHAPTER 20

Wild Ride

OF THE "SIXES" IN
ENTRANCE ISLAND RACE, 1955

FEW YACHTSMEN will not thrill to the vivid action packed recital by P. V. O. Evans—Fleet Captain, 1956—of the superb seamanship displayed by the crews of our five Six Metre yachts when a sudden violent storm burst on these open hulled vessels in the middle of the Gulf of Georgia.

The morning of May 7th, 1955, was overcast and the Dominion Meteorological Office forecast was for a continuation of the cloud cover with south or southwesterly winds of from 5 to 7 m.p.h. in the Gulf. Most of the starters bemoaned the light weather forecast and crossed the starting line at 9:00 a.m. anticipating a long and possibly boring race. How wrong they were!

There were ten starters: the Eight Metre *Fulmar,* the five Six Metres, *Alana, Golden Hind, Hecate, Juno,* and *Kini;* the Roeddes *Elusive* and *Treveda,* and *Hereandthere* and *Barracouta* in B class. The distance from Jericho around the Island and back is about 42 miles and in the light going the fleet was soon widely dispersed. Occasional rain fell on the way across but the weather cleared as the boats approached the Island and soon the Eight and most of the Sixes were becalmed a few hundred yards from the Light. Fortunately, or so it turned out later, it was nice and warm and, for refreshment, the odd beer passed from hand to mouth, leaving the thermoses in the Sixes available for future use.

By mid-afternoon the Eight and most of the Sixes were around the Island, *Juno* having hung up on a reef briefly en route, and as they headed home the breeze, while still light, came in from the south and held steady for a time. By five o'clock, with the Metre boats well out in the Gulf and the Cruisers in the neighborhood of the Island, it fell light again and sail drill was the order of the day. Soon after six the breeze came in again from the sou'west, veering steadily to west and, with spinnakers set, it seemed that the fleet was on the way home at last. Shortly after seven o'clock a bank of very dark cloud and a well defined black line on the water were seen approaching from up the Gulf to the northward and most people, thinking it was an extra heavy rain shower, paid little heed. Sudden and violent storms are relatively unknown in this area, particularly in the early summer, and there was no reason for expecting the screaming inferno which, in the space of a minute or two, covered the Gulf from Point Grey to Nanaimo.

The expression "all hell broke loose" is often heard but never could it have been more aptly illustrated. When the storm first struck the wind was about N.N.W. and it caught those with spinnakers set almost straight abeam. If you can picture nine small boats (*Hereandthere* dropped out early in the day), several of them virtually open, many with spinnakers flying and all with crews abruptly aroused from a very leisurely down wind run, trying to douse or reduce sail in a wind of at least 35 m.p.h. and increasing every moment, and a sea rapidly building up to extremely unpleasant proportions, you will have some idea of what it was like. Confusion was everywhere. On *Juno* Denny Wotherspoon and Gordie Baker were on the foredeck trying to get the spinnaker off when a sheet or a guy parted and the sail took charge and before they knew what had happened they were in the water with their ship sailing away from them. Bob Day, the skipper, and Herbie Millham, his only remaining crew member, threw the liferaft overboard but with its high freeboard it went down wind so fast it was soon out of sight; at the same time they were trying to bring the ship under control and sail her back to the rescue. By dint of fine seamanship, and some superhuman work by Herbie, Bob succeeded in finding his men in the rapidly gathering dusk and the wild spray shrouded sea and got them aboard. He was not a moment too soon as darkness descended very quickly and both Denny and Gordie were almost played out. On other boats spinnakers took charge, running gear carried away, sails split, cockpits flooded and engines failed but nowhere else was tragedy so close at hand.

Three of the cruising boats were still on the Vancouver Island side of the Gulf and, after calling for help on the radio phone, two of them were helped into Nanaimo by a local tug which came to their rescue. The other, *Elusive,* her engine ashore for repairs, continued towards Vancouver but, after proceeding for a while, split her main and was in danger of being driven onto the banks in the Fraser River Delta. Her radio phone call for aid was picked up by the Black Ball Ferry and relayed to the *Princess of Nanaimo.* This vessel, beautifully handled, made a lee and stood by until assistance arrived.

The Sixes and the Eight, having no phones, concentrated on getting things as orderly as possible and then started the wildest down hill ride any of them had ever experienced. The wind gradually backed through Norwest to W.N.W., becoming almost due West as the boats got further in towards English Bay. As it backed it blew harder until the strength was such that speeds in excess of 58 m.p.h. were recorded in the gusts at the Airport; and the harder it blew the worse the sea became. It was estimated that the distance between the crests of the seas was as much as 45 feet and the height from trough to crest at least 10 feet. Looking over one's shoulder at that stuff from the helm of a Six Metre is not exactly a soothing experience. With the completely open cockpits of these boats and the low coaming the danger of pooping is very real, and the way that long narrow counter rose, almost gaily, before each sea was amazing and most reassuring.

As the boats flew home, many under Genoa alone, and it was plain that they were capable of coping with wind and sea most of the crews began to notice how cold they were and it was then that they blessed the warm weather earlier in the day. Out came thermoses of soup (in at least one case lashed with sherry) and of coffee (to which a tot of rum gave a worthy lift) and spirits rose. Because of the darkness no one knew where their competitors were and when dim shapes did appear tearing in one direction or the other, they were impossible to identify. It was not safe for anyone to go forward to rig running lights but all had flashlights and kept a good lookout.

As the remainder of the fleet tore in towards the Bay, at speeds that must in many instances have exceeded by several knots the theoretical hull maximum, two problems arose. The first was to find the opposition and the second was what to do after crossing the finish line. The first was solved for two of the contenders when *Alana* and *Kini* crossed one another without warning just off the Bell Buoy. Immediately everything else was forgotten and both boats headed for the finish line as hard as they could go. From about the middle of the measured mile to the finish they sailed side by side, first one roaring ahead on the face of a sea and then, as she dropped into the trough, being passed by the other. So they went, neck and neck, with both crews anxiously peering ahead for the finish line, in as exciting a final sprint as one can imagine. *Kini* finally dashed across the line at 10:30 p.m. about two boat lengths in the lead after 13½ hours and some 42 miles of racing. (*Kini* was sailed by P. V. O. Evans with crew of L. Culter, M. Hunt, S. Rasmussen, and *Alana* by Ches Rickard with Mrs. Rickard and his two daughters, the youngest only 7 years old, and Eric Marsden.) While complete records are lacking it appears almost certain that, despite the light airs experienced earlier in the day, this was the fastest Entrance Island Race ever run. The problem of what to do after the race was over came in for some comment during the dash to the finish and one skipper is reported to have yelled across to the other enquiring how the h - - - they were supposed to stop these bl - - - - things after the race was over. The question answered itself very quickly. There was far too much wind and sea to moor off Jericho Station and even had it been possible to pick up a mooring there was no way to get ashore so *Alana* and *Kini* took off again, this time for the Narrows and Coal Harbour.

At the same time as this was going on *Juno* was having some more excitement of her own. While manoeuvering to pick up Denny Wotherspoon and Gordie Baker one of the backstays had fouled the main making it impossible to come about and, considering it too risky to attempt a jibe, Bob had no option but to keep on going until something stopped him. He carried on as long as he could without being forced to jibe and this took him under the First Narrows Bridge where there was some slight shelter from the wind; there he picked a fairly smooth looking spot on the North Shore and up she went. It took just two seas to lift her high enough up the beach for the crew to walk ashore where they were picked up by the tender to the dredge which was then working further up the channel. By a miracle very little damage was done either to the hull or the rigging.

Almost as exciting and, to some, a good deal more tiring than the race itself was the trip in through the Narrows to Coal Harbour. In the Narrows itself the wind was very fitful, blowing in short and violent gusts from all directions and this, coupled with the presence of the dredge and its various markers made the passage both difficult and frustrating. Once through and into the harbour it was a beat up to the Club moorings in the teeth of a full gale. Sailing a 6 Metre under Genoa alone under these conditions is enough to cause even the strongest crew member to sign off for good. Without the help of a main the boats do not point too high and, of course, when tacking sag off very badly before filling away. This means that progress to windward is very slow and the amount of work required on the winches is heroic. It was indeed a relief to see Stan Brooks, Superintendent, Coal Harbour Station, standing on the wharf ready to lend a helping hand into a convenient berth.

Once ashore all thoughts turned to those who had not yet reported and many wild rumours of founderings and missing craft were heard. Fortunately through the wonderful work of the Air Sea Rescue Unit under Captain Cyril Andrews and the willing and able assistance of a number of towboat crews and the *Princess of Nanaimo,* all boats were eventually accounted for, and what might have been a tragic day in the annals of yachting in the Pacific Northwest turned out to be a good lesson for the future and the source of many tales to be told over a sundowner in the cockpit or a cocktail at Jericho.

CHAPTER 21

Frostbiting

HARDY DINGHY SAILORS
ENJOY WINTER CONTESTS

W HEN THE SNOW STARTS TO FALL, ice commences to form and cold winter winds begin to blow, Frost-bite racing enthusiasts come to life, and start thinking about such things as "room at the mark", "starboard tack right-of-way", and other problems usually associated with fair weather racing. To complete the cycle of year-round racing, the Frost-biters become active at the time their "mother ships" go into hibernation. For fun, thrills and keen racing, winter dinghy sailing is hard to beat, and the "off" season comes to tingling life.

The above introduction to Frostbiting was written in 1950 by Bob Day, who with "Bunny" Whitcroft, "Ace" Lindsay and a few others revived the sport locally about that time. Their enthusiasm quickly spread to our good friends at Victoria following the occasion of a "live" dinghy being lugged bodily into the Commodore's New Year's Day reception at Royal Victoria Yacht Club by certain visitors from the mainland.

Since that time the fleet has shown encouraging improvement and the following year (1951) the first inter-city regatta was arranged between Royal Victoria and ourselves with six boats from each club participating in strong winds at Cadboro Bay. Frequent upsets were the order of the day in the "puffs" whistling over the Upland oaks— the Miller brothers, "Ace" Lindsay, Max Young and Capt. Billie Holmes of Victoria all swam around the first mark in water a chilly 41 degrees.

Since it takes real enthusiasm to sail all winter after an active summer, these skippers are frequently leaders in their respective classes. Many Frost-biters are youngsters and in this league will be found the finest training ground. The experience gained is of value to any skipper. It also gives the power-boater an opportunity to learn and enjoy the art of racing and sailing.

Dinghy racing is almost a separate art. Usually the top dinghy skippers will do very well when they step into a larger boat. The reverse is not always the case. It is a lot colder watching a Frost-bite race than it is taking part in one. Even with a reasonable amount of clothing,

181

one will not find it difficult to keep warm because you have got to keep moving in a dinghy, and this little exercise seems to do the trick. The novice will find he is too warm, but after a race or two it is not difficult to judge the correct amount of clothing.

Races are held in sheltered waters free of too much "slop" in order to keep spray from the inside of the hull. Otherwise one gets the feeling of sitting in a bathtub full of ice water. Races are held each Sunday, but in order to create interest, and give each skipper an opportunity to win a monthly series, it is not necessary to compete every Sunday, as points are scored only on the results of each skipper's best two or three Sundays of the month.

These sailing dinghies have their advantages during the cruising season as well. There is nothing like a sail in the "dink" after a run in a power boat, or on a Sunday morning in Flat Tops, Center Bay or any other favourite rendezvous.

Much pleasure and enjoyment may be secured the year round from these little boats, which also serve the dual purpose of able yacht tenders. For boats of twenty-five feet and over, the Davidson nine-foot dinghy is recommended, and for boats under that length the Sabot pram is ideal. Both are excellent for Frost-biting or sailing at any time of the year.

With the juniors coming along in their Sabots and flatties, plus senior Davidsons, there have been as many as fifty Frostbiters out sailing during the winter season. This division of the Club is providing excellent training for future competitive skippers. For top-flight competition in one-design boats and for over-all genuine camaraderie there is nothing to top this group.

Recognition must go to E. S. (Ernie) Earle and Norm Park for their unstinted service to Frostbiters by acting as start and finish Judges for many years at Coal Harbour and elsewhere. In rain, driving sleet or snow they have shivered in the elements, stomping feet or flapping arms to keep warm while the Frostbiters worked up a sweat skittering around the courses.

Frostbiters racing in Coal Harbour.

Frostbiters, 1964; background, Bayshore Inn, Vancouver.

BURGEES PRESENTED TO ROYAL VANCOUVER YACHT CLUB

Royal Yacht Squadron .... Cowes, England
Royal Cruising Club .... Itchenor, Chichester, England
Royal Danish Yacht Club .... Copenhagen, Denmark
Royal Norwegian Yacht Club .... Oslo, Norway
Royal Yacht Club De Maas .... Rotterdam, Holland
Royal Victoria Yacht Club .... Victoria, B.C.
Royal St. Lawrence Yacht Club .... Montreal, Quebec
Royal Nova Scotia Yacht Squadron .... Halifax, Nova Scotia
Royal Canadian Yacht Club .... Toronto, Ont.
Royal New Zealand Yacht Club .... Auckland, New Zealand
Royal Sydney Yacht Club .... Sydney, Australia
Royal Motor Yacht Club .... Sydney, N.S.W., Australia
Royal Clyde Yacht Club .... Glasgow, Scotland
Royal Brighton Yacht Club .... Brighton, England
Royal Barbados Yacht Club .... Barbados
Royal Ulster Yacht Club .... Belfast, Ireland
Royal Thames Yacht Club .... London, England
Royal Suva Yacht Club .... Suva, Fiji Islands
Royal Windermere Yacht Club .... Windermere, England
Royal Singapore Yacht Club .... Singapore
Royal Yorkshire Yacht Club .... Bridlington, England
Royal Sydney Yacht Squadron .... Sydney, Australia
Royal Yacht Club of Tasmania .... Hobart, Tasmania
Muskegon Yacht Club .... Muskegon, Michigan
Portland Yacht Club .... Portland, Oregon
Seattle Yacht Club .... Seattle, Washington
Maple Bay Yacht Club .... Maple Bay, B.C.
Queen City Yacht Club .... Seattle, Washington
Corinthian Yacht Club .... Seattle, Washington
Oakland Yacht Club .... Oakland, California
San Diego Yacht Club .... San Diego, California
South Shore Yacht Club .... Milwaukee, Wisconsin
St. Francis Yacht Club .... San Francisco, California
Golden Gate Yacht Club .... San Francisco, California
Prince Rupert Yacht Club .... Prince Rupert, B.C.
Los Angeles Yacht Club .... Los Angeles, California
Sussex Motor Yacht Club .... Brighton, England
Skovshoyed Yacht Club .... Copenhagen, Denmark
Havana Yacht Club .... Havana, Cuba
St. George Motor Boat Club .... Sans Souci, Australia
Colne Yacht Club (Brightlingsea) .... Sussex, England
St. George Motor Boat Club .... Sydney, N.S.W., Australia
Hawaii Yacht Club .... Hawaii
Brixham Yacht Club .... Devon, England
Penarth Yacht Club .... Penarth, Wales
Everett Yacht Club .... Everett, Washington
Milwaukee Yacht Club .... Milwaukee, Wisconsin
St. Petersburg Yacht Club .... St. Petersburg, Florida
International Star Class Yacht Racing Ass'n., 13th District .... Czechoslovak, Heet
Rungl Svenska Segel Salls Kapet .... Royal Swedish Yacht Club
Scarborough Yacht Club .... Scarborough, England
Waikiki Yacht Club .... Honolulu

CHAPTER 22

Post War Commodores

1948 to 1965

T. W. AYRES
Commodore 1948-1949

EIGHTEENTH COMMODORE, T. W. Ayres was an enthusiastic power cruiser yachtsman, having occupied the position of Staff Captain for the years 1945-46-47. His flagship was the M.V. *Arieta*. He later owned the fine 110 ft. converted sub-chaser *Senarietta II*, in which he cruised extensively in Coastal waters, acting also as mother ship to cross-Gulf Frostbiters and other small craft. In *Senarietta II* he won the International Power Boat Race which finished at Vancouver in 1953. During has terms of office a great deal of replacement work was done at the Coal Harbour Station. Under the direction of his Rear Commodore Alex Aitken extensive replacement of floats was undertaken and the piling renewed under the main wharf. It was at this time that extra piling was driven and decking provision made for the area which later was utilized for the establishment of The Mermaid Inn (Coffee House at Coal Harbour). Extensive water surveys were made by Rear Commodore Aitken of the "Cabbage Patch" shoal area of our water lot and designs were drawn to extend mooring for shallow-draft vessels in that area; however club finances did not permit of this added moorage at that time. It was also during the tenure of Commodore Ayres that modernization of the Bar facilities at Jericho Clubhouse were instituted under the direction of Vice Commodore Frank Wilgress, which provided workable facilities for Stewards Jayes and his assistant Frank, now our capable and very efficient Steward. Commodore Ayres for years made his *Senarietta II* available for the club's annual impressive Remembrance

Day observances and has endeared himself to the older members who many years ago formed the Eight Bells Club. This organization of sea lovers attends to the last rites of those wishing to have their ashes scattered on the waters of English Bay. Commodore Ayres presented the Tom Ayres Trophy to the club and was elected to Honorary Life Membership in 1957.

M.V. ARIETA, 1948.

M.V. SENARIETA II, 1949.

E. A. TOWNS
Commodore 1951

NINETEENTH COMMODORE, E. A. Towns had held the position of Vice Commodore in 1950 after serving on the Executive Committee for a number of years. His flagship was the power cruiser *Nirvana*. Commodore Towns headed a very enthusiastic group of Flag Officers which included W. Clarke Gibson, E. D. Stone, J. C. Williamson and R. W. R. Day. Work on the Junior Room at the Jericho Wharf, which was commenced in Past Commodore Capt. B. L. Johnson's 1950 term, was completed, and improvements in the kitchen facilities at the Jericho Clubhouse and in docking arrangements at Coal Harbour were carried out. This year, co-operating with the Burrard Yacht Club, the R.V.Y.C. arranged the starting details for the International Cruiser Race which had Vancouver as its starting point for the first time in history. Also this year, W. H. (Bud) Day imported from Norway the first Dragon in Canada, D KC I., which he named the *Lady Nan*. This trim yacht was later owned by Pat Leslie in 1956 and since 1957 by Jack Shepherd, renamed *Cam*. This year Bill Cunningham in *Cambria* won the Buscombe Trophy and his sister, in the same yacht, carried off the Julian Cup. The Beaver Cup went to Ken Glass in *Gometra* and the Macneill Trophy was awarded to Dr. Bob McCaffrey in *Hymac*. The Commodore's Cup was won by Ken Glass in *Gometra* and the Harry Marshall Trophy gained by Harry Bird in *Dolphin*. The Butt Trophy was won by junior A. Lilly in *Cambria* and the Vice Commodore's Cup for the Ballenas Island race went to Lorne Culter in *Miss Lee*.

The Dewees Trophy for the power boaters was awarded to Bob Day in *Gremlin* and Harry Bird achieved the doubtful distinction of being given the Bird Rock award.

M.V. NIRVANA IV, 1951.

W. CLARKE GIBSON
Commodore 1952

TWENTIETH COMMODORE was W. Clarke Gibson, eldest of the four Gibson brothers, well-known loggers, lumbermen and fish canners, pioneer developers of the Northwest coast of Vancouver Island. When Commodore Gibson took over leadership the club's finances were at a low ebb and the bank loan raised to build the junior quarters on the Jericho wharf had not yet been retired. Commodore Gibson immediately instituted improved administrative policies at the Jericho Clubhouse and hired a capable experienced catering manager, Victor Waram, to develop the dining-room services to the membership. His flagship, *Norsal*, was always available for club ceremonies, and he instituted the Annual Staff Outing, giving our employees a full day trip on coastal waters which is much enjoyed and appreciated. *Norsal* frequently functioned as mother ship for the juniors, transporting their smaller craft 'cross gulf and not only during his term as Commodore but every season since then Mr. Gibson has been most generous in placing his fine commodious yacht at the disposal of the club for its Annual Crippled Children's Outing and trips for the Sea and Air Cadets.

This year *Cambria*, sailed by Bill Cunningham, again won the Buscombe Trophy, and Mrs. M. C. Fox, sailing *Tsolum*, won the Julian Cup. Percy Burr in *Oho* won the Beaver Cup, and the Macneill Trophy went to Bill Morrow's *Elusive*. The Commodore's Cup was awarded to *Oho* and the Harry Marshall Trophy went to *Barracouta*, sailed by Ken J. McRae. The Butt Trophy for juniors was won by

Jerry Palmer in *Gometra,* and the Vice Commodore's Cup went to Bill Morrow's *Elusive.* The Minerva Trophy was won by Palmer and Glass in *Gometra,* and the Fraser River Lightship Trophy by Stan Davies in *Hymac.* The power boat Dewees Trophy was won by Ken Mair in *Gleniffer* and Miss Jill Biller's *Duende* earned the Bird Rock award.

M.V. NORSAL,

KENNETH G. GLASS
Commodore 1953-1954

TWENTY-FIRST COMMODORE K. G. Glass joined the club in 1931 and was the first recorded Junior Commodore in 1935, although it is known that club records are incomplete and that there were probably Junior Commodores appointed previous to that date. A keen and successful sailor of smaller yachts. Ken was quickly accepted when he volunteered for naval service at the start of World War II, and he spent the war years overseas in command of various vessels in the North Atlantic and West African Coast. He returned with the rank of Lieut.-Commander. His flagship was the famous *Gometra*—the "gold ship" whose story is related elsewhere in the History. Having been active in the junior group as a boy, he naturally took special interest in the juniors' welfare and the first steps were taken to give juniors the "ear" of the senior Executive by appointing a member of that body to the position of Hon. Junior Commodore—Mr. E. J. Palmer. It was Commodore Glass who first proposed the extension of the upstairs Lounge to the full width of the Clubhouse, although this improvement was not carried out till some years later. Special evening events and dinners were extensively instituted during his regime, and club revenues showed very satisfactory improvement. The Buscombe Trophy was won in 1953 by D. M. MacDonald in *Amberjack* and in 1954 by Sven Rasmussen in *Halvan*. The Julian Cup went to Mrs. Sandy Martin in *Alana* in 1953, and in 1954 to Mrs. Sid Miller. The Beaver Cup was won by Bill Morrow's *Elusive* in 1953 and by Glass and Palmer in

Gometra, 1954. The Macneill Trophy went to T. L. Daniels' *Miss Lee* in 1953 and to Len Murrell's *Trevida* in 1954. The Commodore's Cup was won by Bill Morrow's *Elusive* in 1953 and by Chas. Bayne in *Fulmar*, 1954. The Harry Marshall Trophy was won by Ken McRae in *Barracouta* both years and the Butt Trophy to Jack Kingscote sailing *Cambria* in 1953 and *Gometra* in 1954. The Dewees Trophy was won by Jack White, 1953, in *Arrow II*, and by Tom Pakenham, *Geva*, in 1954. Bird Rock honours went to Bob Day in *Acrasia* in 1953 and to Doug Maitland in *Kini*, 1954.

Sloop GOMETRA, 1953.

J. D. MAITLAND,
D.S.C., C. DE GUERRE
WITH PALM
Commodore 1955

TWENTY-SECOND COMMODORE, J. D. (Doug) Maitland, was an active sailor before he was into his "teens", as was to be expected of the son of our tenth Commodore, the distinguished yachtsman Ron Maitland. Doug became a junior member when he was 9 years old in 1925, and by the time he was 12 he sailed his Flattie *Dynamite* to International Flattie Championship at the P.I.Y.A. Regatta here in 1928, beating out the best from Seattle, Victoria and Bellingham Yacht Clubs. He crewed in the exciting R Class races of the late twenties and his name appears on most of our perpetual trophies during the thirties. Among the first to go overseas for naval service in the Second World War, he quickly earned command of a motor gunboat, as did his two pals Cornelius (Corny) Burke and Tommy Ladner, and was sent with them to the Mediterranean where their exploits gained them major decorations and naval recognition as "The Three Musketeers" (see chapter on World War II). Returning as Lieut.-Commander, he took up his old sport of sailing and was Vice Commodore in 1953 and 1954, when with three other members he imported the fine McGuier designed Clyde built 6 Metre sloop *Kini*. Some of the keenest racing in the club's history followed with importation of five other 6 Metres— *Alana*, *Juno*, *Golden Hind*, *Ca Va* and *Hecate*. It was in 1955 that the *Kini* led by a boat's length to win the furious finish of the Entrance Island Race in which two of *Juno's* crew were swept overboard midgulf (see Wild Ride of the Sixes.) Commodore Maitland encouraged participation by the juniors as crews in our major racing fixtures and next year, as Past Commodore, took a leading part in assisting to set up the present highly successful Junior Training Programme. In 1961 he and Commodore Temple H. Wright acquired the fine power cruiser *Cora May* and later he assumed full ownership, renaming the yacht *Wanderer.*

6 Metre Sloop KINI, 1955.

J. M. KERR
Commodore 1956

TWENTY-THIRD COMMODORE, J. M. (Mac) Kerr, joined the club in 1936 and served as a Flag Officer in the position of Rear Commodore in the years 1953 and 1954. He held the position of Vice Commodore in 1955 and did much to increase the efficiency of the Jericho Clubhouse operation. He held the position of Hon. Measurer in 1944. It was during his term of office as Commodore that the Executive Committee finally approved the sum of Three Thousand Dollars to launch the Junior Training Programme which had been set up by the Committee headed by Ray A. Delaplace. In the late thirties he was active in the C Class cruising yachts in his Hi Ho Class *Elomar,* and his flagship while Commodore was the power cruiser *Alola.* Major improvements to the upstairs ladies' lounge at Jericho were approved this year, and a sum of $25,000 was allotted to extend the lounge westward as proposed originally in 1953 by then Commodore K. G. Glass. This work was completed and the enlarged lounge in use by the Fall, greatly increasing the club's revenue in the process. About this time the new type aluminum roofed boat houses began to make their appearance at the Coal Harbour Station and a start was made to gradually eliminate the somewhat unsightly collection of miscellaneous structures serving as protection for our every growing fleet of power cruisers. While an active season of sailing events was run off, several of our major trophies were not contested. There was no award for the Buscombe Trophy, the Nacneill Cup nor the Harry Marshall Trophy. The Spencer Class did not finish within time racing for the Fraser River Lightship Trophy, but the B Class in that event was won by *Barracouta*, sailed by Harry Herlihy, and in the C Class race around the White Rocks the Jericho Trophy went to *Yahda*, sailed by H. Hollick Kenyon. The Julian Cup for the ladies' race was won by Mrs. Ches Rickard in *Alana* and the Butt Trophy for junior skippers went to Bill Falcus in *Kini*. The Dewees Trophy was captured by Bill Killam in *Porpoise II* and the Bird Rock award was presented to Gerry Palmer, sailing *Gometra*. Past Commodore Kerr was elected an Honorary Life Member in 1964.

M.V. ALOLA, 1956.

ELMER J. PALMER
Commodore 1957, 1958

JOINING THE CLUB in 1949, Elmer J. Palmer led the club for two terms to become the twenty-fourth Commodore, after having served as Fleet Captain in 1955 and Vice Commodore in 1956. Co-owner of the *Gometra* for several years with Past Commodore Ken Glass, he assumed full ownership of the yacht in 1953. *Gometra* was his flagship, and until recently he raced her in all major sailing events and still cruises coastal waters in this fine vessel. Previous to assuming Flag office Elmer took an active interest in the juniors, being Hon. Junior Commodore for two terms, and was one of the Committee which set up the training programme now in effect. In his first years term a special meeting was held, at which a group of power cruiser owners, headed by Bob Gibson, put up a strong plea for additional modern shelters at Coal Harbour, and it was decided that these would be proceeded with, the owners putting up the cost of construction to apply against their yearly moorage rental, the club to finally have clear ownership of the structures. Rear Commodore Stanley Davies contributed much to the successful accomplishment of this plan, which has considerably extended our sheltered moorage facilities. In 1958 Commodore Palmer was also elected Commodore of P.I.Y.A., with W. H. (Bud) Day, Vice Commodore. The club was host to the P.I.Y.A. Regatta this year, and a fine turn out of yachts enjoyed exceptional sailing weather for the event. Also, the club was honored by being host club for the 1958 Sears Cup Regatta in August, when for the first time this North

American Junior Championship event was held on the Pacific Coast in Canada. Extensive improvements were made at the Jericho Wharf, and Commodore Palmer donated a fine enlarged landing float to the facilities which were overtaxed, largely due to the increasing participation in sailing events by the junior membership.

Sloop GOMETRA, 1957.

G. G. FLEMING
Commodore 1959

TWENTY-FIFTH COMMODORE, Mr. G. C. Fleming, was essentially a power cruiser enthusiast and his flagship was the *Tulsequah,* a well built, roomy cruising yacht which he designed and supervised construction. He had been Rear Commodore for 1955 and 1956, and was Vice Commodore for 1957 and 1958. He was thus very familiar with Coal Harbour Station problems and had taken a leading part in planning and supervising construction of the ladies' lounge extension at Jericho. His programme of instituting additional social events and special dinners at Jericho Clubhouse, in which he was ably assisted by Stan Davies, Vice Commodore, did much to build up the club's financial reserves, which were now in healthy condition. This summer the Club was honored with a visit by Prince Philip's Dragon Class *Bluebottle,* which was sailed in a number of Dragon Race events on English Bay by her sailing master, Surgeon-Lieut. Coles. Jack Sheperd's *Cam* won the elimination tests to compete with *Bluebottle,* but was defeated by the Royal yacht in two straight races. In July the club was host to the finish of the International Power Boat Race in which the leading R.V.Y.C. participant was Dr. R. E. McKechnie's *Mamita,* which won the Tom Ayres Trophy in this event. The Dewees Trophy that year went to Ken Mair's *Gleniffer.* The Buscombe Trophy was not awarded in 1959, but the *Mary Bower,* sailed by Ken McRae, gained the Beaver Cup, and *Vogad,* sailed by Dr. Jack McMillan, won the Macneill Trophy. The Commodore's Cup went to Bob Ross, sailing *Concerto,* and *Vogad* took the Harry Marshall Trophy and the Keyes Trophy for the Fraser River Lightship Race. The Minerva Trophy was won by *Mary Bower* and the Julian Cup by Mrs. R. D. Ross in *Concerto*. The Butt Trophy went to Doug Helmer in *Tricia* and the Bird Rock award was earned by John Grubbe in *Dolphin*.

M.V. TULSEQUAH, 1959.

STANLEY DAVIES
Commodore 1960

JOINING THE CLUB in 1934, Stan Davies became Junior Commodore in 1938 and was one of the keenest sailors amongst the younger members during the thirties. He was the twenty-sixth Commodore of the Club. He also held the post of Hon. Junior Commodore in 1955, as well as being Fleet Captain in 1954 and 1955, Rear Commodore 1957 and 1958, and Vice Commodore in 1959. During his boyhood Stan built and sailed a number of fine smaller yachts and later won a number of major trophies with *Hymac*, one of the 34 ft. Roedde Class yachts. He imported *Amita*, the Fife of Fairlie designed, Clyde built, 8 Metre sloop in 1954, and she was his flagship in 1960. As Fleet Captain in 1954-55 he led sailing and racing activities to a new high, and his terms as Rear Commodore, in charge of Coal Harbour, witnessed major improvements in our mooring facilities. For many years he edited and enlivened Sea Breeze, our monthly informational news-letter to members, and he continues to maintain his interest in the advancement and welfare of the junior membership. It was during Commodore Davies' term that the deck of the Jericho Wharf was enlarged under the capable direction of member Maurice J. (Shorty) Hunt. Tugboat Island acquired as the club's first off-short station at a cost of $27,000, this sum being raised by average assessment on the membership of $36 each. This year saw the inauguration of the Nor-Pac Ocean Race from the Columbia River to Port Townsend, Wash., which was the site of the P.C.Y.C.-P.I.Y.A. Regatta and in which R.V.Y.C.'s *Troubadour*, owned and sailed by Phil Graham, took part. This year, in the Swiftsure Classic, Pat Leslie's *Tricia* was the winner in the BB Class, and Bob Ross' *Concerto* came home first in the AA Class. Also this year, Dave Miller won the world's Flattie Championship in *Silver Wings*, crewed by his father Sid, who twenty-two years previously, in 1938, won the same title in the same Flattie, crewed by Janet, his wife. *Winsome* won the Buscombe Trophy; *Hawk*, the Beaver Cup; *Aida*, the Macneill Trophy; *Mary Bower*, the Commodore's Cup; *Dolphin*, the Harry Marshall Trophy; *Tricia*, the Keyes Trophy; *Alcion*, the Minerva Trophy; and the Julian Cup went to Mrs. Jean Sturdy in *Kini*. The Butt Trophy was won by *Marchessa*, and the Bird Rock award went to Tom Sturgess for a faux-pas in his *Lightning*.

Eight Metre Sloop AMITA, 1960.

TEMPLE H. WRIGHT
Commodore 1961, 1962

TWENTY-SEVENTH COMMODORE, "Temp" joined the club in 1936 and soon took a leading part in stimulating juniors' sailing activities by occupying the post of Hon. Junior Commodore in the years 1938, 1939 and 1940. He was also active in C Class racing with his 26 ft. sloop *Marlou*. In 1938 he acquired *Alexandra* and endeared himself to lovers of fine sailing craft by rebuilding this historic 31-year-old R.V.Y.C. champion. In 1939 he was awarded the Club Championship in 9 Metre yachts, winning the Stock Exchange Trophy. He and his brother Owen were among the first group of R.V.Y.C. sailors to be accepted for overseas service, and left in the Spring of 1940 for naval training in England, soon to receive his commission, and was assigned to active service with Tribal Class cruisers (see R.V.Y.C. in World War II). He was active on the Executive Committee before going overseas, being Hon. Hydrographer in 1938, and occupied the position of Rear Commodore in 1946 and 1947. In 1955 he presented the Yuno Trophy to the club—it is the mounted compass of the yawl *Yuno*, owned by his father in the early years of the club. He also presented the mounted tiller of *Alexandra* as a Perpetual Trophy to encourage competition in the hardy Frostbiters dinghy racing class. Commodore Wright initiated modernization of Jericho Clubhouse furnishing and appointments, and led a progressive effort to construct a new building which was defeated by a General Meeting as being somewhat ahead of its time. Commodore Wright has the distinction of being second only to the renowned tenth Commodore Ron Maitland in the number of yachts he has owned and operated. Pacific Motor Boat, in October, 1929, credited the latter with a total of sixteen yachts, and he may have owned quite a few more before his decease in 1937. "Temp's" record of nine ships so far, could well be increased. They are:

1935-37 *Marlou* (sail)	1957-60 *Maori II* (power)
1937-45 *Alexandra* (sail)	1961-62 *Stromboli* (sail)
1946-48 *Amberlack* (sail)	1961-62 *Cora May* (power)
1948-55 *Kennett II* (power)	1962-64 *De Anza* (power)
1956-57 *Firewind* (power)	

Further maintenance work at Jericho Wharf was completed in 1961, including widening and renewing of joists and decking of the approach to the dock, etc.

Illness forced Commodore Wright to relinquish his duties for a portion of his second year term, and Vice Commodore Ken J. McRae carried on in his enforced absence. It was in March, 1962, that a strong Building and Development Committee was appointed to bring in recommendations for future construction at Jericho, which were filed eighteen months later (see following Commodores).

Dragon Class Sloop STROMBOLI, 1961.

KENNETH J. McRAE
Commodore 1963

ENTHUSIASTIC YACHTSMAN Ken. McRae was our twenty-eighth Commodore. He joined the club in 1950 and in 1957 held the position of Fleet Captain and was Vice Commodore 1961 and 1962. His flagship was the power cruiser *Mutineer,* although he had owned and sailed the fine yacht *Mary Bower* for eight years since importing her from England where she was built 1939 in Solent Shipyards from designs by Robert Clark. He skippered the *Mary Bower* in the trans-Pacific Race to Honolulu in 1961, being the first Canadian yacht entry that year. He was Acting Commodore for the latter half of 1962 due to the illness of Commodore T. H. Wright, and led club affairs for a very active eighteen months with much success. Following the enthusiastic reception by the membership of the redecorated upstairs lounge and model room, his House Committee, under Vice Commodore F. R. Killam, carried out modernization of the main floor areas and the completion of these improvements resulted in the highest revenues from member services in the history of the club. Commodore McRae also served as Commodore of the Pacific International Yachting Association and our club was host to the P.I.Y.A. annual Regatta this year when the largest attendance to this event was recorded. Although the Building Committee had completed its eighteen months' study of projected development plans, their report and recommendations had just been placed in members' hands prior to our Annual Meeting, and Commodore McRae's Executive Committee recommended that study and discussion on these plans should be left to two Special Meetings scheduled for November after the Annual General Meeting. This year a full and active racing programme was enjoyed despite unseasonable weather: John Grubbe won the Buscombe Trophy in *Veleda*, the Beaver Cup went to John Long in *Mary Bower*, the Macneill Trophy to Stuart Foley in *Comtessa*, the Commodore's Cup to Lol Killam in *Velaris*, the Harry Marshall Trophy to John Brandlmayr in *Coho*, the Keyes Trophy to R. G. Lundy in *Mareda*, the Minerva Trophy to Dr. J. E. Balmer in *Fulmar*, and the Julian Cup to Mrs. Megan Balmer in *Fulmar*, the Butt Trophy to Alec Foley in *Comtessa*, and no yacht nor skipper earned the infamous Bird Rock award. Dewees Power Boat Award went to Dr. Bob McKechnie in *Mamita*, the Sam Cromie Memorial to Les Simmers in *Walithy*, the Tom Ayres Trophy to Bill Killam in *Porpoise II*, the Bent Propeller award to Harry Milne in *Corvels*, and the Pakenham award went to the Burrard Yacht Club.

M.V. MUTINEER, 1963.

F. R. KILLAM
Commodore 1964

TWENTY-NINTH COMMODORE F. R. (Bill) Killam joined the club in 1951 and immediately took keen interest in the power boat section of our activities in his K5, soon to be replaced with *Porpoise II*. His flagship as Commodore was the fine power cruiser *Porpoise III*. He had served as Staff Captain in 1959 and 1960, Rear Commodore in 1962 and Vice Commodore in 1963. Immediately on assuming the post of Commodore presided a series of discussion meetings on the new Building and Development plans proposed by the Special Committee for the club. These culminated in a Special General Meeting held November 30th at which the membership overwhelmingly approved plans to proceed with Breakwater and Marina development at Jericho. Commodore Killam had worked hard in the preceding months co-operating with the Building Committee which was chaired during its extended life by Elmer Palmer, Ralph Farris and Colin Campbell, who concluded and tabled the recommendations. Immediate steps were taken to implement the plan but neighboring residents' opposition occasioned delays to its fruition. Meanwhile sailing and power boat activities proceeded apace. Twenty-seven new ships were added to the fleet bringing the total to 429 (241 power, 188 sail). Due to an increase in non-resident members' dues there was a slight falling off in total membership, but the total membership at the end of the fiscal year was reported at 1,696, practically a capacity figure, and of which the junior membership accounted for 271. This season the Buscombe Trophy was won by Art Way in *Maredea*, the

Beaver Cup by Colin Campbell in *Alcion*, the Macneill Trophy by Dr. J. A. McMillan in *Oonah*, the Commodore's Cup by Lol Killam in *Velaris*, the Harry Marshall Trophy by Stu Foley in *Comtessa*, the Keyes Trophy by Art Way in *Maredea*, the Minerva Trophy by Dr. J. E. Balmer in *Fulmar*, the Gyles White Rocks Trophy by S. B. Watts in *Jester*, the Entrance Island Trophy by Ralph Farris in *Hawk*, the Julian Cup by Miss Nora Way in *Maredea*, the Butt Trophy by B. Killam in *Velaris* and the Bird Rock award was gained by Chas. Bayne in *Spirit*. Power boaters recorded the *Porpoise II* as winner of the Dewees Trophy, skippered by Commodore F. R. Killam; the R.V.Y.C. team took the Pakenham Trophy, Tom Ayres Trophy went to Len Sewell in *Dorleen*, the Bent Propeller Trophy to Ron Runge in *RIOT IV*, and the Sam Cromie Memorial to Hew Brooke in *Maryllice*. In the international field Len Sewell was the winner in the big annual cruiser race and Les Simmers won the tough 980-mile Alaska race in *Walithy*.

M.V. PORPOISE III, 1964.

LYALL O. BELL
Commodore 1965

THIRTIETH COMMODORE Lyall Bell joined the club in 1939 and is also
a power boat enthusiast, his flagship being the cruiser *Four Bells*. He
held the position of Staff Captain in 1962, Rear Commodore in 1963,
and was Vice Commodore in 1964. Under his leadership the Sailing
and Power Boat Committees have laid out an extensive programme
of racing and cruising activities, the results of which are not yet
recorded history. Already this year, within a month of our opening
day, May 8th, several exciting overnight races have been held and
this year saw a turnout of twenty-one R.V.Y.C. yachts for the Swiftsure
Classic, the largest ever, in which a number of our ships had extremely
rough going. Pat Leslie's fine ship *Tricia* took second place overall,
being second in the BB Class; *Fulmar* was second in the A Class, and
the two-time Swiftsure winner *Winsome III* came in third in the BB
Class and eighth overall. *Cam*, sailed by Steve Tupper, won the Duke
of Edinburgh Trophy of the Canadian International Dragon Council,
emblematic of the International Dragon Class Championship, in a series
of races held on English Bay in June, 1965. Already this year our
juniors are showing their class, Colin Park having placed first in the
1965 Canadian Sabot Championships.

At a Special General Meeting held in June the membership gave authority to purchase Alexander Island for the sum of $15,000. It had been leased to the club in recent years by Captain B. L. Johnson for a nominal $1.00 annually.

M.V. FOUR BELLS, 1965.

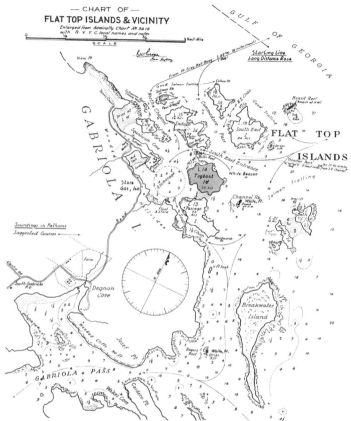

Chart of Flat Top Islands, showing Tugboat Island.

View of Silva Bay from Tugboat Island.

CHAPTER 23

Club Expansion

AND TUGBOAT AND
ALEXANDER ISLANDS

THE DECISION TO SEEK a new headquarters for the R.V.Y.C. in the Jericho Beach area was made in 1924, when A. M. Dollar was commodore. A committee to study the possibility of acquiring property was set up under the chairmanship of G. F. Gyles, to whom is due much of the credit for the success of the move. Even at that time there were members who feared that the club was faced with bankruptcy if it accepted the heavy obligations of moving from the Coal Harbour station to the remote western section of the city. There were others who feared there was not sufficient good anchorage at Jericho.

However the committee's recommendations were accepted by the majority of the membership, and at the annual meeting in February 1925, the committee was authorized to raise $25,000. Raising such a sum . . . which would seem small in these days . . . caused some head shaking among members. G. F. Gyles solved the problem, however, by preparing a bond issue of $30,000 at six per cent interest, which was one per cent above the then normal rate. The bonds were purchased by members, and the entire issue was eventually redeemed through the drawing of lots.

Arrangements to lease the Jericho property from the provincial government were completed late in 1925. The property then comprised only one and a half acres with a 200 foot frontage on Point Grey Road. The original lease was for 21 years, and the property was eventually purchased. Further land was purchased from the government in 1937 through the issuance of another bond issue for $15,000. Construction of the new clubhouse was well underway during 1926, and for a while the club had no permanent quarters of its own, for arrangements were made to lease the Stanley Park clubhouse for use by the navy reserve unit. The club retained the moorings, landing floats, motor boat berths, and other facilities at Coal Harbour. G. F. Gyles, who had done so much to arrange for the move to Jericho, was elected commodore in 1927, so that he had the well-deserved honour of being the first commodore in the new quarters. The new club was officially opened in

June 1927 in time for the international regatta in early July, which got the new site off to a fine start.

The move to Jericho brought an increase in membership, and also a considerable increase in the number of juniors. Proper recognition of the junior element of the club was first given early in 1931, when a junior section was organized under the supervision of Harold Jones. Their skipper was Bunny Whitcroft; first mate, Doug Maitland; second mate, Ken Glass; third mate, Charles Clark; and committee members were David Oppenheimer and Bill Cameron. The juniors decided to hold a dance in order to raise funds for furnishings and for sailing equipment. Prominent among the juniors were Forrest Rogers, who had been sailing the R Class yacht *Turenga* for several years; Stuart Dollar, who raced the sloop *Snooky;* and Doug Maitland, who had won the international championship in the 18 foot Flattie Class. Among those who assisted the juniors with lectures on navigation and seamanship were R. M. Maitland, Capt. B. L. Johnson and Claude Thicke. Ron Maitland, at this time, was a member of the racing rules committee of the North American Yacht Racing Union.

Despite the prevailing depression, the club found itself in good financial condition when accounts were presented at the 1932 annual meeting. The old clubhouse in Stanley Park had finally been sold to the federal government, and the mortgage on the new clubhouse had been paid off. The rank of staff captain was created at this time, to have charge of the power boat division of the club.

Two interesting additions to club facilities have been the acquisition of Tugboat Island and Alexander Island, to act as club rendezvous. Tugboat Island is one of the Flat Tops, consisting of 28 acres. It was acquired by means of a $36 assessment of members. There is a house and wharf at the property, which is maintained throughout the year by a watchman. Alexander Island, which lies in Centre Bay, Gambier Island, is a popular rendezvous because of its easy accessibility from the Jericho station.

The island was originally owned by our second commodore, R. H. Alexander, after whom it is named, and in recent years it was owned by Past Commodore Captain B. L. Johnson. In 1960 Captain Johnson gave the club a lease of the island for a nominal $1.00 yearly rental, and in 1965 the club decided to acquire the title to the property for which a general meeting approved the sum of $15,000.

CHAPTER 24

R. V. Y. C.

POST WAR ACTIVITY

AND PERSONALITIES

WHEN HOSTILITIES CEASED and activity in yacht cruising and racing again became possible, every year saw an increase in club membership and yacht ownership. The fine new Roedde Class was commissioned and a number of well-known yachts were brought out from Nova Scotia. Outstanding amongst these were the "Bird" Class yachts, *Hawk*, *Swallow*, *Blue Heron*, and *Buccaneer III*. Leaders in this expansion were J. C. (Jim) McPherson, Vans Macdonald, Bill Smith; also Mike Senyi brought out the *Fiska*, and Jack Horan the *Westwind*.

Two yachts that were purchased on the east coast and brought out to join the R.V.Y.C. sailing fleet, the 43-foot *Gometra* and 38-foot *Buccaneer V*, have quite romantic histories.

Gometra has a niche in history as the "gold ship", which was used to bring the gold reserves of the Royal Norwegian government, amounting to 15 million pounds, from Norway to Canada during the war, thus preventing it from falling into the hands of the Nazis. She was built for a retired British admiral in Scotland by Milne and Sandbanks, and was named *Gometra* after a small islet off the Isle of Arran. In the summer of 1939 she was cruising off the west coast of Norway, and when war was declared in September, her owner decided to leave her at Trondhjem for the duration. Also stranded in the same port was the 28-foot cutter *Sinbad*, built at Southampton in 1910. There they might have wasted the war years away, had not the Germans treacherously invaded Norway in the spring of 1940.

After a gallant defence against strong odds, the Norwegian king and government were forced to flee from Oslo, taking with them the gold reserves, which eventually arrived at Trondhjem. It was decided the gold should be sent to Canada for safekeeping, but there was the big danger that the freighter carrying the precious cargo might be torpedoed on the way.

It was then that somebody had a brilliant idea. Why not stow the gold into the hulls of the yachts *Gometra* and *Sinbad*, which were conveniently at hand, and then stow the yachts on the freighter's deck? If the mother ship was torpedoed, the two yachts would be cut adrift, and since they had all their sailing gear aboard, and experienced crews standing by, perhaps with a bit of luck they could be sailed into a safe haven.

There was little time to lose. The Germans were closing in on Trondhjem. The gold was hastily but carefully stowed into the yachts, which were towed down the Trondhjemfjord by a small motor patrol vessel, to where a Norwegian freighter was impatiently waiting for the gold cargo. Special cradles had been built on deck to hold the yachts, so that they would easily float off, or be pitched off in a case of emergency. Special flooring was also built into the cockpits of the yachts by the ship's carpenter, so that no matter how they hit the water they would right themselves and stay afloat.

So *Gometra* and *Sinbad* were conveyed safely across the Atlantic to Halifax, their hulls the floating crates for a nation's gold. They remained there for the remainder of the war. *Gometra* was purchased by Gus Ortengren from the Norwegian government after the war and brought her to Vancouver. He sailed her for several seasons and then sold her to the late Ken Glass and Elmer Palmer.

The *Buccaneer V* was formerly the American-built *Gwen* (originally *Buccaneer*), and her notoriety comes from the fact that she was stolen from her moorings near Boston by five German submarine officers during the Second World War. They had escaped from a nearby prisoner-of-war camp, and they sailed her up to Chester Basin, southwest of Halifax, where they wrecked her. She was subsequently salvaged and purchased by Bill Smith, who brought her to Vancouver. She was then sold in 1945 to Fred Mills, who renamed her *Gwen* and sailed her under R.V.Y.C. colours, and later she was sold in 1951 to Vernon Kirkby, who gave her the name *Buccaneer V*.

A notable feature of the 1950's in R.V.Y.C. history was the large number of fine imports from Europe and Eastern Canada, particularly in the 8 metre and 6 metre classes, and the development of a Dragon Class fleet and the popular Lapworth designed "L 36" light displacement sloops.

In 1953 Sandy Martin imported the 6 metre *Alana* from Clydeside, a Fyfe designed boat built in 1930. She came by freighter and arrived in perfect condition. Later he sold her to Ches Rickard and he and his brother-in-law Hugh Mann bought the 6 metre *Hecate*. Both of these are now out of the fleet. Sid and Phil Miller, who ruled for five years as undisputed world champion Flattie racers, and later on top Star Class racers, found their 6 metre, the *Ca Va*, in Denmark. She had been built by a Danish syndicate in 1938 to represent Danish interests in international Gold Cup racing, but was not finished when war broke out. Other 6 metres were brought in by syndicates. Peter Evans,

Bill Dolmage, Doug Maitland and Lorne Culter brought out *Kini* from Scotland. Bob Day, John Frazee and Denny Wotherspoon purchased the *Juno II*. Lorne Kyle owns the modified 6 metre *Golden Hind III*, built in 1948 at Teignmouth, England, originally imported by Ted Courbould.

The first of the 8 metre class to come out from the Old Country was imported by Jack Smith of Victoria. Next was the mahogany-hulled *Fulmar*, built 1930 at Fairlie, Scotland, and brought out by Charles Bayne. These were quickly followed by Stan Davies' *Amita*, the late Ted Field's *Pandora of Rhu*, built in 1938 at Ardmaleish, and Bob Ross' *Concerto*, built at Fairlie in 1937. The *Velaris* was built to this class in 1953 by W. H. Alcock at Crofton, and was sold to Lol Killam in 1962.

The largest of the post war yachts is the 72-foot 12 metre *Jenetta*, built in 1939 at Ardmaleish, Scotland. She was imported in 1953 by Wavell and Doug Urry, who sailed her for a season in the Old Country before shipping her home. Another notable post war production was Harold Jones' 66-foot sloop *Spirit*, built at Vancouver Shipyards.

After the Second World War there was an enormous increase in the number of power boats added to the R.V.Y.C. fleet. Some of the larger vessels were converted naval patrol craft, while the greatly increased interest in power boating that swept the continent led to the acquisition by many members of powerful outboard vessels.

Among notable additions to the fleet in post-war years were Tom Ayres' big *Senarietta II*, commodore's flagship in 1948-49; George Norgan's *Bali Hai*, Max Bell's *Campana*, Harry Reifel's *Casa Mia*, H. R. MacMillan's *Marijean*, Fred Brown's *Invader*, Don Cromie's *Tempest IV*, D. M. Hartnell's *Xanadu* and F. E. Lewis' *Stranger*.

Other personalities who have contributed much time and effort in furthering the club's interests include F. R. (Frank) WILGRESS, for twelve years our Hon. Treasurer, from 1936 to 1947, and Vice Commodore in 1948. A well known Vancouver banker, he was a "natural" for this position, in which he holds a record for long time service second only to Art Jefferd's tops of twenty-one years as Hon. Hydrographer. He joined the club in 1929 and sat on the Executive for several years before assuming the post of Hon. Treasurer. In addition to handling the club's "money-bags", he gave yeoman help to F. Burton Brooke ("Brookie") on the "Urry Maru" for many years in the somewhat thankless chore of Starter and Race Judge. He was elected to Honorary Life Membership in 1952.

CEDRIC J. DILL joined the club in 1928 and on his Star boat *Ariki* was one of the keen racing enthusiasts of the "thirties" in this class. He devoted much time to the training of juniors and in the winter months gave lectures on racing tactics and efficient small boat handling. Frequently a member of the Executive Committee, he was

Hon. Measurer in 1935-36-37 and held the post of Fleet Captain in 1940 and 1944, and was elected Vice Commodore in 1949. He was active in the Naval Training and Patrol section of the club during the war years and served as an Officer again in 1958-59-60, capably handling the position of Honorary Treasurer. In addition to his Star boat activities he raced successfully in the Spencer Boat Class, winning many trophies in *Ariki*, which he acquired in 1938 and sailed up to the war years. In 1946 he brought the 29 ft. sloop *Ariel* from the east coast and sailed her for several years. Now he has "graduated" to the motor boat class and commutes to his Bowen Island summer home in M.V. *Flight*. He was elected to Honorary Life Membership in 1960.

COL. COLIN C. FERRIE joined the club in 1916 and like his father before him is an Honorary Life Member of the club. He was elected to that honour in 1957, twenty years after his father had attained that distinction. Colin is a power cruiser enthusiast, being the owner of that fine senior cruiser *Rhinegold*, built 1911 and still going strong. He holds the record for attendance at all club cruises, Remembrance Day services and important club functions, and is as meticulous in flag etiquette and ceremonial as he is in the maintenance of his historic yacht. He served the club as Staff Captain for the years 1936 to 1938 and was Rear Commodore in 1939.

CEDRIC GYLES, also like his father, was elected to Honorary Life Membership in 1962. He joined the club in 1920 and skippered the R Class sloop *Riowna* in the contests for the Lipton Cup in the "twenties", see Lipton Cup Races. He frequently served on the club Executive and was Fleet Captain in 1939 and Honorary Treasurer for the years 1952 to 1956.

F. J. (Bunny) WHITCROFT joined in 1929 and was one of the keen group of juniors who crewed in the R Class racers and sailed Flatties and Stars to their hearts' content around English Bay and up Howe Sound, occasionally venturing across the Gulf to Nanaimo and the Flat Tops in the open boats (approximate distance across the English Channel at Dover). In 1939 he owned the Star *Stardust*, and probably owned others before that. His service overseas was in the artillery in Italy and other areas. Returning, he rebuilt the old West Coast Lifeboat *Tofino Belle*, and in recent years has operated a number of smart run-abouts, products of his own yards, West Coast Salvage & Contracting Co. Ltd., which he and other interests purchased from the late E. F. (Jack) Cribb. "Bunny" is a keen Frostbiter, having taken a part, along with Bob Day, "Ace" Lindsay and others, in reviving interest in the hardy sport of Dinghy Racing. His name is engraved on many dinghy trophies, and in 1960 he presented the F. J. Whitcroft Golf Trophy to the club for annual competition. He was a member of the Executive Committee in 1961 and 1962.

GEORGE A. CRAN (History Editor) joined the club in 1933

and for a few years sailed *Bearcat,* a 16-foot cat boat, before acquiring *Hi Ho II,* 26-foot sloop designed by Halliday and built for him by Tom Taylor. It was the first of a class of 26-foot sloops which were subsequently named the Hi Ho Class. He was elected Hon. Secretary in 1952 and held the position for six years till 1957. During that time he instituted modern business practices in office procedure, had a decorative design created for Honorary Life Membership Certificates by Ron Jackson, and was responsible for getting the concrete fireproof vault built which by now is crammed with irreplacable records and needs to be enlarged. Not always on the side of the Executive, George follows after the renowned Ian McKenzie, Sidney Smith and Roy Ginn as perennial critic of policies and procedures at Annual Meetings. He cruised the 26-foot power boat *Cosmo II* from 1953 to 1958 and was elected to Honorary Life Membership in 1964.

R. H. R. (Bob) DAY joined in 1931, was one of the most active juniors and went on to be a winning Star sailor in his *Nomana.* He made a name for himself with the Air Force in World War II, becoming Squadron Leader and gaining the D.F.C. Returning, he took up his favourite sport of yachting, swinging over to power cruisers. He owned the cruisers *Chinthe, Gremlin, Acrasia* and *Malecite,* and took keen interest in Predicted Log Racing, winning the Dewees Trophy with *Gremlin* in 1951 and with *Malecite* in 1958 and 1961. His *Acrasia* was awarded the Bird Rock Trophy in 1953, the first time that "distinction" went to a power boater and gained the Order of the Bent Propeller in 1961 with *Malecite.* Bob held the position of Staff Captain in the years 1951-52-53. In 1955 he imported the Nicholson designed six metre *Juno II* from England and displayed superb seamanship when, with his remaining crew member Herbie Millham, he succeeded in coming about in a howling gale, rescuing "Denny" Wotherspoon and "Gordie" Baker (see chapter, "Wild Ride of the Sixes"). In 1961 he initiated the VanIsle Race which circumnavigates Vancouver Island, and in 1960 presented the R. W. R. Day Golf Shield for annual competition by club members.

W. H. (Bud) DAY joined in 1934, and like his brother Bob was also a winning Star Boat sailor in his *Taseko.* He served overseas in the Air Force with the Radar Division in England, and returning became Honorary Secretary to the Pacific International Yachting Association in 1945, which post he held for twelve years. He was also Honorary Secretary to the Pacific Coast Yacht Council for 1950-51-52. He has served several terms on our club Executive and his organizing ability has been much in demand when we host the P.I.Y.A. Regattas every four years. He imported the first Dragon Class yacht brought to Canada in 1951 which he named *Lady Nan,* and in her won the Dragon Series at the P.I.Y.A. Regatta in Seattle, 1951. This yacht, lated renamed *Cam,* continues to be a consistent winner, now owned and sailed by Jack Shepherd. Bud is a member of the club Historical Committee.

O. H. BELL joined in 1937 and was active in the power boat class, owning at various times the cruisers *Latona*, *Latona A* and *Latona B*. He was a veteran of the First War and was a tower of strength on the Executive during the Second World War years, occupying the position of Vice Commodore from 1944 to 1947. He took part in the naval training and patrol activities of the club in the war years and initiated the Family Cruise and Children's Week-End in his first year as Vice Commodore. This annual event, which culminates in an impressive open air Service at the Anglican Church, Artaban Camp, is always very well attended, as many as fifty yachts and up to three hundred adults and children taking part. Vice Commodore Bell also instituted efficiencies in our Jericho Clubhouse operation and added a distinctly nautical touch to the decorations by arranging for framing and hanging approximately fifty burgees presented to the club by Royal and other Yacht Clubs from all over the world. His son Lyall is our thirtieth Commodore.

RON JACKSON joined in 1933 and was a partner in the original *Carita* with the late Bill Roedde. He served on the Executive Committee several years and was Honorary Hydrographer in 1939. He designed the very attractive certificate which is presented to Honorary Life Members on their election to that honour.

J. C. (Jim) McPHERSON joined the club in 1936 and held the position of Staff Captain in 1939. At various times he owned a number of power cruisers, including the Hong Kong built *Gleniffer*, which although launched in 1912 is still actively cruising, skippered by her present owner Ken. F. Mair. In his earlier years, before coming to Vancouver around 1910 to engage in the real estate business, Mr. McPherson had been captain of several vessels, both sail and steam, on the east coast, and had engaged in ship trade to Mediterranean and West Indies ports in the barquentine *Gaspe*. Contrary to a popular belief amongst local yachtsmen, Jim was not a "Cape Horner", according to his son D. C. (Doug) McPherson, current active power boater who owns and skippers *Sea Dream*. Although not a "Cape Horner" Capt. McPherson was a very efficient sailor because of his apprenticeship "before the mast" and kept his vessels, including the *Hawk*, in tip-top shape. In 1946 he brought the 47 ft. sloop *Hawk* to the Pacific Coast from Nova Scotia, and also had a hand in bringing out other Bird Class yachts designed by Roue, the designer of the famous *Bluenose*. These trim vessels included *Buccaneer III*, *Swallow*, *Blue Heron*, and they did much to enliven the big cruiser class long distance and English Bay races.

E. S. (Ernie) EARLE is one of the stalwarts who have done much for the club in the field of Race Starting, Race Recording and

Judging. He originally joined the club in 1935 and for a time filled in as Secretary-Manager during a staff shake-up. He returned to club membership in 1952 and took a keen interest in assisting Art Jefferd on the Starting Tower for a number of years until Art expressed a desire to retire. Ernie followed him as Hon. Hydrographer in 1961. Well trained in his duties, Ernie was an efficient starting and judging official, and his services are even now much in demand at major sailing events when the large number of yachts taking part creates hectic activity on "Urry Maru". For his services as Hydrographer to the English Bay Star Fleet he, as well as Art Jefferd, are Honorary Life Members of that active fleet. Ernie is most appreciated perhaps by the Frostbiters for his unfailing services as Starter and Judge at Coal Harbour, at Victoria Regattas and elsewhere, turning out to start them off in all weathers—mostly wet, cold and miserable.

A. W. (Nye) NYBLOM joined in 1937 and for many years skippered the sloop *Ganessa*, which he acquired in 1938 from Jim Longley. He was active in C Class racing and won the Frank Parsons Trophy for the English Bay Series in the years 1940, 1947, 1950, 1951 and 1952, and was awarded the "coveted" Bird Rock Trophy in 1947. "Nye" devoted a lot of time and effort to junior training, and was Honorary Junior Commodore for the five years of World War II. He was Honorary Measurer of the club in 1942 and 1943 and Honorary Treasurer in 1949, also a member of the Executive Committee for several years thereafter, his American citizenship precluding him from holding a Flag Office in the club.

Another hardy sailing enthusiast, N. T. (Norm) PARK, also gets the "nod" from the Frostbiters for his interest in their activities and Norm's work for several years as Honorary Junior Commodore is deeply appreciated by the Executive and the fathers and mothers of the hundreds of fortunate juniors who have received their sailing training from instructors under Norman's direction.

DR. R. E. (Bob) McKECHNIE joined in 1946. He is a power cruiser enthusiast, and in his fine yacht *Mamita* has been a consistent winner of Predicted Log Racing. He won the Dewees Trophy in 1957 and again in 1963, the Sam Cromie Memorial Trophy in 1962, and has ranked high in the International Power Boat Annual Races. He was Staff Captain in 1955 and 1956 and Vice Commodore in 1960. Active in the formation of the B.C. Yacht Council, he represented the club for some time on that body, and a few years ago wrote and produced a very authoritative booklet on Flag Etiquette.

W. E. (Bill) CUNNINGHAM joined in 1933 and was one of the efficient junior skippers of the "thirties". He served in the air force during the war years and in 1948 designed and built the fine 30 ft. B Class sloop *Cambria*, with which, over the years, his name has been inscribed on many club trophies. He has served the club well on the

Executive Committee and was Honorary Measurer in 1938 and Fleet Captain in 1952.

KEN MacKENZIE, who joined in 1943, is the well-known "dour" Scottish skipper of the trim 32-foot B Class sloop *Ealasaid,* one of the best kept yachts in the fleet, and winner of many trophies including the famous Lipton Cup. Ken built *Ealasaid* himself around 1927 from designs by Tom Halliday, and still actively sails her, having changed her rig over the years and raising the cabin to give full headroom. Many club year books have incorrectly recorded the name *Ealasaid,* leaving out the first "a". Ken points out that the name is Gaelic, which is to be expected, and it means Elizabeth.

W. R. (Bill) MORROW joined in 1931 and for some years he owned the old time power cruiser *Margaree.* In 1948 he built the 34 ft. Roedde Class *Elusive* and very actively sailed her till 1956. Swiftsure records available now only go back to 1952, but *Elusive* was entered in every year till 1955. In 1952 he was third in the B Class, first in B Class in 1953 and fifth overall. In 1954 he was again first in B Class and was second overall. In the 1955 Swiftsure he did not finish. In 1950 he and John Burnett presented the Burn-Mor Match Trophy and in 1952 he won the Macneill Trophy, Vice Commodore's Cup and the Spencer Class award. In 1953 he won the Vice Commodore's Cup and the Entrance Island Race. In 1955 he won the Fraser River Lightship Trophy and the Vice Commodore's Cup.

DR. J. A. (Sammy) SAMPSON joined the club in 1937. His yacht was the power cruiser *Tequilla,* and he was Staff Captain in 1940-41-42. He was active in the formation of the Naval Training Section of the club along with Fleet Captain Ced. Dill in 1940, and continued as leader of that group till disbanded in 1944. It was under Dr. Sampson that the group of six club power cruisers assisted naval authorities to round up approximately 1100 Jap owned fishing vessels and intern them at Annacis Island, Fraser River, see Chapter 18.

DR. J. E. (Jack) BALMER joined in 1947 and became Fleet Captain in 1963, and was re-elected to the post in 1964. He acquired the 8 metre sloop *Fulmar* in 1956 and has an excellent record of wins. In 1963 he won Minerva Trophy, W. O. Bell Trophy, Navigator's Trophy and Jack Cribb Memorial Trophy on the Snake Island Race, and Mrs. Megan Balmer won the Julian Cup. He repeated his record again in 1964 but the Julian Cup that year went to Mrs. Way in *Maredea. Fulmar* entered the Swiftsure in recent years and in 1965 came second in the A Class.

J. G. (Jack) WILLIAMSON joined in 1935, and his first yacht was the C Class *Jollilu.* He later had the power cruiser *Lorelei,* and in 1947 built the 34 ft. Roedde Class sloop *Fantasie II.* Jack served on the Executive for several terms and was elected Fleet Captain in 1949, 1950 and 1951. He won the Spencer Trophy in 1948 and again in 1953. Active in promoting class boat competitive racing, Jack was a leader in the Roedde Class, having assisted the late Bill Roedde to develop the design finally put on the boards by naval architect Tom Halliday. Nowadays Jack and Olive prefer to cruise the Gulf Islands, but they take an active part in all club cruises and functions, never failing to turn out for the Remembrance Day services.

S. (Stu) FOLEY joined in 1932 and was one of the very active group of young sailors sailing Stars and Flatties in the "thirties". He is one of the trio of airline pilots in the club who are very highly rated racing skippers—the others being Ches Rickard and Pat Leslie. Stu was stationed in Eastern Canada for a considerable time, but returning to permanent home in Vancouver he built the sleek 32 ft. Seafair sloop *Comtessa* in 1956 and has the following club trophies to his credit: 1957, Keyes Trophy; 1963, Macneill Trophy; 1964, Harry Marshall Trophy; and in 1958 his son Alec won the Butt Trophy in *Comtessa*, repeating the win in 1963.

J. P. (Pat) LESLIE joined in 1948, sailing the Star *Polaris* with success. He later owned the *Flamingo*, and for a couple of years the Dragon KC I. *Cam*. In 1958 he built the 36 ft. L36 Class sloop *Tricia* and entered in his first Swiftsure Race in 1959, placing third in the BB Class and a very worthy third overall. He was elected Fleet Captain in 1959 and was Honorary Measurer 1960-61-62. In the Swiftsure of 1960 he placed first in the BB Class and second overall, and in the 1961 event came fifth in BB and seventh overall. In Swiftsure 1962 he tied with S. B. Watts in *Jester* for third place in BB and fifth overall, being eleventh in BB in 1963 and third in BB in 1964. In the 1965 Classic he placed second in BB and second overall. Pat's record of club wins is most impressive: In 1960 he won Keyes Trophy, Empire Trophy, Gulf of Georgia Trophy and Harbour Lights award. In 1961 he again won the Keyes Trophy, White Islands Race, Entrance Island Race (which he also won in 1959), the Gulf of Georgia Trophy, also the Jack Cribb Memorial. He won the 1963 Schooners and Yawls Trophy and *Tricia* also won the Butt Trophy, sailed by Doug. Helmer, in 1959.

C. L. (Ches) RICKARD joined in 1950, and his *Winsome III* belongs in the club "Hall of Fame" for twice winning the Swiftsure Classic in consecutive years 1961 and 1962, and its second place in 1963 (if the protest against *Thetis* by another yacht had been allowed, Ches would have had three consecutive Swfitsure wins to his credit). Ches served on the club Executive in 1957 and has been active in the Honorary Junior Commodore's Committee. When he owned and sailed the six metre *Alana* she was one of the only two yachts to finish the Entrance Island Race of 1955, coming only two lengths behind *Kini* (see Wild Ride of the Sixes). His daughter Joan won the Butt Trophy in 1955 and Mrs. Wyn Rickard won the Julian Cup in 1955 and 1956 in *Alana*. The club Six Metre Championship went to *Alana* in 1956, sailed by Pat Leslie. *Winsome III* is also carved on the trophies for both the White Rocks and Entrance Island races in 1960.

R. D. (Bob) ROSS joined in 1954 and his first yacht in the club was the 26 ft. sloop *Flying Walrus*. In 1956 he acquired *Concerto* from Ced. Gyles, who had imported this sleek 48 ft. eight metre sloop from the Clyde, where it was built in 1937. In *Concerto,* Bob has made a name for himself as a racing skipper as the following record of his wins will show: In 1957, Commodore's Cup; 1958, Redskin Trophy; 1959, Commodore's Cup and Gulf of Georgia Trophy, also this year Mrs. Ross won the Julian Cup; 1960, W. O. Bell Trophy; 1962, Beaver Cup and Harbour Lights Trophy; and in 1963 the Burn-Mor Match Trophy. He also has a fine record in Swiftsure racing. In 1964 he acquired the fine roomy *Coral Reef* from Art Way and re-named her *Penelakut*. She came eighth in the A Class in the 1965 Swiftsure Classic.

L. H. (Lol) KILLAM joined in 1946 and was active in the powerboat fleet from 1950 to 1960 in his 62 ft. cruiser *Wyrill*. He is an enthusiastic Frostbiter, and his name is on many of their trophies. In 1960 he acquired the 48 ft. A Class sloop *Velaris,* and has a fine record of race victories with her. In 1961 he won the Commodore's Cup, W. O. Bell Trophy and the Harbour Lights Trophy; his son Hayden also won the Butt Trophy. In 1963 *Velaris* also won the Commodore's Trophy and the Gulf of Georgia award. In 1964 he again won the Commodore's Cup and his son "Bunker" the Butt Trophy. *Velaris* is also a regular entrant in the Swiftsure Classic, placing fifteenth in the A Class in 1961, second in the A's in 1962, eighth in A's 1963, fifth in A's 1964, and tenth overall and tenth in A's in 1965. *Velaris* is this year entered in the Victoria to Honolulu Race. Lol was Fleet Captain of the club in 1961 and 1962.

N. R. (Norm) McCARVILL joined in 1957 and is skipper of the fine yacht *Spirit* in all the major racing and cruising events on the club calendar. He is a keen yachtsman, and the contests between our two largest active racing yachts, Phil Graham's *Troubadour* and *Spirit,* have enlivened discussion at the famous "five o'clock club" for the last seven years, their crews being frequently present AND vocal. In 1961 Norm entered the Acapulco Race from Los Angeles and had a very strenuous passage down the coast to enter that event. He keeps *Spirit* in tip-top shape, maintaining her in the style set by her co-designer and builder, the late Past Commodore Harold A. Jones. Mrs. McCarvill (nee Beverley Jones) is also a first rate skipper, having won the Julian Trophy sailing *Spirit* in the 1947 ladies' race.

P. D. (Phil) GRAHAM joined in 1955, and in 1958 imported from Europe the 65 ft. yawl *Troubadour,* which he kept in active commission until sold in 1965 to California. An enthusiastic yachtsman, he sailed *Troubadour* in all club fixtures and branched out to "blue water" sailing with his entries in the Trans-Pacific Honolulu Race in 1961 and the tough NorPac races to and from the mouth of the Columbia River and Port Townsend, Wash. He has regularly entered the Swiftsure Classic, being first yacht home in the 1961 event, thereby winning the City of Victoria Trophy. Phil has done a great deal to stimulate interest in the big cruising-class races with his perennial challenges to *Spirit*, and to him can be attributed the creation of the Snake Island Race, which is now a club fixture. In 1958 he challenged *Spirit* to a matched race over that 58 mile course, which the *Spirit* won, passing *Troubadour* going to windward in the night on the way home. He is also the initiator of the Sisters Islets Race, the distance around being approximately 100 miles. For this new annual fixture Phil presented the Troubadour Trophy, which was won the first year (1963) by *Coho*, sailed by John Brandlmayr. Phil was elected Fleet Captain in 1965.

C. (Chuck) BAYNE joined in 1941 and was active in the junior and intermediate classes. In 1954 he imported the Fife of Fairlie designed, Clyde built 8 metre sloop *Fulmar*, and sailed her for a couple of years, winning the Burn Mor Match Trophy in 1955 and the Redskin Trophy in 1956, having been awarded the Bird Rock Trophy in 1955. He succeeded in acquiring the latter "distinction" again in 1964, sailing *Spirit*.

A. W. (Art) WAY joined in 1941 and took part in the naval training and patrol activities of the club in the war years. He owned the cruiser *Yellow Jacket* for a number of years and built the fine cruiser *Bel Air* in 1953. In 1956 he imported the Robb designed, Shandon built *Delphin* and entered her in the Swiftsure Classic of 1957, placing sixth in the BB Class that year. In 1959 he built the Seaborn designed 46 ft. sloop *Coral Reef* and placed eleventh in the A Class Swiftsure Classic that year. In 1960 he did not finish in the Swiftsure but in 1961 came fourth in the A Class, beating out seven other R.V.Y.C. entries. In 1962 he placed thirteenth in the A Class Swiftsure but he won the Commodore's Cup in our local Entrance Island race. In 1964 he acquired the *Maredea*, making the fine sailing record of the following wins: Buscombe Trophy, Schooners and Yawls Trophy, Keyes Trophy, Empire Trophy, Troubadour Trophy, and Mrs. Nora Way won the Julian Cup. In the 1964 Swiftsure he placed tenth in the BB Class, in 1965 he was fifth in the BB's.

E. D. (Doug) STONE joined in 1944 and had previously been an active Star boat sailor with Kitsilano Yacht Club. He has an extensive background in yacht designing, having at one time been engaged in that profession in New York City. He comes from a long family of boat builders, and annually visits the family boat works in England. He, along with the late E. F. (Jack) Cribb, imported the Uffa Fox designed *Fleet Fairy* from England in 1952. Although a trim 33 ft. open sloop she did not perform too well in the light English Bay airs, and has not been in commission for some years. Doug was Rear Commodore in 1951 and 1952, and has always taken a keen interest in junior sailing activities. For some years he has headed the Sea Cadet movement in British Columbia, and is a member of the club Historical Committee.

D. M. (Doan) HARTNELL joined the club in 1954, and is also a power cruiser enthusiast, having owned *Xanadu*, the rebuilt U.S. sub-chaser of the First War, and now the fine cruiser *Takulli*. He was Staff Captain in 1963 and Rear Commodore in 1964, and is now Vice Commodore in 1965. He is an active worker on the club cruises, and has developed fine participation in the new winter cruises and the Children's Day events.

A. F. (Bud) ROULSTONE joined in 1949 and was Honorary Junior Commodore in 1951. He was active in the small boat classes, sailing 14 ft. International Dinghies, Flatties, Dragons, and at one time *Stromboli*, which was originally built for Past Commodore Temp. Wright. He was also a capable Frostbiter, and his name is on many trophies for the small boat classes. He presented the Stromboli Trophy in 1961 and in 1963 won the Canadian Flying Junior Class Series at Lake Louis, Quebec, with the aggregate of 535 points, to pick up the Vanier Trophy, out-scoring a fleet of 102 boats although he had never sailed a Flying Junior before. Bud was Honorary Hydrographer in 1962.

R. C. (Ron) RUNGE joined in 1946 and is a keen power cruiser enthusiast, his yacht being *Riot IV*. He has served on the Executive Committee and has been active on several House Committees and on Rear Commodore Committees. He was elected Staff Captain in 1965.

COLIN D. CAMPBELL joined in 1950 and over the succeeding years has been an active cruising and racing skipper in *Blue Wave*, a 33 ft. yawl, and since 1961 in *Alcion*, the fine 47 ft. A Class sloop. He has recently headed the Breakwater Committee and has been active on House Committees, having been elected to the Executive Committee in 1963, 1964 and 1965.

T. F. (Bill) ORR joined the club in 1951, and is a power cruiser enthusiast. He has owned the *Senerietta II* and now owns the *Malecite*, which he frequently places at the disposal of the Eight Bells Club, and his fine ship is always available to transport materials and supplies to our off shore stations at Tugboat and Alexander Islands. He has taken a keen interest in the development of these club assets and is affectionately known as "Mayor of Tugboat Island". He was elected Rear Commodore in 1965.

Three champion power cruiser operators, A. L. (Les) SIMMERS, *Walithy;* L. G. (Len) SEWELL, *Dorleen;* and DR. H. (Hew) BROOKE, *Maryllice,* have gained distinction for themselves and have brought honours to the club by their expert performance in Predicted Log Races. They captured all three major power cruiser events in 1964— the International Alaska Race, the International Cruiser Race and the

Gulf of Georgia Race—and they are all set to repeat the feats again this year.

JAYES—the perfect English butler—who assumed the position of Steward when the Jericho Clubhouse was opened in 1927, gave an air of graciousness and distinction to our club dining room and was a landmark at the premises for many years till he retired in 1950. He was succeeded in the position by his assistant, FRANK CAVALIERO, who carries on today as our efficient head Steward. Frank joined the club in 1938, receiving leave of absence during the war years for navy service. He supervised the officers' mess at H.M.C.S. *Discovery* for a short time and had active service for eighteen months on frigates in the North Atlantic Convoy Patrol. Returning in 1945, he has carried on in the best traditions and is a "prime favourite" with all members.

STANLEY BROOK, who was appointed to look after our Coal Harbour Station in 1922, retired in 1960 after 38 years of faithful, conscientious service to all active members, big, little, experienced or amateur yachtsmen—all were alike to him—they could always count on Stan. to see that their boats were safely riding at moorings and they knew that they could call on him for the little personal attentions that mean so much to the zealous boat-owner. He presented the Stanley Brook Trophy for Frostbiters in 1955. CAPT. "Denny" RAMSBOTHAM succeeded Stan Brook in 1960 as Superintendent at Coal Harbour. He is a qualified ship's captain, a navy veteran, and before joining the staff was skipper of the well-known Gibson brothers yacht *Norsal*. Capt. "Denny" watches over his charges at the moorings like a mother hen guards her chicks, and is a dependable source of sage counsel for budding navigators or inexperienced "novice" boat-owners.

Flag Officers who have served the club since its inception in 1903 are listed in Chapter Thirty-two. Meanwhile the following table records the members, not otherwise mentioned, who have given service on the Executive Committee for the years stated:

1946 Gus Ortengren, Ted LePage.
1948 George L. Cran
1949 Dr. R. P. (Bob) McCaffery, Dr. C. D. Helmer, B. R. (Bert) Tupper
1950 R. H. R. (Bob) Young
1951 Claude S. Thicke, G. Hazen Phillips
1961 and 1962 E. B. Dueck, J. M. (Ace) Lindsay
1963 D. C. (Doug) McPherson
1964 G. Alan Martin, P. D. Graham.
1965 L. Dampier, Geo. Glanville, Alec. J. Forsyth, G. Alan Martin.

Previous to 1957 the Flag Officers always gave their reports verbally at the Annual General Meetings, usually reading them, then passing the documents to the Commodore. Presumably they were intended to reach the Hon. Secretary's hands for inclusion in the official minutes.

Over the years, some did and some didn't—so to save long "harangues" at Annual Meetings the Hon. Secy. of that year (your editor) adopted the modern plan of including all Flag Officers' reports in the printed Annual Report and Financial Statement mailed to the membership in advance of the Annual Meeting. This not only simplified procedure but definitely put the reports in print where they can be studied and referred to in succeeding years.

A review of the last eight years sail and power boat activities is therefore at hand, and is recorded in condensed form herewith.

1957 Fleet Captain Ken J. McRae reported—

". . . early in the year our Frostbiters, under the Chairmanship of J. M. (Ace) Lindsay, invaded Victoria and annexed the H. A. Wallace Trophy, symbol of the Inter City Team Championship . . . *Gometra, Delphin, Treveda* and *Mary Bower* did well in the Swiftsure Classic, *Treveda* achieving 1st in the B Class and *Mary Bower* 3rd in A Class . . . over sixty yachts took part in the English Bay Invitational Regatta, but the representation from other clubs was disappointingly small . . . the P.I.Y.A. Regatta was held at Port Townsend, Wash., and few R.V.Y.C. yachts participated, possibly due to the poor sailing conditions encountered two years ago, and which were repeated this year . . . Angus Roulstone took first prize in the International Dinghy Class and the Canadian six metres won the International Team Race for the first time in four years . . . there was a good turn out to the Labour Day Regatta at Maple Bay, and our club won the H. Wallace Trophy for interclub competition from Victoria this year . . . Dr. Cec. Helmer credibly represented us at the Mallory Cup Eliminations in Seattle, and George Mason and crew made an excellent showing in the Royals Regatta at Toronto, losing first place by only one quarter of a point . . . Ray Delaplace was successful in winning the Venture Trophy in International Competition for the 14-foot Dinghies."

1957 Staff Captain F. S. Clendenning reported—

". . . the Easter Cruise up the Fraser River to Pitt Lake was repeated again this year and the popular Family Cruise or Children's Week End again held at Camp Artaban, Gambier Island . . . only seriously handicapped children were included in the Children's Day Cruise and this year a Fishing Derby provided additional fun . . . our team won the Inter Club Predicted Log event, retaining the Pakenham Trophy by a large margin . . . a new Thanksgiving "Wind-up" Cruise enjoyed a large turnout and will be a permanent fixture in the future."

1958 Fleet Captain H. J. Burnett reported—

". . . more and more power boat skippers are turning out for the Frostbite events, and this year won the majority of prizes . . .

although Easter was early this year the large turnout for the race to Flat Tops was most gratifying, but the early events in English Bay were poorly attended, and it is recommended that no events be scheduled in future prior to Opening Day . . . there were nine entries from the club in the Swiftsure Race, *Cresset*, sailed by Gerry Palmer coming fourth in the BB Class and *Gometra*, sailed by Elmer Palmer sixth in the A Class . . . the P.I.Y.A. Regatta was an outstanding success, largely due to the hard work of our Regatta Chairman W. H. (Bud) Day . . . with Mrs. Ann Bottrell as Instructress a series of ladies' sailing classes were successfully held, and our juniors gave an outstanding performance in the Sears Cup and other international events . . ."

1958 Staff Captain F. S. Clendenning reported—
". . . during the winter months a series of successful events were held in the Jericho Clubhouse—Stag Party and Auction Sale, Photo Night and others . . . the Easter Cruise to Pender Harbour was blessed with calm and fine weather, as was the Children's Week End at Camp Artaban . . . the Children's Day Cruise was highlighted by entertainment aboard vessels of the R.C.N. Destroyer Escort Squadron through the courtesy of Rear Admiral H. S. Rayner and Captain J. Pratt . . ."

1959 Fleet Captain J. P. Leslie reported—
". . . the Swiftsure Classic drew a record entry of eleven yachts from our club; *Mary Bower* won in A Class, *Concerto* second in AA Class and *Tricia* third overall . . . David Miller, with his father, participated in the World's Flattie, and the Kirkland brothers in the World's Star Championships in California . . . George Mason and Maurice Hunt represented Canada in Stars in the Pan American Games in Chicago, while our junior team of David Miller, Colin Park, Ken Baxter and Jon Fladgate sailed for the Pacific Northwest in the North American Junior Championships at Noroton, Conn. . . . *Bluebottle*, the Dragon Class yacht owned by H.R.H. Duke of Edinburgh, skippered by Surgeon-Lt. R. Coles and Clive Smith, visited our waters and was the centre of intensive racing culminating in a match against *Cam*, which she won. Two more Dragons joined the fleet this season . . . Bill Burgess won the Star Class eliminations in a close contest against local and two eastern teams, and will represent our club at the 1960 Olympics . . . nine large yachts were added to our fleet this season: *Coral Reef, Gabrielle, Heather, Novara, Toroa, Tramontana, Tricia, Trima* and *Winsome* . . ."

1959 Staff Captain F. R. (Bill) Killam reported—
". . . a new innovation was a Mid Winter Cruise to Centre Bay, Gambier Island, very successfully organized by R. W. R. (Bob) Day . . . the Easter Cruise planned for Pender Harbour was diverted to Camp Artaban because of the weather, and 37

cruisers participated with 94 adults and 48 children, and was an unqualified success thanks to Lyall Bell's efforts . . . the Family Cruise to Camp Artaban was attended by over fifty ships, 125 adults and 125 children . . . prompted by Harbour and Naval Authorities our club participated with Burrard Yacht Club and West Vancouver Yacht Club in patrolling a lane from Pier B to Pt. Atkinson for the passage of Her Majesty Queen Elizabeth on the H.M.C.S. *Assiniboine* . . . with Burrard Yacht Club we were hosts to the finish of the annual International Cruiser Race when over 100 ships and crews were accommodated under the able direction of Dr. R. E. (Bob) McKechnie . . . predicted log racing was very active with five Harbour races, the International Cruiser Race in which our seven entries did well, the Dewees and Pakenham Trophy Races . . . 36 members enrolled in an excellent navigation course organized and conducted by W. J. (Bill) Johnson . . . improved procedure for radio communication with cruisers was arranged with D.O.T. through the good offices of John Dunn . . . a greater variety of competitive power boat events is recommended, also the acquisition of a club property within reasonable cruising distance of Vancouver . . ."

1960 Fleet Captain Denis F. Wotherspoon reported—
    ". . . David Miller, with his father Sid, won the World's Flattie Championships, which were hosted by our club in English Bay with twenty-five Flatties participating, including many former World's Flattie champions . . . David, with Colin Park, Ken Baxter and Bob Lance, travelled to Green Lake, Wisconsin, and won the Sears Cup, emblematic of the North American Junior Sailing Championships . . . Ron Maitland, Alec Fergusin, Alec Foley and Don Martin made an impressive showing at the Junior Olympic Regatta held in Montreal . . . Cec Helmer represented our club in the Mallory Cup eliminations at Seattle, and Audree Rees the Adams Cup eliminations also held there, unfortunately without success . . . eighteen Lightnings and eleven Dragons have added a colorful spectacle and increased interest to our week-end racing . . . Phil Graham entered his *Troubadour* in the strenuous Norpac Race from the mouth of the Columbia River to Port Townsend, Wash. . . . Alf Loomis, an Editor of "Yachting", and John Guzwell, who sailed *Trekka* around the world, also Walter Chapelle, gave interesting addresses to the membership . . ."

1960 Staff Captain F. R. (Bill) Killam reported—
    ". . . the Mid Winter, Easter, Children's and Thanksgiving Cruises were well attended, as was also the special annual cruise for crippled children . . . a Harbour Patrol was organized and successfully concluded during the visit of U.S.S. *Coral Sea* . . . four R.V.Y.C. cruisers took part in the International Cruiser Race, one in the

Alaska Race, seven in the Dewees Trophy Race, six in the Gulf of Georgia Race, four in the Pakenham and four in the Thanksgiving Races . . . acquisition of Tugboat Island at Silva Bay was promoted and successfully concluded and the value to the club of this property was amply proven by its popularity throughout the season . . . through the generosity of Capt. B. L. Johnson, Alexander Island in Centre Bay, Gambier Island, was made available to the club . . ."

1961 Fleet Captain L. H. (Lol) Killam reported—
". . . statistically speaking, during the past year there were more boats, more races, and more wins than ever before. More of our members travelled farther afield and the R.V.Y.C. was well represented in national and international races . . ."

1961 Staff Captain Robert Gibson reported—
". . . your Tugboat Island Station was host this year to over 350 registered members' boats with some 1400 guests aboard . . . on the occasion of the arrival of the largest passenger vessel ever to visit Vancouver, the *Canberra*, your power boat committee organized a harbour patrol in conjunction with the National Harbours Board . . . the first Van-Isle predicted log race and family cruise programme around Vancouver Island was instigated through the efforts of R. W. R. (Bob) Day, and the result would indicate that this would be a bi-annual event . . ."

1962 Fleet Captain L. H. (Lol) Killam reported—
". . . another successful year of sailing and racing . . . club events well attended . . . in international racing your club showed once again that it has many capable ships and crews . . . a number of fine new vessels were added to the fleet this year and more are being built . . ."

1962 Staff Captain Lyall O. Bell reported—
". . . although the weather left much to be desired, we have had a successful year . . . all the organized events and cruises were well attended . . . Tugboat Island has proven a wonderful offshore station and was continuously used by many boating members . . . Alexander Island floats and ramps were completed, and special thanks go to Captain Bill Dolmage . . ."

1963 Fleet Captain Dr. J. E. Balmer reported—
". . . a full and active racing season has just been completed and an enlarged schedule of events carried out in generally damp weather and unsettled winds . . . your club hosted a successful P.I.Y.A. Regatta which was well attended, as well as a number of other regattas, both national and international, for different racing classes . . . (club yachts to the record number of nineteen entered in the Swiftsure Classic, *Winsome III* winning second place overall,

Nyon third in BB Class, with *Long Gone* fourth and *Jester* fifth in that class) . . ."

1963 Staff Captain D. M. Hartnell reported—

". . . a very successful year was enjoyed in the Predicted Log Racing schedule and outstanding showings were made in the International, Pakenham and Dewees Trophy Races . . . the hosting of the International Power Boat Association added to the enjoyment of the racing schedule and will be brought to conclusion with the Association Annual Meeting to be held here in December . . . our off-shore stations continue to receive increasing use by a large number of members and a permanent caretaker has been retained for Tugboat Island, where additional floats to be constructed by our Coal Harbour employees will be installed next year . . ."

1964 Fleet Captain Dr. J. E. Balmer reported—

". . . in generally poor weather our fleet has had an active season and all events enjoyed a good attendance . . . the 104-mile Sister's Island Race, scheduled for the second time this year, had a good entry list . . . the Lightning and Dragon fleets were depleted somewhat this year . . . twelve R.V.Y.C. yachts entered the Swiftsure Classic, *Tricia* placing third in the BB Class and *Sanderling* sixth, with *Fulmar* fourth in the A Class and *Velaris* fifth . . . the North American Intercollegiate Championships and the Canadian Junior Championships were held here for the first time this year . . ."

1964 Staff Captain J. D. Overholt reported—

". . . top honours went to Len Sewell on *Dorleen* in the Pacific Coast senior annual predicted log race, the International Cruiser Race, with the fantastically small error of .725 per cent . . . in the Alaska Race—world's longest regularly run predicted log event—trophy went to Les Simmers and wife Babe for a record shattering low error of 2.22 per cent over the rugged 980-mile course, their *Walithy* being the first Canadian boat to win the classic since our own *Limit*, skippered by E. B. Deane, won it in 1908 . . ."

Special series Dragon Class races, 1959, in honour of visit of BLUEBOTTLE, No. K192, owned by H.R.H. Duke of Edinburgh.

CHAPTER 25

Juniors make History

FOR R.V.Y.C.

JUNIORS HAVE BEEN A PART of the Royal Vancouver Yacht Club ever since it was first formed in 1903. In the main they were generally children of the original members. O. L. Spencer, son of the first Hon. Secy., was said to be the first junior member who joined shortly after the Club was formed. The first yearbook, published in 1906, stated that the age limit for juniors was between seventeen and twenty years of age, and the list of junior members at this time included the following:

Bell-Irving, H. B.	Macneill, Cyril	Wainright, Lionel
Austin, Ernest	Scott, Douglas	Wainright, Victor
MacLean, E. W. Jr.	Taaffe, W. J.	

Within three years, the number of junior members had increased to twenty-six, including

Austin, E.	Maitland, R. M.	Rochester, E. P.
Bell-Irving, R. J.	MacLean, E. W. Jr.	Scott, Douglas
Bradshaw, R.	McLennan, R. P. Jr.	Stone, H. A.
Carter, H. E.	Macneill, Cyril	Taaffe, Frank
Clement, C.	Patterson, H. P.	Taylor, H.
Deane, E. R.	Ramsey, H. V.	Templeton, Edwin
Farrell, G.	Ramsey, T. M.	Wainright, Lionel
Hoy, Bert	Roedde, Walter	Webster, H.
Jefferd, A. H.	Roedde, Wm. A.	

Records of the actual formation of the Junior Division are vague but it is generally felt that the first Junior Division was initiated in 1925. The actual formation of a junior executive, in 1935, was thought to have been piloted by Harold Jones and headed by Jr. Commodore Ken Glass. Hon. Junior Commodore Temple Wright reported on an organizational meeting of the junior executive in February, 1939. It included Jr. Commodore Bud Day, Jr. Vice-Commodore Tom Bolton, Jr., Secretary Ernest Thompson, and Jr. Fleet Captain Dana Ramsey. At this meeting it was decided that the juniors adopt a uniform consisting of white ducks and sweater with crest. Junior membership had reached approximately one hundred and forty, and monthly general meetings were held at that time.

War greatly disrupted junior activity in the following years and in 1944 Hon. Junior Commodore A. W. Nyblom reported that there were forty-four juniors in active service.

With the end of the war juniors again became active, and Hon. Junior Commodore Robert Maitland conducted a winter instruction programme, which was well attended. Junior enthusiasm was on the increase and in 1946 J. Elsey skippered *Whirlwind* at the International Comet Races in Maryland. The following year, Bruce Carter, also in *Whirlwind,* represented the club in the Comet World Series. It was during this period that the club purchased two Comets, *Red Devil* and the *Trident,* for junior use. In later years the *Red Devil* was sold to John Williams, and until recently it was still actively sailed.

Commodore B. L. Johnson saw the need for extended junior facilities and it was at his urging that the junior clubroom and other facilities on the floats at Jericho were erected during the winter of 1949-50.

Also at this time the beautiful Frederick & Nelson Trophy was presented as a perpetual trophy to develop junior sailing talent. The winners over the ensuing years have been

1950	Stuart Shelley	1955	Laurel Tupper	1960	Doug Helmer
1951	Bob Little	1956	John Purdy	1961	Colin Park
1952	John Yuill	1957	Glen Smith	1962	Not Awarded
1953	Diana Wilson	1958	Steve Tupper	1963	Bob Lance
1954	Dennis Pennell	1959	Audrey Roscoe	1964	Tim Meakin

To further develop all-round seamanship amongst the juniors, Past Commodore Capt. B. L. Johnson donated to the Club a One Thousand Dollar Bond, the yearly interest from which to be awarded annually to the junior (12 to 17 years of age, boat owner or skipper) most outstanding, based on merits and demerits as designated. The winners have been

1954	Dennis Pennell	1957	Dave Miller	1960	Colin Park
1955	Steve Tupper	1958	Dave Miller	1961	R. Maitland
1956	Steve Tupper	1959	Dave Miller	1964	Colin Park

In 1956, with the introduction of the Junior Training Programme (see following chapter), and the subsequent interest in the Flattie Class sloops, junior participation increased tremendously. For the first time, Royal Van. was represented in the North American Junior Championships Eliminations. A crew headed by Steve Tupper with crews Bill Falcus and John Dill placed fourth in the races, held in Bellingham. A full racing schedule was enthusiastically followed, and highlights included the introduction of a Point to Point Long Distance Race from Royal Van. to Snug Cove. David Miller, with crew Dick Roscoe, placed first. The Passage Island Race, another first, provided a thrilling ride for all. That fall, Royal Van. juniors were also invited to enter the McCurdy Challenge Cup. Steve Tupper, Bill Falcus, Colin Park and Dave Miller placed first in these races, which were held in Seattle.

R.V.Y.C. juniors are keen Frostbite cailors, and in 1955 the Kitten Class Trophy was assigned for international competition at the annual winter regatta held between individuals from Pacific Northwest yacht clubs in Seattle, Victoria and Vancouver. Team racing at the winter regatta was allotted the W. Clarke Gibson Trophy, and the winners have been

	Kitten Trophy (individual)	Clarke Gibson Trophy (team)
1957	Steve Tupper	R.V.Y.C.
1958	Steve Tupper	R.V.Y.C.
1959	Rae Ellen Ramey	Corinthian Y.C., Seattle
1960	Dave Miller	R.V.Y.C.
1961	Jeff Steinborn (C.Y.C.)	R.V.Y.C.
1961	Colin Park	R.V.Y.C.
1962	Don Martin	Seattle Y.C.
1964	Don Martin	R.V.Y.C.
1965	Bob Crossley	R. Victoria Y.C.

In the North American Junior Sailing Championship for the Sears Cup, held for the first time in English Bay August, 1958, Dave Miller, with crew Steve Tupper, Colin Park and alternate Paul Sturdy, placed second. The contest was sailed in Flatties (see chapter on Flatties).

During this year the junior clubroom was renovated and lockers for junior use were installed.

The P.I.Y.A. was also hosted by Royal Van., and juniors made an excellent showing in the Flattie Class. Dave Miller in *Silver Wings* placed first, Steve Tupper skippering *Wing Ding* placed second, and Colin Park at the helm of *Schuss* placed fourth. Dave and Steve went on to sail in the Flattie World Championships held in Seattle, where Dave placed second and Steve seventh.

1959 saw junior sailors travelling farther afield. At the Sears Cup Finals in Noroton, Connecticut, Dave Miller and crew Colin Park, Ken Baxter and Jon Fladgate placed third. The Flattie World Championships at Lake Cachuma, California, saw Dave Miller, sailing his *Silver Wings,* place fourth. Again that year the junior made a good showing in the Flattie Class at the P.I.Y.A. in Bellingham.

1960 proved an outstanding year. In the World Flattie Championships here on English Bay, Dave Miller, sailing *Silver Wings,* the boat in which his father with his mother crewing had won this same championship in 1938, placed first. No sooner was the prizegiving over than Dave packed his bags and with Colin Park, Ken Baxter and Bob Lance took off for the Sears Cup Finals in Green Lake, Wisconsin, there again to place first. Meanwhile Ron Maitland, Alex Harrison, Alex Foley and Don Martin were headed back to Montreal for the Canadian Junior Olympic Regatta. This was the first time this regatta was held, and the youngsters made an excellent showing. Ron and Alex placed fourth in a fleet of forty Flying Junior Dutchmen, while Alex Foley and Don placed second in a fleet of twenty Fireflies.

By 1961, junior membership numbered three hundred and six, and the Flattie Class, now renamed Geary 18's after the class designer Ted Geary, was very active. The Geary 18 World Championships at Lake Arrowhead, California, saw Colin Park place seventh in *Tammie*. Dave Miller, Colin Park, Alex Harrison and Tim Meakin headed off to St. Petersburg, Florida, to defend their Sears Cup title, placing third in heavy winds. At the same time Alex Foley and Don Martin were in Montreal taking another crack at the Canadian Jr. Championship title, which they managed to win this time.

Also introduced that summer was the exchange of a junior sailor from Royal Van. with one from the Jr. Yachting Associations of Long Island. Alan Sturgess came back with glowing reports of his summer experiences. Peter Tufts, the representative from the east, will be remembered by many for his enthusiasm and friendship.

The North American Intercollegiate Championships started off the round of highlights in 1962. Dave Miller, Bob Healey, Colin Park and Owen Wright combined their efforts to place third amongst the ten top college teams in North America in the races in Newport, California. Next on the list, Colin Park, sailing *Tammie,* placed second by a disheartening quarter point in the Geary 18 World Championships in Coos Bay, Oregon. Meanwhile, Alan Sturgess was in the process of finishing third in the Pacific Coast Lightning Championships held in Seattle. Shortly afterwards, Norm Angus and Bob Crossley, sailing in Halifax, placed eighth in the Canadian Junior Sailing Championships. Back at home several new series were added to an already bulging racing schedule. The first OK Dinghy Regatta was held on July 21 and 22. An Okanagan Yacht Club Challenge was set up in which we send a team to the Okanagan in the early summer and they send a team to race here later in the summer. The Intermediate Challenge, strictly for those between the ages of seventeen and twenty, was raced for against Royal Victoria Yacht Club.

Again in 1963, the North American Intercollegiate Championships heads the schedule. "A" Division team, Dave Miller, Doug Race and Paddy Maitland, and "B" Division team, Colin Park, Paul Walters and Marylile Martin, combined efforts to take fifth place in the races sailed in Cambridge, Mass. An exchange with the Junior Yachting Association of Long Island Sound was again successful. Ron Maitland went east and John Saunders came west. In the list of individual glories: Colin Park took the North American OK Dinghy Championship in Seattle; Dave Miller, sailing *Glisten,* placed sixth in a field of sixty-seven entries at the Star Class North American Championships in Rye, N.Y.; a week later, in Chicago, Dave was in seventh position when dismasted in the fourth race of the Star World Championships;

late in August third place went to Don Martin, Alex Foley and Tim Meakin in the Sears Cup Finals in Newport, California.

1964 was a busy year for many of the juniors. June 14-19 saw the U.B.C. Sailing Club and the Royal Vancouver Yacht Club co-hosting the North American Intercollegiate Sailing Championships. Perhaps the best thankyou possible to those who had worked and planned so long was to see the U.B.C. team of Colin Park, Doug Helmer, Rich Helmer and Alex Foley finish the winners. With all the preparation work North American Intercollegiate President Colin Park did have time, however, to hop over to La Rochelle, France, for an OK Dinghy Invitational Regatta, in which he placed seventh. Colin came home to take the OK Dinghy Class North American Championships here on English Bay in his new boat *Mariah*. Canadian Olympic Trials followed closely in Kingston, Ontario. In these, Dave Miller, with his crew Bill West, sailing *Glisten,* won the right to represent Canada at the Olympics in Tokyo, Japan. Barry Clark and Alex Harrison, sailing with Steve Tupper on *Audax*, placed sixth in the Dragon Class. It seemed that Dave had just returned home from the trials when he had to hop a plane back again to sail Bonar Davis' Star *Simba* in the Star World Championships in Boston, Mass. Unfortunately dismasting put him out of contention in the series. In the Sears Eliminations in Eugene, Oregon, Bob Crossley, with crew Robbie Black, placed third. Alan Drinkwater and Frank Mantle represented Royal Van. in the Canadian Junior Championships here on English Bay.

This is but a resume of the highlights of junior activity in recent years. Throughout the past few years the Junior Division, with the help and guidance of the seniors, have maintained a full schedule of activities all year round. As to the 1965 list of highlights—the first one is already in. Colin Park placed first in the Canadian Sabot Championships. As to the future—we shall see!

Junior training programme in 16 Flying Juniors.

JUNIOR EXECUTIVE

	1935	**1936**	**1937**
Hon. Jr. Commodore	Harold A. Jones	T. M. Ramsay	Cedric J. Dill
Jr. Commodore	Ken. Glass	F. J. Whitcroft	J. D. Maitland

	1938	**1939**	**1940**
Hon. Jr. Commodore	Temple H. Wright	Temple H. Wright	Temple H. Wright
Jr. Commodore	Stanley Davies	Bud Day	Dana Ramsay
Jr. Vice Commodore	Bud Day	Tom Bolton	
Jr. Secy.-Treasurer	Don Brooke	Ernest Thompson	George Dill
Jr. Fleet Captain	Terry Thompson	Dana Ramsay	John Barltrop

	1941	**1942**	**1943**
Hon. Jr. Commodore	E. F. (Jack) Cribb	A. W. Nyblom	A. W. Nyblom
Jr. Commodore	George L. Cran		Jeff Morris
Jr. Vice Commodore			Don Wilson
Jr. Secy.-Treasurer			Leroy Elsey
Jr. Fleet Captain			Doug Woodley

	1944	**1945**	**1946**
Hon. Jr. Commodore	A. W. Nyblom	A. W. Nyblom	Robert R. Maitland
Hon. Jr. Fleet Captain			H. E. Wylie
Jr. Commodore			Charles Bayne
Jr. Vice Commodore			Donald Warner
Jr. Fleet Captain			John Lillico
Jr. Secy.-Treasurer			James Hughes

	1947	**1948**	**1949**
Hon. Jr. Commodore	R. W. R. Day	Dr. Cecil Helmer	Dr. C. D. Helmer
Jr. Commodore	Charles Bayne	Howard Eckman	Bruce Carter
Jr. Vice Commodore	Jock Ferrie	James Hamilton	Ronald Kelly
Jr. Fleet Captain	Howard Eckman	Bruce Carter	Robert Little
Jr. Secy.-Treasurer	Bruce Carter	Miss Diane Bancroft	Miss J. Gyles
Jr. Hon. Measurer		Gerry Reynolds	Ted Protheroe

	1950	**1951**	**1952**
Hon. Jr. Commodore	S. G. Foley	Bud Roulstone	E. J. Palmer
Jr. Commodore	L. Ortengren	*Stuart Shelley	John Yuill
Jr. Vice Commodore	E. J. R. Boulter	*Miss Audrey Wilson	Peter Shields
Jr. Fleet Captain	S. Shelley	Bob Little	Rod Madison
Jr. Secretary	Miss A. Wilson	Miss Sheila Astbury	Miss Diana Wilson
Jr. Measurer	F. H. Stearman	Jim Cain	Gordon Mitchell

*There were TWO Junior Commodores elected in 1951 due to Stuart Shelley moving away after his term started. By election, Miss Audrey Wilson—the first GIRL to fill the post—was confirmed as Junior Commodore and accomplished her duties very acceptably; in addition, she married during her term of office, becoming Mrs. W. M. Robson.

	1953	**1954**	**1955**
			Stanley Davies
Hon. Jr. Commodore	E. J. Palmer		J. H. K. Miller
Jr. Commodore	Bruce Bennett	Rod R. Maddison	G. VanNorman
Jr. Vice Commodore	Rusty LePage	John W. Purdy	L. J. Baker
Jr. Fleet Captain	Rod Maddison	Jack Kingscote	Sonia Baker
Jr. Secretary	Miss D. Wilson	Sally Cross	S. McG. Tupper
Jr. Measurer	Gordon Mitchell	Stephen Tupper	

	1956	**1957**	**1958**
Hon. Jr. Commodore	R. A. Delaplace	C. L. Rickard	N. T. Park
Jr. Commodore	John Purdy	G. Smith	Stephen Tupper
Jr. Vice Commodore	Rod Maddison	Bill Falcus	John Dill
Jr. Fleet Captain	Brian Lake	S. Tupper	Doug. Helmer
Jr. Secretary	Laurel Tupper	Miss Laurel Tupper	Audrey Roscoe
Jr. Measurer	Bill Falcus	J. Dill	Colin Park

	1959	**1960**	**1961**
Hon. Jr. Commodore	N. T. Park	N. T. Park	N. T. Park
Jr. Commodore	Miss Laurel Tupper	Doug. Helmer	Bob Lance
Jr. Vice Commodore	Dick Roscoe	Miss Audrey Roscoe	Miss Audrey Roscoe
Jr. Fleet Captain	Dave Miller	Richard Helmer	Colin Park
Jr. Secretary	Miss Audrey Roscoe	Miss Paddy Maitland	Miss Diane Sturdy
Jr. Measurer	Colin Park	Bruve Lance	Alan Sturgess

	1962	**1963**	**1964**
Hon. Jr. Commodore	K. G. Clark	Darrel D. Jones	Darrel D. Jones
Jr. Commodore	Paul Sturdy	Bob Lance	Tim Meakin
Jr. Vice Commodore	Miss Audrey Roscoe	Miss Mary Lile Martin	John Grubbe Jr.
Jr. Fleet Captain	Alan Sturgess	Colin Park	Don Martin
Jr. Secretary	Miss Diane Parsons	Miss Diane Parsons	Miss Diane Sturdy
Jr. Treasurer	Bob Lance	Don Martin	Norman Angus

	1965
Hon. Jr. Commodore	G. Alan Martin
Jr. Commodore	Norman Angus
Jr. Vice Commodore	Miss Valerie Hennell
Jr. Fleet Captain	Bob Crossley
Jr. Secretary	Miss Sue Maitland
Jr. Treasurer	Miss Mary Fladgate

SUPERVISED JUNIOR
TRAINING PROGRAMME
AT R.V.Y.C.

IT IS SAID that sailors are "born, not made", but modern organized and supervised training goes a long long way to making champion sailors —as witness the fine crop of racing skippers being turned out by our regular summer programme of junior training and the history of their achievements just related.

Previous to 1956 our training of juniors was decidedly "hit or miss". Older juniors tried to whip younger juniors into shape and to an extent they certainly succeeded, but it was largely a case of a good skipper training a good crew and a not-so-good skipper being less successful in his training tactics.

The senior Executive Committee was very conscious of this, but it remained for a few fathers of budding sailor sons and daughters agitating for hiring professional qualified help, to get action in establishing a sound basic training programme.

Under Commodore J. M. Kerr in 1956 a strong honorary junior committee was appointed, headed by Ray A. Delaplace and consisting of Past Commodore J. D. Maitland, Bert Tupper, E. S. Earle and Bonar Davis, and these are the men who studied, planned and organized the present highly successful annual junior training programme, which embodies qualified instruction in water safety, swimming, and the rudiments of seamanship. Three thousand dollars was allotted to the setting up of the programme and the construction of four eighteen foot Flatties. Later several additional Flatties were donated anonymously by seniors.

The programme started on July 1st and ended on Labour Day, under the capable leadership of Bob Morford, a graduate of Physical Education at U.B.C. Three juniors: Stephen Tupper, Audrey Roscoe and Bill Falcus, assisted Mr. Morford, and the four Flatties and three Cadets were used as training boats. As well as a full programme of instruction at the Jericho Station, swimming instruction was given twice a week at Empire Pool. The thirty students were examined at the end of the summer and awarded the rank of Skipper, Able-seaman and Leading-seaman according to their stage of advancement.

In the following year the programme continued to grow under the leadership of Mr. Bud MacFarlane. Two new Flatties were added to the fleet. Steve Tupper, Audrey Roscoe and Dick Roscoe acted as instructors.

In 1958, when Mr. Fred Root took over the programme, three new Flatties were purchased, bringing the total fleet to nine Flatties and three Cadets. Audrey Roscoe, Steve Tupper and Dick Roscoe, with Mrs. Root, assisted Fred. Mr. Root lead the programme for the three succeeding years and it was under his leadership in 1961 that the programme, now handling more than one hundred students, was divided up into senior, intermediate and junior classes. The nine Flatties were completely refurbished and the staff was enlarged to accommodate the high enrollment. Steve Tupper and Audrey Roscoe again assisted, along with three other juniors: Tim Irwin, Bob Lance and Paul Sturdy.

It was in 1962, under the leadership of Stephen Tupper, that the programme was first divided into two one-month sections with approximately one hundred students in each term. Eight new Flying Junior Dutchmen were purchased, to bring the total number of boats to seventeen. Junior instructors this year included Audrey Roscoe, Marylile Martin, Alex Harrison, Paul Sturdy and Diane Sturdy. The following year eight more Flying Juniors were purchased and the nine Flatties were sold to club members. In 1964 Jack Kingscote lead the programme for a successful summer, while Stephen Tupper will again take it over for the coming season. Eight new Flying Juniors have been purchased, while the first eight have been sold to club members.

The Junior Programme has achieved many things. First and foremost it has taught many youngsters the pleasure of sailing and how to do it safely. It has been instrumental in producing top international junior sailors, notably Colin Park and David Miller. A third achievement is not perhaps the aim of the programme; the majority of instructors over the years have been "older" junior members—perhaps teaching others to sail has taught them something about sailing and about getting along with people.

The brilliant splash of colour on English Bay fronting our Jericho Clubhouse presented during July and August by the smart well-cut sails of the junior training ships naturally caught the attention of lady members entertaining at the clubhouse, and a number of them in 1958 expressed desire to take part in such an obviously enjoyable sport. Accordingly Mrs. Ed Bottrell, an expert handler of small boats, volunteered to organize a Ladies' Sailing Programme, which was launched that year with a limited number of participants.

In 1963 the Ladies' Sailing Programme was headed by Mr. Steve Tupper, with 30 members' wives participating in classes on Tuesday evenings and Wednesday afternoons. The lively Flying Juniors were used to give the ladies a basic knowledge of sailing and to give them a chance to take part in the exciting, enjoyable sport. Next year Jack Kingscote supervised the Ladies' Programme, with 40 ladies taking part, and this year (1965) the class will be under the supervision of Mr. Steve Tupper.

CHAPTER 26

Post War Sailing Yachts

FROM 1938 ON

AIDA—26 ft. sloop, built 1958 at New Westminster. Owned by H. B. Vogel from 1958 on.

ALANA—36 ft. 6 Metre sloop, built in Great Britain. Imported by Sandy Martin 1952, owned by Ches Rickard 1954-56.

ALCION—47 ft. A Class sloop, built from Monk designs by Chappel Boat Works in 1947. Owned by Mr. McGregor 1947 to 1950, M. Young 1950 to 1953, L. A. Watts 1954 to 1959 and by Colin D. Campbell from 1959 to date.

AMBERJACK—32 ft. PC sloop, Kettenburg design, built Vancouver Shipyard 1946 for Temple H. Wright. Owned by Stu Foley 1948 to 1951, D. M. MacDonald 1951 to 1962; he circumnavigated Vancouver Island in her.

AMITA—48 ft. 8 Metre sloop, Fife of Fairlie design, built 1930 on Clyde. Imported by Stan Davies 1954, was flagship for Commodore Davies in 1961. Sold to F. K. Dennison and Sven Rasmussen 1961-65.

ANN—B Class sloop owned by J. H. Buchannan 1949-.

APACE—41 ft. BB Class sloop, owned by J. Bowron 1956 to 1958.

AQUILLA ex **WILDCAT**—26 ft. Hi-Ho Class sloop, Halliday design, built by Taylor Shipyard. Owned by W. J. Polglase 1958 to 1960.

ARGONAUT—30 ft. sloop. Owned by C. R. Fogal 1957 to 1960.

ARIEL—29 ft. B Class sloop, designed by J. Alden, built at Halifax, N.S. Brought out by Cedric Dill 1946, owned by Lorne Kyle 1948 to 1954, E. H. Killam and M. H. Moan 1963 to date.

ARIKI—30 ft. Spencer Class sloop, designed by Halliday, built at Boeing's Shipyards, Vancouver, in 1937 for R.V.Y.C. syndicate. Owned by C. J. Dill 1938 to 1941.

AUDAX—29 ft. Dragon Class sloop, Johann Anker design, built in Norway. Imported by Ken G. Clark 1961 and raced consistently to date.

BARRACOUTA II—35 ft. B Class sloop, design by Boyce, built Chappell Yards. Owned by Wright Chappell 1948-51, K. J. McRae 1951-53, H. Herlihy 1954-60.

BALLERINA—29 ft. Dragon Class sloop, Johann Anker design, built in Norway. Imported by J. S. Smith 1962.

BENORA—C Class sloop, built by Harry Herlihy in 1938, who sailed her till 1943 when sold to Gus Ortengren, who sailed her till 1947.

BENORA II—36 ft. L36 Class sloop, Lapworth design, built for H. Herlihy 1960.

BLOWFLY ex **MOLLIE BONN,** ex **OLE,** ex **TWO BITS**—J. Anker design, built by Aage Birch, Humblebaek, Denmark. Imported 1956 by Jorgen Baers of Victoria, owned by H. Horne 1957-62, A. W. Baker 1962-64, and now by H. J. (Johnnie) Burnett of Thetis Island, Gulf Islands, B.C.

BLUE HERON—47 ft. A Class sloop, W. G. Roue design, built 1929 at Shelbourne, N.S. Owned by Dr. S. L. Williams 1953-.

BLUE WAVE—33 ft. B Class yawl, built by Rodd & Sons, Victoria. Owned by Colin D. Campbell 1950-60.

BUCCANEER III—47 ft. A Class sloop, designed by W. G. Roue, built 1929 at Shelbourne, N.S. Brought to Pacific Coast by Bill Smith in 1946, who sold to H. A. Wallace 1948, owned by Russell K. Baker 1956-60, Vic Grimson 1961-.

BUCCANEER V ex **GWEN**—34 ft. yawl, built 1939 at East Boothbay, Maine. Brought to Pacific Coast by Mr. Bill Smith and sold by him to Fred O. Mills 1945, who sold to Vernon and Evelyn Kirkby 1951. Mr. Kirkby changed her name to Buccaneer V and still sails her.

BRIS—31 ft. sloop, designed by Von Hellesborg and built in Denmark. Brought to Pacific Coast by Sven Rasmussen in 1956, who sailed her till 1961 when sold to J. S. Motherwell in 1962, who still owns her.

CAM ex **LADY NAN**—29 ft. Dragon Class sloop (first Dragon in Canada, and numbered D KC1), designed by J. Anker, Norway. Imported by W. H. (Bud) Day in 1951. Owned by J. P. Leslie 1956 and from 1957 to date by Jack Shepherd.

CAMBRIA—30 ft. B Class sloop, designed, built and owned by W. E. (Bill) Cunningham 1948 to date.

CA VA now **TRIM**—38 ft. 6 Metre sloop, built 1938 in Denmark. Imported 1953 by Phil and Sid Miller.

CAVALIER—29 ft. sloop, designed by Roger de Quincy and built in St. George Yard, Walberswick, England, in 1953. Imported 1955 by Capt. B. L. Johnson and still sailed by him.

CIRRUS—34 ft. ketch, designed and built by Ray Delaplace 1961.

COHO—35 ft. sloop, designed by J. Brandlmayr Ltd., built by Spencer Boats Ltd. in 1962. Owned by J. Brandlmayr and sold in 1963 to Mr. R. Glube, Royal Nova Scotia Yacht Squadron, and re-named Rochelle II.

COMTESSA—32 ft. Seafair sloop, designed by Ben Seaborn. Owned by Stu Foley 1962 to date.

CONCERTO—48 ft. 8 Metre sloop, designed by Fife of Fairlie, built on the Clyde in 1937. Imported from Scotland by Cedric Gyles 1955. Owned by Bob Ross 1956 to 1963, A. R. Booth 1964-.

CORAL REEF now **PENELAKUT**—46 ft. sloop, designed by L. Ben Seaborn, built Vancouver for A. W. (Art) Way 1959, who sailed her till 1963. Bought by R. D. (Bob) Ross in 1964.

CHERE AMIE—28 ft. sloop, designed by T. Halliday and built at Taylor Boat Works for Dr. J. C. Grimson in 1939, who sailed her till 1950.

CONDOR V—30 ft. B Class sloop, designed by R. H. Richards and built at Pelagic Yard, Victoria. Owned by J. S. Motherwell in 1964.

DELPHIN—40 ft. cruiser 8 Metre sloop, designed by A. C. Robb and built 1952 at Shandon, Scotland. Imported by A. W. (Art) Way 1956. Owned by E. Chisholm 1958-1962, T. W. Donovan 1963-1965, sold to Capt. R. Oliver 1965.

DIANA—29 ft. Dragon Class sloop, designed by J. Anker, Norway. Owned 1956-57 by J. Vangolen.

DOLPHIN II—35 ft. sloop, designed by Boyce, built by Chappell Boat Works. Owned by Wright Chappell 1950, sold to Harry J. Bird in 1952, who sold to Cardo B. Smalley 1953. Owned by John Grubbe 1956 to 1963.

DOROTHY—B Class sloop, designer and builder unknown. Owned by G. W. Burnett 1948 to 1956.

ELOMAR—26 ft. Hi-Ho Class sloop, designed by T. Halliday, built at Taylor's Boat Yard 1940 for J. M. Kerr, who sold to L. A. Watts in 1945. Owned by Dr. Hugh Ross from 1948 to date.

ELUSIVE—34 ft. Roedde Class sloop, designed by Halliday, built by Taylor Boat Yard for W. R. Morrow in 1948, who sailed her till 1956. Owned by K. Y. Lochhead from 1957 to 1964.

ERRANT I—26 ft. Hi-Ho Class sloop, designed by Halliday, built by Tom Taylor Boat Yard. Owned by Keith C. Middleton from 1948 to 1961. Sold out of club.

ESCAPEE—39 ft. cutter, built by Talbot-Lehman, Sydney, N.S.W. in 1940. Owned by Phil (Phip) Brock 1948 to 1950, C. Patey 1950 to 1957, H. J. Burnett 1957 to 1963, R. Sykes 1963-.

EVERYWHERE—26 ft. Hi-Ho Class sloop, designed by Halliday, built at Taylor Boat Yard. Owned by R. Vittery 1948, C. Campbell 1956-.

FAEM—36 ft. L36 Class sloop, designed by Lapworth, built Vancouver for D. and M. Findlay in 1961.

FAIR LADY II.—32 ft. Seafair Class sloop, designed by Seaborn, built Vancouver 1960 for A. C. Loach.

FANTASIE II—34 ft. Roedde Class sloop, designed by Halliday, built by T. Taylor for Jack G. Williamson in 1947. Owned and sailed continuously by Jack and Olive Williamson to date.

FINTRA II—34 ft. sloop, built in 1933 at Fairlie, Scotland. Owned by Ortengren and Granger 1954 to 1956.

FISKA—30 ft. schooner, built at Halifax, N.S. Owned 1946 by Miklos Senyi.

FLEET FAIRY—33 ft. sloop, designed by Uffa Fox, built at Cowes, Isle of Wight. Owned by E. D. Stone and Jack Cribb 1952, since then by E. D. (Doug) Stone.

FLYING WALRUS—26 ft. sloop, owned by I. J. Davidson 1951-53, R. D. Ross 1954-1955, and E. N. R. Elliott from 1956 to 1960.

FOIL—29 ft. Dragon Class sloop, designed by Anker, built in Norway. Owned by Mrs. Jill Sims (nee Biller) 1959 to date.

FULMAR—48 ft. 8 Metre sloop, designed by Fife of Fairlie, built 1930. Imported by Charles Bayne 1954, who sailed her till 1956 when sold to Dr. J. E. Balmer, who still sails her.

FUNDY II ex **SHANGRA-LA**—26 ft. Hi-Ho Class sloop, designed by Halliday, built and owned by Sid Humphries 1941. Sold to Ned Ashe, Victoria, 1948, who sold her to Walter Walsh, 1948. Owned by K. M. Lightbody 1952 to 1954, C. S. Walker 1956 to date.

GANESSA—28 ft. C Class sloop, designed by Halliday and built by J. A. Longley in 1934, who sold her to A. W. Nyblom in 1938. "Nye" sailed her actively till 1954. Owned 1955 by Stu Watts. Terry Towns owned her 1955 to 1957.

GABRIELLE II—48 ft. yawl re-rigged 1964 to sloop, designed by K. H. Reimers, built 1947 at Hastholmsvarvet, Sweden. Imported by P. R. Sandwell in 1958 and sailed by him to date.

GEORGE KITAMIKE—38 ft. sloop, built Vancouver. Owned by Hamish Davidson 1962-.

GINI II—32 ft. sloop, owned by Ian Ross 1962-.

GOLDEN HIND III—37 ft. 6 Metre sloop built by Morgan Giles Ltd. in 1948 at Teignmouth, Eng. Owned by Capt. M. G. Corbeil 1955, and from 1955 on by Lorne S. Kyle.

GOMETRA—43 ft. sloop, designed by Milne, built on Clyde. The famous "Gold Ship" (see story elsewhere in History). Brought to Pacific Coast by J. G. (Gus) Ortengren 1948. In 1950 Ken Glass and E. J. Palmer owned her, and in 1953 Elmer J. Palmer, who still sails her.

GWEN ex **BUCCANEER**, now **BUCCANEER V.** (see).

HALCYON II—35 ft. cutter, designed by Monk, built 1949 by Nicholson, Victoria. Owned by T. T. (Terry) Towns 1957 on.

HAWK—47 ft. Bird Class sloop, designed by W. G. Roue, designer of the famous Bluenose, built 1929 at Shelbourne, N.S. Brought to Pacific Coast 1946 by J. C. (Jim) McPherson who sailed her until 1956, when sold to Ralph Farris who still owns her.

HAZEL MAID—39 ft cutter, designed by Robt. Clark and built at Shoreham, Eng. Imported in 1957 by R. H. (Rollie) Ellison, who still sails her.

HECATE—36 ft. 6 Metre sloop, designed by Nicholson, built in Great Britain. Imported by Sandy Martin 1954 and sold to Seattle 1958.

HI HO—26 ft. C Class sloop after which the Hi-Ho Class was named. Designed by Halliday and built by Tom Taylor for George A. Cran in 1938. Sold to M. J. (Mike) Lucas in 1951, who sold her out of the club in 1957.

HILMAR—22 ft. D Class sloop, owned by Claude and Eileen Hill 1941, J. K. Sloan, S. Burke and D. A. Sloan 1946-51, H. W. Eckman 1951-53, Ted Suttle 1953-.

HULDRA ex **KAREN WELLS**—25 ft. sloop, built at Poole, Eng. Imported 1959 by Per T. Christoffersen, who still sails her.

HYMAC—34 ft. Roedde Class sloop, designed by Halliday, built by Tom Taylor for Dr. Robt. McCaffery in 1948, who sold her to Stan Davies in 1951. Sold to N. S. Vallance 1954, who sold her out of the club in 1958.

HALF MOON—26 ft. C Class sloop, owned by Hamish Davidson in 1946 and L. G. D. Fraser 1947-1955.

IDYLOURS—29 ft. C Class sloop. Owned by Dr. Jack MacMillan from 1952-55, Lloyd Campbell from 1956 to 1958.

ISHBELL—22 ft. sloop, owned and sailed by Justice Sidney Smith.

JENETTA—71.5 ft. 12 Metre sloop, designed by Alfred Mylne for Sir William Burton in 1938, built 1938-39 by Bute Slip Dock Co., Isle of Bute, Scotland. Bought in 1953 by D. P., F. W. and Victoria M. Urry when on a visit to the U.K. Converted to ketch rig by the Urrys in consultation with designer Robt. Clark and next season brought to Vancouver on deck of freighter. On the death of D. P. Urry in 1961 she has been owned and sailed by F. Wavell and Victoria M. Urry to date.

JESTER ex **HEATHER VI**—36 ft. L36, designed by Lapworth, built 1959 by Tom Taylor for J. Innes. Owned by S. B. Watts 1961 to date.

JUNO II—37.5 ft. 6 Metre sloop, designed by Nicholson, built at Gosport, Eng., in 1948. Imported by R. W. R. (Bob) Day in 1955, who sold her to D. F. (Denny) Wotherspoon 1956, who sold to the U.S. 1963.

KRIS—29 ft. Dragon Class sloop, designed by Anker, built in Norway. Owned by R. W. Butt, K. Downey and D. Skibbe 1964-.

KANTAKI—32 ft. cutter, owned by D. Barraclough 1964-.

KAINUI—25 ft. sloop, owned by B. S. Lowe 1961-.

KAISUN II—38 ft. sloop, built by Tom Taylor for Stan Davies in 1961.

KALLISTE—28 ft. sloop, designed by Laurent Giles & Partners Ltd., built 1938 at Lymington, Eng. Imported by Norm Park 1954, who still sails her.

KINI—37.5 ft. 6 Metre sloop, designed by McGuier, built on the Clyde in 1937. Imported by J. D. Maitland, P. V. O. Evans, W. G. Dolmage and L. B. Culter in 1954. Bought by Walter Sturdy in 1958, who sold her out of the club in 1959.

LEMOLO—36 ft. Evergreen Class sloop, built in New Westminster 1963. Owned by Hugh P. Brady to date.

LADY NAN—See Cam.

LALONGA—30 ft. C Class sloop, designed by R. V. James, built by James for Cardo B. Smalley in 1958, who sailed her till 1960.

LONG GONE—36 ft. L36 sloop, designed by Lapworth. Owned by J. G. Innes 1961-.

LADY LUCK—30 ft. Spencer Class sloop, built at Boeings Shipyard 1937 for R.V.Y.C. syndicate, designed by Halliday. Raffled to A. C. Taylor 1937.

MARCELLE II—32 ft. sloop, designed by Halliday, built by Frank E. Godwin in 1950 and owned by him to date.

MARCHESA ex **CAMIRAM**—32 ft. Seafair Class sloop, designed by L. Ben Seaborn, built for Mackenzie Bowell in 1956. Owned by G. A. Martin from 1957 to date.

MAREDEA—36 ft. L36 class sloop, designed by Lapworth, built for R. G. Lundy 1959 to 1963. Art Way 1964 to date.

MARY BOWER—49 ft. cutter, designed by Robt. Clark, built in Solent Shipyards, Eng. Imported by K. J. (Ken) McRae 1955 and sailed by him till 1962, when sold to J. V. Long.

MASKEE—29 ft. Dragon Class sloop, designed by Anker and built in Norway. Owned by G. Horder 1957 to 1960.

MISS LEE—34 ft. Roedde Class sloop, designed by Halliday, built by Tom Taylor for L. B. Culter 1948. Sold to T. L. Daniels 1952, who sold her out of the club in 1956.

MOLLIE BONN—See Blowfly.

MARLIN I now **VOGAD I**—30 ft. Spencer Class sloop, designed by Halliday, built at Boeing Shipyards by R.V.Y.C. syndicate. The winner of this ship was Bob E. Cromie in 1937. He sold to Jack MacDougal.

NEPTUNE—28 ft. C Class sloop, designed by Laurent Giles & Partners Ltd. of Lymington, Eng., and built in Kaj Christensen Yard, Vejle, Denmark, in 1960. Imported by J. V. and Alice Christensen 1961 and still sailed by them.

NERITA—C Class sloop owned by W. H. Alcock in 1938.

NIKE—29 ft. Dragon Class sloop, designed by Anker, built in Norway. Owned by R. J. Casson and S. Bowman 1960, and by R. J. Casson 1965.

NOVARA—28 ft. S28 sloop, owned by J. Brandlmayr 1959-60.

NUTMEG—36 ft. L36, designed by Lapworth, owned by W. L. Moore 1957-1959.

NYON ex **TRIMA**—36 ft. L36, designed by Lapworth, built by T. Taylor, Vancouver.

OHO—39 ft. sloop, designed by Olin Stevens, built New Westminster in 1948 for Percy R. Burr, who still owns her.

ONNA—33 ft. sloop, owned by P. R. Sandwell 1955 to 1957.

OONAH—34 ft. sloop, owned by Evans Wasson 1956 to 1962. Owned by Dr. Jack MacMillan since 1963.

ORM—29 ft. Dragon class sloop, designed by Anker, built in Norway. Owned by J. Fleming 1961 and in 1962 by C. Jukes.

PALADIN—29 ft. Dragon sloop, designed by Anker, built by Borensen of Denmark in 1938. Owned by T. I. Hughes 1961 to 1962 and by Dr. C. D. Helmer in 1964.

PANDORA OF RHU—48 ft. 8 Metre sloop, designed by Sir T. C. Glen Coats, built on the Clyde in 1938. Imported by E. R. R. Field in 1954, sold to D. P. Gray 1958, who sold to Jack Sloan 1961.

PINK CLOUD—40 ft. Newporter, cutter. Owned by Gwynne Austin, non-resident member in Seattle, 1963.

PENELAKUT—See Coral Reef.

PUFF ex **BALLOCHMYLE** ex **TWO BITS**—29 ft. Dragon Class sloop, designed by J. Anker, built by Aage Birch, Humblebaek, Denmark. Owned 1961-1963 by Dr. T. V. Jones, in 1964 by Rob Stewart, and in 1964 by John J. West.

RESTLESS—23 ft. yawl, designed by Foster, built in Vancouver. Owned 1946 by Dr. J. Scott Baxter, in 1947 by W. Campbell, 1948 to 1955 by D. C. B. Duff.

REVERIE—45 ft. cruising yawl, built at Assam, India. Sailed out from U.K. by Rev. John Antle in 1941, who owned her till 1948. Owned by C. Bayne in 1949, and by Dr. J. Balmer from 1951 to 1955.

ROMAYNE—53 ft. ketch, brought from Europe by Ed. Chisholm in 1956, who sailed her till 1959.

RUNA—30 ft. sloop, owned by R. F. B. Taylor 1957 to date.

REBEL—26 ft. C Class sloop, owned by Roy Anderson 1943 to 1958.

RRIENA—26 ft. Hi Ho Class sloop, designed by Halliday, built by Taylor for K. G. (Ken) McCandless in 1938.

SANRONAN—28 ft. sloop, owned 1960 by W. F. Kent. Ian Rogers owned in 1965.

SARCEE ex **KO NO MAURI**—32 ft. sloop, owned by C. Bailey 1961 to 1965.

SERAPIS—36 ft. L36 Class sloop, designed by Lapworth and built by T. Taylor and Pieter Rook in 1963 for A. J. F. Forsyth.

SERENDIPITY—28 ft. sloop, designed by Herreshof, built by Tom Taylor for Dr. W. J. Polglase in 1962.

SIR RON—30 ft. Spencer Class sloop, designed by Halliday, built at Boeing's Shipyards, Vancouver, in 1937 for R.V.Y.C. syndicate. Owned by J. D. Maitland 1938-1940.

SKOAL—26 ft. aux. sloop, designed by Aage Utzon, built in Denmark 1938. Owned by W. D. Kinsey 1965.

SPIRIT—66 ft. sloop, designed by Monk, modified by H. A. Jones, built Vancouver Shipyards in 1946 for Harold A. Jones, who sailed her till 1955. Now owned by Norman and Beverly McCarvill.

SPRAY—29 ft. Dragon Class sloop, designed by Anker, built in Norway. Owned 1960-1962 by John Fleming, by C. A. Jukes in 1963.

STAGHOUND ex **SHIRLEY JANE**—40 ft. motor sailer, built by E. F. (Jack) Cribb in 1954, who sold to J. M. (Ace) Lindsay in 1956, who sold to George and Bunty Donaldson in 1958, who still own her.

STROMBOLI–29 ft. Dragon Class sloop, designed by Anker, built Vancouver Shipyards in 1961 for Temple H. Wright. Sold in 1963 to C. Bayne, sold to Seattle 1964.

SWALLOW–47 ft. Bird Class sloop, designed by W. G. Roue, built 1929 at Shelbourne, N.S. Brought to Pacific Coast by J. Vans Macdonald in 1946, who sailed her for several years before selling her to Honolulu.

SERENA–32 ft. PC sloop, designed by Kettenburg, built at Vancouver Shipyards 1946 for J. A. Longley and Dr. H. G. Baker, who owned her till 1949. Owned by Mrs. V. Fox in 1952 and C. (Chuck) Bayne 1953 and 1954.

SUNDOWNER ex **ANCHORITE**–40 ft. BB Class yawl, designed by Knud Riemers, built Posnam, Costa Rica, and Wilmington, Calif. in 1959. Owned by P. M. and D. L. Amcotts, non-resident members, Kaneohe, Hawaii.

SANDERLING–36 ft. L36, designed by Lapworth, built by Taylor for Art and Jean Meakin in 1964.

SIKI–24 ft. C Class sloop, owned by Chris Justice in 1964.

TAHUNA–C Class sloop owned in 1938 by Arthur Cox.

TAI SHAN–29 ft. sloop, owned by H. N. Ellis 1951-1957.

TJEP–29 ft. Dragon Class sloop, designed by Anker, built in Norway. Owned by J. Barltrop 1955-1957 and R. F. Burgess from 1958 to date.

TOM BOY II–34 ft. Roedde Class sloop, designed by Halliday, built by Taylor for T. W. Baird in 1948, who sailed her till 1950. Owned by H. G. Barkes 1951-53, A. G. Shockley from 1954 to date.

TOROA–32 ft sloop, owned by Pete and Audrey Rees 1958 to date.

TREVEDA–34 ft. Roedde Class sloop, designed by Halliday, built by Taylor for Len Murrell in 1947. Sailed consistently by Len to date.

TRICIA–36 ft. L36 Class sloop, designed by Lapworth, built by Tom Taylor for J. Pat Leslie in 1958, who still sails her.

TROUBADOUR ex **THETIS**–65 ft. yawl, built by Abeking & Rasmussen in Bremen, Germany, 1924. Imported by Philip D. Graham in 1958, who sailed her actively till 1965, when sold to California.

TWO BITS–See Puff.

TSOLUM–28 ft. C Class sloop, designed by Mower, built by F. Thompson, who sailed her till 1947 when sold to H. J. Burnett, who sold to M. J. Lucas in 1957. Sold to Victoria in 1960.

TIFFANY–40 ft. BB Class yawl, owned by John Bowron 1964 on.

TRAMONTANA–28 ft. S28 sloop, owned by S. deKeserdy 1959-1961.

TRIM see **CA VA**

VELADA–36 ft. L36 Class sloop, designed by Lapworth, built by Taylor for John Grubbe 1963.

VELARIS—48 ft. A Class sloop, designed by Halliday, built at Crofton, V.I., by W. H. Alcock in 1953. Owned by L. H. (Lol) Killam 1960 on.

VELEDA—36 ft. L36 sloop designed by Lapworth. Built 1963 by Taylor for John Grubbe.

VOGAD—34 ft. Roedde Class sloop, designed by Halliday, built by Tom Taylor for H. R. (Bert) Tupper in 1947, sold to Dr. Jack MacMillan in 1956, who sold out of the club in 1962.

VOGAD I ex **MARLIN I**—30 ft. Spencer Class sloop, designed by Halliday, built at Boeing's 1937 for R.V.Y.C. syndicate and won by R. E. Cromie, sold to Jack MacDougal. Owned by Bert Tupper 1939.

WAYFARER II ex **MOSCA**—32 ft. sloop, designed by Rodd, built at Canoe Cove Shipyard for Dr. D. C. B. Duff in 1955, who still owns her.

WESTWIND—28 ft. C Class sloop, designed by P. Rhodes, built by Taylor in 1960 for Cardo and L. Smalley.

WHEREAWAY—37 ft. sloop, owned by Don Smith 1957.

WHANI WHANI—29 ft. motor sailer, owned by C. F. Harley 1962 on. Non-resident member.

WINSOME III—36 ft. L36 Class sloop, designed by Lapworth, built by Taylor for Ches. L. Rickard in 1958, who still sails her.

WINSOME TWO—28 ft. C Class sloop, owned by Stanley Davies 1938.

WINSTON—36 ft. Evergreen Class sloop, built at New Westminster in 1948 for Capt. B. L. Johnson, who sailed her till 1955.

WADA—32 ft. ketch, designed by G. F. Waddington, built in Sidney, V.I., in 1929. Owned by T. B. Edwards from 1939 to 1949. Sold to Acapulco.

YAHDA—30 ft. C Class sloop, designed by E. Monk of Seattle, built by Woodruff & Simmonds Ltd., Vancouver, for Chris McGregor in 1949. Owned by H. Hollick-Kenyon from 1953 to 1958.

THUNDERBIRDS—26 ft. sloops
Jehara—H. and J. Dye, 1962-.
Kalara—Larry Walters, 1962-.
Gypsy—A. R. Booth and C. Hood, 1962-.
Qa-Yel—Bob and Jo Jarvis, 1964-.
Rota—Dr. W. Otto, 1962-.
Swahlee—Jim and Liba Tyherst.
Tiki III—Russell and Marion Baker, 1964-.

CAL 20s—20 ft. sloops
Blowhard—Michael Power, 1963-.
Cal-Tiki—J. Don Black, 1963.
Mary Hester—Dr. Mac MacPherson, 1964-.
Sinbad—Sam and Margaret Toy, 1964-.

CHAPTER 27

Post War Power Cruisers

FROM 1938 ON

Vessel	Owners	Vessel	Owners
Abegweit	Ian Shaw	Caprice	K. A. Cruise
	C. B. Storch	Campanero	T. P. Barnett
Aleta	Morris Wilson	Carol II	R. Outtrem
Alva May	W. K. I ıssell	Cherfoli	T. V. Roote
Aquajoy	W. M. Bennett	Chinthe	R. W. R. Day
Acrasia	A. L. Cunningham	Cito	R. H. R. Young
	A. Gordon Bennett	Clairlyn	Dr. R. E. McKechnie
	R. W. R. Day	Clipper IV	K. Cruise
Alansana	P. W. Field		L. Killam
	R. Carfrae		Dr. J. A. McMillan
Algir	H. Cobold		Frank Bernard
Allaverdy	Capt. Roy Roberts	Corinata	W. W. Davidson
Aljo	J. G. Chutter	Coryels	J. V. W. Phillips
Aquarius	L. G. Golman	Cottonwood	L. A. Lewis
Almaro	J. Pearcy	Cover Girl	J. H. Howe
Arab	J. Newell	Cream Puff	W. M. Campbell
Arandee	R. J. Spry	Curlew	C. Wallace
	Dr. A. Francis	Cygnus	J. L. Helliwell
Arieta	T. W. Ayres	Danae	Massey Goolden
Arrow II	Jack White	Daveth	D. R. L. Rolfe
Atonic	O. A. Peterson	Deidree	W. S. Day
Avalon	E. W. Keenleyside	Deirdre II	C. H. Grinnell
Barbara B	F. L. Bott		Dr. F. Emmon
Barmar	J. C. Adams	Demijohn	H. Rendell
	W. Fred Evans	Diana Joan	Gerry D. Wilson
Bee Bee	A. M. McGavin	Dorisar	Basil H. Rae
Blue Horizon	T. W. Hethrington		L. C. de Merrall
Bonnie Pat	G. H. Gadd	Dorothy Vose	F. W. Leadbetter
Bradscott	K. F. R. Mair	Dot	W. K. Tremble
Breezin Thru	C. Wallace	Earlmar	E. B. Finning
Brendan	R. E. Leary	Eileen	T. Hamilton
Broxburn	L. A. Prosser	Eldee	L. D. Dueck
Bunty II	R. M. Andrews	Emmart	A. R. Tomlinson
Cahuenga	Dr. R. E. McKechnie		B. Atkins
Caleano	G. F. Sweet	Far West	Stan Burke
			Dr. Max Johnson

Vessel	Owners	Vessel	Owners
Fifth Fusilier	G. R. Nightingale	L. & H.	S. Darnborough
Fifer	Capt. W. M. Crawford	Lorraine	W. G. Mackenzie
	Hon. C. Wallace (Col.)	Lotis	G. Robin Hackett
Fiona II	Dr. B. J. Hallowes	Lylann	A. W. Way
Foamcrest	M. D. Campbell	Machigonne	E. W. I. Keenleyside
Free Enterprise	W. T. Money	Mahero	Roy Corbett, Seattle
Friendship	C. W. Copp	Maiha	D. Dwyer
Geva	G. E. Morrison		A. G. Smith
	Tom Pakenham	Mallard	R. H. Buchannan
Geva II	T. H. Pakenham	Malibu Teepee	T. F. Hamilton
Giggla	R. Walkem	Manona	H. Rendell
Gipsy Jean	J. May	Margaret V.	J. H. Pearcy
	O. Leigh-Spencer	Marie	Stan Morton
Gipsy Queen	G. E. Watt	Mareen	A. Simpson
Giljean	G. E. Haskamp	Minisa	J. A. Bellerby
Happy Days	Les R. Grant	Marijean	H. R. MacMillan
Harwood	A. L. McLennan	Maristan	Stan Morton
Hop A Long	J. V. Long	Mar-O-Mia	D. M. Campbell
Hulakai	Dr. J. E. Harrison	Maora I.	E. Webster
Hyak	O. Leigh-Spencer	Marrimac	J. W. McAndless
Hymac	Dr. R. D. McCaffery	Marshall Wells	J. McAdam
Icarus	W. A. Sudbury	Mary Ann	M. A. Stewart
	W. Fred Evans	Martinet	Stan Burke
Ianda	A. C. Cox	Maureen	Joe W. Wilkinson
Invader	Harry F. Reifel	Mayfly	Dr. J. McMillan
Jervis II	E. W. Sampson	Medosa I.	D. Saunders
Joleen	J. Jenkins, Bellingham	Ministik	R. M. Pye
Kauki Lani	F. T. Nicholson	Mira Booka	A. E. Jukes
Lady Joan	T. W. Baird	Miss Vancouver	H. R. Nickson
Lady Luck	J. Stuart		D. P. Dewees
Lady Vici	James Abbott	Navarre	Blake Hunt
La Caprice	Harold A. Jones	Nelverbil	V. Hoyle
Latona	O. H. Bell		Stan Leith
Latona A	O. H. Bell	New Yorker	L. H. Killam
Latona B	O. H. Bell	Nirvana II	E. A. Towns
	Mrs. F. C. Hoad	Nodlew	J. B. Smith
Lamalchi	Roy W. Ginn	Nonchalant	F. M. Kelly
Leannan	Mrs. E. E. Rose		J. C. McPherson
Leeward	Dr. R. E. McKechnie	Norda	D. Mitchell
Lei Lani	J. R. Smith	Noreanne	Norm W. Hullah
Lenora	Roy W. Ginn	Nyanza	C. L. Welch
Letitia II	Gordon Oliver	Ochichak	F. Crossman
Lorelei	W. Fred Evans	Odalisque	E. W. I. Keenleyside
	Jack Williamson		W. Clarke Gibson

Vessel	Owners	Vessel	Owners
Onaway	John Egan	Stranger	F. E. Lewis
Panda II	A. F. H. Head	Sulhamar	J. W. C. Duck
Papoose	R. M. Andrews	Surfco	E. D. Stone
	W. T. Money	Tagalong	A. D. DesBrisay
Pegasus	K. Alexander	Taihoa	W. Oliphant Bell
Pleasure	J. B. Hoffar	Tally Ho II	W. J. Lynott
	Dr. S. F. Kirkpatrick		G. E. D'Arcy
Pursuit II	K. G. McCandless	Teco II	E. D. Taylor
Raskew	Dr. J. Harrison	Tee Dee	T. A. Dutton
Ray Mac	W. G. Dolmage	Temiscouta	G. St. John
Reverie	H. Shergold	Tempest I	C. C. Teeple
Rip Tide	R. Gibson		D. C. Cromie
Ripple Point	W. G. Dolmage	Tempest II	Sam P. Cromie
	J. D. Maitland		G. W. Swney
Riot	R. C. Runge	Tequila	Dr. J. A. Sampson
Ronaldsway	E. A. Riddell	Toriann	C. H. Grinell
Rosjon	J. R. Storey	Trasnagh II	C. Frew
Runabout	K. L. MacKenzie	Twin Isles	R. M. Andrews
Pride of the West	L. A. Lewis	Tyee	B. Atkins
Saga	Percy Jenner	Victory IV	E. D. Stone
Salt Mist	J. A. Moody	Wapalu	W. Schoffield
Sandona	G. A. Hayes	Wawee III	C. A. Price
Saronia	J. S. Halse	Wee Yat	Jack Storey
Sea Gypsy	Dr. G. Dreaske	Wendy B	W. Bain
Sea Rover	G. Mort. Fergusson	West	W. R. Johnson
Sea Shell	T. A. Richardson	Wilsa	Frank Griffiths
Serapis	A. N. Skill	Wi-Ski	Sam P. Cromie
Shal-O-Mar	H. A. Borgerson	Yellow Jacket	Art Way
Sinbad I	A. S. Hudson	Yorkhome	R. J. Hyndman
Siskin	R. Carfrae	Young Carruthers	W. G. Dolmage
Skylark	Dr. G. Ellsperman	Zanthus	Jack K. Storey
Snooper	R. Q. Maxwell	Zephrus	C. H. Knox
Sokum	Capt. A. Lane	Zephyr	D. C. MacLure

M.V. MALACITE, T. F. (Bill) Orr.

M.V. MARBORENE, R. A. Osborne.

M.V. VITABELLA II, George D. Glanville.

M.V. TAKULLI, Doan M. Hartnell.

CHAPTER 28

Blue Water

CRUISING and RACING

Probably the most extended and unique cruise ever undertaken by a member of the club was the voyage of Roy G. Selman from Vancouver to Sarnia, Ont. in the 43 ft. power cruiser *B for Bob* around 1952.

Roy, Harry Proctor and another man cruised down the West Coast to San Pedro and shipped the vessel through the Panama Canal on a freighter to Puerto Rico. Mrs. Selman accompanied Roy to Puerto Rico where an engineer joined them and they took off for Miami, Florida. They put in at St. Thomas, Virgin Islands, after some severe weather and Mrs. Selman disembarked, flying to Miami to await *B for Bob's* arrival there.

Mr. and Mrs. Selman and the engineer cruised up the East Coast to New York, thence up the Hudson River and via Lake Champlain to the St. Lawrence. They proceeded up river and via Lake Ontario to Sarnia, Ont., their destination — Roy's birthplace.

Later they proceeded via the Erie Canal to the Hudson and down the East Coast to Great Bridge, Virginia, where they left the ship in fresh water storage for the winter months.

Next summer Mr. and Mrs. Selman boarded *B for·Bob* at Virginia and took off for Tampa, Florida, where it was freighted to San Francisco. Roy and his brother Bert powered up the West Coast,.returning to home waters with a log covering several thousand miles of memorable cruising.

Another wanderer was the 39 ft. cutter *Escapee*, built at Sydney, N.S.W. in 1940. Acquired by P. H. G. (Pip) Brock in 1948 he and a crew of Bob Fortune and J. O. Wells set off from Vancouver for a cruise of the fabled South Seas on May 23, 1948. They sailed to San Francisco, then to Honolulu, and before returning to Vancouver October 2nd, 1949 they cruised the following islands south of the equator — Fanning Island, Samoa, Suva, Fiji Islands, Lau Group, Tonga, Raratonga and Tahiti.

H. R. McMillan's *Marijean* cruises regularly down the West Coast to Acapulco, Mexico. Many interesting species of tropical fish have been obtained by Dr. Murray Newman for Stanley Park Aquarium through the co-operation of Mr. McMillan.

Blue water racing has attracted some of the more adventurous club members including Ken J. McRae, Phillip D. Graham, Dr. Derek Simpson and P. R. Sandwell, who have taken part in the 1961 and 1965 Trans Pacific Races from Los Angeles to Honolulu, Hawaii.

1961, *Mary Bower*, skipper Ken J. McRae, finished sixth in C Class, which had ten entries, and came twenty-seventh overall, 41 entries. Elapsed time 12 days, 23 hours, 57 minutes, 41 seconds. Corrected time 10 days, 15 hours, 13 minutes, 53 seconds.

1961, *Troubadour*, skipper P. D. Graham, finished tenth in A class which had thirteen entries, and came twenty-ninth overall, 41 entries. Elapsed time 11 days, 20 hours, 10 minutes, 54 seconds. Corrected time 10 days, 17 hours, 3 minutes, 6 seconds.

1965, *Gabrielle II*, skipper P. R. Sandwell. Elapsed time 13 days, 07 hours, 38 minutes, 11 seconds. Corrected time 10 days, 16 hours, 54 minutes, 58 seconds. B Class position tenth, twelve entries.

1965, *Nyon*, skipper Dr. Derek Simpson. Elapsed time 15 days, 06 hours, 34 minutes, 42 seconds. Corrected time, 11 days, 09 hours, 25 minutes, 08 seconds. D Class position 14th, 15 entries.

In 1962 Norman McCarvill sailed *Spirit* to third place A Class in the Acapulco Race from Los Angeles, and he also took part in the 1964 event, crewing on *Caper*, which placed second in B Class and third overall.

This year, 1965, John Innes in *Long Gone* and Lol Killam in *Velaris* raced from Neah Bay, Juan de Fuca Strait, to Kahului, Maui, Hawaii, in what is hoped to become a regular bi-annual fixture from the Pacific Northwest to Hawaii. They experienced good weather all the way and made the following times:

Long Gone, skipper John Innes. Elapsed time 15 days, 16 hours, 29 minutes, 27 seconds.

Velaris, skipper Lol Killam. Elapsed time 16 days, 2 hours, 30 minutes.

Noreana of Wight, skipper Ron Ramsay, R.Vic.Y.C. Elapsed time 17 days, 12 hours.

Many club members have had a taste of dipping into the long green rollers when rounding the Swiftsure mark in the annual Swiftsure Classic. Close at hand is the grim "Graveyard of the Pacific" where 243 wrecks are charted by George Nicholson in his vivid book, *Vancouver Island's West Coast 1762 - 1962* (now in its third printing), and on the other hand is rugged Cape Flattery.

It is around the latter Cape and down to the mouth of Columbia River that the bi-annual Nor Pac Race gives those that relish that sort of thing just about every condition of wind, tide, rain and fog that can be experienced anywhere in the world.

Phil Graham skippered *Troubadour* in the 1960 Nor Pac Race, placing third in very rough going. There were four entries, *Sea Fever* of Seattle placed first, and *Maruffa* of Seattle came second.

In the 1962 race, which *Troubadour* also entered, only *Sea Fever* finished, all other yachts did not finish.

In 1964 the event was changed from a race to a cruise, the one participant from our club being *Penelakut*, skippered by owner Bob Ross.

CHAPTER 29

Other Yachting Organizations

SINCE WORLD WAR II THE R.V.Y.C. and other northwest clubs in the P.I.Y.A. have broadened their horizons widely, with active affiliation and participation in a number of other organizations.

PACIFIC COAST YACHTING ASSOCIATION

This group is made up of regional associations from British Columbia to Southern California, and sponsors the annual Pacific Coast Championship Regatta, which was held at our club in 1950. The late Harold A. Jones was commodore of the association in that year. In the early years of the association, in the 1920's, Capt. James Griffiths of Seattle and Ronald M. Maitland of Vancouver were strong supporters.

NORTH AMERICAN YACHT RACING UNION

The N.A.Y.R.U. was the "national" governing body of sailboat racing in both Canada and the U.S.A. for many years until the late 1950's, when both countries joined the International Yacht Racing Union coincident with the adoption of one world wide code of racing rules. The N.A.Y.R.U. sponsors four North American Championships:

Mallory Cup—Senior Men
Adams Cup—Senior Ladies
Sears Cup—Juniors
O'Day Cup—Single-handed sailing

Our club members have competed in all of these events, including David Miller, who won the Sears Cup in 1959. The final championship races for this cup were held at the R.V.Y.C. in 1958 and were recognized as an official sports event of the British Columbia Centennial programme.

CANADIAN YACHTING ASSOCIATION

The C.Y.A. is responsible for many phases of sailboat racing in Canada, including:

Publication of the official racing rules, and hearing appeals from decisions of local protest committees under these rules.

Sponsoring Olympic and Pan American Games trials, and selecting the representatives from our country for these events, and for raising funds to assist with the cost of taking part.

Sponsoring the annual Junior Championship, which was held at our club in 1964, and assisting with similar events for Sea Scouts, Boy Scouts, university sailing clubs, etc.

Our club members have been active in the organization and racing, Bud Day, Bud Roulstone, Ralph Farris and Frank Hahn having served as Vice Presidents representing B.C., and the following members have represented Canada in the Star Class:

> 1956 Olympics, Melbourne—E. Pennell and G. Parsons
> 1959 Pan American Games, Chicago—G. Mason and M. Hunt
> 1960 Olympics, Naples—W. Burgess, W. West
> 1964 Olympics, Tokyo—D. Miller and W. West

COUNCIL OF B.C. YACHT CLUBS

This group was formed to deal with legislative and other matters involving various levels of government, and has been active in looking after the interests of B.C. yachtsmen in such things as:

Promotion of provincial marine parks at Plumper's Cove, Keats Island, Montague Harbour, and development of launching ramps at many locations.

Protection of pleasure boat anchorages from undue encroachment by log storage and other commercial interests.

Liaison with Ottawa on small vessel safety regulations, equipment standards, etc.

Past Commodore J. M. (Mac) Kerr, Dr. R. E. (Bob) McKechnie and Past Commodore Elmer Palmer are three club members who have taken an active part in the Council activities.

INTERNATIONAL POWER BOAT ASSOCIATION

This Association sponsors the annual International Power Boat Race, attracting an entry of 100 to 150 ships, and the Alaska race, held in alternate years.

THE VENERABLE BOAT OWNERS' ASSOCIATION

This group within a group was formed about 1957 as a result of an incident at an Easter Cruise in Pender Harbour.

A number of the members' boats, including the *Deirdre, Bonaventure II,* the old *Four Bells, Hope Point III* and the *Truant* arrived in Pender Harbour together, and as they came around the point, the daughter of a member who owned one of the more glamorous boats exclaimed "Here comes the Turtle Fleet".

It was then decided to form this group within a group whose only requirement was that their vessels must be over a quarter of a century old. There are no rules or regulations or any other such thing—not even DUES!

A pennant was designed as a house flag incorporating a turtle on a log against a red background. Any members' boats passing the half century mark gets a chevron for his pennant. It might surprise members to know the number of vessels in the club which qualify for this house flag!

"Captain Domo" Doug McPherson, from whom this item was obtained, was unable to state the number of vessels in this "cozy" group; however he recalls that two dozen pennants were ordered and presumably are proudly flown. There are probably quite a few additional yachts in the club that could qualify, and since no dues are involved there is no particular reason why those who are entitled to do so should not acquire an additional "honor" flag to add to their hoist.

M.V. GLENIFFER, K. F. R. (Ken) Mair.

M.V. WANDERER, ex Cora May, Past Com. J. D. Maitland.

CHAPTER 30

Perpetual Trophies

OF THE ROYAL VANCOUVER YACHT CLUB

TROPHY	YEAR	DONOR
Buscombe Trophy	1905	F. and G. Buscombe
C. O. Julian Trophy	1906	C. O. Julian
Alexandra Cup	1907	Hon. James Dunsmuir *Lieutenant Governor of B.C.*
Beaver Cup	1908	R. H. Alexander
MacNeill Trophy	1908	C. B. MacNeill
Chaldecott Cup	1909	F. F. Chaldecott
Rand Cup	1912	C. D. Rand
Redskin Trophy (formerly Rand Cup)	1955	Mrs. Ramsay
Commodores' Cup	1912	B. T. Rogers
(re-presented)	1939	Mrs. W. E. Graveley
Rogers Trophy	1920	Mrs. B. T. Rogers
Roedde Challenge Cup	1923	G. A. Roedde
Dewees Trophy	1924	W. P. Dewees
Star Fleet Capt. Cup	1925	English Bay Star Fleet
Schooners and Yawls under 30'	1925	Unknown
Yawls under 30'	1928	Unknown
Harry Marshall Trophy	1929	Mr. & Mrs. Alexander Marshall
Keyes Trophy	1929	Eleanor Keyes
Stock Exchange Trophy	1929	Vancouver Stock Exchange
Butt Trophy	1931	W. J. Butt
Bird Rock Trophy	1932	Royal Vancouver Yacht Club
Minerva Trophy	1935	H. A. Wallace
W. O. Bell Trophy	1935	William Oliphant Bell
Catherine Day Trophy	1935	W. S. Day
English Bay S. Class	1936	Spencer Class Syndicate
White Rocks Trophy	1937	G. F. Gyles
Duncan Bell-Irving Trophy	1937	Duncan Bell-Irving
H. A. Jones Trophy	1937	Harold A. Jones
Harry Wylie Shield	1937	R.V.Y.C. Star Boats
Vice Commodore's Cup	1938	Harold A. Jones
Entrance Island Trophy	1938	Austin C. Taylor
Jericho Trophy	1939	Royal Vancouver Yacht Club
Harry Gale Trophy	1939	Harry Gale
Port of Vancouver Trophy	1939	Kenneth J. Burns
Frank Parsons Trophy	1940	Frank Parsons

TROPHY	YEAR	DONOR
Akhurst Trophy	1940	W. A. Akhurst
Watt Trophy	1946	Gordon Watt
Boultbee Sweet & Co. Trophy	1946	Boultbee Sweet & Co.
Vancouver Diamond Jubilee Trophy	1946	City of Vancouver
Weston Founders Trophy	1947	W. P. Weston
Burn-Mor Match Trophy	1950	J. Burnett and Wm. Morrow
Junior Perpetual Trophy	1950	Frederick & Nelson
Empire Trophy	1951	F. H. Clendenning
Stanley Brook Trophy	1952	Stanley Brook
Pakenham Trophy	1952	T. H. Pakenham
Hamish Davidson Trophy	1953	Hamish Davidson
B. L. Johnson Trophy	1954	Capt. B. L. Johnson C.B.E., D.S.O., R.C.N.
Yuno Trophy	1955	Temple H. Wright
Gyles Trophy	1955	G. F. Gyles
Venture Trophy	1955	R. C. Stevenson
Temple Wright Trophy	1955	Temple H. Wright
Kitten Class Trophy	1955	Unknown
W. Clarke Gibson Trophy	**1955**	W. Clarke Gibson
Tom Ayres Trophy	1957	T. W. Ayers
Order of the Bent Propeller	1957	R. A. Osbourne
The Flattie Trophy	1958	B. R. Tupper
Gulf of Georgia Trophy	1959	Royal Vancouver Yacht Club
Harbour Lights Trophy	1960	R. Farris and R. Ross
R. W. R. Day Golf Shield	1960	R. W. R. Day
F. J. Whitcroft Annual Golf Trophy	1960	F. J. Whitcroft
R.V.Y.C. Race Committee Trophy	1960	E. S. Earle
Stromboli Trophy	1961	A. F. (Bud) Roulstone
Navigator's Trophy	1962	T. M. Ramsay
English Bay Trophy	1962	Burgess, Bowman & Clark
Ernestine Jefferd Memorial Trophy	1962	A. H. Jefferd
Jack Cribb Memorial Trophy	1962	Eva Cribb
Samuel Patrick Cromie Memorial Trophy	1962	Don C. Cromie
Townley Trophy	1962	F. L. Townley
Hazen Phillips Trophy	1963	Mrs. Hazen Phillips
Albert Austin Trophy	1963	Bert Austin
Troubador Trophy	1963	Philip D. Graham
Petersen Trophy	1963	Carl Petersen
Miller Bros. Trophy	1963	Phil and Sid Miller

The Buscombe Trophy

PRESENTED 1905 BY
FREDERICK &
GEORGE BUSCOMBE

For the fastest boat over the
English Bay Course
under time allowance.
Designated for Special Sloops
in 1949.
Re-designated for BB Class in 1960.

WINNERS

1905	*Madeleine*	A. Austin Jr.	1952	*Cambria*	W. E. Cunningham
1906	*Onaway*	W. McDougall	1953	*Amberjack*	D. M. MacDonald
1907	*Britannia*	F. G. N. Seaton	1954	*Halvan*	S. Rasmussen
1908	*Alexandra*	E. B. Deane	1955	*Halvan*	S. Rasmussen
1909	*Madeleine*	W. J. Thicke	1956		
1910	*Kittymouse*	S. Busby	1957	*Bris*	S. Rasmussen
1911	*Spirit*	Cao Brothers	1958	*Bris*	S. Rasmussen
1912	*Alexandra*	E. B. Deane	1959		
1913	*Asthore*	R. W. Purves	1960	*Winsome*	C. Rickard
1914	*Gazeka*	R. M. Maitland	1961	*Tricia*	J. P. Leslie
1915	*Gazeka*	R. M. Maitland	1962	*Jester*	J. B. and L. A. Watts
1949	*Amberjack*	S. G. Foley	1963	*Veleda*	John Grubbe
1950	*Amberjack*	D. D. MacDonald	1964	*Maredea*	A. W. Way
1951	*Cambria*	W. E. Cunningham			

The C. O. Julian Trophy

**PRESENTED 1906 BY
C. O. JULIAN**

Lady Skippers' Race.
All handicap classes.

WINNERS

Year	Boat	Skipper
1906	*Cheemaun*	Miss Jessie McGeachie
1907	*Wideawake*	Miss Sophie Thicke
1908	*Madeleine*	Miss Violet Thicke
1909	*Asthore*	Miss Olive McLennan
1910	*Tillicum*	Miss Marion Shaw
1911	*Wideawake*	Miss Sophie Deane
1912	*Spirit*	Mrs. R. C. Cao
1913	*Alexandra*	Miss Louise Deane
1914	*Spirit II*	Miss Marion Mawdsley
1915	*Spirit II*	Miss Helen McDonald
1920	*Gwendolyn*	Miss E. Irwin
1921	*Turenga*	Miss Jean Murray
1922	*Patricia*	Mrs. W. G. McKenzie
1924	*Spirit*	Miss Shirley Woodward
1925	*Tamahnowus*	Mrs. E. W. Templeton
1926	*Riowna*	Mrs. Cedric H. Gyles
1927	*Spirit*	Miss Shirley Woodward
1928	*Minerva*	Mrs. H. A. Wallace
1929	*Spraydrift*	Mrs. Hoskins
1930	*Alexandra*	Mrs. P. G. Sills
1931	*Cresset*	Mrs. F. W. Urry
1932	*Minerva*	Mrs. Isabelle Dickson
1933	*Riowna*	Miss Gwynneth Gyles
1934	*Lady Van*	Miss E. Wylie
1935	*Spirit*	Mrs. H. A. Jones
1936	*Westward Ho*	Miss Mary Sutton
1937	*Tamahnowus*	Miss B. Pedlow
1938	*Lady Van*	Miss E. Wylie
1939	*Lady Van*	Miss Dorothy Wylie
1940	*Cresset*	Mrs. Cowan
1946	*Spirit*	Mrs. H. A. Jones
1947	*Spirit*	Miss B. Jones
1948	*Amberjack*	Mrs. Wm. Dunn
1949	*Amberjack*	Mrs. C. Gyles Jr.
1950	*Cresset*	Mrs. F. W. Urry
1951	*Cambria*	Miss M. Cunningham
1952	*Tsolum*	Mrs. M. C. Fox
1953	*Alana*	Mrs. S. Martin
1954	*Ca Va*	Mrs. S. Miller
1955	*Alana*	Mrs. Wyn Rickard
1956	*Alana*	Mrs. Wyn Rickard
1957	*Gometra*	Miss Gail Palmer
1958	*Kini*	Mrs. C. Bayne
1959	*Concerto*	Mrs. R. D. Ross
1960	*Kini*	Mrs. Jean Sturdy
1961	*Kini*	Miss Diane Sturdy
1962	*Coral Reef*	Mrs. A. W. Way
1963	*Fulmar*	Mrs. Megan Balmer
1964	*Maredea*	Miss Nora Way

The Alexandra Cup

PRESENTED 1907 BY
THE HONORABLE JAMES DUNSMUIR
LIEUT. GOVERNOR OF BRITISH COLUMBIA
FOR INTERNATIONAL COMPETITION

WINNERS

1907	*Spirit*	E. L. 'Ted' Geary	1909 Series called off after first race as
		Seattle Yacht Club	the new American contender *Spirit*
1908	*Alexandra*	E. B. Deane	*2* exceeded the required measure-
		Royal Vancouver Yacht Club	ment.

The Beaver Cup

PRESENTED 1908 BY
R. H. ALEXANDER

Fashioned in part from a portion of the timber originally in the hull of the Hudson's Bay Company Steamer *Beaver* which was the first steamer upon the Pacific Ocean, wrecked at Prospect Point, Stanley Park, July 26th, 1888.

For cruiser type vessels in annual race around White Islets and Baleneas Island. Object of the trophy is to induce the building of a good staunch type of boat with fair accommodation for a suitable crew on a trip that may last some days.

WINNERS

Year	Boat	Winner
1906	*Verona*	C. O. Julian
1907	*Minerva*	C. B. MacNeill
1908	*Ivanhoe*	C. A. Godson
1909	*Minerva*	P. H. Thompson
1910	*Minerva*	P. H. Thompson
1911	*Minerva*	P. H. Thompson
1913	*Uwilna*	R. H. Alexander
1914	*Gazeka*	R. M. Maitland
1915	*Gazeka*	R. M. Maitland
1917	*Minerva*	P. H. Thompson
1920	*Minerva*	W. E. Graveley
1921	*Onoma*	J. P. Fell, Lt. Col.
1922	*Minerva*	Thompson and Graveley
1923	*Tamahnowus*	W. O. Templeton
1924	*Elsa May*	G. F. Gyles
1925	*Minerva*	Thompson and Graveley
1926	*Andi-Lailey*	Ernest Rogers
1927	*Onoma*	Ian Mackenzie
1928	*Tamahnowus*	W. O. Templeton
1929	*Andi-Lailey*	E. T. Rogers
1930	*Westward Ho*	B. L. Johnson
1931	*Anywhere*	C. H. Elliott
1932	*Anywhere*	C. H. Elliott
1933	*Maratea*	W. O. Bell
1934	*Minerva*	H. A. Wallace
1935	*Minerva*	H. A. Wallace
1936	*Minerva*	H. A. Wallace
1937	*Westward Ho*	B. L. Johnson
1938	*Uwhilna*	F. O. Mills
1939	*Westward Ho*	B. L. Johnson
1940	*Cresset*	D. P. Urry

Racing discontinued till

Year	Boat	Winner
1946	*Cresset*	D. P. Urry
1947	*Spirit*	H. A. Jones
1948	No Race	
1949	*Gometra*	G. Ortengren
1950	*Oho*	P. R. Burr
1951	*Gometra*	K. G. Glass
1952	*Oho*	P. R. Burr
1953	*Elusive*	W. R. Morrow
1954	*Gometra*	Glass and Palmer
1955	*Oho*	P. R. Burr
1956	*Mary Bower*	K. J. McRae
1957	*Gometra*	E. J. Palmer
1958	*Gometra*	E. J. Palmer
1959	*Mary Bower*	K. J. McRae
1960	*Hawk*	Ralph Farris
1961	*Mary Bower*	K. J. McRae
1962	*Concerto*	Bob Ross
1963	*Mary Bower*	John Long
1964	*Alcion*	Colin Campbell

The MacNeill Trophy

**PRESENTED 1908 BY
C. B. MacNEILL
For International Championship**

Originally intended for international racing in the 18 ft. Class at annual Pacific International Yachting Association regattas. Horace Stone's *Adanac* was the original winner in 1908. No further contests held in this class.

Awarded as Star Championship in 1923 to Harry Wylie's *Astrea*.

Designated for Roedde Class White Rocks Race in 1937.

Re-designated for B Class English Bay Regatta 1958.

WINNERS

Year	Boat	Owner
1908	*Adanac*	Horace Stone
1923	*Astrea*	H. B. Wylie
1937	*Carita*	W. A. Roedde
1938	*Lady Luck*	J. M. Lindsay
1939	*Carita*	W. A. Roedde
1940	*Ariki*	C. J. Dill

Racing discontinued till

Year	Boat	Owner
1947	*Serena*	Baker and Longley
1948	*Hymac*	Dr. R. P. McCaffrey
1949	*Carita II*	W. A. Roedde
1950	*Carita II*	W. A. Roedde
1951	*Hymac*	Dr. R. P. McCaffrey
1952	*Elusive*	W. R. Morrow
1953	*Miss Lee*	T. L. Daniels
1954	*Trevida*	L. Murrell
1955	*Trevida*	L. Murrell
1956	No entries	
1957	No entries	
1958	*Dolphin II*	J. R. Grubbe
1959	*Vogad*	Dr. J. A. McMillan
1960	*Aida*	H. Vogel
1961	*Aida*	H. Vogel
1962	*Coho*	J. Brandlmayer
1963	*Comtessa*	Stuart Foley
1964	*Oonah*	Dr. J. A. McMillan

The Chaldecott Cup

PRESENTED 1909 BY
F. F. CHALDECOTT

Won 1909 by *Minerva*
P. N. Thompson.

Won 1910 by *Minerva*
P. N. Thompson.

Designated in 1949 for annual
C Class Cruiser competition
in Popham Island Race.

WINNERS

1949	*Elomar*	Dr. H. Ross	1959	No Race	
1954	*Ganessa*	A. W. Nyblom	1960	No Race	
1955	*Tsolum*	H. J. Burnett	1961	No Race	
1956	*Tsolum*	H. J. Burnett	1962	No Race	
1957	*Tsolum*	H. J. Burnett	1963	*Jehara*	Harry Dye
1958	*Yahda*	H. H. Kenyon	1964	*Kalara*	L. A. Walters

The Rand Cup

PRESENTED 1912 BY
C. D. RAND

For series of 3 races—
21 ft. Class—Inlet Course.

WINNERS

| 1912 | *Redskin* | H. V. Ramsay |
| 1913 | *Redskin* | H. V. Ramsay |

NOW KNOWN AS

The Redskin Trophy

PRESENTED 1955 BY
MRS. RAMSAY
IN MEMORY OF
H. V. RAMSAY

WINNERS

1955	*Pandora of Rhu*	E. R. Field
1956	*Fulmar*	C. Bayne
1957	*Pandora of Rhu*	E. R. Field
1958	*Concerto*	R. D. Ross

Re-allocated to Lightning Class in 1961.

WINNERS

| 1961 | No. 6948 | P. Pangman |
| 1962 | *Pastime* | A. Thomson |

The Commodores' Cup

**PRESENTED 1912 BY
B. T. ROGERS**

**RE-PRESENTED 1939 BY
MRS. W. E. GRAVELEY**

For Cruiser Race Point Grey
to Entrance Island and return.

WINNERS

1912	*Ailsa I*	R. M. Maitland	1955	*Oho*	P. R. Burr
1913	*Tamerlane*	W. G. Breeze	1957	*Concerto*	R. D. Ross
1914	*Gazeka*	R. M. Maitland	1958	*Hawk*	Ralph Farris
1949	*Hawk*	J. C. McPherson	1959	*Concerto*	R. D. Ross
1950	*Swallow*	Vans MacDonald	1960	*Mary Bower*	Ken McRae
1951	*Gometra*	K. G. Glass	1961	*Velaris*	Lol Killam
1952	*Oho*	P. R. Burr	1962	*Coral Reef*	A. W. Way
1953	*Elusive*	W. R. Morrow	1963	*Velaris*	Lol Killam
1954	*Fulmar*	C. Bayne	1964	*Velaris*	Lol Killam

The *Rogers Trophy*

PRESENTED 1920 BY
MRS. B. T. ROGERS

Originally for Kitten Class
Championship for Season.

Allocated 1947 to 14 Ft.
Dinghies. English Bay Series.

Re-allocated 1961 to Lightnings.

WINNERS

1920	H. B. Bell-Irving		
1921	J. Winslow		
1922	T. Pattison		
1923	W. P. Weston		
1925	R. G. Matheson		
1927	C. P. Leckie		
1928	Ben Elliott		
1947	*Gin Fizz*	W. Cunningham
1950	*Lizabeth*	R. Baker
1955	*Hoyden*	A. Roulstone
1961	*Pastime*	Adrian Thomson
1962	*Pastime*	Adrian Thomson
1963	*Thunderbird*	Geoff Ince
1964	*Thunderbird*	Geoff Ince

The Roedde Challenge Cup

PRESENTED 1923 BY
G. A. ROEDDE

Original Deed of Gift
destroyed by fire.

Trophy was raced for by
the Star Fleet since 1923
but in 1937 under
a new Deed of Gift signed
by William A. Roedde,
son of the original donor,
the trophy was designated as
THE ROEDDE STAR FLEET
CHAMPIONSHIP TROPHY,
emblematic of CHAMPIONSHIP
in the R.V.Y.C. Star Fleet.

WINNERS

1923	*Stella Maris*	R. W. Purves	1946	*Clear Sky*	P. and S. Miller
1924	*Corona*	T. Patterson	1947	*Victory*	H. Eckman
1925	*Stella Maris*	R. W. Purves	1948	*Clear Sky*	P. and S. Miller
1926	*Stella Maris*	R. W. Purves	1949	Records destroyed	
1927	*Auriga*	Phillips and Kerr	1950	Records destroyed	
1928	*Auriga*	Phillips and Kerr	1951	*Totem*	C. D. Helmer
1929	*Auriga*	Phillips and Kerr	1952	*Totem*	C. D. Helmer
1930	*Auriga*	Phillips and Kerr	1953	*Spitfire*	George Parsons
1931	*Auriga*	Phillips and Kerr	1954	*Marina*	E. Pennell
1932	*Auriga*	Phillips and Kerr	1955	*Wisp*	Ken Watt
1933	*Nomana*	P. D. Gordon	1956	*Clear Sky*	D. C. McPherson
1934	*Nomana*	Stuart Foley	1957	*Sparkle*	George Mason
1935	*Astrea*	H. E. Wylie	1958	*Scram*	I. and K. Kirkland
1936	*Nomana*	Stuart Foley	1959	*Ghost*	George Mason
1937	*Nomana*	R. W. R. Day	1960	*Windor*	W. West
1938	*Auriga*	Phillips and Kerr	1961	*Scram*	W. Burgess
1939	*Auriga*	G. Hazen Phillips	1962	*No Mo*	George Mason
1940	*Clear Sky*	P. and S. Miller	1963	*Glisten*	David Miller
	Racing discontinued till		1964	*Glisten*	David Miller

The Dewees Trophy

PRESENTED 1924 BY
W. P. DEWEES

For annual Gulf Power Boat Race.
Promoting cross gulf.
Predicted Log racing.

WINNERS

1924	*Mandalay S.*	Geo. Beaching	1953	*Arrow II*	J. G. White
1925	*Jolly Mac*	W. J. Butt	1954	*Geva*	T. Pakenham
1933	*Rhinegold*	C. C. Ferrie	1955	*Seaward*	Kai Wohlleben
1934	*Saronia*	J. S. Halse	1956	*Porpoise II*	F. R. Killam
1935	*Avalon*	E. Keenleyside	1957	*Mamita*	Dr. R. E. McKechnie
1936	*Nyanza*	C. L. Welch	1958	*Malecite*	R. W. R. Day
1937	*Gerald C.*	G. H. Rae	1959	*Gleniffer*	Ken F. Mair
1939	*Caprice*	K. A. Cruise	1960	*Porpoise II*	F. R. Killam
1940	*Taihoa*	W. O. Bell	1961	*Malecite*	R. W. R. Day
1948	*Kennett II*	T. H. Wright	1962	*Porpoise II*	F. R. Killam
1951	*Gremlin*	R. W. R. Day	1963	*Mamita*	Dr. R. E. McKechnie
1952	*Gleniffer*	K. F. R. Mair	1964	*Porpoise III*	F. R. Killam

The Star Fleet Captains Cup

PRESENTED 1925 BY THE ENGLISH BAY STAR FLEET

Star Class.
Popham Island Race.

WINNERS

1926	*Mercury*	H. E. Wylie	1947	*Clear Sky*	P. and S. Miller
1927	*Stella Maris*	R. W. Purves	1948	*Clear Sky*	P. and S. Miller
1928	*Corona*	T. L. Patterson	1949	*Totem*	Dr. C. D. Helmer
1929	*Uranus*	P. D. Gordon	1950	*Clear Sky*	Miller Bros.
1930	*Auriga*	Phillips and Kerr	1951	*Clear Sky*	P. and S. Miller
1931	*Astrea*	H. E. Wylie	1952	*Spitfire*	George Parsons
1932			1953	*Spitfire*	George Parsons
1933	*Nomana*	P. D. Gordon	1954	*Victory*	C. Shields
1934	*Astrea*	H. E. Wylie	1955	*Black Hawk*	Ron Marsden
1935	*Nomana*	Stuart Foley	1956	*Black Fish*	J. B. Shepherd
1936	*Ariki*	C. J. Dill	1957	*Duz*	Bonar Davis
1937	*Nomana*	R. W. R. Day	1958	D.N.F.	
1938	*Auriga*	Phillips and Kerr	1959	*Scram*	I. and K. Kirkland
1939	*Auriga*	G. Hazen Phillips	1960	No entry	
1940	*Windor*	George Parsons	1961	No entry	
	Racing discontinued till		1962	*Surf*	Ian Kirkland
			1963	*Scram*	Bill Burgess
1946	*Windor*	K. G. Watt	1964	*Scram*	Bill Burgess

Schooners and Yawls under 30'

PRESENTED IN 1925
DONOR UNKNOWN

WINNERS

1953	*Spitfire*	George Parsons
1954	*Sabot Class*	C. D. Helmer
1956	*Sabot Class*	Bill Falcus

Re-designated in 1963 to BB Class.

1963	*Tricia*	J. P. Leslie
1964	*Maredea*	A. W. Way

Yawls under 30'

PRESENTED IN 1928
DONOR UNKNOWN

Sailed for by 14 ft. Dinghy Class.
Later by the 6 Metre Class
and since 1962
by the Dragon Class.

WINNERS

1937	*Viva*	R. A. Gray	1957	*Juno*	D. Wotherspoon
1938	*Hot Rum*	W. Cunningham	1958	*Juno*	D. Wotherspoon
1939	*Hot Rum*	H. Givens	1959	*Ca-Va*	S. and P. Miller
1940	*Hot Rum*	H. Givens	1960	*Kini*	Dr. W. Sturdy
1946	*Gin Fizz*	Wm. Cunningham	1961	*Kini*	Dr. W. Sturdy
1947	*Gin Fizz*	Wm. Cunningham	1962	*Two Bits*	Dr. T. V. Jones
1955	*Kini*	J. D. Maitland	1963	*Audax*	Ken Clark
1956	*Kini* P. V. O. Evans, L. B. Cutler,		1964	*Cam*	J. Shepherd
	W. C. Dolmage, J. D. Maitland				

The Harry Marshall Trophy

**PRESENTED 1929 BY
MR. & MRS.
ALEXANDER MARSHALL**

For boats of 30 ft. water line
or under of Yawl or Schooner rig.

B. Class.

White Rocks Race.

WINNERS

1929	*Maratea*	W. O. Bell	1953	*Barracouta*	K. J. McRae
1930	*Maratea*	W. O. Bell	1954	*Barracouta*	K. J. McRae
1931	*Maratea*	W. O. Bell	1955	*Carita II*	Dr. C. Helmer
1932	*Maratea*	W. O. Bell	1956	No entries	
1933	*Nelmar*	Alex. J. Marshall	1957	*Vogad*	Dr. J. A. McMillan
1934	*Ailsa II*	J. W. Wilkinson	1958	*Vogad*	Dr. J. A. McMillan
1935	*Maratea*	W. O. Bell	1959	*Vogad*	Dr. J. A. McMillan
1936	*Nelmar*	Alex. J. Marshall	1960	*Dolphin*	J. Grubbe
1937			1961	*Ealasaid*	K. Mackenzie
1938			1962	*Coho*	J. Brandlmayr
1939	*Armida*	T. Ramsay	1963	*Coho*	J. Brandlmayr
1940	*Maratea*	J. A. Longley	1964	*Comtessa*	S. Foley
1951	*Dolphin*	Harry J. Bird			

The Keyes Trophy

PRESENTED 1929 BY
ELEANOR KEYES

For sloops of the largest class
for the last official race
of the season, around
Fraser River Lightship.

Re-allocated to B Class
and later to BB Class.

WINNERS

1929	*Alexandra*	B. L. Johnson	1950	*Serena*		V. Fox
1930	*Spirit II*	H. A. Jones	1954	*Winston*	Capt. B. L. Johnson	
1931	*Spirit II*	H. A. Jones	1955	*Ealasaid*		Ken Mackenzie
1932	*Spirit II*	H. A. Jones	1956	*Barracouta*		H. Herlihy
1933			1957	*Comtessa*		S. Foley
1934	*Spirit II*	H. A. Jones	1958	*Golden Hind II*		Lorne Kyle
1935	*Alexandra*	Harold M. Cline	1959	*Vogad*	Dr. J. A. McMillan	
1936			1960	*Tricia*		J. P. Leslie
1937	*Spirit II*	H. A. Jones	1961	*Tricia*		J. P. Leslie
1938	*Lady Van*	H. E. Wylie	1962	*Nyon*	Dr. Derek Simpson	
1948	*Amberjack*	Stuart Foley	1963	*Maredea*		R. G. Lundy
1949	*Winston*	Capt. B. L. Johnson	1964	*Maredea*		A. W. Way

The Stock Exchange Trophy

PRESENTED 1929 BY
THE VANCOUVER
STOCK EXCHANGE

For 9 Metre Yachts
"such as Alexandra, Spirit, Spirit II,
and R Class such as Lady Van,
Lady Pat, Riowna, Turanga,
also 6 Metre and 8 Metre Yachts".
Re-designated for 6 Metre
in 1955 Club Championship Series.

WINNERS

1929	*Lady Pat*	R. M. Maitland	1954	*Hecate*	Sandy Martin
1930	*Lady Pat*	R. M. Maitland	1955	*Kini*	J. D. Maitland
1931	*Lady Pat*	R. M. Maitland	1956	*Alana*	J. P. Leslie
1932	*Alexandra*	W. Cline	1957	*Ca-Va*	P. and S. Miller
1933	*Riowna*	G. F. Gyles	1958	*Ca-Va*	P. and S. Miller
1934	*Riowna*	G. F. Gyles	1959	*Juno*	D. Wotherspoon
1935	*Riowna*	G. F. Gyles	1960	*Ca-Va*	P. and S. Miller
1936	*Lady Van*	H. E. Wylie	1961	*Kini*	W. Sturdy
1937	*Riowna*	G. F. Gyles	1962	No Race	
1938	*Spirit II*	H. A. Jones	1963	No Race	
1939	*Alexandra*	T. H. Wright	1964	No Race	

The
Butt Trophy

**PRESENTED 1931 BY
W. J. BUTT**

Junior Skippers Race.
All Handicap Classes.

WINNERS

1931	*Westward Ho*	Doug. McLeod	1951	*Cambria*	A. Lilly
1932	*Gamine*	Derek Wilks	1952	*Gometra*	Jerry Palmer
1933	*Lady Van*	Ewing Macauley	1953	*Cambria*	Jack Kingscott
1934	*Turenga*	Russell Baker	1954	*Gometra*	Jack Kingscott
1935	*Riowna*	Thomas Eakins	1955	*Alana*	Joan Rickard
1936	*Armida*	Dana Ramsay	1956	*Kini*	W. Falcus
1937	*Carita*	Ed. Lewis	1957	*Kini*	Brian Lake
1938	*Lady Van*	Gerald Wood	1958	*Comtessa*	Alex. Foley
1939	*Lady Van*	Gerald Wood	1959	*Tricia*	Doug Helmer
1940	*Cresset*	Henry Strubin	1960	*Marchesa*	Don Martin
1941	*Mareta*	Jas. Stuart	1961	*Velaris*	Hayden Killam
1945	*Spirit*	Bob Cave	1962	*Coho*	D. Miller
1947	*Serena*	H. Eckman	1963	*Comtessa*	A. Foley
1948	*Amberjack*	H. Eckman	1964	*Velaris*	B. Killam
1950	*Vogad*	Stephen Tupper			

The Bird Rock Trophy

**PRESENTED 1933 BY
T. M. RAMSAY**

For the biggest FAUX-PAS.

WINNERS

Year	Boat	Winner	Year	Boat	Winner
1932	*Ailsa I*	T. M. Ramsay	1948	*Pursuit II*	K. C. McCandless
1933	*Minerva*	H. A. Wallace	1950	*Elusive*	W. R. Morrow
1934	*Andi-Lailey*	P. T. Rogers	1951	*Dolphin*	Harry J. Bird
1935	*Hereanthere*	Geo. Askew	1952	*Duende*	Miss Jill Biller
1936	*Westward Ho*	Capt. B. L. Johnson	1953	*Acrasia*	R. W. R. Day
1937	*Fuzilier*	Kenny McLennan	1954	*Kini*	Doug. Maitland
1938	*Cresset*	D. P. Urry	1955	*Fulmar*	C. Bayne
1939	*Sir Ron*	D. Maitland	1956	*Gometra*	Gerry Palmer
1940	*Ariki*	C. J. Dill	1957		Cliff Frew
	Danny	B. D. L. Johnson	1958	*Escapee*	John Burnett
	Carita	W. A. Roedde	1959	*Dolphin*	J. Grubbe
	Tequilla	Dr. J. A. Sampson	1960		Tom Sturgess
1941	*Uwhilna*	F. O. Mills	1961	*Tricia*	Ed. Botterell
1943	*Anywhere*	C. H. Elliott	1962	*Spirit*	Norm. McCarvill
1944	*Spirit II*	H. A. Jones	1963		
1946	*Hawk*	J. C. McPherson	1964	*Spirit*	C. Bayne
1947	*Ganessa*	A. W. Nyblom			
	Rebel	Dr. Roy Anderson			

The
Minerva Trophy

PRESENTED 1935 BY
H. A. WALLACE

For competition each season
by A Class concurrent
with The Keyes Trophy.
Course to be around the
Fraser River Lightship
and return to English Bay.

WINNERS

1935	*Mareta*		W. O. Bell
1936	Two races sailed. No Contest.		
1937	*Cresset*		Doug. Urry
1938	Race sailed. No Contest.		
1939	*Armida*		T. M. Ramsay
1940	*Gamine*		H. T. Frederickson
1947	*Spirit*		H. A. Jones
1948	*Oho*		P. R. Burr
1949	*Oho*		P. R. Burr
1950	*Oho*		P. R. Burr
1952	*Gometra*		Palmer and Glass
1954	*Jenetta*	F. W. and D. P. Urry	
1955	*Mary Bower*		K. J. McRae
1956	*Barracouta*		H. Herlihy
1957	*Buccaneer*		R. K. Baker
1958	*Buccaneer*		R. K. Baker
1959	*Mary Bower*		Ken McRae
1960	*Alcion*		L. A. Watts
1961	*Alcion*		Colin Campbell
1962	*Spirit*		Norm. McCarvill
1963	*Fulmar*		Dr. J. E. Balmer
1964	*Fulmar*		Dr. J. E. Balmer

The W. O. Bell Trophy

PRESENTED 1935 BY
WILLIAM OLIPHANT BELL

For sail boats of the Snipe Class.
Re-allocated in 1958 for A Class.

WINNERS

1935	*Westwind*	R. Slade	1947	*Aloha*		J. Rattenbury
1936	*Scandal*	N. Horton	1958	*Buccaneer III*		R. K. Baker
1937	*Waterwitch*	David Gray	1959	*Hawk*		R. Farris
1938	*Flamingo*	Miss C. Dill	1960	*Concerto*		R. Ross
1939	*Flamingo*	Miss C. Dill	1961	*Velaris*		L. Killam
1940	*Blueboy*	Dana Ramsay	1962	*Concerto*		R. D. Ross
1941	*Aloha*	Geoff. Morris	1963	*Fulmar*	Dr. J. E. Balmer
1946	*Aloha*	J. Rattenbury	1964	*Fulmar*	Dr. J. E. Balmer

The Catherine Day Trophy

**PRESENTED 1935 BY
W. S. DAY**
(named for his daughter)

For competition
amongst Snipe Class,
boats to be eligible
must have finished
1st, 2nd or 3rd place in any
series of races held during the year.
Re-designated 1955 for
Club Championship
in Davidson Frostbite Dinghy class.

WINNERS

1935	*Ace*	Gordon Wallace	1950	*Blue Boy*	R. R. Maitland
1936	*Scandal*	N. Horton	1955	T. Heiberg	
1937	*Scandal*	N. Horton	1956	F. J. Whitcroft	
1938	*Flamingo*	Miss C. Dill	1958	M. J. Lucas	
1939	*Retlaw*	Wm. Plommer	1962	F. R. Killam	
1946	*Aloha*	J. Rattenbury	1963	David Miller	
1947	*Demon*	M. Merrick	1964	Colin Park	

English Bay Spencer Class Trophy

**PRESENTED 1936 BY
THE SPENCER SYNDICATE
(COL. VICTOR SPENCER,
COL. K. A. McLENNAN,
CAPT. WILLIAM CRAWFORD,
W. A. ROEDDE)**

For S. Class Yachts, series of races
in English Bay (no handicap).
Sailed for by the Roedde Class
and re-allocated to
the Dragon Class in 1957.

WINNERS

1937	*Carita*	W. A. Roedde	1955	*Vogad*	B. R. Tupper
1938	*Ariki*	C. J. Dill	1956	*Carita*	Dr. C. Helmer
1939	*Ariki*	C. J. Dill	1957	*Cam*	J. P. Leslie
1940	*Vogad*	B. R. Tupper	1958	*Cam*	J. Shepherd
1947		Baker and Longley	1959	*Tjep*	R. F. Burgess
1948	*Fantasie*	J. G. Williamson	1960	*Tjep*	R. F. Burgess
1950	*Miss Lee*	Lorne Culter	1961	*Two Bits*	T. Jones
1952	*Elusive*	W. R. Morrow	1962	*Two Bits*	T. Jones
1953	*Fantasie*	J. G. Williamson	1963	*Audax*	Ken Clark
1954	*Hymac*	Stanley Davies	1964	*Cam*	J. Shepherd

The Duncan Bell-Irving Trophy

also known as

Fraser River Lightship Trophy

**PRESENTED 1937 BY
DUNCAN BELL-IRVING**

This trophy is the Riding Light of the R.M.S. Empress of Japan, famous C.P.R. Steamships Trans-Pacific liner 1891 - 1922. For S Class yachts (now B Class) rating 22.6 to be sailed for concurrently with the Minerva Trophy, around Fraser River Lightship and return to English Bay.

WINNERS

1937	*Graceful*		1955	*Elusive*	W. R. Morrow
1938	Race sailed — No contest.		1958	*Vogad*	Dr. J. A. McMillan
1939	*Ariki*	C. J. Dill	1959	*Vogad*	Dr. J. A. McMillan
1940	*Ariki*	C. J. Dill	1960	*Vogad*	Dr. J. A. McMillan
1947	*Hymac*	Dr. R. P. McCaffey	1961	*Ealasaid*	K. Mackenzie
1950	*Carita II*	W. A. Roedde	1962	*Coho*	J. Brandlmayr
1952	*Hymac*	Stanley Davies	1963	*Coho*	J. Brandlmayr
1954	*Hymac*	Stanley Davies	1964	No Contest.	

The White Rocks Trophy

PRESENTED 1937 BY
G. F. GYLES

For sloops of water line length
20 to 36 ft.
No handicap greater than
1 Minute per mile.

To be competed for each season
concurrent with the
Harry Marshall Trophy.

Re-allocated 1960 to BB Class.

WINNERS

1953 *Cambria*	W. E. Cunningham	1962 *Jester*	S. B. and L. A. Watts
1954 *Halvan*	S. Rasmussen	1963 *Maradea*	R. G. Lundy
1960 *Winsome*	C. Rickard	1964 *Jester*	S. B. Watts
1961 *Tricia*	J. P. Leslie		

The Harold A. Jones Trophy

PRESENTED 1937 BY HAROLD A. JONES

For National Class Dinghies.
Won three times and
permanently held by
W. E. CUNNINGHAM,
who re-presented it in 1949
for annual competition
in 14 Ft. International Dinghies.

WINNERS

| Annual Championship Series | | 1954 | *Sabot Class* | C. D. Helmer |
| 1953 | *Spitfire* | George Parsons | 1955 | *Sabot Class* | Fred Davies |

The Harry Wylie Shield

PRESENTED 1937 BY THE ENGLISH BAY STAR FLEET IN RECOGNITION OF THE EFFORTS OF HARRY E. WYLIE ON BEHALF OF THE FLEET

For English Bay
Fleet Championship,
registered Star Class boats
in any recognized Yacht Club
in English Bay.

WINNERS

1937	*Nomana*	R. W. R. Day	1954	*Totem*	K. Kirkland
1938	*Taseko*	W. H. Day	1955	*Totem*	K. Kirkland
1939	*Nomana*	R. W. R. Day	1956	*Black Hawk*	Ron Marsden
1940	*Auriga*	Phillips and Kerr	1957	*Duz*	Bonar Davis
1946	*Spitfire*	Geo. Parsons	1958	*Sparkle*	George Mason
1947	*Clear Sky*	P. and S. Miller	1959	*Windor*	W. West
1948	*Clear Sky*	P. and S. Miller	1960	*Cetus*	Bonar Davis
1949	*Flamingo*	J. P. Leslie	1961	*No Mo*	Dave Miller
1950	*Totem*	C. D. Helmer	1962	*Scram*	Bill Burgess
1951	*Spitfire*	Geo. Parsons	1963	*No Mo*	George Mason
1952	*Totem*	C. D. Helmer	1964	*Gypsy*	Ken Kirkland
1953	*Marina*	E. H. Pennell			

The Vice-Commodore's Cup

PRESENTED 1938 BY HAROLD A. JONES

For B. Class yachts race around Ballenas Island.

WINNERS

1938	*Nelmar*	Alex. Marshall	1956		
1939	*Armida*	T. M. Ramsay	1957	*Dolphin*	J. R. Grubbe
1940	*Gamine*	H. T. Frederickson	1958	*Vogad*	Dr. J. A. McMillan
1949	*Maratea*	Dr. A. R. Anthony	1959	*Barracouta*	H. Herlihy
1950	*Ealasaid*	Ken. McKenzie	1960	*Dolphin*	J. R. Grubbe
1951	*Miss Lee*	Lorne Culter	1961	*Elusive*	K. Lochead
1952	*Elusive*	W. R. Morrow	1962	*Coho*	J. Brandlmayr
1953	*Elusive*	W. R. Morrow	1963	*Coho*	J. Brandlmayr
1954	*Barracouta*	K. J. McRae	1964	No contest.	
1955	*Elusive*	W. R. Morrow			

The Entrance Island Trophy

PRESENTED 1938 BY AUSTIN C. TAYLOR

For competition in the
Roedde Class race
around Entrance Island.
Re-allocated as overall trophy
in 1959.

WINNERS

1938	*Ariki*	C. J. Dill	1954	*Hymac*	Stanley Davies
1939	*Ariki*	C. J. Dill	1955	*Kini*	P. V. O. Evans
1940	*Carita*	Roedde and Jackson	1959	*Tricia*	J. P. Leslie
1949	*Carita II*	W. A. Roedde	1960	*Winsome*	C. Rickard
1950	*Miss Lee*	Lorne Culter	1961	*Tricia*	J. P. Leslie
1951	*Miss Lee*	Lorne Culter	1962	*Coho*	J. Brandlmayr
1952	*Trevida*	Len Murrell	1963	*Hawk*	Ralph Farris
1953	*Elusive*	W. R. Morrow	1964	*Hawk*	Ralph Farris

The Jericho Trophy

**PRESENTED 1939 BY
ROYAL VANCOUVER
YACHT CLUB**

For C. Class Race
around the White Rock Islands.

WINNERS

1939	*Benora*	H. Herlihy	1958	*Tsolum*	M. J. Lucas
1940	*Benora*	H. Herlihy	1959	No Race.	
1947	*Naivette*	J. Barltrop	1960	No Race.	
1949	*Rebel*	Dr. Roy Anderson	1961	No Race.	
1954	*Yahda*	H. H. Kenyon	1962	No Race.	
1955	*Tsolum*	J. Burnett	1963	*Kalara*	Larry Walters
1956	*Yahda*	H. Hollick Kenyon	1964	No Contest.	
1957	*Elomar*	Dr. H. M. Ross			

The Harry Gale Trophy

PRESENTED 1939 BY MAYOR HARRY GALE

Originally presented in 1920 to
the Crescent Beach Country Club
for competition by Yacht Clubs
of the Pacific Northwest.

Presented 1939 to
the Royal Vancouver Yacht Club.
Allotted to Star Class,
then D. Class
and now to C. Class,
Fraser River Lightship Race.

WINNERS

1939	*Nomana*	R. W. R. Day	1956	*Tsolum*	
1940	*Auriga*	Phillips and Kerr	1957	*Tsolum*	M. J. Lucas
1949	*Rebel*	Dr. Roy Anderson	1958	No race.	
1950	*Marquita*	W. J. Johnson	1959	*Tramontana*	
1951	*Duende*	Miss Jill Biller	1960	*Tramontana*	
1952	No entry.		1961	No entry.	
1953	No entry.		1962	Race called — time limit.	
1954	No entry.		1963	*Kalara*	Larry Walters
1955	No entry.		1964	*Kalara*	Larry Walters

The Port of Vancouver Trophy

**PRESENTED 1939 BY
KENNETH J. BURNS**

For Club Championship
in 14 Ft. Dinghies.

Re-allocated in 1960 to Lightnings.

WINNERS

1939	*Aeolus*	H. Harrison	1958	*Hoyden*	A. Roulstone
1940	*Hot Rum*	H. Givins	1960	*Thunderbird*	G. Ince
1947	*Gin Fizz*	W. E. Cunningham	1961	*Pastime*	A. Thomson
1955	*Hoyden*	A. Roulstone	1962	*Pastime*	A. Thomson
1956	*Hoyden*	A. Roulstone	1964	*Skua*	Lyall Acheson
1957	*Jolly Olly*	V. W. Ruskin			

The Frank Parsons Trophy

**PRESENTED 1940 BY
FRANK PARSONS**

For C. Class 23.5 rating or
D. Class 20.0 rating or over
for series of races in English Bay.
Trophy is titled English Bay Series
Perpetual Trophy.

WINNERS

1940	*Ganessa*	A. W. Nyblom	1956	*Tsolum*	H. J. Burnett
1946	*Elomar*	L. A. Watts	1957	*Errant*	K. C. Middleton
1947	*Ganessa*	A. W. Nyblom	1958	*Tsolum*	M. J. Lucas
1949	*Elomar*	Dr. Hugh Ross	1959	*Tramontana*	S. de Keseredy
1950	*Ganessa*	A. W. Nyblom	1960	No entry.	
1951	*Ganessa*	A. W. Nyblom	1961	No R.V.Y.C. winner.	
1952	*Ganessa*	A. W. Nyblom	1962	No entry.	
1953	*Tsolum*	H. J. Burnett	1963	*Everywhere*	W. Colin Campbell
1954	*Ganessa*	S. Watts	1964	No Contest.	
1955	*Elomar*	Dr. Hugh Ross			

The Akhurst Trophy

PRESENTED 1940 BY
W. A. AKHURST

For Comet Class.

Re-allocated to Geary 18's
(Flatties) B.C. Championship.

WINNERS

1940	*Cienta*		W. Brealey
1941	*Alita*		W. Brealey
1946	*Waterwitch*		Miss Jill Biller
1947	*Whirlwind*		B. Carter

1948	*Whirlwind*		B. Carter
1950	*Warrior*		John Green
1957	*Mischief*		Steve Tupper

The Watt Trophy

PRESENTED 1946 BY GORDON WATT

For R.V.Y.C. Star Class race rounding Kitsilano Tugboat Buoy and Point Grey Bell Buoy. Changed to Bowyer Island Race in 1955 and in 1957 to English Bay Series.

WINNERS

1946	*Spitfire*		Geo. Parsons
1947	*Clear Sky*		P. and S. Miller
1948	*Clear Sky*		P. and S. Miller
1949	*Clear Sky*		P. and S. Miller
1950	*Duz*		S. Davies
1951	*Ariki*		E. Perry
1952	*Flamingo*		L. Ortengren
1953	*Duz*		S. Davies
1954	*P.D.Q.*		W. West
1955	*Totem*		K. Kirkland

1956	No entry.		
1957	*Sparkle*		George Mason
1958	*Scram*		I. and K. Kirkland
1959	*Scram*		I. and K. Kirkland
1960	*Diggin*		T. Hope
1961	*Cetus*		Bonar Davis
1962	*Scram*		Bill Burgess
1963	*Scram*		Bill Burgess
1964	*Gypsy*		K. Kirkland

The Boultbee Sweet & Co. Trophy

**PRESENTED 1946 BY
BOULTBEE SWEET & CO.**

For Comet Class.

Passage Island Race.

Re-allocated after 1950 for
Geary 18 (Flatties).

WINNERS

1946	*Lady Gay*	G. Frost	1961	*Tammy*	C. Park
1947	*Spectar*	K. Parsons	1962	No Race	
1948	*Whirlwind*	Bruce Carter	1963	No Race	
1950	*Warrior*	John Green	1964	No Race	
1957	*Rock 'N Roll*	David Miller			

Vancouver Diamond Jubilee Trophy

PRESENTED 1946 BY THE CITY OF VANCOUVER

For International Competition.

WINNERS

1946	*Intrepid*	Corinthian Yacht Club		1953	*Pompero*	Seattle Yacht Club
1947	*Angelica & Polho*			1954	Royal Victoria Yacht Club	
		Seattle Yacht Club		1960	Royal Vancouver Yacht Club	
1948	*Lemolo*	Seattle Yacht Club		1963	*Seraphis*	Royal Vancouver
1949	*Lemolo*	Corinthian Yacht Club				Yacht Club
1950	*Bolero*	Seattle Yacht Club		1964	*Khorasan*	Royal Vancouver
1951						Yacht Club
1952	*Panacea II*					
		Y.R.A. San Francisco Bay				

The Weston Founders Trophy

PRESENTED 1947 BY
W. P. WESTON, A.R.C.A.

For race to or from Howe Sound.
To perpetuate the names
of the original Star Boats
and Members organized in 1922
as the English Bay Star Fleet.

Star #117 *Corona,* T. Pattison
Star #118 *Astrea,* H. E. Wylie and
H. H. Simmonds
Star #119 *Centaur,* W. J. Alcock
Star #120 *Stella Maris,* R. W. Purves
Star #129 *Auriga,* G. Hazen Phillips
and R. M. Kerr
Star #130 *Argo,* J. Winslow
Star #145 *Mercury,* A. N. Wolverton
Star #212 *Daphne,* D. P. Weston,
A.R.C.A.

WINNERS

1947	*Ariki*				
1950	*Totem*	E. Perry	1956	*Totem*	I. and K. Kirkland
1952	*P.D.Q.*	C. D. Helmer	1957	*Totem*	K. P. Kirkland
1953	*P.D.Q.*	D. Shafer	1963	*Windor*	Bill West
1954	*P.D.Q.*	D. Shafer	1964	*Spitfire*	Alan Vittery
		D. Shafer			

The Burn-Mor Match Trophy

PRESENTED 1950 BY
JOHN BURNETT &
WM. MORROW

For an open handicap race with Yachts starting at designated times. All Handicap Classes.

WINNERS

Year	Yacht	Skipper	Year	Yacht	Skipper
1953	Amberjack	D. M. McDonald	1959	Cetus	Bonar Davis
1954	Barracouta	Ken J. McRae	1960	Kaliste	N. T. Park
1955	Fulmar	C. Bayne	1961	Rampage II	R. Duggan
1956	Carita II	Dr. C. D. Helmer	1962	Cetus	Bonar Davis
1957	Thunderbird	G. Ince	1963	Concerto	R. D. Ross
1958	Kaliste	N. T. Park	1964	Simba	Bonar Davis

The Frederick & Nelson Trophy

PRESENTED 1950 BY FREDERICK & NELSON CO. SEATTLE

Junior Perpetual Trophy.

For the Junior Member proving most meritorious in all Club activities.

WINNERS

1950	Stuart Shelly	1958	Steve Tupper
1951	Bob Little	1959	Audrey Roscoe
1952	John Yuill	1960	Doug Helmer
1953	Diana Wilson	1961	Colin Park
1954	Dennis Pennell	1962	Not awarded
1955	Laurel Tupper	1963	Bob Lance
1956	John Purdy	1964	Tim Meakin
1957	Glen Smith		

The Stanley Brook Trophy

**PRESENTED 1951 BY
STANLEY BROOK
SUPERINTENDENT,
COAL HARBOUR STATION
1925-1958**

Frostbite Dinghies
New Year's Day Race.

WINNERS

1951	F. J. (Bunny) Whitcroft	1958	Lol Killam
1952	R. W. R. Day and	1959	Bunny Whitcroft
	A. F. (Bud) Roulstone	1960	Lol Killam
1953	Eric Marsden	1961	Bonar Davis
1954	C. D. Helmer	1962	
1955	F. J. (Bunny) Whitcroft	1963	Bonar Davis
1956	C. D. Helmer	1964	Bonar Davis
1957	J. M. Lindsay		

The Empire Trophy

PRESENTED 1951 BY
F. H. CLENDENNING

For a recognized Class
with sail area
not less than 350 square feet.
Originally designated for
Special Sloops.
Re-allocated 1960 to BB Class.
Season's Championship.

WINNERS

1951	Cambria	W. E. Cunningham	1958	Bris	S. Rasmussen
1952	Cambria	W. E. Cunningham	1959		
1953	Amberjack	D. M. MacDonald	1960	Tricia	J. P. Leslie
1954	Halvan	S. Rasmussen	1961	Tricia	J. P. Leslie
1955	Halvan	S. Rasmussen	1962	Jester	S. B. and L. A. Watts
1956			1963	Veleda	John Grubbe
1957	Bris	S. Rasmussen	1964	Maradea	A. W. Way

The Pakenham Trophy

PRESENTED 1952 BY
T. H. PAKENHAM

For Predicted Log Race —
Power Boats — Team Competition.

WINNERS

1952	Burrard Yacht Club
1953	Burrard Yacht Club
1954	Burrard Yacht Club
1955	Burrard Yacht Club
1956	Royal Vancouver Yacht Club
1957	Royal Vancouver Yacht Club
1958	Burrard Yacht Club

1959	Burrard Yacht Club
1960	Burrard Yacht Club
1961	Royal Vancouver Yacht Club
1962	Burrard Yacht Club
1963	Burrard Yacht Club
1964	Royal Vancouver Yacht Club

The Hamish Davidson Trophy

**PRESENTED 1953 BY
HAMISH DAVIDSON**

For Inter-Club racing in
Davidson Frostbite Dinghies.

WINNERS

1953	Royal Victoria Yacht Club	1959	Royal Vancouver Yacht Club
1954	Royal Victoria Yacht Club	1960	Royal Vancouver Yacht Club
1955	Royal Vancouver Yacht Club	1961	Royal Victoria Yacht Club
1956	Royal Vancouver Yacht Club	1962	Royal Vancouver Yacht Club
1957	Royal Vancouver Yacht Club	1963	Royal Vancouver Yacht Club
1958	Royal Vancouver Yacht Club	1964	Royal Vancouver Yacht Club

The
B. L. Johnson
Trophy

**PRESENTED 1954 BY
CAPTAIN B. L. JOHNSON,
C.B.E., D.S.O., R.C.N.**

Presented concurrent
with donation of $1000 Bond,
interest from which
to purchase Prize each year
for Junior 12 - 17 years age
(boat owner or skipper)
most outstanding based on merits
and demerits as designated.

WINNERS

1954	D. Pennell		1959	D. Miller
1955	S. Tupper		1960	Colin Park
1956	S. Tupper		1961	R. Maitland
1957	D. Miller		1964	Colin Park
1958	D. Miller			

The Yuno Trophy

PRESENTED 1955 BY TEMPLE HALL WRIGHT

Trophy is the compass
of the yawl *Yuno*,
a ship of the R.V.Y.C. Fleet
in 1906.

Originally designated for
the 6 Metre Class.
Total Points for
three distance races.
Re-allocated 1962
to the Dragon Class.

WINNERS

1955	*Kini*	J. D. Maitland	1960	*Juno*	D. F. Wotherspoon
1956	*Juno*	D. F. Wotherspoon	1961	*Kini*	W. Sturdy
1957	*Ca-Va*	P. and S. Miller	1962	*Stromboli*	Temple H. Wright
1958	No Contest.		1963	*Tjep*	Bob Burgess
1959	No Contest.		1964	*Cam*	Jack Shepherd

The Gyles Trophy

PRESENTED 1955 BY GEORGE F. GYLES

For the season's championship in the 6 Metre Class. Re-allocated in 1962 to the Dragon Class, First Evening Series.

WINNERS

1955	*Kini*	J. D. Maitland	1960	Not awarded.	
1956	*Juno*	D. Wotherspoon	1961	*Kini*	W. Sturdy
1957	*Ca-Va*	P. and S. Miller	1962	*Tjep*	Bob Burgess
1958	*Juno*	D. Wotherspoon	1963	*Tjep*	Bob Burgess
1959	Not awarded.		1964	*Audax*	Ken Clark

The
Venture Trophy

PRESENTED 1955 BY
R. C. STEVENSON,
MONTREAL, P.Q.
HONORARY COMMODORE,
CANADIAN DINGHY
ASSOCIATION

For 14 Ft. Dinghy Championship.
Re-allocated 1962
to Lightning Class.

WINNERS

1955	A. F. (Bud) Roulstone, Skipper; Bruce Mairs, Crew.	1959	
1956	Norm. Cole, Skipper; Bud Thees, Crew.	1960	
		1961	
1957	Ray Delaplace, Skipper; Steve Tupper, Crew.	1962 *Pastime*	Adrian Thomson
		1963 *Thunderbird*	Geoffrey Ince
1958		1964 *Thunderbird*	Geoffrey Ince

The Temple H. Wright Perpetual Trophy

PRESENTED 1955 BY TEMPLE HALL WRIGHT

Trophy is the original tiller
of the yacht *Alexandra,*
mounted as a perpetual trophy.
Presented to encourage
Dinghy Sailing and Racing
on the waters of the
Pacific Coast of Canada.
Davidson Frostbite Class,
Invitational Regatta.

WINNERS

1955	J. M. Lindsay, Victoria, B.C.	1960	Lol Killam, Vancouver, B.C.
1956	F. J. Whitcroft, Vancouver, B.C.	1961	Ned Ashe, Victoria, B.C.
1957	F. J. Whitcroft, Vancouver, B.C.	1962	Ches. Rickard, Vancouver, B.C.
1958	Lol Killam, Vancouver, B.C.	1963	Ches. Rickard, Vancouver, B.C.
1959	Pat Leslie, Vancouver, B.C.	1964	Bonar Davis, Vancouver, B.C.

The Kitten Class Trophy

DONATED IN 1955
DONOR UNKNOWN

For Junior International,
Christmas Regatta.

WINNERS

1955	Steve Tupper	1962	Colin Park, Don Martin
1958	Steve Tupper	1963	Don Martin
1959	Rae Ellen Ramey	1964	Don Martin
1961	Jeff Steinborn		

The
W. Clarke Gibson
Trophy

**PRESENTED 1955 BY
W. CLARKE GIBSON**

Sabot Class.
Junior Class —
Inter-Club Championship.

WINNERS

1955 Larry Baker
Re-allocated to Frostbite Dinghy,
Junior Division, International Re-
gatta.

1962 Seattle Yacht Club Team
1964 Royal Vancouver Yacht Club
Team

The
Flattie Trophy

PRESENTED 1958 BY
BERT R. TUPPER

To be raced for annually
at the English Bay Regatta
by Flattie Class or other
designated class or event.

WINNERS

1958	*Sea Jet*	Ron Maitland	1962	*Rock 'N Roll*		P. Sturdy
1959	*Silver Wings*	D. Miller	1963	No. 1075		C. Helmer
1960	*Silver Wings*	D. Miller	1964	No Contest.
1961	*Rock 'N Roll*	P. Sturdy

The Tom Ayres Trophy

**PRESENTED 1957 BY
T. W. AYRES**

As a perpetual trophy
for the R.V.Y.C. yacht
with the best score in the
Annual International Cruiser Race.

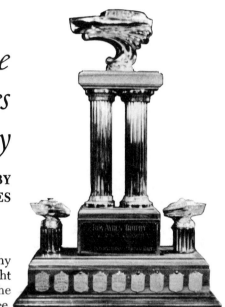

WINNERS

1957	*Porpoise II*	F. R. Killam	1961	*Smitty*	Tom Trapp
1958	*Gleniffer*	K. F. R. Mair	1962	*Mamita*	Dr. R. E. McKechnie
1959	*Mamita*	Dr. R. E. McKechnie	1963	*Porpoise II*	F. R. Killam
1960	*Porpoise II*	F. R. Killam	1964	*Dorlen*	D. & L. Sewell

The Order of the Bent Propeller

**PRESENTED 1957 BY
R. A. OSBORNE**

for the Power Boat committing
the greatest error in
seamanship or navigation.

WINNERS

1958	*Staghound*	J. M. Lindsay	1962	*Porpoise II*	F. R. Killam
1959	*Let's Go*	W. Dunn	1963	*Coryels*	Harry Milne
1960	*Gleniffer*	K. F. R. Mair	1964	*Riot IV*	Ron Runge
1961	*Malecite*	R. W. R. Day			

The
Gulf of Georgia
Trophy

PRESENTED 1959 BY
ROYAL VANCOUVER
YACHT CLUB

Long Distance Racing Series.

WINNERS

1959	*Concerto*	Bob Ross	1962	*Coho*	J. Brandlmayr
1960	*Tricia*	Pat Leslie	1963	*Velaris*	Lol Killam
1961	*Tricia*	Pat Leslie	1964	*Jester*	S. B. Watts

The Harbour Lights Trophy

**PRESENTED 1960 BY
RALPH FARRIS &
ROBERT D. ROSS**

For Evening Harbour Series.

WINNERS

1960	*Tricia*	Pat Leslie	1963	*Hawk*	Ralph Farris
1961	*Velaris*	Lol Killam	1964	*Fulmar*	D. J. E. Balmer
1962	*Concerto*	Bob Ross			

The
R. W. R. Day
Golf Shield

PRESENTED 1960 BY
R. W. R. DAY

WINNERS

1960	Robt. Kidd	1962	Carl Carlson
1961	Robt. Kidd	1963	Sir Robert Cave-Browne-Cave

The
F. J. Whitcroft
Annual Golf
Trophy

PRESENTED 1960 BY
F. J. WHITCROFT

WINNERS

1960 Brian Hopkins   1962 Peter Bagshaw
1961 D. F. Wotherspoon

The
R. V. Y. C.
Race Committee
Trophy

**PRESENTED 1960 BY
E. S. EARLE**

For Championship in
Tri-City Combined Events,
(best combined score),
Frostbite Dinghies
with less than 200 sq. ft. sail.

WINNERS

1960	F. R. Killam		1963	F. R. Killam
1961	Bonar Davis		1964	Bonar Davis
1962	Ches. Rickard			

The Stromboli Trophy

PRESENTED 1961 BY A. F. (BUD) ROULSTONE

For Dragon Class
Season's Championship.
Highest total points
in one racing season—
each series to be counted
as one race—
best four out of five races.

WINNERS

1961	*Stromboli*	T. H. Wright	1963 *Audax*	Ken Clark
1962	*Tjep*	Bob Burgess	1964 *Cam*	Jack Shepherd

Navigator's Trophy

PRESENTED 1962 BY
TOM RAMSAY

For A Class, Snake Island Race.

WINNERS

1962 *Mary Bower*	Ken McRae	1964 *Fulmar*	Dr. J. E. Balmer
1963 *Fulmar*	Dr. J. E. Balmer		

The English Bay Trophy

**PRESENTED 1962 BY
S. J. BOWMAN, R. F. BURGESS,
K. G. CLARK**

For Dragon Class
English Bay Invitational Regatta.

WINNERS

1962	*Tjep*	R. F. Burgess	1964	*Audax*	Ken Clark
1963	*Audax*	Ken Clark			

The Ernestine Jefferd Memorial Trophy

**PRESENTED 1962 BY
ARTHUR H. JEFFERD**

For Star Class
Season's Championship.
Two 3-race Series and
two 5-race series as designated.

WINNERS

| 1961 | *Scram* | B. Burgess | 1963 | *Simba* | Bonar Davis |
| 1962 | *Cetus* | Bonar Davis | 1964 | *Gypsy* | Ken Kirkland |

The Jack Cribb Memorial Trophy

**PRESENTED 1962 BY
EVA CRIBB**

For cruising class yachts
in the Snake Island Race
(overall winner)
classes AA, A, BB, B, C,
with sail area
of not less than 350 sq. ft.

WINNERS

1961	*Tricia*	Pat Leslie	1963	*Fulmar*	Dr. J. E. Balmer
1962	*Jester*	S. B. and L. A. Watts	1964	*Fulmar*	Dr. J. E. Balmer

The Samuel Patrick Cromie Memorial Trophy

PRESENTED 1962 BY
DON C. CROMIE

For the Winner of the Gulf of Georgia Predicted Log Race (member of any recognized Yacht Club). Canadian Inter-Club.

WINNERS

1962	*Mamita*	Dr. R. E. McKechnie	1964	*Marillyce*	Hew Brooke
1963	*Walithy*	Les Simmers			

The Townley Trophy

**PRESENTED 1962 BY
FRED L. TOWNLEY**

For competition in sailing
by crews in Junior Training
during the programme.

WINNERS

1962   Bruce Gordon
1963   Alan Drinkwater

1964   Hunt Gordon

The
Albert Austin
Trophy

**PRESENTED 1963 BY
ALBERT AUSTIN
(Charter Member)**

For the R.V.Y.C. yacht
in cruising class
with the best overall
in the Ballenas Island Race.

WINNERS

1963 *Spirit*   Norm McCarvill   1964 *Kalara*   L. H. Walters

The Hazen Phillips Trophy

**PRESENTED 1963 BY
MRS. HAZEN PHILLIPS**

For Championship in
R.V.Y.C. Midsummer Regatta,
English Bay Star Fleet.

WINNERS

1963	*Glisten*	Dave Miller	1964	*Glisten*	Dave Miller

The
Petersen Trophy

**PRESENTED 1963 BY
CARL PETERSEN**

Star Class October Series—
Annual Challenge Trophy.

WINNERS

1963 *Windor*   Bill   West   1964 *Scram*   Bill Burgess

The
Troubadour
Trophy

PRESENTED 1963 BY
PHILIP D. GRAHAM

For cruising type boats
in the Sisters Island Race—
overall winner.

WINNERS

1963 *Coho*   J. Brandlmayr 1964 *Maredea*   A. W. Way

The Miller Brothers Trophy

PRESENTED 1963 BY PHIL and SID MILLER

For the Star Class "B" Division Championship of the English Bay Star Fleet.

Boats having a record of finishing worse than fourth are allowed to compete, though all boats start at the same time.

WINNERS

1963 *Totem*   Ron Grenough, K.Y.C.   1964 *Blackfish* S. Prinsenberg, K.Y.C.

The
Dr. Bob
McKechnie
Predicted
Log Race Trophy

For the British Columbia yacht
with the lowest percentage
of error of all
British Columbia skippers
competing in the
International Power Boat Race
conducted by I.P.B.A.

**PRESENTED 1958 BY
DR. R. E. McKECHNIE**

WINNERS

1958 *Gleniffer*	Ken Mair	1962 *Tampico*	R. H. Smith
1959 *Mamita*	Dr. R. E. McKechnie	1963 *Kedaro*	W. E. Fowler
1960 *Tecora*	Len Sewell	1964 *Dorleen*	Len Sewell
1961 *Smitty*	Tom Trapp		

CHAPTER 31

Honorary Life Members

OF THE
ROYAL VANCOUVER YACHT CLUB

	Joined	Elected	Office held
*W. E. Graveley	1903	1907	Commodore 1903-04-05.
*R. G. Macpherson	1903	1906	Liaison between Ottawa and London, Eng.
*Rev. J. Antle	1903	1948	
*W. A. Akhurst	1905	1940	Hon. Secretary 1912-17-18-19.
*H. F. Burton-Brooke	1908	1928	Hon. Secretary 1928-29-35-36-37-39-40-42.
*F. M. Chaldecott	1903	1930	Charter Member.
*W. B. Ferrie	1903	1937	Charter Member.
*C. B. MacNeill	1903	1938	Commodore 1909-10.
*Alex Marshall	1906	1938	Vice-Commodore 1919-27, Rear Comm. 1911, Hon. Treas. 1914.
*F. T. Schooley	1904	1937	Fleet Capt. 1933-34, Hon. Meas. 1916-17-18. Commodore 1919.
*Tom Pattison	1910	1938	
*G. F. Askew	1905	1948	Builder of early yachts.
C. G. Thicke	1906	1950	Hon. Treasurer 1915-16-29-30-31-33.
*Capt. B. L. Johnson, c.b.e., d.s.o.	1904	1951	Commodore 1929-30-36-50, Vice Comm. 1925-26-28-31, Rear Comm. 1921-22-23.
*Albert Austin	1903	1954	Charter Member.
*W. G. Breeze	1905	1948	Vice Commodore 1914-15, Rear Comm. 1912-13, Hon. Secy. 1924-46-47-48-49, Hon. Treas. 1909-10-11,17-18-19.
*W. A. Roedde	1905	1945	Rear Commodore 1945, Fleet Capt. 1941-42-43, Hon. Hydrographer 1934-35-36.
*W. J. Thicke	1906	1959	Rear Commodore 1909-10, Hon. Meas. 1919.
A. H. Jefferd	1909	1951	Hon. Hydrographer for 21 years, 1940 to 1960.
T. M. Ramsay	1907	1958	Fleet Captain 1935-36.
*F. O. Mills	1910	1964	Fleet Captain 1921.
Col. C. C. Ferrie	1916	1957	Rear Commodore 1939, Staff Capt. 1936-37-38.
*G. F. Gyles	1918	1953	Commodore 1922-23-27-28-40-41, Vice Comm. 1921-35-43, Hon. Treas. 1925.
*H. A. Jones	1919	1953	Commodore 1939-44-45-46-47, Vice Comm. 1938, Fleet Captain 1932-37.
* J. A. Longley	1919	1958	Commodore 1942, Rear Comm. 1940-41, Fleet Capt. 1938, Hon. Hydrographer 1937.
C. H. Gyles	1920	1962	Fleet Captain 1939, Hon. Treas. 1952-53-54-55-56.
*H. E. Wylie	1919	1947	Hon. Hydrographer 1924.
*Hon. E. W. Hamber	1923	1953	Commodore 1931-32-33-34-35.
J. S. Halse	1925	1960	Commodore 1943, Vice Comm. 1942, Staff Capt. 1935, Hon. Secretary 1938-41-58-59-60.
H. J. Bird	1925	1964	Hon. Treasurer 1950-51.
*E. F. Cribb	1926	1956	
*D. P. Urry	1925	1956	Rear Commodore 1935-36-37-38, Hon. Meas. 1932-33-34.
*Mrs. A. H. Jefferd	1927	1955	
C. J. Dill	1928	1960	Vice Commodore 1949, Fleet Capt. 1940, Hon. Meas. 1935-36-37.
* F. R. Wilgress	1929	1952	Hon. Treasurer for twelve years 1936-47.
* W. S. Day	1930	1959	Commodore 1937-38, Vice Comm. 1936, Hon. Treasurer 1933-34-35.
G. A. Cran	1933	1964	Hon. Secretary 1952-53-54-55-56-57.
J. M. Kerr	1936	1964	Commodore 1956, Vice Comm. 1955, Rear Comm. 1954.
T. M. Ayres	1940	1957	Commodore 1948-49.

*Deceased.

333

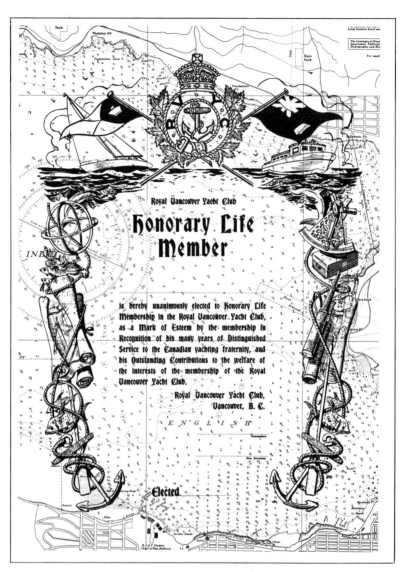

Hon. Life Certificate designed by Ron. Jackson.

LIFE MEMBERS OF THE ROYAL VANCOUVER YACHT CLUB

Joined	Member	Purchased	Joined	Member	Purchased
1903	C. S. V. Branch	1904	1903	H. M. Leggatt	1904
1903	G. S. Bushby	1904	1903	O. Moseley	1904
1903	E. B. Deane	1904	1903	C. C. McCaul	1904
1903	A. French	1904	1903	J. H. Senkler	1904
1903	Capt. A. Grant	1904	1903	Capt. P. N. Thompson	1904
1903	Commodore		1903	W. E. Thompson	1904
	W. E. Graveley	1904	1903	A. G. Thynne	1904
1903	Wm. Hodson	1904	1934	G. L. Cran	1955

CHAPTER 32

Officers of the
Royal Vancouver Yacht Club
1903-1965

	1903	1904	1905
Commodore	W. E. Graveley	W. E. Graveley	W. E. Graveley
Vice Commodore	W. Hodson	W. Hodson	P. N. Thompson
Captain	C. S. V. Branch	P. N. Thompson	G. G. Bushby
Hon. Secy.-Treasurer	O. L. Spenser	O. L. Spenser	O. L. Spenser

On receiving the Royal Warrant in 1906 two additional officers were elected, and a third in 1907

	1906	1907	1908
Commodore	R. H. Alexander	R. H. Alexander	A. G. Thynne
Vice Commodore	A. G. Thynne	A. G. Thynne	R. H. Alexander
Rear Commodore	A. French	P. N. Thompson	A. French
Hon. Secretary	C. O. Julian	C. O. Julian	J. J. Banfield
Hon. Treasurer	J. S. Gall	J. S. Gall	J. S. Gall
Hon. Measurer	G. G. Bushby	G. G. Bushby	W. McDougall
Hon. Hydrographer		W. H. Archer	W. H. Archer

	1909	1910	1911
Commodore	C. B. MacNeill	C. B. MacNeill	H. O. Alexander
Vice Commodore	F. Buscombe	R. H. Alexander	Maj. H. D. Hulme
Rear Commodore	W. J. Thicke	W. J. Thicke	A. Marshall
Hon. Secretary	J. J. Banfield	R. W. Holland	R. W. Holland
Hon. Treasurer	W. G. Breeze	W. G. Breeze	W. G. Breeze
Hon. Measurer	W. McDougall	W. McDougall	W. McDougall
Hon. Hydrographer	W. H. Archer	W. H. Archer	W. H. Archer

	1912	1913	1914
Commodore	B. T. Rogers	B. T. Rogers	B. T. Rogers
Vice Commodore	Maj. H. D. Hulme	A. H. Nicholl	W. G. Breeze
Rear Commodore	W. G. Breeze	W. G. Breeze	R. M. Maitland
Hon. Secretary	W. A. Akhurst	Maj. H. D. Hulme	Col. H. D. Hulme
Hon. Treasurer	J. D. Small	J. D. Small	A. Marshall
Hon. Measurer	W. McDougall	E. B. Schock	A. J. C. Robertson
Hon. Hydrographer	E. B. Schock	R. W. Purves	R. W. Purves

	1915	**1916**	**1917**
Commodore	B. T. Rogers	B. T. Rogers	B. T. Rogers
Vice Commodore	W. G. Breeze	W. A. Bauer	R. W. Holland
Rear Commodore	R. M. Maitland	R. W. Holland	J. Emerson
Hon. Secretary	Col. H. W. Hulme	G. C. Van Horne	W. A. Akhurst
Hon. Treasurer	C. S. Thicke	C. S. Thicke	W. G. Breeze
Hon. Measurer		A. Marshall	A. Marshall
Hon. Hydrographer	R. W. Purves	J. A. Leckie	

	1918	**1919**	**1920**
Commodore	B. T. Rogers	F. T. Schooley	H. O. Bell-Irving
Vice Commodore	R. W. Holland	A. Marshall	A. E. White
Rear Commodore	J. Emerson	A. E. White	R. W. Purves
Hon. Secretary	W. A. Akhurst	W. A. Akhurst	C. R. Sneyd
Hon. Treasurer	W. G. Breeze	W. G. Breeze	F. O. Mills
Hon. Measurer	A. Marshall	W. J. Thicke	J. Winslow
Hon. Hydrographer			

In 1921 an additional officer was elected

	1921	**1922**	**1923**
Commodore	H. O. Bell-Irving	G. F. Gyles	G. F. Gyles
Vice Commodore	G. F. Gyles	R. M. Maitland	R. M. Maitland
Rear Commodore	Comm. B. L. Johnson, D.S.O.	Comm. B. L. Johnson, D.S.O.	Comm. B. L. Johnson, D.S.O.
Fleet Captain	F. O. Mills	J. H. Willard	P. Whitehead
Hon. Secretary	R. M. Maitland	W. J. Butt	A. M. Dollar
Hon. Treasurer	H. B. Bell-Irving	A. M. Dollar	W. J. Butt
Hon. Measurer	J. Winslow	E. B. Schock	Comm. A. St. V. Keyes, R.N.
Hon. Hydrographer	R. W. Purves	R. W. Purves	

	1924	**1925**	**1926**
Commodore	R. M. Maitland	A. M. Dollar	A. M. Dollar
Vice Commodore	A. M. Dollar	Comm. B. L. Johnson, D.S.O.	Comm. B. L. Johnson, D.S.O.
Rear Commodore	W. J. Butt	W. J. Butt	W. J. Butt
Fleet Captain	R. W. Purves	P. Whitehead	W. Templeton
Hon. Secretary	W. G. Breeze	E. A. Woodward	A. L. Bell
Hon. Treasurer	A. L. Bell	G. F. Gyles	R. F. Marpole
Hon. Measurer	G. H. Phillips	Comm. A. St. V. Keyes, R.N.	T. Holliday
Hon. Hydrographer	H. E. Wylie	R. W. Purves	R. W. Purves

	1927	**1928**	**1929**
Commodore	G. F. Gyles	G. F. Gyles	Comm. B. L. Johnson, D.S.O.
Vice Commodore	A. Marshall	Comm. B. L. Johnson, D.S.O.	P. Whitehead
Rear Commodore	W. J. Butt	R. W. Ginn	R. W. Ginn
Fleet Captain	P. Whitehead	P. Whitehead	H. A. Wallace
Hon. Secretary	R. M. Maitland	H. F. Burton Brooke	H. F. Burton Brooke
Hon. Treasurer	R. F. Marpole	R. M. Merrick	C. S. Thicke
Hon. Measurer	L. T. Alden	L. T. Alden	L. T. Alden
Hon. Hydrographer	R. W. Purves	R. W. Purves	R. W. Purves

	1930	1931
Commodore	Comm. B. L. Johnson, D.S.O.	Hon. E. W. Hamber
Vice Commodore	E. W. Hamber	Comm. B. L. Johnson, D.S.O.
Rear Commodore	R. W. Ginn	R. W. Ginn
Fleet Captain	H. A. Wallace	H. A. Wallace
Hon. Secretary	R. J. Bushell	R. J. Bushell
Hon. Treasurer	C. S. Thicke	C. S. Thicke
Hon. Measurer	L. T. Alden	L. T. Alden
Hon. Hydrographer	R. W. Purves	D. P. Urry

In 1932 one additional officer was elected

	1932	1933	1934
Commodore	Hon. E. W. Hamber	Hon. E. W. Hamber	E. W. Hamber
Vice Commodore	R. W. Ginn	R. W. Ginn	R. W. Ginn
Rear Commodore	H. A. Wallace	G. McClay	G. McClay
Fleet Captain	H. A. Jones	A. Marshall	A. Marshall
Staff Captain	J. L. Northey	J. L. Northey	W. Higbie
Hon. Secretary	P. Whitehead	J. W. MacDougall	J. W. MacDougall
Hon. Treasurer	C. S. Thicke	W. S. Day	W. S. Day
Hon. Measurer	D. P. Urry	D. P. Urry	D. P. Urry
Hon. Hydrographer	R. W. Purves	H. H. Simmonds	W. A. Roedde

	1935	1936	1937
Commodore	E. W. Hamber	Comm. B. L. Johnson, D.S.O.	W. S. Day
Vice Commodore	G. F. Gyles	W. S. Day	K. A. McLennan
Rear Commodore	D. P. Urry	D. P. Urry	D. P. Urry
Fleet Captain	T. M. Ramsay	T. M. Ramsay	H. A. Jones
Staff Captain	J. S. Halse	C. C. Ferrie	C. C. Ferrie
Hon. Secretary	H. F. Burton Brooke	H. F. Burton Brooke	H. F. Burton Brooke
Hon. Treasurer	W. S. Day	F. R. Wilgress	F. R. Wilgress
Hon. Measurer	C. J. Dill	C. J. Dill	C. J. Dill
Hon. Hydrographer	W. A. Roedde	W. A. Roedde	J. A. Longley

	1938	1939	1940
Commodore	W. S. Day	H. A. Jones	G. F. Gyles
Vice Commodore	H. A. Jones	S. A. Smith	S. A. Smith
Rear Commodore	D. P. Urry	C. C. Ferrie	J. A. Longley
Fleet Captain	J. A. Longley	C. H. Gyles	C. J. Dill
Staff Captain	C. C. Ferrie	J. C. McPherson	Dr. J. A. Sampson
Hon. Secretary	J. S. Halse	H. F. Burton Brooke	H. F. Burton Brooke
Hon. Treasurer	F. R. Wilgress	F. R. Wilgress	F. R. Wilgress
Hon. Measurer	W. Cunningham	J. A. Longley	W. S. Miller
Hon. Hydrographer	T. Wright	R. Jackson	A. H. Jefferd

	1941	**1942**	**1943**
Commodore	G. F. Gyles	J. A. Longley	J. S. Halse
Vice Commodore	H. F. Burton Brooke	J. S. Halse	G. F. Gyles
Rear Commodore	J. A. Longley	R. W. Ginn	R. W. Ginn
Fleet Captain	W. A. Roedde	W. A. Roedde	W. A. Roedde
Staff Captain	Dr. J. A. Sampson	Dr. J. A. Sampson	Dr. J. A. Sampson
Hon. Secretary	J. S. Halse	H. F. Burton Brooke	F. Insley
Hon. Treasurer	F. R. Wilgress	F. R. Wilgress	F. R. Wilgress
Hon. Measurer	D. P. Urry	A. W. Nyblom	A. W. Nyblom
Hon. Hydrographer	A. H. Jefferd	A. H. Jefferd	A. H. Jefferd

	1944	**1945**	**1946**
Commodore	H. A. Jones	H. A. Jones	H. A. Jones
Vice Commodore	O. H. Bell	O. H. Bell	O. H. Bell
Rear Commodore	H. T. Frederickson	W. A. Roedde	T. H. Wright
Fleet Captain	C. J. Dill	J. C. Horan	J. C. Horan
Staff Captain	F. R. Bartlett	T. W. Ayres	T. W. Ayres
Hon. Secretary	K. G. McCandless	K. G. McCandless	W. G. Breeze
Hon. Treasurer	F. R. Wilgress	F. R. Wilgress	F. R. Wilgress
Hon. Measurer	J. M. Kerr	W. M. Reid	T. B. Edwards
Hon. Hydrographer	A. H. Jefferd	A. H. Jefferd	A. H. Jefferd

	1947	**1948**	**1949**
Commodore	H. A. Jones	T. W. Ayres	T. W. Ayres
Vice Commodore	O. H. Bell	F. R. Wilgress	C. J. Dill
Rear Commodore	T. H. Wright	A. S. Aitken	A. S. Aitken
Fleet Captain	J. A. Longley	W. W. Walsh	J. G. Williamson
Staff Captain	T. W. Ayres	K. F. R. Mair	K. F. R. Mair
Hon. Secretary	W. G. Breeze	W. G. Breeze	W. G. Breeze
Hon. Treasurer	F. R. Wilgress	R. K. Baker	A. W. Nyblom
Hon. Measurer	R. E. Anderson	R. E. Anderson	R. E. Anderson
Hon. Hydrographer	A. H. Jefferd	A. H. Jefferd	A. H. Jefferd

	1950	**1951**	**1952**
Commodore	Capt. B. L. Johnson, C.B.E., D.S.O.	E. A. Towns	W. C. Gibson
Vice Commodore	E. A. Towns	W. C. Gibson	K. G. Glass
Rear Commodore	W. G. Dolmage	E. D. Stone	E. D. Stone
Fleet Captain	J. G. Williamson	J. G. Williamson	W. E. Cunningham
Staff Captain	G. H. Oliver	R. W. R. Day	R. W. R. Day
Hon. Secretary	R. J. Bicknell	R. J. Bicknell	G. A. Cran
Hon. Treasurer	H. J. Bird	H. J. Bird	C. H. Gyles
Hon. Measurer	R. E. Anderson	R. E. Anderson	R. Delaplace
Hon. Hydrographer	A. H. Jefferd	A. H. Jefferd	A. H. Jefferd

	1953	**1954**	**1955**
Commodore	K. G. Glass	K. G. Glass	J. D. Maitland, D.S.C., C. DE G.
Vice Commodore	J. D. Maitland, D.S.C., C. DE G.	J. D. Maitland, D.S.C., C. DE G.	J. M. Kerr
Rear Commodore	J. M. Kerr	J. M. Kerr	G. G. Flemming
Fleet Captain	S. Davies	S. Davies	E. J. Palmer
Staff Captain	R. W. R. Day	G. G. Flemming	Dr. R. E. McKechnie
Hon. Secretary	G. A. Cran	G. A. Cran	G. A. Cran
Hon. Treasurer	C. H. Gyles	C. H. Gyles	C. H. Gyles
Hon. Measurer	R. Delaplace	R. Delaplace	H. J. Burnett
Hon. Hydrographer	A. H. Jefferd	A. H. Jefferd	A. H. Jefferd

	1956	**1957**	**1958**
Commodore	J. M. Kerr	E. J. Palmer	E. J. Palmer
Vice Commodore	E. J. Palmer	G. G. Flemming	G. G. Flemming
Rear Commodore	G. G. Flemming	S. Davies	S. Davies
Fleet Captain	P. V. O. Evans	K. J. McRae	H. J. Burnett
Staff Captain	Dr. R. E. McKechnie	F. S. Clendenning	F. S. Clendenning
Hon. Secretary	G. A. Cran	G. A. Cran	J. S. Halse
Hon. Treasurer	C. H. Gyles	A. H. Pinkham	C. J. Dill
Hon. Measurer	H. J. Burnett	H. J. Burnett	M. J. Lucas
Hon. Hydrographer	A. H. Jefferd	A. H. Jefferd	A. H. Jefferd

	1959	**1960**	**1961**
Commodore	G. G. Flemming	S. Davies	T. H. Wright
Vice Commodore	S. Davies	Dr. R. E. McKechnie	K. J. McRae
Rear Commodore	F. S. Clendenning	F. S. Clendenning	W. G. Dolmage
Fleet Captain	J. P. Leslie	D. Wotherspoon	L. H. Killam
Staff Captain	F. R. Killam	F. R. Killam	R. Gibson
Hon. Secretary	J. S. Halse	J. S. Halse	J. S. Halse
Hon. Treasurer	C. J. Dill	C. J. Dill	G. Fawcett
Hon. Measurer	M. J. Lucas	J. P. Leslie	J. P. Leslie
Hon. Hydrographer	A. H. Jefferd	A. H. Jefferd	E. S. Earle

	1962	**1963**	**1964**
Commodore	T. H. Wright	K. J. McRae	F. R. Killam
Vice Commodore	K. J. McRae	F. R. Killam	L. O. Bell
Rear Commodore	F. R. Killam	L. O. Bell	D. M. Hartnell
Fleet Captain	L. H. Killam	Dr. J. E. Balmer	Dr. J. E. Balmer
Staff Captain	L. O. Bell	D. M. Hartnell	J. D. Overholt
Hon. Secretary	R. K. Baker	R. K. Baker	C. E. Morris
Hon. Treasurer	G. Fawcett	R. G. Brodie	R. G. Brodie
Hon. Measurer	J. P. Leslie	L. Brandlmayr	A. J. Forsyth
Hon. Hydrographer	A. F. Roulstone	M. J. Hunt	M. J. Hunt

	1965	**1966**	**1967**
Commodore	L. O. Bell	D. M. Hartnell	D. M. Hartnell
Vice Commodore	D. M. Hartnell	T. F. Orr	T. F. Orr
Rear Commodore	T. F. Orr	Philip D. Graham	A. J. B. Forsyth
Fleet Captain	P. D. Graham	A. J. B. Forsyth	John H. Long
Staff Captain	R. C. Runge	D. C. McPherson	Robert Gibson
Hon. Secretary	C. E. Morris	J. D. Overholt	J. D. Overholt
Hon. Treasurer	R. G. Brodie	Robert G. Brodie	P. R. Wilson
Hon. Measurer	A. Meakin	G. M. Palmer	K. Y. Lochhead
Hon. Hydrographer	B. Davis	J. H. Long	Stephen Tupper

	1968	**1969**	**1970**
Commodore	T. F. Orr	A. J. B. Forsyth	Robert Gibson
Vice Commodore	A. J. B. Forsyth	Robert Gibson	W. E. Simpson
Rear Commodore	Robert Gibson	W. E. Simpson	R. A. Orr
Fleet Captain	K. Y. Lochhead	A. H. Meakin	W. G. Burgess
Staff Captain	W. E. Simpson	G. A. Healey	S. Bardach
Hon. Secretary	R. D. Ross	E. P. Bowser	E. P. Bowser
Hon. Treasurer	W. D. Kinsey	W. D. Kinsey	A. L. Andrews
Hon. Measurer	Paul T. Cote		R. F. Burgess
Hon. Hydrographer	David S. Miller	D. S. Miller	
Jericho Port Capt.		K. Y. Lochhead	K. Y. Lochhead
Offshore Stations Officer		R. A. Orr	T. F. Orr

Honorary Life Members (Continued from page 333)

*Oswald Moseley	1903	1966	Charter Member.
J. D. Maitland, D.S.C. C. de G. with Palm.	1925	1970	Commodore 1955, Vice Commodore, 1953, 1954.
*Temple H. Wright	1936	1967	Commodore 1961, 1962 Rear Commodore 1946, 1947
O. H. Bell	1937	1965	Vice Commodore 1944-45-46-47.
W. Clarke Gibson	1941	1969	Commodore 1952, Vice Com. 1951.
Elmer J. Palmer	1949	1965	Commodore 1957, 1958 Vice Comm. 1956, Fl. Capt. 1955.
E. S. Earle	1952	1967	Hon. Hydrographer 1961.

Life Members

1944	Dr. J. D. Longley	....	1969	1955	Temple M. Wright	 1968
1953	Lyall O. Bell	....	1968	1961	Owen F. Wright	 1968
1954	Russell G. Fraser	....	1970			

ANNALS OF
The Royal Vancouver Yacht Club

SUPPLEMENT
1966-1970

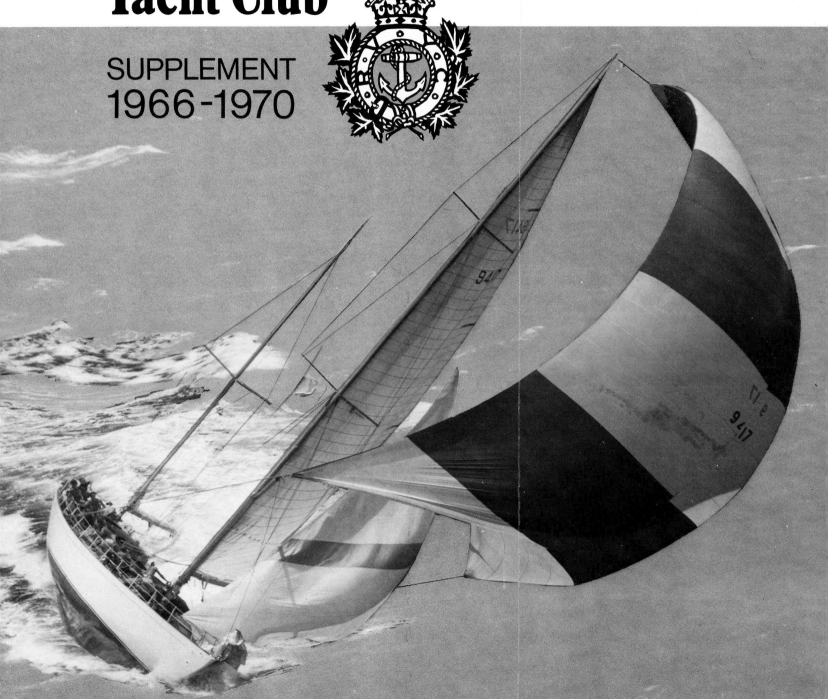

Annals

of the

Royal Vancouver Yacht Club

1966-1970

As the first edition of R.V.Y.C. Annals 1903-1965 is now out of print, it was decided to publish a second edition from the original plates. A review of the last five years has been added making the complete Annals available in one volume.

Information presented herein has been obtained from reliable sources and any inaccuracies should be reported to the R.V.Y.C. History Committee. Acknowledgement is gratefully extended to the R.V.Y.C. History Committee and the following

Commodore Robert Gibson, Past Commodores K. J. McRae, F. R. Killam, D. M. Hartnell, T. F. Orr and A. J. B. Forsyth; Dr. J. Balmer, W. G. Burgess, E. E. Jefferys, J. Long, A. H. Meakin, D. C. McPherson, N. C. Thomson, T. J. Trapp, Bob Orr, Maurice Hunt, Dr. M. M. MacPherson and Stephen Tupper.

Compiled and Edited
by
George A. Cran

Published under the supervision of the History Committee of the Royal Vancouver Yacht Club

Evergreen Press, Vancouver, B.C.
Copyright, 1965, 1971, R.V.Y.C.

341

Contents

CORRECTIONS ON FIRST EDITION

Page 135 Ken Watt's name omitted from list of prominent Star sailors; he skippered *Twilight, Windor* and *Wisp* in the forties.

Page 206 Add that Commodore K. J. McRae also owned and sailed *Barracouta II* from 1951 to 1955.

Page 238 Transpose Jr. Commodores 1935, 1936; F. J. Whitcroft was Jr. Commodore in 1935.

Bob Day and not Bud Day was Jr. Vice Commodore and Jr. Commodore in 1938 and 1939.

Also note correction in years 1951 and 1952.

Page 246 *Kalliste* was imported by H. Wrohan in 1947 and sold to Norm Park in 1954.

SUPPLEMENT COVER PICTURE Killer gust of 60 knots hits Geo. O'Brien's *Mir* off Diamond Head a few hundred yards from finish of 1969 Trans-Pacific Yacht Race from Los Angeles to Honolulu. Seconds later she was dismasted yet her crew succeeded in clearing wreckage; rigging a small spinnaker they crossed the line stern first (See page 369) first foreign yacht to finish.   *Photo courtesy Pacific Yachting*

CHAPTER 33

Annals

OF ROYAL VANCOUVER YACHT CLUB

1966-1970

SINCE PUBLICATION of the original volume of Annals covering 1903 to 1965 the club has experienced unprecedented growth in moorage installation, registration of sail and power yachts and general service facilities: membership has reached a total of 1,771—virtually a capacity figure—and the members' equity has been increased from $320,575 to $693,969, a very substantial 116%.

In this period no less than $1,082,482 has been expended in physical improvement and capital asset replacement, a record that few if any established yacht clubs on the North American continent can equal. This sum was provided partially from operating profit, two general assessments, increase in entrance fees and dues and a bank loan authorized to a maximum of $300,000 of which $165,000 has been drawn down to date (January 1971) to be repaid over a four year period commencing in 1973.

Many years of planning lie behind these figures—planning and concentrated application not only by recent Commodores, Flag Officers and Committees but by those dedicated members who held office in the early sixties, culminating so far in an outlay of $374,688 at Coal Harbour station, $588,284 on the new Jericho Marina, $82,372 on Jericho Clubhouse, $29,294 at Tugboat and $7,844 at Alexander Island stations.

While the actual total membership increased a modest 5½% in the five year period there has been a great upsurge in boating activity, a much greater percentage of members acquiring yachts and participating in sailing, cruising and predicted log events. Also the quality of members' vessels is higher; there are sleeker racing machines, more efficient and commodious cruising yachts and capable power vessels with the most modern, sophisticated navigational equipment: and, too, the sailing fraternity was swelled by the graduating sailors from our very successful Junior Training programme attended by approximately two hundred keen budding skippers annually.

Faced with these developments it was vital for the club Executives to extend and improve our facilities and to implement our long cherished plans to fully use our Jericho waterlot and Coal Harbour moorage basin. This latter was plagued by, among other things, shallow water and heavy silting, deteriorating floats and obsolete wiring and the Jericho waterlot was absolutely unprotected from Westerly, North and Easterly winds to being unsuitable for permanent all season moorage. As far back as 1935 the late Mr. Jack Cribb designed an offshore rip-rap rock breakwater construction similar to the Fraser River North Arm Jetty, the estimated cost of $275,000 being considered at that time to be beyond our means as some Jericho Clubhouse bonds were still outstanding. The coming of World War Two was a further setback. Meanwhile in 1962 and 1963 a Development and Building Committee headed at various times by Past Commodore Elmer Palmer, the late Ralph Farris and Colin Campbell spent over eighteen months co-relating conflicting interests and perfecting plans which retiring Commodore Ken McRae recommended for members' study and discussion so that work could proceed if approved early in 1964.

Commodore F. R. (Bill) Killam (1964) then carried the ball and after two Special General Meetings which wholeheartedly supported him, invited local nearby residents to view our plans with the expectation of their approval. This was not forthcoming unfortunately, largely due to the inclusion in the artist's sketch of several rows of power boat shelters, also public misconception of our development plans, stirred up in 1961, when we requested the City to sell back to us the Highbury Street-end. This property we had leased from 1926 to 1948 and had given up to the City for incorporation into Pioneer Park—and since that time been largely unused.

So, as it was apparent that we could only moor sail boats in the projected Jericho Basin, it was obvious that we would either have to apply for enlargement of Coal Harbour moorage or else substantially increase its capacity by extensive dredging. With the advent of Canadian Armed Forces Consolidation it was hoped that we would be able to acquire a lease on ex Deadman's Island—H.M.C.S. Discovery: accordingly Commodore Doan M. Hartnell (1966) headed a delegation to Ottawa but it was unsuccessful, being told that the naval branch of the Services would continue to use the island as a sea-cadet training centre.

Plans for the Jericho Marina were then redrawn, eliminating power boat shelters and confining our breakwater structure to the limits of our water-lot, within which area it was estimated we could moor approximately 275 sail boats leaving Coal Harbour mainly for power boat moorage.

COAL HARBOUR BASIN MODERNIZED

Early in 1966 under the immediate supervision of energetic Rear Commodore Philip D. Graham and with the invaluable assistance of Wavell Urry, plans for dredging the entire Coal Harbour basin to minus 7 ft. at zero tide were laid and immediately carried out, replacing and rearranging the main and finger floats, also renewing and installing all electrical wiring in plastic conduits under float decks. D Section was completely replaced with 450 ft. of new main float and 15 finger floats all of styrofoam flotation parts built with chemically treated preservative. Piling was put at outer ends of finger floats eliminating unsightly piling along the main walks and additional styrofoam flotation placed under main walks and shelters now held up with obsolete saturated logs. Also this year saw the end of the unsightly privately owned power boat shelters the last 14 of which were replaced by new member-financed structures.

In Commodore Hartnell's second year (1967), under Rear Commodore Alex Forsyth, modernization plans were further implemented. Two hundred and twenty lineal feet was added to "A" Section and forty feet to "E" Section, four hundred feet of new finger floats were built and styrofoam placed under older sections. Eight club-owned log-supported shelters were renovated with styrofoam flotation and the Mermaid Inn interior and exterior were painted and improvements made to the galley. In addition, as pilferage was becoming an increasing problem, a new gate was installed at the head of the ramp. Our work crew also constructed a 34 ft. by 65 ft. float to house the club-owned Flying Juniors; this was installed alongside our old pier at Jericho. In 1968 under the direction of Rear Commodore Bob Gibson a further 450 ft. of main floats were installed and 700 ft. of floats constructed for installation out at Jericho where breakwater piling was being driven.

R.V.Y.C. Coal Harbour Station 1970

In 1969 under the direction of Rear Commodore W. E. (Al.) Simpson an additional 350 ft. of new floats were constructed and installed making provision for berthing 64 new vessels, and 22 new member-financed shelters were erected. In 1970 under the direction of Rear Commodore Bob Orr, five 40 ft., five 50 ft. and six 60 ft. shelters were built and floodlighting of certain dark areas in the basin and a watchman's time-clock system installed. Replacements were made on the Marine Ways and contract let for the construction of a new floating lift. A new master plan has been completed to enable maximum use of the water-lot and discussions are being continued with the Parks Board relative to member parking facilities.

JERICHO MOORAGE BASIN DEVELOPMENT

Although temporarily set back in 1964 our plans for protected moorage at Jericho were never shelved and in 1967 Commodore Doan Hartnell and Executive commissioned Wavell Urry and the engineering firm of Swan Wooster to design breakwater protection and moorage facilities in the area contained in our Jericho water-lot of 12.49 acres. An overwhelming percentage of sail boat owning members pledged that they would utilize all year moorage at Jericho and at a Special General Meeting plans submitted were approved and authorization given to proceed with the work. In 1968 through the initiative of Commodore T. F. (Bill) Orr and past Commodore Doan Hartnell, approval to proceed was obtained from the National Harbours Board and the Provincial Government authorities and the pile driving work commenced, being completed during the year, 896 ft. north along the westerly and 200 ft. east along the northerly boundary. While this work was proceeding it was realized that it would be necessary to extend the north protection to the full width of the water-lot and authorization was given to continue the piling a further 472 ft., giving maximum protection against the north-westerly swells. Concrete main floats were nestled alongside and we were in operation early in 1969 awaiting dredging of the basin before installation of bisecting and finger floats. In July 1969 we were hosts to the Annual P.I.Y.A. Regatta at which 284 sail boats were registered and the new Jericho protected basin proved very useful as the majority of them rafted up inside whereas at former regatta weeks skippers would not risk anchoring offshore but trekked through the Narrows to tie up in Coal Harbour overnight.

With the increased activity at Jericho, car parking became a No. 1 problem especially over week-ends: by late 1969 and early 1970 approximately 90 sail boats were permanently moored in the unfinished basin. Permanent placing of east-west main floats and finger floats had been delayed until dredging was completed and this was held up pending City Council approval of our placing the fill on the rocky foreshore, otherwise it had to be barged out to sea and dumped. Under Commodore Alex Forsyth we received Parks Board approval to create a substantial parking area along the base of the bank fronting Pioneer Park all within our actual water-lot which extends to high water line coming right up to the bank thus impeding public thoroughfare. There was no usable public access to the foreshore within five city blocks—from Dunbar Street to Jericho Bathing Beach and following Parks Board policy of pumping sand on the foreshore along Beach Avenue and at Third Beach and Spanish Banks The Board had no objections to our covering marine slime, worm and shell growth on the rocks at this point, especially as we made provision for a public walkway along the foot of the Bank from Alma Road westerly to join up with the Jericho Tennis Club foreshore where the bank disappears. The City Planning Department also gave their approval but before issue of the necessary permit we were required to appear before the Board of Variance because some public objection had been raised. The club won this decision and Development Permit No. 50923 was issued. We then appeared before City Council and obtained their approval, also the approval of the Provincial Minister of Lands whose department owns the entire foreshore of English Bay. Unfortunately a wave of public protest was stirred up by "Open Line" radio commentators and distorted "faked" photographs were published in temporary publications, the regular editions of The Sun and The Province being struck and were not published for three months at that time. The agitation thus stimulated resulted in one City Council member—Alderman Sweeney—changing his vote at a subsequent City Council meeting and the permit granted us was suspended. However, the club proceeded to complete the dredging and the contractors dumped the material outside the Harbour limits at great additional cost to the club. Installation of finger floats on the northerly half of the basin was proceeded with under Commodore Bob Gibson early in 1970, but at this date, January 1971, the placing of east-west permanent floats with abutting finger floats has not yet been completed.

Despite the frustrating negotiations constantly being carried on with City officials our major parking problem has not yet been solved, although somewhat alleviated by blacktopping portions of our front and side lawns to provide space for 20 additional cars.

R.V.Y.C. Jericho Moorage Basin 1970

JERICHO CLUBHOUSE IMPROVEMENTS

Looking back a few years it was in 1961 when the late Past Commodore Temple H. Wright made strenuous efforts to swing the membership behind his progressive plans to demolish the decaying clubhouse structure built in 1926-7 and replace it with a modern building fully equipped with up-to-date facilities in more spacious areas and meeting rooms that would better serve members' requirements. While fully sympathetic with his plans the Special General Meeting voted to concentrate on developing boating facilities rather than dissipating our resources on non-essential social services. It was decided instead, to replace failing wooden beams with steel, and to modernize the interior as much as possible and to carry on the old building for another ten years at least. This was done spending $80,000, under the direction of Commodore Ken McRae and Vice Commodore Bill Killam. (See page 206). In 1966-67 Commodore Doan Hartnell's house committee headed by Vice Commodore Bill Orr and including Alex Andrews, the late Ron Runge and others, supervised the reconstruction and redecorating of the Dining Room and certain other areas at a cost of approximately $30,000. In 1968, under Commodore Bill Orr and Vice Commodore Alex Forsyth new equipment was installed in the galley and the exterior of the building painted. In 1969 the club office was completely renovated, with new ceiling, office furniture and drapes; a new piano was bought for the lounge and in the basement showers were tiled and lockers installed. Meanwhile a new Board Room was constructed downstairs and Junior quarter remodelled and furnished. In 1970 the old Board Room area was converted into a sailors' Lounge and in the hustle and bustle of rearranging the downstairs floor, much to the grief of our old-timers and historically minded members, our complete collection of Past Commodores' framed photographs was removed, discarded and destroyed.

Unquestionably, creditable work has been done in smartening and brightening up the old clubhouse within the limits of the $80,000 expended in the last five years; of course we are hopelessly crowded on annual Commodore's Reception Days, Annual Meeting and Special General Meeting days but these are not too frequent and anyway a good full house makes for a swinging party. Much of the picturesque nautical atmosphere has been lost, however, with the removal of irreplaceable sailing photographs of our original yachts, especially the historic twin etchings of the Imperial German Navy surrender to the British Grand Fleet in Scapa Flow donated by the late Past Commodore G. F. Gyles, and the striking photo of His Majesty Edward VIII's yacht Britannia in full sail on the Solent, donated by the late Captain Sir Joe Hobbs of fond memory.

But all is not lost—within the confines of our Marine room the worthy "five o'clock faithful" have still managed to hang on to the miscellaneous array of half-models hung around the room and recently D. C. (Doug) McPherson resurrected a rare photo of a group of seven or eight of the old "A" Class yachts racing off the Clubhouse in the early forties, which he kindly donated and which will be protected by the faithful to the last drop (of their blood). Another gracious gesture, deeply appreciated by the older sailing members, was the refurbishing and remounting in a special glass case by H. A. (Hubie) Wallace, of a model of his famous old yacht Minerva, which presently occupies a place of honour in the main Lounge.

The club lost a familiar figure in the person of efficient, ever cheerful Head Steward, Frank Cavaliero who retired in 1970; in 1938, Frank took over from the late impeccable Jayes and for over three decades was the continuous outstanding personal link between the membership and the staff at Jericho. In the ever changing flow of Secretary-Managers, office personnel and indeed club Executives, the presence of Frank in the Bar and Dining Room was a solid contact with past good times; he will be genuinely missed. He was succeeded by George Barrié our present efficient Head Steward. Also, Capt. Denny Ramsbotham Superintendent at Coal Harbour retired owing to ill health and was succeeded by Walter Gwyer in 1967.

Meanwhile, in the past five years the grim reaper has taken heavy toll of well known long time members. In 1966 twenty-two members passed on including Ken Mair, G. W. O'Brien Sr., Mr and Mrs. Bob Henry, Frank Wilgress, Will Vivian, Tommy Pakenham, A. W. Nyblom:

in 1967 sixteen members, including O. B. Allan, Capt. A. C. Crawford, Sid. Darnborough, Robin Hackett, Senator Stan McKeen, Fred Townley, Mrs. G. A. Cran and Charter Member Oswald Moseley:

in 1968 seven members, including Charter Member Albert Austin, Past Commodore Wm. S. Day, and our first Fleet Captain Fred O. Mills;

in 1969 thirteen members, including Past Commodore Capt B. L. Johnson C.B.E., D.S.O., Ron Runge, W. P. Weston and Ed Chisholm:

in 1970 seventeen members, including Past Commodore Temple H. Wright, Mackenzie Bowell, K. B. Woodward, Mrs. B. L. Johnson and Mrs. L. W. Warcup.

R.V.Y.C. Jericho Club House 1970

AMERICA'S CUP CHALLENGE

THE most outstanding and exciting news in our club history and in Canadian yachting is the challenge of the America's Cup by the Royal Vancouver Yacht Club. This challenge has been made on behalf of the Canadian Challenge Syndicate headed by our member George O'Brien.

The following is a copy of the challenge:

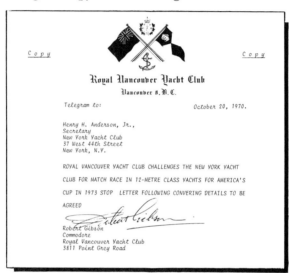

This challenge by the Royal Vancouver Yacht Club is only the third challenge by Canada in the one hundred and nineteen (119) years of reign by the New York Yacht Club. The 1st challenge was by the Royal Canadian Yacht Club in 1876, when the *"Countess of Dufferin"* was badly beaten by the American *"Madeline"*. In 1881, the Bay of Quinte Yacht Club sent the 70' Centreboard sloop *"Atlanta"* against the New York Yacht Club *"Mischief"* with the same sad results.

In the spring of 1970 Geo. O'Brien, with the challenge in mind, purchased the *Dame Pattie*, the 1967 Australian Challenger which was defeated by the *Intrepid*. He rechristened her *"Endless Summer"* and she is the only top flight 12 metre in Canada, and will be a valuable trial horse for the new Canadian Challengers.

Since his acquisition of *"Endless Summer"* he has campaigned her actively and with much success, particularly his victory in the 1970 Swiftsure Race. In October of 1970 *"Endless Summer"* was defeated 2 to 1 in a three race match series with *Columbia* for the Californian Cup, at Marina del Ray, California.

Much was learned from this series both in match racing tactics and requirements of sails and equipment for this type of competition. We wish Geo. O'Brien and his syndicate every success in this tremendous challenge.

CHAPTER 34

Commodores

ROYAL VANCOUVER YACHT CLUB 1966-1970

DOAN M. HARTNELL
Commodore 1966, 1967

THIRTY-FIRST COMMODORE Doan M. Hartnell joined the club in 1954 and held the offices of Rear Commodore 1964 and Vice Commodore 1965 previously being active in the Power Boat and House committees. A capable administrator, he is also an enthusiastic power boater owning and sailing successively the fine large motor vessels *Xanadu* a 94.5 ft. converted U.S. sub-chaser built in 1917, *Takulli* his flagship in 1966, 1967 and the roomy sleek new *Takulli* launched in 1969. Under Commodore Hartnell's leadership long planned expansion of club facilities was instituted and completed. He headed a delegation to Ottawa attempting to acquire *H.M.C.S. Discovery* for club use (old Deadmans Island), and on learning that those facilities were not available to us either in part or in whole, focused our expansion activities on development work in Coal Harbour moorage, and modernising the Jericho Clubhouse. With substantial reserve funds in hand improvements were authorized and completed totaling $172,386.00, distributed $119,218 for dredging, new floats and wiring at Coal Harbour: $33,490 remodeling and refurbishing dining room at Jericho: $18,617 for new pavilion at Tugboat Island and $1,061 for floats at Alexander Island. Meanwhile the club enjoyed a very active season of racing, cruising and power boat predicted log racing. *Mary Bower's* fantastic finish to win the first boat home trophy in the Swiftsure classic was the highlight of the race, in which five club boats were included in the first ten winners. In the tough Norpac Race *Mary Bower* took first and *Velaris* second overall.

Many successful cruises were held by the power boat division, club teams winning both the Century 21 and Pakenham Races. In the Junior division 196 boys and girls took part in the Junior Training Program and the training fleet was increased to 20 Flying Junior sloops.

In his second year as Commodore, Doan directed and supervised a further $74,463 capital expenditure, distributed $54,445 at Coal Harbour: $12,746 at Jericho: $7,272 at Tugboat and Alexander Islands. Pressure on moorage space at Coal Harbour and warning by Provincial authorities to fully utilize our Jericho waterlot necessitated revision of our plans for that area which had been halted by neighborhood opposition. (See page 208.) Accordingly Mr. Wavell Urry was commissioned to design modified protective moorage for sail boats at Jericho and we were launched on the structural waterfront development which was to take several years to accomplish.

Although rising operating costs had necessitated increased dues and moorage charges in the two years of Doan's Commodoreship these had minimal effect on the total membership which declined only 2% largely in the out-of-town classification leaving the current enrollment at a very substantial 1,670. All divisions of the club enjoyed an active successful season our Juniors being well represented in the numerous Centennial Regattas held in August across Canada.

M.V. Takulli 1966

T. F. ORR
Commodore 1968

THIRTY-SECOND COMMODORE T. F. (Bill) Orr joined the club in 1951 and was elected Rear Commodore 1965 and Vice Commodore 1966, 1967. Experienced businessman, he has been an active participant in Civic and Provincial affairs serving as an alderman on Vancouver City Council for three terms, Vice Chairman Provincial Centennial Committee four terms, and Vice Chairman Barkerville Restoration and Fort Steele Restoration Committees. He is also a keen power boat enthusiast having owned and skippered *M.V. Senarieta II* and *M.V. Malecite* his Flagship, fine converted ex Naval and R.C.A.F. vessels. He gave active direction and supervision to the clubs' continuing modernization and expansion program on which $334,055 was expended this year—Coal Harbour $78,176: Jericho Marine Basin $234,087; Jericho Clubhouse $14,293 and Tugboat-Alexander Island stations $7,519. The immediate result of these improvements was a reversal of the slight downward trend in the membership which by the end of the year reached a total of 1,687.

Highlight of sailing activities this year was the inauguration of the Victoria-Maui International Race jointly sponsored by our club and the Royal Lahina Yacht Club (see page   ) in which our Past Commodore F. R. (Bill) Killam in *Porpoise III* made a clean sweep winning 1st to finish, 1st overall and 1st in Division I. R.V.Y.C. member Paul Cote in *Jeunesse* came 1st in Division III, the Tacoma Yacht Club's *Moonglow III* being winner in Division II.

All races were keenly contested the major trophies being won by the following:—in the "A" class the Beaver cup was won by Bob Ross in *Penelakut*, the Minerva cup by John Long in *Mary Bower*, the W. O. Bell trophy by Ken McRae in *Crusader*, the Navigator's trophy by Bill Killam in *Porpoise III* and the Mary Bower trophy by Lol Killam in *Velaris*. In the "B" class John Brandlmyr in *Coho* won the Buscome, the Empire, the White Rocks and the Henry Memorial trophies, the Keyes trophy went to Ken Lochhead in *Ariel V*, and the Schooners & Yawls under 30 ft. to Ian Hamilton in *Cloudrace*. In the power boat section the Tom Ayres (and Bob McKechnie trophies) were won by Les & Babe Simmers in *Vandal*, and the Skipper of the Year trophy, the Dewees, Sam Cromie and Ken Mair Memorial trophies went to Len Sewell in *Dorleen*. The Pakenham trophy was won by the R.V.Y.C. team but the Century 21 Cup went to the U.S. team.

M.V. Malecite 1968

A. J. B. FORSYTH
Commodore 1969

THIRTY-THIRD COMMODORE A. J. B. (Alex) Forsyth joined the club as a junior in 1938 and was one of that outstanding group of our young pre war sailors who participated in the Active Forces—Alex was a pilot with the Royal Canadian Air Force, one of the fifty-four R.V.Y.C. members in that Service. As one of the juniors assigned to learning the "ropes" on the racing yachts he crewed under H. T. "Freddie" Frederickson in the 30 ft. Alden designed sloop *Gamine* and participated in junior racing events in his miniature star. In 1963 he launched the L36 sloop *Serapis* which was later to be his Flagship. This fine yacht designed by W. Lapworth was built by Taylor Shipyards with finishing work by Pieter Rook. His active work in club affairs started with his election to the post of Honorary Measurer in 1964. In 1965 he was elected to the Executive Committee and was appointed Seabreeze editor. He was elected Fleet Captain in 1966, Rear Commodore in 1967 and Vice Commodore in 1968. In addition to being Commodore in 1969 he was appointed Commodore of Pacific International Yachting Association as it was R.V.Y.C.'s turn to host the International Regatta that year. He was the club's liaison officer on *C.N.A.V. Laymore* the escort vessel on the Victoria-Maui Race in 1968. While Commodore he was a crew member on the R.V.Y.C. team that participated in the first Canadian entry U.S. Congressional Cup races at Long Beach, California and also that year he was a crew member on Dick Sandwell's *Gabrielle III* when she sailed in the United Kingdom events, the Dinard Race, Cowes week and the Fastnet Race.

Aggressively continuing the expansion programme which had been finally launched by the previous three Executives of which he had been an outstanding member, Commodore Forsyth directed and completed the expenditure of construction totalling $264,045, distributed Coal Harbour $93,161; Jericho pier extension $161,806; Jericho Clubhouse $7,553; Tugboat Island $1,525. Member interest in these activities and the necessity for member approval of the required financing called for no less than three General Meetings during the year—an unprecedented number in any one year of the club's 66 year history. Commodore Alex carried these off successfully with minor amendments, receiving overwhelming authority to increase dues, borrow up to $125,000 and make certain necessary changes in the Bylaws. Meanwhile sailing and power boat activities carried on in full force. The P.I.Y.A. Regatta held here that year had a registration of 284 boats, by far the largest attendance ever recorded. This year also saw the inauguration of the new Olympic Soling Class boats, eight fine new vessels of this type having been brought into the club. The power boat fleet were also very active, our R.V.Y.C. teams winning the Pakenham Trophy Race; and the Canadian team in which our members participated recovered the Century 21 Trophy for Canada. Membership also continued to increase, the total at the end of the year being 1,715. This year the elective office of Measurer was dropped and two new elective offices established, Jericho Port Captain and Offshore Stations Officer.

Sloop Serapis 1969

ROBERT GIBSON
Commodore 1970, 1971

THIRTY-FOURTH COMMODORE Robert Gibson originally joined the club as a junior in 1933 sailing Snipes till 1936 rejoining as an active senior member in 1950. He is an avid power boater having owned and skippered the following vessels: 1950 *Arrow II*, 1952 *Argee I*, 1954 *Argee II*, 1957 *Gibson Gal* and 1965 on *Gibson Gal*—51 ft. twin screw Diesel his Flagship 1970 and 1971. Bob is an extremely active and energetic Commodore, his drive and ability to get things done being reminiscent, within living memory, of the late Commodores Harold A. Jones and Temple H. Wright. Active on the Rear Commodore's Committee in 1957 Bob at the Annual General Meeting that year battled out and initiated the member financed shelter programme which has been so successful, finally enabling the club to get rid of the two or three dozen dilapidated old shelters—eyesores at Coal Harbour for years. Elected to office of Staff Captain in 1961 and 1967 he became Rear Commodore in 1968 and Vice Commodore in 1969 but before holding those Flag Offices he had been a force in the power boat and Coal Harbour Committees since 1958. An outstanding effort in 1960 was obtaining Executive approval for an option on the purchase of Tugboat Island which was acquired for $27,000—now one of our finest assets. His enthusiasm and logic at Special General Meetings held in 1969 helped to carry the day for the completion of the Jericho Marina on which a total of $588,284 has now been expended, the last $192,391 being in his year: other capital expenditures being Jericho Clubhouse $14,310: Coal Harbour $48,497 and the offshore stations $1,145.

A full programme of club sailing fixtures was run off including several major events in which the other local yacht club vessels participated on an invitational basis. Six yachts from R.V.Y.C. were entered in the International Victoria-Maui Race (total entries 23) in which Lol Killam's fine new 73 ft. ketch *Graybeard* made a clean sweep 1st to finish, 1st overall and 1st Div. 1. A highlight of the season was the eliminations in the 6 metre class for the St. Francis Yacht Club Challenge Race held on English Bay midsummer in which our *Yam-Sing* was defeated.

Another "highlight" was provided by no less than Commodore Bob himself on the occasion of the annual local Commodores challenge event sailed in Dragons. It seems that Bob, at the tiller on *Puff* leaving the Marina, and turning to acknowledge the encouraging waves of interested spectator "critics" on the Clubhouse verandah, crashed full bore into a moored yacht, presumably forgetting that racing Dragons do not have reverse engines. For this "achievement" Bob was justly awarded the annual Bird Rock Trophy—however he redeemed himself by winning the Commodore's race.

The power boaters had their usual active season. Les and Babe Simmers in *Vandal* won the McKechnie Trophy in the International Cruiser race but the Century 21 Trophy went back to the U.S. team. In addition to initiating the Annual Commodore's Cruise to Tugboat Island, Commodore Bob over the years organized many working parties to the offshore stations, donating kitchen equipment etc. to the new clubhouse on Tugboat Island and in 1967 the impressive Tugboat Island Fishing Derby Trophy. His second year as Commodore has just commenced—no doubt it will be equally successful.

M.V. Gibson Gal 1971

CHAPTER 35

R.V.Y.C.

Offshore Stations

TUGBOAT ISLAND

ALEXANDER ISLAND

.

W HILE OUR ACQUISITION of Tugboat Island in 1960 and Alexander Island in 1965 is recorded in Chapter 23 pages 213-4 of the original Annals few details are given, therefore the following history of the transformation into their present high usefulness and exceptional asset value prepared by Commodore Gibson, Rear Commodore Bob Orr and "reeve" Neil Thomson, is worthy of note—their untiring efforts sparking work parties etc. have been a major factor in this happy development.

TUGBOAT ISLAND

Tugboat Island was purchased in 1960, under Commodore Stan Davies; since then, many significant changes have taken place.

The first work parties commenced in November, 1960, progressing over the next decade with volunteer help, and starting from the water up.

The first float was installed in 1963; the second float was taken over in sections in 1965, on a barge, and assembled on the site. Telephone, power and dock lighting were completed on the Island in the fall of 1965.

The third section was completed in 1966, in Vancouver, and towed to Tugboat by the *Malecite*, and Captain Bill Orr. Number 4 and 5 sections were also built in Vancouver, at the club, in 1967 and towed to Tugboat by the *Gibson Gal* and *Owaissa* under Bob Gibson and Bob Orr. This gave us a total of 1,248 lineal feet of moorage, all installed by volunteer, progressive work parties. A new ramp float and dock were rebuilt in 1968.

The first permanent caretaker of the Island was Mr. Nash, followed by Mr. Al Galbraith and presently Mr. Will Tritchell, who has been primarily responsible for our wonderful trail and fire-fighting programme.

On a $10,000 budget, we progressed to the inception of the present pavilion, complete with fireplace, electric stove and refrigerator and water system, with the official opening ceremonies, under Commodore Doan Hartnell on July 1, 1966.

In February, 1968, again with volunteer labor, a 2,500 gallon water tower was erected on high ground, in lieu of drilling a well for fresh water.

In the same year, a well was drilled but unfortunately, salt water was struck and had to be abandoned. The well having failed, a cistern was constructed under the pavilion and a pumping system installed to pump the water to the water tower, where it flows back to the pavilion by gravity.

The first Commodore's Cruise was inaugurated in 1961 and this is now an annual affair.

The farsighted wisdom in purchasing Tugboat Island is borne out in that 500 to 600 vessels and upwards of 2,500 members and friends visit this delightful rendezvous every year, with its forest trails, secluded beaches and abundance of shellfish.

Tugboat Island Station comes under the jurisdiction of the Offshore Station Officer, who appoints a mayor; the mayor at present is Mr. John Erickson, of the *Noresnne*. The first mayor of Tugboat was Bob Day in 1960-63; Bill Orr in 1963, and Bob Orr from 1964 to 1969.

In conclusion, it should be stated that one of Tugboat's greatest assets has been the fellowship created by its many volunteer work projects, stag cruises, family cruises, frost-bite regattas, and the annual sailing races to and from the Island. It has an international reputation as a termination point for both the P.I.Y.A. and the I.P.B.A. Regattas.

R.V.Y.C.'s Tugboat Island, Silva Bay, B.C.

ALEXANDER ISLAND

Upon acquiring the Island in 1965 from Past Commodore Captain B. L. Johnson, the Island has operated under a Reeve appointed by the off-shore Stations Officer.

Our first Reeve was Douglas C. McPherson followed by Neil C. Thomson since that date, with the exception of 1969 when John Belyea was Reeve.

Much work has been performed at the Island through volunteer member work parties who in 1966 constructed a large outdoor barbecue together with a registration hut and washrooms. Since that time our famous and controversial horseshoe pitch has been installed together with a large picnic and happy hour veranda as well as trails for the nature lovers. Moorage facilities presently comprise two large floats giving a total moorage of approximately 900 feet. A new section is replacing a part of the original moorage during the Spring of 1971 which will add an additional 275 feet of space.

In 1970 an abundance of fresh water was piped to the island from a fresh water spring on Gambier Island and this again was done through volunteer labour.

The close proximity of this Island to Vancouver makes Alexander a popular rendezvous for our members to the extent that an average of 500 vessels with 1800 members visit this delightful spot each year.

R.V.Y.C.'s Alexander Island, Howe Sound, B.C.

CHAPTER 36

Predicted

LOG RACING

F AVORED WITH comparatively sheltered waters stretching seven hundred miles from Puget Sound to the Gulf of Alaska and winding through scenery of unequalled grandeur, it is natural that the major activity of the power boating fraternity centers on cruising and exploring the majestic inlets (fjords to the Norwegians) and intriguing bays and coves scattered in profusion along the entire North Pacific coast. It is logical, however, that the competitive spirit stirring in the breasts of enthusiastic skippers who take pride in their abilities as pilots, navigators and seamen, should express itself in different forms of contest. The Predicted Log Race, the now well recognized and popular contest, is one of those forms. It is great fun and a contribution to better seamanship to compare predicted with actual times of arrival at different points without reference to any time keeping device except immediately after passing those points. The skipper with the least difference between actual and predicted times is the winner.

Top scoring requires accurate chart work, knowledge of currents, wind velocity and direction and an accurate speed curve giving the speed for normal cruising R.P.M.s. Until recently most races were run on a fixed throttle but now change in throttle is allowed without reference to time keeping devices. The standard and special rules for the Gulf of Georgia race and the International cruiser race have remained essentially similar so that both Canadian and U.S. skippers can participate on equal terms.

The top Canadian predicted log race is run by the Gulf of Georgia Predicted Log Race Committee which consists of members from most yacht clubs in British Columbia. The top skipper in this event wins the Sam Cromie Memorial Trophy. A special rule usually requires that about half of the approximate 60 mile course be run in the open Straits of Georgia. Formerly the rules called for some running in darkness but this has been dropped in deference to the hazard this presented to the modern high speed cruisers many of which cruise at speeds up to twenty knots.

Other interclub races are the Spring Race—usually in June—the winner receiving the Ken Mair Memorial Trophy and the leading R.Van.Y.C. vessel the Dewees Trophy. Points are earned in this race for the Skipper of the Year trophy. The Fall Race is usually held in October, the winner earning points for Skipper of the Year.

The International Cruiser Race in July sponsored by the International Power Boat Association is the oldest in North Pacific power yachting between Puget Sound and Gulf of Georgia ports. Points are earned for Skipper trophy and the winning Canadian vessel receives the Bob McKechnie Trophy, the top R.V.Y.C. skipper gets the Tom Ayres Trophy. The Pakenham Trophy raced for in the Fall between teams from local yacht clubs, 4 boats each, goes to the yacht club having the best score between the three top boats in the four boat teams. The Seattle World's Fair Century 21 Trophy is worthy of note in that it is a large and costly prize and it is raced for by six-cruiser Canadian and U.S. teams. Royal Vancouver skippers are usually on the Canadian team.

R.V.Y.C. wins Century 21 International Team Race. Bill Anderson, at left, congratulates the winning team of l. to r., Carl Carlson, Les Simmers, Len Sewell, Bill Killam, Tom Trapp. The 1966 race was from Anacortes to Ladysmith.

CHAPTER 37

Victoria-Maui

INTERNATIONAL YACHT RACES

A BRIGHT NEW STAR in the constellation of Ocean Racing—the Victoria-Maui International Yacht Race—came into being in 1965 when our R.V.Y.C. yachts *Long Gone* and *Velaris* with Royal Victoria Yacht Club's *Noreana of Wight*, raced from Neah Bay in Juan de Fuca Strait to Kahului on the island of Maui, Hawaii (see page 256). The idea of organizing a major ocean race originating from the North Pacific was born in the mind of our member John G. Innes and skipper of *Long Gone* in 1963 and the initial event proved so interesting and successful that it was decided to promote an official race for 1968. Our club undertook to act as Sponsor with the co-operation of Royal Lahaina Yacht Club in Maui, the race to start July 1st off Victoria, B.C. and end off the Black Rock off Kekaa Point on the island of Maui, a distance on the Great Circle Route of 2310 miles.

Fourteen yachts took part in 1968: five were from Royal Vancouver Y.C.—*Porpoise III, Velaris, Gabrielle III, Mary Bower* and *Jeunesse;* from the Royal Canadian Navy Sailing Assn. the *H.M.C.S. Oriole;* and from Royal Victoria Y.C. *Tiffany* and *Cubara;* from Tacoma Y.C. *Moonglow III* and *Rainbird; African Star* from Seattle Y.C.; *Suerte II* from Corinthian Y.C.; and *Cu Na Mara* from Western California Y.C.

Winners were *Porpoise III* R.V.Y.C. Skipper F. R. (Bill) Killam 1st to finish, 1st overall, 1st Division I; *Moonglow III* Tacoma Y.C. Skipper Dave Neilsen 1st Division II; *Jeunesse* R.V.Y.C. Skipper Paul Cote 1st Division III.

The race was started by His Honour J. R. Nicholson Lieutenant Governor of British Columbia on board *H.M.C.S. Mackenzie* off Brotchie Ledge Light, Victoria, B.C. Escort for the fleet was provided by the Canadian Navy with their Oceanographic vessel the *C.N.A.V. Laymore* under the command of Captain McDonald.

Winds varied from North to South down to Latitude 33 where the N.E. trades were encountered which blew from 7 to 35 knots for the balance of the route for those ships that followed a course a bit South of a great Circle Route. Those that chose a more Southerly arc to take advantage of the supposedly prevailing N.W. winds down the coast had very light going down to the tradewind belt.

Porpoise III took 16 days 7 hours 51 minutes.

Planned for Bi-Annual competition the following perpetual trophies were awarded at a traditional Hawaiian Luau held in the Hale Paahoa, Lahaina, a restored historic old prison built in 1852 to hold early unruly whalers who wintered in the old capital of the Hawaiian Islands where also Captain George Vancouver R.N. wintered in the 1790's.

PROVINCE OF BRITISH COLUMBIA TROPHY for the first yacht on corrected time in Division I.

FOUNDER'S (J. G. Innes) TROPHY presented by Maui Chamber of Commerce for first yacht on corrected time in Division II.

COUNTY OF MAUI TROPHY for first yacht on corrected time in Division III.

ROYAL VANCOUVER YACHT CLUB TROPHY to the first over-all winning yacht on corrected time.

GOVERNOR OF HAWAII TROPHY to the first yacht on elapsed time in Division I.

CITY OF VICTORIA TROPHY to the first yacht on elapsed time in Division II.

BLUE GAVEL CLUB TROPHY presented by past Commodores of North American Yacht Clubs to first yacht on elapsed time in Division III.

ROYAL LAHAINA YACHT CLUB TROPHY to first overall winning yacht on elapsed time.

R.V.Y.C.-L.Y.C. COMMEMORATIVE PLAQUE presented to each yacht completing the course.

Twenty-three yachts took part in the next race July 1st 1970 again started by His Honour J. R. Nicholson Lieutenant Governor of British Columbia on board *H.M.C.S. Miramichi*. Escort vessel was Canadian Navy's deep sea tug *C.N.A.V. St Anthony*. Captain Hooper. Eleven Canadian and twelve U.S. yachts participated. From Royal Vancouver Y.C. six yachts entered; *Celeste*, Geo. Scrimshaw; *Drummer Boy*, John Dunfield; *Graybeard*, Lol Killam; *Long Gone*, John Innes; *Porpoise III*, Bill Killam; *Puffin II*, Ed Lund.

Winners, corrected times were 1st to finish, 1st overall and 1st, Div. I *Graybeard*, Lol Killam R.V.Y.C., 1st, Division II, *Satin Doll*, skipper Bush C.Y.C., 1st Division III, *Drummer Boy*, skipper John Dunfield, R.V.Y.C.

Winds were relatively light down to the tradewind belt, although the times made by the fleet were on the average better than in 1968. However the tradewinds were non existent until 100 miles out of Maui, reputed to be the first time this has happened in 50 years.

In spite of the light airs, *Graybeard*, a new 73 ft. fiberglass ketch made a record crossing of 15 days, 00 hours, 45 minutes elapsed time leading the second yacht *Satin Doll* by 4 days, 22½ hours. The third yacht *Drummer Boy* took 21 days, 5½ hours. *Porpoise III* (1968 winner) was fifth ship in the fleet to finish with an elapsed time of 20 days 14 hours.

It is a source of great pride to British Columbians, Vancouverites and the Royal Vancouver Yacht Club that the winners of the first two official Victoria-Maui Races were yachts designed and built in Vancouver by naval architect Peter Hatfield and ICL Engineering Ltd. proving to the world-wide sailing fraternity that not only does Vancouver produce champion sailors but has, in addition, the talent, materials and equipment to be "tops" in yacht designing and construction.

GRAYBEARD 2nd TO FINISH IN CAPETOWN TO RIO 1971 RACE

G RAYBEARD, Lol Killam's beautiful 73 ft. fibreglass ketch carried the flag of Canada and the R.V.Y.C. burgee to world yachting distinction in the 3300 mile Capetown to Rio Janeiro race February, 1971 by being second boat to finish and sixth on corrected time in a fleet of 58 vessels from 19 countries including some of the world's top yachts and skippers.

With an elapsed time of 23 days 19 hours 4 minutes *Graybeard* sailed a course of 3658 miles at an average speed of 6.5 knots. Her best day covered 273 miles and her best speed was 14.5 knots, the worst day being 59 miles and the worst watch 5 miles in 8 hours. Average winds less than 10 knots with only 3 days of good wind at 20 knots. Leading *Graybeard* by 19 hours the 71 ft. *Ocean Spirit*, winner of the Round Britain race, was first boat to finish. For the first time in recorded racing history one of the yachts, the *Pioneer* 33 ft. Capt. W. Schuten, South Africa sank after hitting a whale twelve days out of Capetown; all crew members were rescued by an American freighter.

Reputed to be the largest fibreglass sailing yacht in the world, designed by Peter Hatfield and built in Vancouver she is designed to provide all the comforts of a cruiser and still be a champion in ocean racing contests.

After winning the 1970 Victoria to Maui International Race she continued around the world through the South Seas to Fiji, Port Moresby, Darwin, Australia, Thursday Islands, Seychelles Islands, Durban and Capetown. A crew of five, all R.V.Y.C. members, sailed her under Skipper Lol to Capetown where they were joined by eight more R.V.Y.C. sailors. Her crew in the race consisted of Skipper Lol Killam, Pat Leslie, Ches Rickard, Dr. Jack McMillan, Bob Ross, Bill Vogel, John Hutchinson, Malcolm Wickson, Harvey Carruthers and "Bunker" Killam all members of our club, also well known Pacific Northwest sailors Henry Kotkins, Dave Nielsen, Dr. Govnor Teats, Tom Endersby, Chris Justice and Derek Blair.

CHAPTER 38

Blue Water

RACING AND CRUISING

TRANS PACIFIC YACHT CLUB RACES

SINCE the printing of the Royal Vancouver Yacht Club history, in 1965, there have been two Honolulu races sponsored by the Transpacific Yacht Club in which our members have taken part.

In the first race, the 1967 Transpacific from Los Angeles to Honolulu, our club was well represented by Norm McCarvill, sailing the well known "*Spirit*", (ex *Dyna*), and Phil Graham, making his second Transpacific with his beautiful new sixty-two foot ship, "*Driver*". *Driver* had just been launched a few weeks before Phil sailed her to Los Angeles and the Transpacific was really a shake down event for his new boat.

1967, *Driver*, owner-skipper Phil Graham, finished 8th in A class out of 12 entries and 57th overall in a fleet of 70, elapsed time 13:12:30:11 and corrected time 10:11:27:41.

1967, *Spirit*, owner-skipper Norman McCarvill, finished 12th in B class which had 24 entries and 35th overall in a fleet of 70, elapsed time 13:09:52:49, and corrected time 09:19:12:37.

In the second race, the 1969 Transpacific from Los Angeles to Honolulu was one of the most spectacular, at least from the view point of the Royal Vancouver Yacht Club's only entry, "*Mir*", skippered by owner, George O'Brien. George drove his fine 87 foot ketch very hard for the entire 2,225 miles of this race and encountered more than the usual trouble with spinnakers, blowing out some 4 new sails. Despite these problems, *Mir* had been in third position for nearly the entire race being led by the two new ultra racing machines, *Blackfin* and *Windward Passage*.

When *Mir* hit the infamous Molokai Channel with winds of 40 miles per hour and gusting to 60, the crew were forced to hand the mizzen spinnaker. They still held full main, spinnaker and spinnaker staysail which produced surfing speeds of over 16 knots on their speed indicator as they approached Diamond Head.

Just short of the finish line, a heavy gust of wind knocked the 54 ton *Mir* flat on the water. With the tremendous stresses produced, something had to go, and in a few seconds the main mast came crashing down. The skipper could see, although close to the finish, that they were going to drift past the finish line on the wrong side of the committee boat marking the end of the line. The crew set feverishly to work clearing the decks of the twisted remains of mast rigging and sails, set the spinnaker on the mizzen mast and made history by sailing backward over the finish line to an incredible 3rd boat finish.

This dramatic dismasting didn't daunt O'Brien, the boat was jury rigged in Honolulu with a telephone pole and a spinnaker pole for a boom, for its return voyage to Newport Beach.

1969, *Mir*, owner-skipper George O'Brien 3rd to finish was 7th, in A class, which had 14 entries and 35th overall in a fleet of 72 entries elapsed time 10:03:47:35, corrected time 7:16:39:05.

In the 1970 Tahiti race from Los Angeles to Tahiti, a distance of 3,571 nautical miles, our club was represented for the first time in this event by George O'Brien in *Mir*. *Mir* sailed an excellent race and was in either 1st or 2nd position for most of the time and finally finished 2nd to "*Blackfin*".

1970, *Mir*, owner-skipper George O'Brien, finished 2nd, 4th in class A out of 6 entries, and 9th overall in a fleet of 14, elapsed time 18:13:11:43, corrected time 17:05:09:55.

George O'Brien continued to do well with *Mir* and was 1st to finish out of 19 entries in the 1968 Los Angeles to Mazatlan Race. On corrected time he placed 5th in Class A out of 9 boats.

In the 1969 Los Angeles to Ensenada Race with a total entry of approximately 580 boats, *Mir* finished 2nd (mono-hulls) behind the 12 metre *Newsboy*.

Almost across finish line stern first, mizzen spinnaker is struck as mizzen mast, stayed to carry sail on the other side, threatens to follow mainmast. Few moments of power from comparatively small (1,040 sq. ft.) spinnaker was enough to drag Mir over line.
Credit Pacific Yachting

AUSTRALIAN AND EUROPEAN RACING

Other Blue Water Racing and Cruising events saw several R.V.Y.C. boats participating. Dick Sandwell with his 53' sloop *Gabrielle III*, designed by Sparkman & Stephens and built 1967 by McGruer in Scotland was most active.

On 26th December 1968, *Gabrielle* took part in the Sidney—Hobart Race, in which she placed 15th in Division 1, just ahead of *Ondine*. It was a fairly rough race with 67 starters, of which 13 withdrew. R.V.Y.C. members on board were P. R. Sandwell, G. R Anderson, Esben Poulsson and G. C. Hyatt. In January she took part in the Trumpeter Bay Race in Tasmania, in which she placed 2nd. After cruising in Tasmania she was sailed to Melbourne where she was shipped to London by freighter.

In the summer of 1969, *Gabrielle III* took part in Cowes Week and the R.O.R.C. races: Cowes-Dinard, Channel and Fastnet. In the latter she placed 32nd in Class 1. The race was slow and quiet that year. R.V.Y.C. members on board were Commodore A. J. B. Forsyth, P. R Sandwell, G. R. Anderson, Esben Poulsson and G. C. Hyatt.

After wintering in England, *Gabrielle III* was sailed to Copenhagen at the end of May for a summer of cruising in the Baltic and the Skagerrak, including a voyage across Sweden through the Gota Canal, Lake Vattern and Lake Vanern. She entered two races: Gotland Runt and the Skaw. In the former she placed 4th in Class 1B and from the latter she withdrew with 70% of the fleet, after touching a mark on the course— the Skagen lightship! R.V.Y.C. members on board for the two races were P. R. Sandwell and G. C. Hyatt.

As of this writing *Gabrielle III* is laid up in Denmark. She will be campaigned in European waters again in 1971.

SPIRIT IN TRANS-ATLANTIC RACE

Norman R. McCarvill carried the Royal Vancouver Burgee in many international sailing events in the famous ocean racer *Dyna* which he purchased in September 1966 and rechristened her *Spirit*.

During 1966 to January 1968 Norm raced *Spirit* in all the major races and regattas in the California Area, for a total of 26 first places and set records in 2 long distance races.

In February 1968 before sailing to the East Coast, *Spirit* placed 3rd in A class in the Acapulco Race.

In Long Island Sound, *Spirit* was part of the Canadian Team in the Onion Patch Regatta, but unfortunately the 3rd Canadian boat did not show up. Competing in these races were teams from U.S.A., Britain, Germany, Canada and Argentina, this event is similar to the Admirals Cup in England. Norm McCarvill was 1st overall in the second and largest race from Seawananken Yacht Club, Island Sound around Block Island to Newport, Rhode Island. The 3rd race in Newport was cancelled by the race committee over protests. The 4th race the Bermuda Race, for the first time this race was delayed one day due to a Hurricane.

In this race *Spirit* finished 4th in Class A and 12th boat to finish in a fleet of 152 boats.

In 1968, Norm McCarvill with *Spirit* was the first privately owned Canadian Yacht to enter the Trans-Atlantic Race from Bermuda to Travenmunde Germany, 3667 miles, the longest Ocean Race ever held. *Spirit* finished 4th in Class B, 7th overall and was 3rd boat to finish in a fleet of 32 boats within sight of the new Ondine and Stormvogel the 1st and 2nd boats to finish; the crossing took 22 days.

DRIVER ON WORLD TOUR

Phillip D. Graham's 61 ft. sloop *Driver* has been leisurely touring the world since launching from Osborne Shipyards North Vancouver in 1967 and while it has not yet circumnavigated the globe Skipper Phil will doubtless some time in the future flip around the Horn or more likely slip through the Panama Canal to again breast the Pacific seas thus completing the job. Owner-Skipper Phil sailed *Driver* down to California to take part in the 1967 TransPac to Honolulu. Leaving there in September 1967 with his wife Joan as 1st Mate and a crew of his four sons, "Flip" 18, Chris 14, Bruce 11, Lawrence 7, a tutor and a cook, they cruised the South Seas arriving at Australia in October 1968. Leaving there they crossed the Indian Ocean to Durban and rounded the Cape of Good Hope in March 1969. Thence to the Azores in May 1969 and through the Straits of Gibraltar to Malta Nov. 1969. They cruised the Aegean Sea in the Summer of 1970 being joined by sometime exTroubadour crew members, Freddy McMeans and "Buzz" Buzzelle, for a month of unrecorded cruising. After a cruise up the Adriatic Sea to Yugoslavia, *Driver* was tied up in Malta while Phil and family skied and went to school in Switzerland where their home is now set up in Saanon. As of 1971 Phil and family will cruise the Baltic Sea and Scandinavian Countries; Freddy McMeans will join them in Malta for the four months northern cruising.

GULF OF CALIFORNIA BOISTEROUS

The sunny Gulf of California is no place to sail in the wintertime, Jack and Mitzi Walkem found in their 6000 mile cruise to Manzanillo, Mexico and return. Cruising in their 35 ft. sloop *Bendora* from September 1966 to June 1967, they headed up the Gulf to Guaymas in December encountering bitterly cold 35 to 45 knot winds whistling through the channels of the mid gulf islands. They also found the seas between the tip of Baja California and Mazatlan extremely uncomfortable, being short and choppy despite average 15 knot winds. *Bendora* was double reefed most of the trip down the West Coast, the return being made mostly under power within sight of land to avoid the long haul westward necessary to make British Columbia waters under sail.

Another ex R.V.Y.C. small sized sloop, the 32 ft. *Toroa*, made the long bluewater trip down to Costa Rica and Panama and return in 1962. Well known local sailors, Audery and Pete Rees, report that their cruise in *Toroa* was comparatively uneventful.

CHAPTER 39

Swiftsure Racing

ROYAL VANCOUVER YACHT CLUB ENTRIES IN
SWIFTSURE CLASSIC 1966-1970
Continued from Page 155

	Yacht	Skipper	Position in Class		Overall Position
1966	Ariel V	K. Lochhead	3	(3)	8
	Gabrielle	P. R. Sandwell		(2)	DNF
	George Kitamike	H. Davidson	10	(3)	32
	Jeunesse	P. Coté		(4)	DNF
	Jolly Olly	V. Ruskin	5	(4)	5
	Lollipop	H. Vogel	7	(4)	19
	Long Gone	J. West	11	(3)	33
	Maredea	W. Burgess		(3)	DNF
	Mary Bower	J. H. Long	3	(2)	16
	Pandora of Rhu	J. Klymack		(2)	DNF
	Penelakut	R. Ross		(2)	DNF
	Sanderling	A. Meakin	6	(3)	12
	Serapis	A. Forsyth		(3)	DNF
	Spirit	N. McCarvill		(1)	DNF
	Tricia	P. Leslie	2	(3)	7
	Velaris	L. Killam	4	(2)	17
	Winsome III	C. Rickard	4	(3)	10
1967	Alcion	C. Campbell	7	(2)	21
	Allegra	A. Way		(2)	DFN
	Ariel V	K. Lockhead	7	(3)	13
	Benora II	J. Glass	11	(3)	19
	Cloudrace	I. Hamilton		(3)	DNF
	Concerto	A. Booth	4	(2)	12
	Crusader	K. McRae	2	(1)	6
	Gabrielle II	P. R. Sandwell		(2)	DNF
	Hawk	Bill Killam		(2)	DNF
	Jester	S. Watts		(3)	DNF
	Jeunesse	P. Coté		(4)	DNF
	Jolly Olly	V. Ruskin	8	(4)	36
	Kimji	J. Eastman	6	(4)	30
	Kitamike	H. Davidson		(3)	DNF
	Lollipop	H. Vogel		(3)	DNF
	Maredea	W. Burgess		(3)	DNF
	Mary Bower	J. Long		(2)	DNF
	Mir	G. O'Brien		(1)	DNF
	Nantuk	W. M. Young		(4)	DNF
	Nyon	D. Simpson		(3)	DNF
	Pandora of Rhu	J. Klymak	8	(2)	22
	Penelakut	R. Ross	11	(2)	31
	Sanderling	A. Meakin		(3)	DNF
	Serapis	A. Forsyth		(3)	DNF
	Tricia	P. Leslie	9	(3)	16
	Velaris	L. Killam	3	(2)	10
	Veleda	J. Grubbe		(4)	DNF
	Winsome III	C. Rickard	5	(3)	9

crossed the line 34 sec. ahead in the first race and picked up to 1 minute ahead at the 2nd mark but fell to 40 sec. behind at the 3rd failing to better its position and finishing 2 minutes 30 sec. behind. In the second race *St. Francis IV* crossed the line 2 sec. ahead of *Yam Sing* which fell behind progressively till 3 minutes behind at the 4th mark picking up slightly thereafter and was 58 sec. behind at the finish mark. The third race start was taken by *Yam Sing* by 5 sec. but *St. Francis IV* was 47 sec. ahead at the 1st mark and steadily improved its lead to 1 minute 52 sec. at the finish.

DRAGONS

WHILE local interest in International Star, Lightning and Geary 18 contests declined somewhat in recent years, this was probably due to our most active sailors in those classes having graduated to the Dragon, Soling and cruising groups. However, Star sailing activity was maintained locally as the record of trophy results show. (See page 386). In 1967 Ken Kirkland with Bob Burgess as crew took his *Star Gypsy* to Toronto for the North American Star Championships finishing 25th in a fleet of 44. Carl Petersen also took his Star, *Susan IV* to Toronto and with a local crew finished 30th. In 1968 the N.A. Star Championships were held in San Francisco Bay; Bill West with J. Gosden of K.Y.C. as crew took down *Windor* finishing 19th and Ken & Ian Kirkland in *Gypsy* finished 21st in a fleet of 35 Stars.

In two of the six Olympic classes—Dragons and Solings—our club members have continued to carry on the traditions of top competition and performance in international races and it is interesting to note that most of the following mentioned crews are young sailors who learned their active sailing at our club in our then active programme of junior racing.

In 1966 Steve Tupper and his crew Dave Miller began preparing for the 1968 Olympics. They travelled twice to Eastern Canada that summer and sailed borrowed boats in Toronto, Buffalo and Montreal. These trips resulted in winning the coveted John Foster Dulles Trophy, emblematic of the Great Lakes Championships, and the Davar Quaich Trophy in Montreal. However, the crew was unsuccessful in their major aim which was to qualify for the World Championships to be held in Toronto in 1967.

The unfortunate result of the races in 1966 brought plans for Olympic sailing to a halt as it seemed hard to justify an all out effort if they could not sail in the World Championship in Toronto.

Over the winter of 1968 Steve and Dave decided to try again after an offer was made of a boat to sail in the Trials in Kingston in July. Steve purchased *Antigone* in Toronto and a new effort was mounted. In July the crew moved to Kingston for the Trials. The third crew Tim Irwin joined them there. The trials followed the Canadian Championships in which they sailed only three of the five races and finished third.

The trials were a very close fought series with the Vancouver crew taking five of the first six races resulting in cancellation of the three remaining races.

Paul Phelan who had finished second in the Trials kindly offered our crew the use of his brand new boat *Mia IV*. This was one of the major reasons for their excellent performance. The crew were also very fortunate to be able to borrow a Seville Spar from Dr. Patterson who owned *Argo,* the boat they had sailed in the trials.

The next step was the Dragon North American Championships in Houston, Texas. Following are excerpts from a report made by Steve on the Regatta.

"Houston was a rather interesting place to sail as it had been chosen for its similarity in climate to Acapulco. It was very hot with the temperature in the mid 90's and humidity near 100%."

"We were protested at the start of the third race but managed to win the protest after a three hour hearing. Possibly the greatest excitement of the series came in the fourth race when after a beautiful start and going the right place we found ourselves with a nice lead. Suddenly, there was a horrible crash and we found we had pulled out one of the chainplates on the starboard side." "Because of this we slipped to fourth place." "The last race was a first place finish and a wonderful way to end the series."

The results of the Series were O. J. Young first, Buddy Friedrichs second and Steve Tupper third.

The next Series was the Olympics itself. Dave, Tim and Steve went to Acapulco in early October to get ready for the races. Following are some excerpts of Steve's report after the Games.

"We seemed to stand up to the hot sun fairly well. After several days of sailing off Acapulco it became fairly obvious why small one-design sailing is not popular there. The seas are large, up to 15' and the winds are generally light. This made trying to point the boat in one direction a constant chore."

"The first racing day brought the first of many surprises. Instead of the light winds we all expected, it was blowing 10-12 at the start and continued to increase up to about 18 by the end of the race. We were fortunate enough to place third in this race and felt quite confident as we sailed in from the race."

"However, the next day we slipped to eighth and the following day to thirteenth. Fortunately, this was the low point of the series and we fought back to take a third in the last race and a fourth overall."

The final results of the Games were, Friedrichs, U.S.A. first; Birch, Denmark, second; Borowski, East Germany, third and Tupper, Canada, fourth.

This showing was the best that any Canadian has had in any class since Hubie Wallace won a Silver in 8 Meters and Harry Wylie won a Bronze in Stars in 1932.

In 1969 Steve Tupper sailing *Antigone* was joined in the international races by Bob Burgess sailing *Tjep*. Bob had enjoyed an excellent season in Vancouver winning most of the preseason races. The first international event was held in Vancouver, the Duke of Edinburgh, which Steve won to repeat his victory of 1965 the last time the Series had been held in Vancouver. Following this the P.I.Y.A. regatta saw Bob win. The racing moved to Bellingham the next week for the North American Championships where Burgess came second and Tupper third.

In the summer of 1969 Steve also trailered his boat to Kingston, Ontario for the Canadian Olympic Training Regatta. This regatta attracted all the top Eastern boats, Steve finishing first with the assistance of his crew Miss Paddy Maitland and Kevin Hendry.

In 1970 Bob Burgess finished 2nd in the P.I.Y.A. Regatta which was held in Bellingham and trailering *Tjep* back east, came 7th in the Canadian Championships at Toronto and 8th in the North American Championships held in Kingston, Ont.

SOLINGS

This exciting new class of racing craft appeared on the international yacht racing scene in the middle sixties as a result of the I.Y.R.U. looking for alternative Olympic boats in the three man keel type under 30 ft. overall length, as the 5.5 metre was becoming very expensive. Many designs were produced and prototypes built and, after a series of trials, Norwegian Jan Linge's *Soling* was selected and became an International Class in 1967. It soon became the fastest growing keel boat class in the world, within two years numbering 1200 boats in 31 countries. Several of our keen younger sailors were quick to place orders with the only licensed Soling builder in Canada at Sarnia, Ont. and by spring of 1969 the following group were engaged in strenuous competition on English Bay.

KC 32—*Solong*—Dr. Tec Jones
KC 33—*Lady Meg*—Dr. Jack Balmer (later sold for KC 70, also *Lady Meg*)
KC 34—*Chicanery*—Bill Burgess & Alex Harrison
KC 35—*Roadrunner*—Dave Miller, Paul Cote & John Ekels
KC 45—*Alegrias*—Fred Brodie
KC 51—*Andiamo*—Adrian Thompson, John Purdy & John Yuill
these were joined late 1969 and early 1970 by
KC 57—*Chance*—Bill Dickson
KC 63—*Rainbow*—Bob Brodie
KC 68—*Agnete*—Esben Poulsson
KC 71—*Solan*—Ron Maitland
KC 77—*Sine*—Lloyd Walker
KC 81—*Unnamed*—Ted VanWinckel

These sailors formed a group called Pacific Soling Fleet with Jack Balmer as fleet captain, measurer and general organizer and at the P.I.Y.A. Regatta on English Bay midsummer 1969 gave stiff competition to a representative fleet of Solings from Seattle. Dave Miller in *Roadrunner* placed second the winner being Bill Booth, Seattle in *Flare*.

The 1969 Season's Champion was *Chicanery*, Bill Burgess & Alex Harrison.

In late summer 1969 Jack Balmer trailered *Lady Meg* to the first Soling North American in Milwaukee placing 24th out of 35 contestants, and thence to Kingston, Ont. for the first Canadian Championships at the newly organized CORK Regatta in which he placed 11th out of 30. In 1970 Ron Maitland was elected class Fleet Captain with Fred Brodie Secretary, Lloyd Walker, Measurer.

Dave Miller, with his crew Paul Cote and John Ekels, next trailered to Houston, Texas in 1970 for the Second North American series where they came 10th in a fleet of 38 boats. The winds were light and shifty, the last race being called just minutes before the lead boat would have finished, with Dave in second place.

After Houston came Kiel West in San Francisco Bay where Dave's *Roadrunner* was joined by Fleet Captain Bill Burgess in *Chicanery*. The two Vancouver crews, accustomed to the light winds in English Bay, suffered considerably from gear breakdown in the near gales of San Francisco. Dave, however, ended up fourth and Bill Burgess 17th. In the 1970 CORK Regatta, Kingston, the largest contingent was from Vancouver, Dave Miller and Bill Burgess trailered their boat there, and Tec Jones leased a boat for the series. Lloyd Walker took delivery of his new Danish built boat at Kingston and Jack Balmer purchased a new *Lady Meg* from the Sarnia builders and delivered at the regatta. Hans Fogh from Toronto skippered Jack's boat. The regatta was a real test, with 60 boats entered, winds 25 to 30 knots all week and seas at times up to 12 feet. Stiff competition was provided with past Olympians and world medallists Buddy Melges, Dick Stearns and Don Bever sailing. After the final race was cancelled because the Committee boat could not make it to the start, the results were Buddy Melges first, Hans Fogh second and Dave Miller third.

Following CORK, the Vancouver fleet went to Seattle for the last of a series of four International Regattas. Dave Miller won this regatta, with Esben Poulsson's *Agnete* taking fourth but winning the North Pacific Soling Championship for the best performance in the four regattas.

Late 1970, official word came from the C.Y.A. Olympic Committee that Dave Miller was selected as the leading contestant for the Canadian Olympic Sailing team. Not one Royal Van Soling sailor doubts that the Soling at the '72 Olympics at Kiel, Germany, will fly the colors of the Royal Vancouver Yacht Club, or that whoever it is, he will have a good chance of bringing back a medal for Canada.

CANADA GAMES

In 1969 the first Canada Games were held in Halifax, Nova Scotia. British Columbia sent a sailing team with two crews from our Club, Don Martin with his wife Annabelle sailed in the Flying Junior Class and Tec Jones with crew of Lloyd Walker and Fred Brodie sailed in the Soling. The Host Province of Nova Scotia provided the boats which were rotated between races. Winds for the Series provided a good test ranging from 5 knots to 30 knots. Predominant winds were in the 15-20 knot bracket—one race with gusts of 40 knots. The B.C. team made the top showing of any Province with a Gold Medal gained by the Martins and a Silver Medal by Tec Jones.

MALLORY CUP

In 1970 our club was represented for the first time in the Mallory Cup sailed for the North American Championships. Alan Sturgess took his crew Pat Finnegan and Robbie Black to Maine to sail in this event finishing in eighth place.

FROSTBITING STILL TOPS

EVERYONE talks about the weather but only Frostbiters do something about it. They get out and enjoy it. No amount of hail, rain, sleet or snow seems to deter the Frostbiter from the exhilaration of winter dinghy sailing. As some old salt once said, "Dinghy racing gives an outlet to the spirit that no other type of sailing can provide". Many skippers who participate, claim they enjoy the Frostbite season moreso than they do the summer racing schedule in the larger yachts.

Frostbiting has continued to be a very active part of the R.V.Y.C. winter programme. In 1969, Frostbiters moved from the sheltered Coal Harbour area, out to the more exposed waters beyond the breakwater at Jericho. Here the tidal currents and Northwesterly breezes sometimes whip up conditions just a little too precarious and exciting for these sturdy little sail boats. The D9 (Davidson) is still the dinghy of choice at the R.V.Y.C. for Frostbiting. It has had very little modification since first selected in 1951. Hamish Davidson, manufacturer of the D9 dinghy is himself a very avid and fearless Frostbiter. He has been Frostbiting since it first started at the Club in 1950. Many trophies have been presented to the Frostbite fleet to encourage dinghy sailing. In 1967, Hamish Davidson provided a trophy, known as the Broken Mast trophy, to be awarded to the Frostbiter who makes the biggest "boob" or faux pas of the year. This trophy always provides much amusement and hilarity when presented at the annual Frostbite Dinner.

In addition to the series of races held at Jericho, the Frostbiters have an annual invitational regatta which is held at Silva Bay or Alexander Island. This is always well attended and is one of the highlights of the Frostbite season. Interclub regattas are also held with Royal Victoria Yacht Club, West Vancouver Yacht Club, and Kitsilano Yacht Club. The Frostbite schedule is from November through to the end of March, with Frostbiting every other weekend.

The success of Frostbiting is very dependent on a good race committee. Frostbiters have been most fortunate in having the services of Norm Park and Ernie Earle, who have been very devoted and largely instrumental in making Frostbiting a success at the Royal Vancouver Yacht Club.

For keen competition, sportsmanship, fellowship and just good clean fun, there is nothing to beat Frostbiting.

JUNIOR ACTIVITY 1966-1970

WHILE there has been progressively less ownership of small sailboats by R.V.Y.C. Juniors in recent years, due to high cost of competitive boats and their maintenance, there has been no slackening of their interest and activity in National and International racing events. However there has been a noticeable lack of interest, by Juniors, in the local Junior racing events due to the diminishing number of Juniors owning their own boats, and the higher percentage crewing with their parents.

1966 was not "our" year in the National and International events; although our team did win the W. Clarke Gibson Trophy; the Kitten Trophy went to Ian Smith of Victoria. In the Sears Cup Regionals at Kelowna Ian Maitland, Ken Burns and Morgan Sturdy placed fourth and although several juniors travelled to Halifax, Montreal, Port Carling, Ottawa and Winnipeg for Pre-Centennial Regattas their performance was not spectacular.

It was a different story in the Centennial Year 1967; the Fall McCurdy was won by Royal Van with teams from Bremerton, Seattle, Vancouver and Victoria entered, and in the big Centennial Regatta at Ottawa, Alan Drinkwater and crew Pat Finnegan placed first. Dennis Meakin travelled to the Junior World Championships placing thirteenth. While our Juniors competed in the Sears events they did not place in the eliminations.

1968 followed with the same small core of sailors attempting to keep our name in competition—Alan Drinkwater, Don Martin, Ron Maitland, Hunt Gordon, Bill Cote and Pat Finnegan all taking active part. They carried off the W. Clarke Gibson Trophy and the Kitten January series.

Eight juniors were sent to the C.Y.A. Youth Olympic Training Seminar at Montreal and with the National grading of juniors now in effect it is hoped that choices for the Gold Olympic Team can be made from our group.

In 1969 our teams won both the Clarke Gibson and Kitten Trophies. Alan Drinkwater and Pat Finnegan both attended the Youth Olympic Training Seminar in Montreal. Hunt Gordon travelled to Valleyfield, Quebec for the Flying Dutchman Championship and came fifteenth. He also attended the Canadian Olympic Training Regatta at Kingston and finished twenty-second.

Juniors' interest in local sailing contests pepped up a bit in 1970; they took part in the Spring and Fall McCurdys', the Navvy Jack regatta at Hollyburn and the West Vancouver Yacht Club events, and there was a good turn out at our own Clark Gibson series. They came second at the

Gladwell Series in Victoria and at the Eagle Harbour's series. Four of the popular centre-boarder *Fireballs* were brought into the club reviving activity around the Jericho Marina. While our junior members took part in all International events, the newer younger group did not produce any spectacular performances, although Pat Finnegan and Chris Acheson did well at the C.Y.A. Youth Olympic Training Seminar at Hamilton.

JUNIOR DIVISION EXECUTIVE

	1966	1967	1968
Hon. Jr. Advisor	A. H. Meakin	A. H. Meakin	Dr. F. G. Westgate
Jr. Commodore	Norman Angus	Alan Drinkwater	Bill Cote
Jr. Vice Commodore	Chris Tyrell	Valerie Hennell	Dennis Meakin
Jr. Fleet Capt.	Alan Drinkwater	Dennis Meakin	Tim Slaney
Jr. Staff Capt.		Melanie Hartnell	Susan Healey
Jr. Secy-Treas.	Valerie Hennell	Susan Christopherson	M. Hartnell
	1969	1970	
Hon. Jr. Advisor	Stephen Tupper	E. E. Jefferys	
Jr. Commodore	Bill Cote	Tim Slaney	
Jr. Vice Commodore	Tim Slaney	Fred Long	
Jr. Fleet Capt.	Fred Long	Kevin Finnegan	
Secretary	Pam Gordon	Theo Anglin	

JUNIOR TRAINING PROGRAMME

With the club junior training fleet increased to 20 Flying Juniors, with two powered tenders, our programme of supervised sailing courses during July and August each year continues to be eminently successful. Headed by Stephen Tupper and Paul Cote as Chief Instructors for two years each, and following the strict training procedures laid down by the Canadian Yachting Association, our programme is considered by the C.Y.A. to be a model for other yacht clubs to follow. It has attracted the attention of the Royal Canadian Sea Cadets and last year (1970) our instructors ran a one month course for them. In 1971 two special courses for the Sea Cadets are planned. In addition our special course for Ladies (not necessarily juniors) is well utilized and has led to interesting competition on a Bay area level between lady members of the various clubs. The interest and support given the training programme amply justifies outlay for new equipment and sails, and this year it is hoped to add a number of boats equipped for the thrilling and exciting sport of trapeze sailing. Our training programme is now a well established part of the Vancouver sailing scene.

R.V.Y.C. Junior Training Programme 1966

CHAPTER 41

R.V.Y.C.

ACTIVE IN C.Y.A.

ONTINUING from the item on page 257 describing the functions of the Canadian Yachting Association and listing club members who have acted on its Executive since reorganization in the late forties, Frank Hahn carried on as B.C. Vice President with Al Martin and latterly, Ross Boyer of KYC as Junior Coordinator; he was succeeded in 1968 by Dr. Jack Balmer with Dave Miller as Junior Coordinator.

In June 1968, C.Y.A. B.C. Vice President Jack Balmer chaired a meeting of the Commodores of B.C. yacht clubs which resulted in the reactivation of the B.C. Yachting Association, originally formed by W. E. Graveley in 1891, which foundered after a few years. Seventy years later it was reformed, but this time as a branch of the C.Y.A., to act as the Provincial sailing authority, autonomous in its own right, to govern the twenty-odd member Yacht Clubs in B.C. Jack Balmer was elected the first President with four Directors representing the other B.C. clubs.

The newly formed Association became one of the original members of the B.C. Sports Federation which shares in the interest of the $10,000,000 Provincial Fund set up for the benefit of accredited sports governing bodies, to the extent of approximately $25,000 annually; R.V.Y.C. with its large and active racing group was granted $5,000 by the B.C.Y.A. in 1970, to defray travel expenses for national and international events In addition R.V.Y.C. contributed to C.Y.A. approximately $1,500 that year.

After two years as C.Y.A. Vice President and B.C.Y.A. President, Jack Balmer retired but carries on as a director of both groups. Dick Sharpe of Royal Canadian Navy Sailing Assn., Esquimalt was elected to fill the vacated posts, and Dick Sandwell appointed co-chairman of the C.Y.A. Off-Shore Committee which is developing interest amongst western yachtsmen in future international competitions, Admiral's Cup and Canada's Cup challenges. Member clubs of the B.C.Y.A. by the end of 1970 had increased to 30 in number, and the C.Y.A. was fully national in scope being now actively represented in all 10 provinces. Meanwhile, Jack Balmer was appointed Manager of the '71 Pan-Am sailing team and named liaison between the Pan-Am Committee and the C.Y.A.

Vancouver Area
Racing Council Formed

With public interest and participation in the sport of sailing in English Bay, Howe Sound and adjacent waters growing by leaps and bounds in recent years it became obvious that co-operation in scheduling sailing contests to avoid overlapping should be set up between the local established yacht clubs.

Accordingly, to meet this need the Vancouver Area Racing Council was formed in 1970, consisting of The Royal Vancouver Yacht Club, West Vancouver Yacht Club, Kitsilano Yacht Club and Eagle Harbour Yacht Club with the following stated objectives:

1. to co-ordinate racing schedules for cruising class boats in the Vancouver Area.
2. To promote yacht club membership and racing participation.
3. To prepare and promote a code of racing rules and instructions for universal use in the Vancouver area.

The basis of membership in V.A.R.C. is that a member club has the resources to be able to host a race. The work load of hosting races is distributed amongst member clubs in proportion to the number of participating boats from each club. The participating yacht clubs constitute and belong to V.A.R.C. as opposed to the individual members of participating clubs. A member of a participating club is automatically eligible to participate in V.A.R.C. events, subject to rules as to eligibility contained in the General Racing Instructions.

Member clubs will have two representatives on the Council, one of whom will be the current Fleet Captain of each club who will be responsible for the complete and correct registration each year of his members boats.

Should the Council prove successful it plans to include one design boats in the programme. For the 1971 season a complete schedule of events has been set up covering all established local racing contests in the cruising classes from April to November.

CHAPTER 42

R. V. Y. C.

NEW 1966-1970 PERPETUAL TROPHIES

TROPHY	YEAR	DONOR
Mary Bower Trophy	1966	John Long
Bob & Blanche Henry Memorial Trophy	1966	Alex Forsyth
Who Goofed Trophy	1965	unknown
R. D. Ross Trophy	1966	R. D. Ross
Winsome Trophy	1966	Ches Rickard
C. P. Leckie Trophy	1967	C. P. Leckie
Ken Mair Memorial Trophy	1967	Mrs. K. F. Mair, K. Rafe Mair, L. Leigh Mair
Broken Mast Trophy	1967	Hamish Davidson
Skipper of the Year Trophy	1967	F. R. (Bill) Killam
Tugboat Island Fishing Derby Trophy	1967	Bob Gibson
Victoria-Maui International Yacht Race	1968	Royal Vancouver Yacht Club
Sea-Van Trophy	1968	Ray J. Casson

PERPETUAL TROPHY WINNERS

CLASS "A"

BEAVER CUP

(see page 265)

1965	*Penelakut*	Bob Ross
1966	*Velaris*	Lol Killam
1967	*Mary Bower*	John Long
1968	*Penelakut*	Bob Ross
1969	*Porpoise III*	Bill Killam
1970	*Porpoise III*	Bill Killam

MINERVA CUP

(see page 280)

1965	*Penelakut*	Bob Ross
1966	*Concerto*	Arnold Booth
1967	*Mary Bower*	John Long
1968	*Mary Bower*	John Long
1969	*Porpoise III*	Bill Killam
1970	*Anahera W.V.Y.C.*	Dr. C. Morrison

COMMODORE'S CUP

(see page 269)

Allocated 1964 for White Islets Race

1965	*Alcion*	Colin Campbell
1966	*Mary Bower*	John Long
1967	*Mary Bower*	John Long
1968	*Mary Bower*	John Long
1969	*Porpoise III*	Bill Killam
1970	*Winsome IV*	Ches Rickard

W. O. BELL TROPHY

(see page 281)

1965	*Concerto*	Arnold Booth
1966	*Mary Bower*	John Long
1967	*Mary Bower*	John Long
1968	*Crusader*	Ken McRae
1969	*Mary Bower*	John Long
1970	*Winsome IV*	Ches Rickard

NAVIGATOR'S TROPHY

(see page 321)

1965	*Mary Bower*	John Long
1966	*Velaris*	Lol Killam
1967	*Allegra*	Art Way
1968	*Porpoise III*	Bill Killam
1969	*Porpoise III*	Bill Killam
1970	*Porpoise III*	Bill Killam

CLASS "B B" AND "B" CLASS

BUSCOMBE TROPHY

(see page 262)

1965	*Comtessa*	S. Foley
1966	*Ariel V*	Ken Lochhead
1967	*Winsome III*	Ches Rickard
1968	*Coho*	J. Brandlmayr
1969	*Hyak*	B. Davis & B. Mahy
1970	*Hyak*	B. Davis & B. Mahy

EMPIRE TROPHY

(see page 302)

1965	*Comtessa*	Stu Foley
1966	*Coho*	J. Brandlmayr
1967	*Coho*	J. Brandlmayr
1968	*Coho*	J. Brandlmayr
1969	*Hyak*	B. Davis & B. Mahy
1970	*Rapid*	K. & I. Kirkland

WHITE ROCKS TROPHY

(see page 285)

1965	*Mareda*	Art Way
1966	*Ariel V*	Ken Lochhead
1967	*Cloudrace*	Ian Hamilton
1968	*Coho*	J. Brandlmayr
1969	*Cloudrace*	Ian Hamilton
1970	*Rapid*	K. & I. Kirkland

KEYES TROPHY

(see page 276)
Reallocated to B Class 1966

1965	*Serapis*	A. Forsyth
1966	*Ariel V*	Ken Lochhead
1967	*Coho*	J. Brandlmayr
1968	*Ariel V*	Ken Lochhead
1969	*Sinful W.V.Y.C.*	Bob Harrison
1970	*Solquest W.V.Y.C.*	Fred Russell

SCHOONERS & YAWLS
under 30 ft.

(see page 274)
Reallocated to Ballenas Isle 1966

1965	*Tricia*	Pat Leslie
1966	*Ariel V*	Ken Lochhead
1967	*Ariel V*	Ken Lochhead
1968	*Cloudrace*	Ian Hamilton
1969	*Hyak*	B. Davis & B. Mahy
1970	*Rapid*	K. & I. Kirkland

CLASS "C"

VICE COMMODORE'S CUP

(see page 288)

1965	*Jeunesse*	Paul Cote
1966	*Lollipop*	Hunter Vogel
1967	*Jeunesse*	Paul Cote
1968	*Jolly Olly*	Vern Ruskin
1969	*Jolly Olly*	Vern Ruskin
1970	*Lollipop*	Hunter Vogel

HARRY MARSHALL TROPHY

(see page 275)
Reallocated to C Class in 1966

1965	*Barca Del Vela*	F. Hahn
1966	*Jolly Olly*	Vern Ruskin
1967	*Jolly Olly*	Vern Ruskin
1968	*Jeunesse*	Paul Cote
1969	*Lollipop*	Hunter Vogel
1970	*Lollipop*	Hunter Vogel

DUNCAN BELL-IRVING TROPHY

(see page 284)

1965	*Jeunesse*	Paul Cote
1966	*Jeunesse*	Paul Cote
1967	*Lollipop*	Hunter Vogel
1968	*Jeunesse*	Paul Cote
1969	*Barca Del Vela*	R. Baker
1970	*Chimo II W.V.Y.C.*	G. Coleman

MACNEILL TROPHY

(see page 266)
Reallocated to "C" Class 1966

1965	*Jeunesse*	Paul Cote
1966	*Lollipop*	Hunter Vogel
1967	*Veleda*	John Grubbe
1968	*Lara*	Ken Clarke
1969	*Jolly Olly*	Vern Ruskin
1970	*Jolly Olly*	Vern Ruskin

FRANK PARSON'S TROPHY

(see page 293)
Reallocated in 1970 to Soling Class
English Bay International Series

1965	*Siki*	C. Justin, T. Repard
1966	No Contest.	
1967	No Contest.	
1968	No Contest.	
1969	No Contest.	
1970	*Solo*	Dave Miller

JERICHO TROPHY

(see page 290)
Reallocated in 1970 to Soling Class

1965	*Kalara*	Larry Walters
1966	No Contest.	
1967	No Contest.	
1968	No Contest.	
1969	No Contest.	
1970	*Solo*	Dave Miller

CHALDECOTT CUP

(see page 267)
Reallocated to Soling Class for
Club Championship

1965	No Contest.	
1966	No Contest.	
1967	No Contest.	
1968	No Contest.	
1969	No Contest.	
1970	*Solong*	Dr. Tec Jones

HARRY GALE TROPHY

(see page 291)
Reallocated in 1970 to Soling Class for
Fleet Championship

1965	No Contest.	
1966	No Contest.	
1967	No Contest.	
1968	No Contest.	
1969	No Contest.	
1970	*Agnete*	Esben Poulsson

STOCK EXCHANGE TROPHY

(see page 277)

1965	No Contest.	
1966	No Contest.	
1967	*Hanko*	Brian Lake
1968	*Hanko*	Brian Lake
1969	No Contest.	
1970	No Contest.	

DRAGONS
YUNO TROPHY

(see page 306)

1965	*Kris*	Butt, Downey & Skibbe
1966	*No Contest*	
1967	*Kriss*	Butt, Downey & Skibbe
1968	*Antigone*	Steve Tupper
1969	*Tjep*	Bob Burgess
1970	*Tjep*	Bob Burgess

ENGLISH BAY
S CLASS TROPHY

(see page 283)

1965	*Cam*	Steve Tupper
1966	*Tjep*	Bob Burgess
1967	*Cam*	Del Black
1968	*Antigone*	Steve Tupper
1969	*Tjep*	Bob Burgess
1970	*Tjep*	Bob Burgess

STROMBOLI TROPHY

(see page 320)

1965	*Cam*	Steve Tupper
1966	*Kris*	Butt, Downey & Skibbe
1967	*Kris*	Butt, Downey & Skippe
1968	*Antigone*	Steve Tupper
1969	*Tjep*	Bob Burgess
1970	*Tjep*	Bob Burgess

GYLES TROPHY

(see page 307)

1965	*Nike*	Ray Casson
1966	*Kris*	Butt, Downey & Skibbe
1967	*Puff*	Fred Field
1968	*Tjep*	Bob Burgess
1969	*Tjep*	Bob Burgess
1970	*Tjep*	Bob Burgess

YAWLS under 30 ft.

(see page 274)

1965	*Kris*	Butt, Downey & Skibbe
1966	*Kris*	Butt, Downey & Skibbe
1967	*Kris*	Butt, Downey & Skibbe
1968	*Tjep*	Bob Burgess
1969	*Tjep*	Bob Burgess
1970	*Tjep*	Bob Burgess

ENGLISH BAY TROPHY

(see page 322)

1965	*Cam*	Steve Tupper
1966	*Kris*	Butt, Downey, Skibbe
1967	*Kris*	Butt, Downey, Skibbe
1968	*Antigone*	Steve Tupper
	Jinx	M. Rattery
1969	*Paladin KYC*	Ron Whitfield
1970	*Tjep*	Bob Burgess

STARS
ROEDDE CHALLENGE CUP

(see page 271)

1965	*Simba*	Bonar Davis
1966	*Simba*	John McCarvill
1967	*Gypsy*	K. & I. Kirkland
1968	No Contest.	
1969	No Contest.	
1970	No Contest.	

STAR FLEET CAPTAIN'S CUP

(see page 273)

1965	*Westwyn*	Bill Burgess
1966	*Gypsy*	K. & I. Kirkland
1967	*Gypsy*	K. & I. Kirkland
1968	No Contest.	
1969	No Contest.	
1970	*Fiorella KYC*	J. Heywood

WATT TROPHY

(see page 295)

1965	*Simba*	Bonar Davis
1966	*Simba*	Bonar Davis
1967	*Gypsy*	K. & I. Kirkland
1968	*Scram KYC*	S. Prinsenberg
1969	*Aquarius KYC*	S. Prinsenberg
1970	*Aquarius KYC*	S. Prinsenberg

HARRY WYLIE SHIELD

(see page 287)

1965	*Spindrift*	Paul Sturdy
1966	No Contest.	
1967	*Scram KYC*	S. Prinsenberg
1968	*April KYC*	G. Schleigel
1969	*April KYC*	G. Schleigel
1970	*Aquarius*	S. Prinsenberg

WESTON FOUNDERS' TROPHY

(see page 298)

1965	*Simba*	Bonar Davis
1966	No Contest.	
1967	No Contest.	
1968	No Contest.	
1969	No Contest.	
1970	No Contest.	

ERNESTINE JEFFERD
MEMORIAL TROPHY

(see page 323)

1965	*No Mo*	George Mason
1966	*Gypsy*	K. & I. Kirkland
1967	*Scram KYC*	S. Prinsenberg
1968	*Gypsy*	K. & I. Kirkland
1969	*Aquarius*	S. Prinsenberg
1970	*Aquarius*	S. Prinsenberg

HAZEN PHILLIPS TROPHY

(see page 328)

1965	*Glisten*	Carl Petersen
1966	*No Mo*	George Mason
1967	No Contest.	
1968	No Contest.	
1969	*Aquarius*	S. Prinsenberg
1970	*Aquarius KYC*	S. Prinsenberg

PETERSEN TROPHY

(see page 329)
1965	Scram KYC	S. Prinsenberg
1966	Spindrift	Paul Sturdy
1967	Gypsy	K. & I. Kirkland
1968	Gypsy	K. & I. Kirkland
1969	Simba KYC	L. Warshawski
1970	Galadriel KYC	Fred Dill

LIGHTNINGS

PORT OF VANCOUVER TROPHY

(see page 292)
1965	No Contest.	
1966	No Contest.	
1967	No Contest.	
1968	No Contest.	
1969	Skua	Chris Acheson
1970	Skua	Chris Acheson

REDSKIN TROPHY

(see page 268)
1965	No Contest.	
1966	No Contest.	
1967	No Contest.	
1968	No Contest.	
1969	Frolic	G. Ince
1970	No Contest.	

ROGERS TROPHY

(see page 270)
1965	Coka K.Y.C.	Hart Long
1966	No Contest.	
1967	No Contest.	
1968	No Contest.	
1969	Skua	Chris Acheson
1970	Frolic K.Y.C.	G. Ince

VENTURE TROPHY

(see page 308)
1965	Thunderbird	G. Ince
1966	Thunderbird	G. Ince
1967	Thunderbird	G. Ince
1968	No Contest.	
1969	Frolic	G. Ince
1970	Don Clarke S.Y.C.	

GEARY 18 (FLATTIES)

BERT TUPPER TROPHY

(see page 312)
1965	No Contest.	
1966	Bob Crossley	
1967	Little John	J. McAllister
1968	Branco H.Y.C.	Dave Russell
1969	No Contest.	
1970	Redwings C.Y.C.	B. Lefaux

BOULTBEE SWEET TROPHY

(see page 296)
1965	No Contest.	
1966	No Contest.	
1967	No Contest.	
1968	Little John	J. McAllister
1969	No Contest.	
1970	"896" C.Y.C.	Doug Wood

AKHURST TROPHY

(see page 294)
1965	No Contest.	
1966	No Contest.	
1967	No Contest.	
1968	No Contest.	
1969	Catchup	Bill & Allen Cullen
1970	"896" C.Y.C.	Doug Wood

SPECIAL TROPHIES

W. J. BUTT TROPHY

(see page 278)
1965	Comtessa	Alex Foley
1966	Lollipop	Dennis Meakin
1967	Mary Bower	Fred Long
1968	Cloudrace	John McCarvill
1969	Hyak	Bruce Andrews
1970	Hyak	Dennis Meakin

C. O. JULIAN TROPHY

(see page 263)
1965	Winsome III	Lynn Rickard
1966	Coho	Pat Brandlmayr
1967	Coho	Pat Brandlmayr
1968	Cloudrace	Annabelle Martin
1969	Cloudrace	Carol Park
1970	Hyak	Elaine Davis

BIRD ROCK TROPHY

(see page 279)
1965	Benora II	Philip Graham
1966	Velaris	Lol Killam
1967	Mary Bower	John Long
1968	Lollipop	Hunter Vogel
1969	Mary Bower	John Long
1970	Puff	Robt. Gibson

BURN-MOR MATCH TROPHY

(see page 299)
1965	Kalara	Larry Walters
1966	Comtessa	Stu Foley
1967	Winsome III	Ches Rickard
1968	Coho	J. Brandlmayr
1969	Hyak	Davis & Mahy
1970	Endless Summer	Geo. O'Brien

ENTRANCE ISLAND TROPHY

(see page 289)
1965	Gypsy G	J. Brandlmayr
1966	Mary Bower	John Long
1967	Mary Bower	John Long
1968	Serapis	Alex Forsyth
1969	Coho	J. Brandlmayr
1970	Hyak	Davis & Mahy

HARBOUR LIGHTS TROPHY

(see page 316)

1965	*Winsome III*	Ches Rickard
1966	*Mary Bower*	John Long
1967	*Mary Bower*	John Long
1968	*Coho*	J. Brandlmayr
1969	*Coho*	J. Brandlmayr
1970	*Winsome III*	S. Rasmusson

GULF OF GEORGIA TROPHY

(see page 315)

1965	*Maradea*	Art Way
1966	*Ariel V*	Len Lochhead
1967	*Mary Bower*	John Long
1968	*Coho*	J. Brandlmayr
1969	*Hyak*	Davis & Mahy
1970	*Rapid*	K. & I. Kirkland

JACK CRIBB MEMORIAL

(see page 324)

1965	*Mary Bower*	John Long
1966	*Surfer*	Tony Repard
1967	*Jolly Olly*	Vern Ruskin
1968	*Porpoise III*	Bill Killam
1969	*Hyak*	Davis & Mahy
1970	*Porpoise III*	Bill Killam

ALBERT AUSTIN TROPHY

(see page 327)

1965	*Tricia*	Pat Leslie
1966	*Ariel V*	Ken Lochhead
1967	*Ariel V*	Ken Lochhead
1968	*Jolly Olly*	Vern Ruskin
1969	*Jolly Olly*	Vern Ruskin
1970	*Rapid*	K. & I. Kirkland

TROUBADOUR TROPHY

(see page 330)

1965	*Tricia*	Pat Leslie
1966	*Mary Bower*	John Long
1967	*Mary Bower*	John Long
1968	*Jolly Olly*	Vern Ruskin
1969	*Rapid*	K. & I. Kirkland
1970	*Aphrodite W.V.Y.C.*	B. McColl

FROSTBITE DINGHIES

CATHERINE DAY TROPHY

(see page 282)

1965	Phil Miller
1966	No Contest
1967	Bonar Davis
1968	Hamish Davidson
1969	Bob Burgess

TEMPLE H. WRIGHT TROPHY

(see page 309)

1965	No Contest.
1966	No Contest.
1967	Bonar Davis
1968	Don Martin
1969	Norm Marcus R.Vic.Y.C.

HAMISH DAVIDSON TROPHY

(see page 304)

1965	Royal Vancouver Yacht Club
1966	No Contest.
1967	Royal Vancouver Yacht Club
1968	Royal Vancouver Yacht Club
1969	Royal Victoria Yacht Club

R. VANC. RACE COMM. TROPHY

(see page 319)

1965	Phil Miller
1966	No Contest.
1967	Bonar Davis
1968	Bonar Davis
1969	Norm Marcus R.Vic.Y.C.

STANLEY BROOK TROPHY

(see page 301)

1965	Brian Lake
1966	Bill Killam
1967	Bill Killam
1968	Bonar Davis
1969	Don Martin

JUNIOR DIVISION

JUNIOR PERPETUAL TROPHY

(see page 300)

1965	Valerie Hennell
1966	Norm Angus
1967	Alan Drinkwater
1968	Alan Drinkwater
1969	No Award
1970	K. Finnegan

CAPT. B. L. JOHNSON TROPHY

(see page 305)

1965	Alan Drinkwater
1966	Dennis Meakin
1967	Pat Finnegan
1968	Pat Finnegan
1969	No Award
1970	F. Long

R. W. R. DAY GOLF SHIELD

see page 317

1965	R. H. Talling
1966	No Contest
1967	R. W. R. Day
1968	N. Hume McLennan
1969	R. H. Talling
1970	No Contest

F. J. WHITCROFT ANNUAL GOLF TROPHY

see page 318
1965   Lyall O. Bell
1966   Not Awarded
1967   Not Awarded
1968   Not Awarded
1969   Not Awarded
1970   Not Awarded

TOWNLEY TROPHY

(see page 326)
1965   Harry Billingsley
1966   July—Harry Billingsley
        August—R. Harrison
1967   July—Peter Bourne
        August—Kervin Finnegan
1968   July—Kerwin Finnegan
        August—Kervin Finnegan
1969   July—J. Billingsley
        August—Colin Moore
1970   July—Ken Billingsley
        August—Ross Griffin

JUNIOR FROSTBITE DIVISION
HAROLD A. JONES TROPHY

(see page 286)
1965   Dennis Meakin
1966   Dennis Meakin
1967   No Contest.
1968   No Contest.
1969   No Contest.
1970   T. Holland

W. CLARKE GIBSON TROPHY

(see page 311)
1965   Royal Vancouver Yacht Club
1966   Royal Vancouver Yacht Club
1967   Corinthian Yacht Club Seattle
1968   Royal Vancouver Yacht Club
1969   Royal Vancouver Yacht Club
1970   Seattle Yacht Club

KITTEN CLASS TROPHY

(see page 310)
1965   Royal Vancouver Yacht Club
1966   Royal Victoria Yacht Club
1967   Royal Vancouver Yacht Club
1968   Royal Victoria Yacht Club
1969   Royal Vancouver Yacht Club
1970   Mark Laura, S.Y.C.

POWER BOAT RACES
DEWEES TROPHY

(see page 272)
1965   *Marillyce*   Dr. H. Brooke
1966   *Dorleen*   Len Sewell
1967   *Dorleen*   Len Sewell
1969   *Dorleen*   Len Sewell
1969   *Tsona*   Dave Manning
1970   *Tsona*   J. Williamson

PAKENHAM TROPHY

(see page 303)
1965   Burrard Yacht Club
1966   Royal Vancouver Yacht Club
1967   Burrard Yacht Club
1968   Royal Vancouver Yacht Club
1969   Royal Vancouver Yacht Club
1970   Burrard Yacht Club

TOM AYRES TROPHY

(see page 313)
1965   *Dorleen*   Len Sewell
1966   *Vandal*   Les Simmers
1967   *Dorleen*   Len Sewell
1968   *Vandal*   Les Simmers
1969   *Smitty*   Tom Trapp
1970   *Vandal*   Les & Babe Simmers

ORDER OF BENT PROPELLER

(see page 314)
1965   *Ubique*   Claude Thicke
1966   *Nanaimo Chief* Bunny Whitcroft
1967   *Wakeena*   Jack Harrison
1968   *John Antle*   Ralph Smith
1969   *Vandal*   Les Simmers
1970   *Thunderbird*   Jack Charles

SAM CROMIE MEMORIAL TROPHY

(see page 325)
1965   Bill Anderson B.Y.C.
1966   *Kenkath*   Carl Carlson
1967   *Dorleen*   Len Sewell
1968   *Dorleen*   Len Sewell
1969   *Smoothy*   F. Nickel V.C.C.
1970   *Smoothy*   F. Nickel V.C.C.

BOB McKECHNIE TROPHY

(see page 332)
1965   *Dorleen*   Len Sewell
1966   *Vandal*   Les Simmers
1967   *Dorleen*   Len Sewell
1968   *Vandal*   Les Simmers
1969   *Smitty*   Tom Trapp
1970   *Vandal*   Les & Babe Simmers

CENTURY 21 TROPHY
(International Team Race)

1965   Canadian Team
1966   Canadian Team
1967   Canadian Team
1968   U.S. Team
1969   Canadian Team
1970   U.S. Team

The
Mary Bower
Trophy

PRESENTED 1966 BY
JOHN LONG

For Sisters Island Race.

WINNERS

1966	*Mary Bower*	John Long	1969	*Porpoise III*	Bill Killam
1967	*Mary Bower*	John Long	1970	No Contest.	
1968	*Velaris*	Lol Killam			

The
Bob and *Blanche*
Henry *Memorial*
Trophy

PRESENTED 1966 BY A. J. B. (ALEX) FORSYTH

For Sisters Island Invitational Race.

WINNERS

1966	*Ariel V*	Ken Lochhead	
1967	*Cloudrace*	Ian Hamilton	
1968	*Coho*	J. Brandlmayr	

1969	*Rapid*	K. & I. Kirkland	
1970	*Loon*	Frank Hahn	

For Junior Faux Pas.

The Who Goofed Trophy

DONATED 1965
DONOR UNKNOWN

WINNERS

1965	Mary Fladgate & Sue Dunn
1966	Chris Tyrell
1967	Bill Cote
1968	John McCarvill
1969	Bill Cline
1970	D. Andrews

For Best Intermediate
Sailor in Training
Programme.

The R. D. Ross Trophy

PRESENTED 1966 BY
R. D. ROSS

WINNERS

1966	July—Dennis Battrum
	August—Fred Long
1967	July—Michael Miller
	August—Terry McConkey
1968	July—John Stockton
	August—David Warren
1969	July—Tim Delaney
	August—D. Boyle
1970	July—Paul Louie
	August—Stephen Dunn

The Winsome Trophy

PRESENTED 1966 BY CHES RICKARD

WINNERS

1966	*Ariel V*	Ken Lochhead
1967	*Cloudrace*	Ian Hamilton
1968	*Cloudrace*	Ian Hamilton
1969	*Hyak*	B. Davis & B. Mahy
1970	*Rapid*	K. & I. Kirkland

For Snake Island Race.

The C. P. Leckie Trophy

PRESENTED 1966 BY C. P. LECKIE

WINNERS

1966	*Gypsy*	K. & I. Kirkland
1967	*Ariel C.Y.C. Seattle*	Alan Holt
1968	*Colleen C.Y.C.*	Tom Nylund
1969	*Frolic C.Y.C.*	Bill Buchan
1970	*Glisten K.Y.C.*	G. Schagel

For Stars Labour Day Invitational 3 Races.

The Ken Mair Memorial Trophy

**PRESENTED 1967 BY
MRS. K. F. MAIR
K. RAFFE MAIR
L. LEIGH MAIR**

WINNERS

For the winning boat in Spring Predicted Log Race, any club.

1967	*Jaro*	Les Marshall B.Y.C.
1968	*Dorleen*	Len Sewell
1969	*Tsona*	Dave Manning
1970	*Tsona*	Jack Williamson

The Broken Mast Trophy

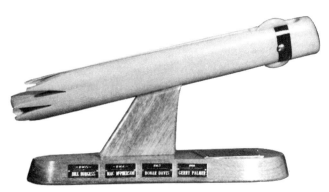

**PRESENTED 1966 BY
HAMISH DAVIDSON**

WINNERS

For Frostbites biggest Faux Pas.

1966	Mac McPherson
1967	Bonar Davis
1968	Ralph Farris
1969	Gerry Palmer

The Skipper of the Year Trophy

**PRESENTED 1967 BY
F. R. (BILL) KILLAM**

WINNERS

For Skipper having highest
number of points for
the year, any club.

1967	*Dorleen*	Len Sewell
1968	*Dorleen*	Len Sewell
1969	*Smoothy*	Frank Nickel
1970	*Smoothy*	Frank Nickel

The Tugboat Island Fishing Derby Perpetual Trophy

**PRESENTED 1967 BY
ROBERT GIBSON**

WINNERS

1967	Bob Gibson
1968	Bob Day
1969	Doan Hartnell
1970	Ron Cliff

For the largest salmon caught.

The Sea Van Trophy

**PRESENTED 1968
BY RAY J. CASSON**

For International
Dragon Team
Racing

WINNERS

1968	Vancouver Dragon Fleet
1969	Seattle Dragon Fleet
1970	Seattle Dragon Fleet

The Victoria - Maui International Race Province of British Columbia Trophy

**PRESENTED 1968 BY
ROYAL VANCOUVER
YACHT CLUB**

For the First yacht
on corrected time
in Division I.

WINNERS

1968	*Porpoise III*	F. R. (Bill) Killam
1970	*Graybeard*	Lol Killam

Lol Killam's ketch Graybeard   Denis Manson photo

First to finish in the 1966 Swiftsure Classic, "Mary Bower," at left, leads "Diamond Head" across the line by one second.

R.V.Y.C. SAILBOATS

Name	Sail No.	Length	Rig Type	Owners
After Me			Sloop	D. Purdie
Ahmic		34'	Sloop	Doug & Anne Courtmanche
Alcion	415	46'	Sloop	Douglas Hall
Alii Nui		22'	Sloop	Victoria Cox
Allegra	241	42'	Sloop	John & Beverley Louie
Andante	9443	51'	Sloop	Art & Nora Way
Applecheeks		31'	Sloop	Dr. H. M. Bell
Aquarius		26'	Sloop	Alex & Ruth Chisholm
Aralon	768		Sloop	R. C. Nelson
Ariel	411	29'	Sloop	Marv Moan
Ariel V	175	39'	Sloop	Ken & Kathleen Lochhead
Artu		26'	Sloop	Ian G. Clements
Ashanti	441	25'9"	Sloop	Vernon & Pam Forster
Avalon		30'	Sloop	Richard & Louise Nelson
Baron Rouge		37'	Sloop	John & Liz Armour
Beluga		25'	Sloop	Fenner & Stephanie Douglas
Benora II	461	36'	Sloop	Harry & Agnes Herlihy
Blue Heron	399	47'	Sloop	Dr. Seriol & Wilma Williams
Blue Mist		46'	Cutter	Gordon Crebbin
Bluey	97007		Sloop	D. Findlay
Bob-O-Link		28'	Sloop	E. Wasson
Caia		23'	Sloop	Bob & Mary Laird
Calabash		30'	Sloop	Claude & Sandra Cronhelm
Cal-Tiki	157	20'	Sloop	J. W. Gill
Cambria		31'	Sloop	Bill & Effie Cunningham
Cavalier	49	30'	Sloop	George H. Halls
Celeste		58'	Sloop	George Scrimshaw
Centaur	CR205	26'	Sloop	Foster K. Dennison
Cerce		34'	Cutter	Carl Kenning
Ceres		25'	Sloop	Dr. James M. Ritchie
Chico Viento	9423	32'	Sloop	Eric & Charlotte Sandberg
Cirrus	105	34'	Ketch	Ray & Hazel Delaplace
Claire d'Lune		45'		Dr. Wm. H. White
Cloudrace	239	32'	Sloop	Wm. Miles
Coho	711	51'	Sloop	John & Pat Brandlmayr
Comtessa	117	32'	Sloop	S. G. Foley
Copepod		21'	Sloop	Tom Killam
Cresset	3	40'	Cutter	Gerry & Dorina Palmer
Crusader	711	51'	Sloop	Ken & Eunice McRae
Diomedea		36'	Sloop	Dr. D. M. Warner
Doran II		37'	Sloop	Alvin & Eileen Narod
Driftwinds		38'	Sloop	D. H. Burnett
Driver	409	61'	Sloop	Philip & Joan Graham
Drummer Boy	439	34'	Sloop	John Dunfield
Ealasaid		32'	Sloop	R. F. Morris
Eilioh Mor	V24-12		Sloop	R. Mackay
Elsinore		30'	Sloop	David Goldie
Elusive	345	34'6"	Sloop	Dr. Ronald & Marcia Boyd
Faem	571	36'	Sloop	Keith & Anne Thomson
Fantasie	9	34'	Sloop	Jack & Ollie Williamson
Flame		48'	Sloop	Warren & Patsy Nesbit
Fleet Fairy		33'	Sloop	Douglas & Alma Stone
Fulmar	23	48'	Sloop	Steve & Stephanie Vagvolgi
Furiant		40'	Yawl	Dave & Marie Moffet
Gabrielle III	401	53'	Sloop	Dick & Agnete Sandwell
George Kitamike	119	38'	Sloop	Hamish Davidson
Gini II	229	32'	Sloop	Ian & Joyce Ross
Glomerulus		31'	Sloop	J. D. Longley
Golden Hind III	13	37'	Sloop	Lorne Kyle
Gometra	5	43'	Sloop	R. W. Butt
Greybeard	9999	73'	Ketch	Lol & Rose Killam
Haida Raven	705	31'	Sloop	William Wagner
Hawk	9001	47'	Sloop	Bettie Farris
Huba		28'	Sloop	G. K. D. Stuart
Hyak	11	32'	Sloop	Bill Mahy & Bonar & Elaine Davis
Jenetta		71'	Ketch	Wavell & Victoria Urry
Jester	129	36'	Sloop	Stuart & Wendy Watts
Jeunesse	235	35'	Sloop	Paul & Bette Coté
Jivaro			Sloop	W. C. T. Edwards
Jolly Olly	303	28'	Sloop	Vern & Olly Ruskin
Kainui		25'	Sloop	Brian Lowe
Kala	15	28'	Sloop	Dr. Bill & Betty Alto
Kalliste	35	28'	Sloop	Norm & Pat Park
Kana-O	413	26'	Sloop	P. H. White

R.V.Y.C. SAILBOATS

Name	No. Sail	Length	Type Rig	Owners
Kandah	427	37'	Sloop	Chris & Helen McGregor
Kantaki		32'	Cutter	Denis & Rita Barraclough
Keewaydin II		41'	Sloop	H. O. Murphy
Kimchow		40'	Sloop	Douglas & Helen Gardiner
Kimje	177	42'	Sloop	Jim & Joy Eastman
Kotare		20'	Sloop	James & Gertrude Gardiner
Lara	125	30'	Sloop	Ken & Alice Clark
Larus		31'	Sloop	Gordon Tener
Lollipop	225	30'	Sloop	Hunter Vogel
Long Gone		42'	Sloop	Jim & Shirley Innes
Loon	445	34'	Sloop	Fank Hahn
Lur		30'	Sloop	John & Judy Burnett
Lutra		30'	Sloop	Harold Wrohan
Ma Coeur		28'	Sloop	R. J. Miller
Ma Coeur	501		Sloop	Bob & Marg Miller
Maid Silya	301	40'	Ketch	Elmer & Katharine Palmer
Mary Bower	7	49'	Sloop	John & Evelyn Long
Mary Hester	217	20'	Sloop	Dr. Mac MacPherson
Maverick III	567	32'	Sloop	Bas & Gillian Cobanli
Mintaka		30'	Sloop	Ted & Daisy MacDonald
Mir	9417	76'	Ketch	George W. O'Brien
Molly Hogan II		30'	Sloop	Dana & Norma Ramsay
Moomba	429	32'	Sloop	Doug & Joan Sudbury
Nantuk	179	35'	Sloop	Maury & Mary-Margaret Young
Neechiemose		47'	Ketch	Terry & Ann Towns
Neptune		28'	Cutter	Jack & Alice Christensen
Nighean Alvinn		30'	Sloop	Thomas & Gladys Cartmill
Nona		25'	Sloop	Don & Jean Black
Ole II	223	35'	Sloop	Bill & Paula Locke
Olympus	359	30'	Sloop	A. J. F. Johnson
Ouija		26'	Sloop	Robert Jr. & Mary-Lou Gibson
Pandora of Rhu	431	49'	Sloop	John Klymak
Paniolo	51	36'	Sloop	Dr. Gordon & Ruth Westgate
Pelekan		26'	Sloop	R. A. Clarke
Penelakut	19	45'	Sloop	Bob & Sheila Ross
Plymouth Girl		25'	Sloop	James & Cynthia Sandilands
Poof		22'	Sloop	**G. L. & Dorothy Cran**
Porpoise III	397	47'	Sloop	Bill & Kay Killam
Puffin II	561	36'	Sloop	Harvey & Marion Carruthers
Quest III		28'	Sloop	Bob & Bubs Forrest
Rapid	421	37'	Sloop	Ian & Ken Kirkland
Rhubarb	75	30'	Sloop	Robbie & Barbara Brown
Running Shoe		30'	Sloop	John & Betty Jarman
Sabre II		37'	Sloop	Bill & Jill Armstrong
Saeter		30'	Sloop	Craig & Margaret Neylen
Santa Clara		30'	Sloop	Frank & Barbara Bunnell
Sanderling	169	36'	Sloop	Art & Jean Meakin
Saumure		30'	Sloop	Ralph & Marney Brine
Seata		26'	Sloop	T. Slaney
Seawyf	57	35'	Sloop	Peter & Shirley Vida
Second Chance		27'	Sloop	W. F. Dickson
Serapis	103	36'	Sloop	Alex & Margaret Forsyth
Seren		30'	Sloop	D. P. Jones
Serendipity	227	28'	Sloop	J. B. Alexander
Skana	703	31'	Sloop	Alan & Margaret Martin
Smilee		48'	Sloop	Ken McLean
Snow Goose		25'	Sloop	Mary Light
Standfast	437	31'	Sloop	Tony & Sue Liebert
Summer Winds	9777	47'	Sloop	Ed & Louise Prescesky
Sunbird	9447			
Sundance Kid	12		Sloop	B. R. Sibbald
Surfer	207		Sloop	Tony & Margaret Repard
Sweetpea	218	24'	Sloop	Tony & Tee Kingsmill
Sylvia	279	35'	Sloop	Roy F. Hooley
Tabasco		30'	Sloop	David & Bittie Jacox
Tae Ping	491	39'	Sloop	C. Paul Daniels
Tahn	37	26'	Sloop	George & Shirley Mason
Tahuna		33'	Sloop	R. Jerome
Tamar II		33'	Sloop	Stanley & Doreen Heaps
Tehani		24'	Sloop	James Magnall
Tekilome		47'	Ketch	D. E. Holland
Tekilomé		37'	Ketch	Douglas & Phyllis Holland
The Roving Eye		28'	Sloop	Gordon & Doris Harris
Tom Boy		34'	Sloop	Alf Shockley
Treveda	405	34'	Sloop	Len & Edna Murrell
Tricia	123	36'	Sloop	Pat & Yvonne Leslie
Unnamed			Sloop	R. Gibson Jr.
Vogad		36'	Sloop	Hugh & Jocelyn MacNeil
Vogad	RI	35'	Sloop	Harry & Jean Fahrni
Westerly Twenty-Five		25'	Sloop	Foster K. Dennison
Whereaway	39	37'	Sloop	Don & Joyce Smith

R.V.Y.C. SAILBOATS

Name	Sail No.	Length	Rig Type	Owners
Wickaninnish		30'	Sloop	Bill & Karen Kinsey
Windborne II	435	30'	Sloop	Glendon & June Hagerman
Wingsong		30'	Sloop	D. A. V. MacDonald
Winsome III	33	36'	Sloop	David E. Frisby
Winsome IV	701	37'	Sloop	Ches & Win Rickard
Wynsonaire	139	34'	Sloop	T. F. Horton
Yola	425	30'	Sloop	George & Vivian Parsons
Zuna II		37'	Sloop	George Scrimshaw

MOTOR SAILERS

Name	Sail No.	Length	Rig Type	Owners
Dawn Star		42'		Stanley & Muriel Davies
Marcelle		32'	Sloop	Frank & Vera Godwin
Pink Cloud		40'		Gwynne & Yvnn Austin
Staghound		40'	Ketch	George & Bunty Donaldson

12 METRES

Name	Sail No.	Length	Rig Type	Owners
Endless Summer			Sloop	George O'Brien

6 METRES

Name	Sail No.	Length	Rig Type	Owners
Ca-Va	KC12	36'	Sloop	Phil & Wynn Miller and Sid & Janet Miller

THUNDERBIRDS

Name	Sail No.	Length	Rig Type	Owners
Amphritrite	731	26'	Sloop	Sid & Sylvia Wilkinson
Minstrel		26'	Sloop	Tom & Ruby Cram
Orielle	T266	26'	Sloop	Bruce & Jane Sibbald
Qa Yel	211	26'	Sloop	Bob & Jo Jarvis
Scherzo		26'	Sloop	R. K. Glass
Tiki III		26'	Sloop	N. Donaldson
Tiny Bubbles	820	26'	Sloop	W. R. Emerton
Tolowa	67	26'	Sloop	Roger Ovens

DRAGONS

Name	Sail No.	Length	Rig Type	Owners
Antigone	KC95	29'	Sloop	Steve & Anne Tupper
Baaz	KC72	29'	Sloop	Allan Goldsmith
Foil	KC81	29'	Sloop	Colin & Jill Sims
Puff	KC53	29'	Sloop	Fred & Bev Field
Scampie	KC83	29'	Sloop	Ray Casson
Tjep	KC32	29'	Sloop	Bob & Joan Burgess

SOLING

Name	Sail No.	Length	Rig Type	Owners
Agnete	KC68	26'9"	Sloop	Esben Poulsson
Algerias	KC45	26'9"	Sloop	Fred Brodie
Andiamo	KC51	26'9"	Sloop	John Purdy, Adrian Thomson & John Yuill
Chance	KC57	26'9"	Sloop	Bill Dickinson & Claude Maurice
Chicanery	KC34	26'9"	Sloop	Bill & Margo Burgess & Alex Harrison
Highlife	KC35	26'9"	Sloop	Dave Miller, John Ekels & Paul Coté
Lady Meg II	KC70	26'9"	Sloop	Jack & Megan Balmer
Rainbow	KC63	26'9"	Sloop	Bob & Suzanne Brodie
Solan	KC71	26'9"	Sloop	Ron Maitland
Solong	KC32	26'9"	Sloop	Tec & Jacqueline Jones
Signe	KC77	26'9"	Sloop	Lloyd & Arlene Walker
Unnamed	KC81	26'9"	Sloop	C. Van Winckel

STAR

Name	Sail No.	Length	Rig Type	Owners
April	4565	22'8"	Sloop	Vic Baker
Blackfish		22'8"	Sloop	Bruce Andrews
Cephei		22'8"	Sloop	R. N. P. Evans
Gypsy	4720	22'8"	Sloop	Ian & Ken Kirkland
Prudence		22'8"	Sloop	Dave Williams
Totem	2371	22'8"	Sloop	Barney Perry
Windor	913	22'8"	Sloop	Bill & Norma West
Unnamed	5505	22'8"	Sloop	Bruce & Gregory Cline

LIGHTNINGS

Name	Sail No.	Length	Rig Type	Owners
Atrain	6917	19'	Sloop	Fred McMeans
Blue J	8882	19'	Sloop	Ted & Mary Lou Jefferys
Hawk	3253	19'	Sloop	A. Sturgess
Joker	10522	19'	Sloop	J. C. Gilley
Let-It-Be	5146	19'	Sloop	W. P. Wallace
Martini	11645	19'	Sloop	M. Scriabin
Skua	8066	19'	Sloop	Dr. Bill Acheson

R.V.Y.C. SAILBOATS

Name	Sail No.	Length	Rig Type	Owners
FLYING DUTCHMEN				
Aries	KC56	20'	Sloop	Al Sturgess
Beta	KC72	20'	Sloop	Alan & Eric Drinkwater
Faszination		20'	Sloop	Doug & Jeanette Helmer
I.R.A.		20'	Sloop	Don & Louise Andrew
Qui Echappe		20'	Sloop	Hunt Gordon
Touche II	KC152	20'	Sloop	Bob & Anne Andrew
GEARY 18's				
Catchup	1114	18'	Sloop	Bill & Alan Cullen
Kelly		18'	Sloop	Kerry Mulhern
Little John	1197	18'	Sloop	Jack & Merelyn McAllister
Stella G	1324	18'	Sloop	Lawrence M. Hall
Tom Jones	913	18'	Sloop	T. B. Anderson
FLYING JUNIORS				
Anaham	1467	13'6"	Sloop	Mike Robinson
Casey Too	420	13'6"	Sloop	Leslie Rollins
Haida	1494	13'6"	Sloop	Chris Bernard
Havoc	417	13'6"	Sloop	Neil Iverson
Impunity	562	13'6"	Sloop	John & Kay Biller
John B	701	13'6"	Sloop	Peter Bull
Joker		13'6"	Sloop	Patrick Finnegan
Linus II	1488	13'6"	Sloop	Russell Jones
Miss Peach	702	13'6"	Sloop	Brad Reynolds
Pam	318	13'6"	Sloop	John Sloan
Pegassus	413	13'6"	Sloop	Gordon Main
Penny	561	13'6"	Sloop	Bob Ross
Sea Serfer	1570	13'6"	Sloop	Fred Long
Snark	KC1102	13'6"	Sloop	J. Swanson
Wee II	1691	13'6"	Sloop	Bill Kennedy
Wingding		13'6"	Sloop	T. Newmarch
Unnamed		13'6"	Sloop	Sean Donovan
Unnamed		13'6"	Sloop	James Miller
Unnamed		13'6"	Sloop	Colin Baker
Unnamed		13'6"	Sloop	Melanie Hartnell
Unnamed		13'6"	Sloop	Debby Evans
Unnamed		13'6"	Sloop	Bud Miller
Unnamed		13'6"	Sloop	Theo Anglin
Unnamed		13'6"	Sloop	John Yuill
Unnamed	1652	13'6"	Sloop	Roger Dower
Unnamed	KC1095	13'6"	Sloop	J. D. Little
Unnamed	KC230	13'6"	Sloop	T. Delaney
Unnamed	KC1585	13'6"	Sloop	P. D. Everett
O.K. DINGHIES				
Chip	KC36	13'2"	Cat	Robbie Black
Unnamed	KC22	13'2"	Cat	W. Horner
ENTERPRISE				
Ecliptic	E-12690	13'	Sloop	John & Diane Ross
Unnamed		13'	Sloop	G. Mann
MISCELLANEOUS				
High Jinks		11'		Dave Nairn
Nan		12'	D12	Bud Day
Sandpiper		14'	Sloop	P. Fahrni
Sea Wizard		12'		E. B. Hall
Sidewinder			Aquacat-Cat	Peter & Sheila Shuley
Ta'ria		12'	D12	Steve Rendell
Tine		15'	Snipe	Ken & Justine Dakin
Whisper		19'		Norman Collingwood
Unnamed		13'4"		Sean Donovan
Unnamed	KC162		Shark-Cat	W. Edwards
Unnamed		13'3"	Blue Jay	Mary-Clare Chapman
Unnamed	6467		Aquacat-Cat	E. Chisholm
Unnamed	KC5139		Fireball	Don Boyle
Unnamed		16' F'ball	Sloop	R. C. H. Davidson
Unnamed		16' F'ball	Sloop	S. Bayley
Unnamed		16' F'ball	Sloop	D. Purdy
Unnamed		16' F'ball	Sloop	D. Pettigrew

R.V.Y.C. SAILBOATS

Name	Sail No.	Length	Rig Type	Owners
FROSTBITERS				
Endless Winter	5	9'	Cat	David & Lynett Hendry and Vern Forster (Syndicate)
Unnamed	24	9'	Cat	Robert Burgess
Unnamed	111	9'	Cat	Hamish Davidson
Unnamed	½	9'	Cat	Bonar Davis
Unnamed	1	9'	Cat	Ralph Farris
Unnamed	17	9'	Cat	Alex Forsyth
Unnamed	143	9'	Cat	John Hutchinson
Unnamed	155	9'	Cat	F. R. Killam
Unnamed	11	9'	Cat	L. H. Killam
Unnamed	33	9'	Cat	Dr. Tec Jones
Unnamed		9'	Cat	Robert K. Lester
Unnamed	117	9'	Cat	Dr. J. A. McMillan
Unnamed	14	9'	Cat	Dr. M. M. McPherson
Unnamed	13	9'	Cat	Eric Marsden
Unnamed	101	9'	Cat	Phil Miller
Unnamed		9'	Cat	Sid Miller
Unnamed	22	9'	Cat	Len Murrell
Unnamed	102	9'	Cat	Gerry Palmer
Unnamed	36	9'	Cat	Keith Thomson
Unnamed	4	9'	Cat	Ches Rickard
Unnamed	15	9'	Cat	Lloyd H. Walker
SABOTS				
Mellow Yellow		8'	Cat	J. Watts
Nini		8'	Cat	Niels Anthonsen
Smartie Blue II		8'	Cat	W. A. Puckering
Tobias		8'	Cat	Mike Robinson
Toby		8'	Cat	S. Toy
Unnamed		8'	Cat	Kim Alfreds
Unnamed		8'	Cat	Harry Billingsley
Unnamed		8'	Cat	Greg Cline
Unnamed		8'	Cat	David Nairn
Unnamed		8'	Cat	J. Montague

Solings in English Bay — a Dale Lawrence photo

R.V.Y.C. POWER BOATS

Boat	Owners
Aia Kai	George Treit & Bruce Mathew
Alados	John & Beulah Swerdfeger
Ala Wai	Hal & Mary Alice Johnson
Alibi III	Roy & Marnie Summerfield
Anchorite	Clarke & Dorothy Gibson
Aquillon	A. O. Manson
Arfrene	Arthur Monahan
Arrow II	Jack & Toni White
Ballygally	Clarke & Pat Simpkins
Banook	Ed & Lorraine Bowser
Barbet	Howie & Ellenor Russell
Bardonilla	Wilson & Jesslyn Mackin
Beausoleil	Gerry & Hazel Thompson
Betsy Karen	Ray & Betsy Arnatt
Black Dolphin	Thornton & Bea Grenfell
Blink Bonnie	John & Evelyn Lock
Bonanza	Jack & Daphne Taylor
Breezin Thru	Gil & Joan Arnold
Brenda	Stu & Helen Gilmour
Brenhines IV	R. A. Osborne
Cadenza	John Steede
Caminante	Alex & Dorothy Healey
Campana	Max Bell
Canadian Fifer	Dr. J. M. Graham Ritchie
Cape D'Or	Russell & Larry Marshall
Capesterre	Sid & Muriel Rooney
Caprice	Bert & Thelma Cruise
Caramia	Sherman & Hedy Bardach
Carefree	Doug & Dorothy Welch
Caribbean	John & Renate Morgan
Caroma	Bob McGregor
Carpe Diem	Dick & Eleanor Malkin
Casa Mar	Karl Springer
Cavalaire	Hugh & Nancy Mann
Cazador	John Van Kleeck
Cee Aer	Bob Hall
Cha Cha III	Robert & Suzanne Brodie
Chunky Too	S. H. Wallace
Cleodoxa	Stan & Isobel Morton
Con Dios	John & Peggy Roseborough
Coral Seas	G. Lougheed
Corsair I	Ken & Frances Sulley
	and Penn & Mary Lou Taylor
Coryels	Harry & Vera Milne
Cover Girl	Tom & Phyllis Hethrington
Cox'n I	T. E. Ladner
Coya	John & Cecyl Simpson
Crystal Sea	Arthur & Helen Christopher
Cul de Sac	L. B. Culter
Dalarna	Harry & Pearl Gillespie
Dalkeith Doll	Fred Edy
Daphnia	J. G. Gould
De Anza III	Hubie Wallace
Deirdre II	Frank & Helen Emmons
Dione	Loring & Robin Foster
Dolphin Gal	R. L. DeProy
Donzi	Bill & Beth Wright
Dorado	J. M. Lecky
Dorlen	Len & Dorothy Sewell
Dream Along	Stanley & Ina Guile
Elanat	Vic & Joan MacLean
Eldorado II	Jack & Jean Overholt
Errant	Keith & Muriel Middleton
Escapada	Trevor & Margie Jordan-Knox
Evohn	Ken & Barbara Small
Fifer	Col. Clarence Wallace
Fleetwood	Bruce & Lois Buchanan
Flight	Ced. & Pat Dill
Flying Spray II	Jack & Stella Gillis
Four Bells	Lyall & Kay Bell
Framac	Tillie & Tucker Battle
Free Enterprise	C. H. Naphtali
Friendship	Finn & Osa Petersen
Fusilier	Fred & Lorna Clendenning
Gibson Gal	Bob & Barbara Gibson
Gillcrest	Jerry & Barbara Rendell
Gladsong II	Paddy & Gladys Morris
Gogama	A. Wm. Everett
Go Go Girl	Ronald & Gloria Young
Golden Hind II	Arthur & Sylvia Naylor
Graywing	Gordon & Joan Wheatley
Green Parrot	Hume & Jane McLennan

Boat	Owners
Griffin III	Beldon Stafford
Halcyon	C. Effinger
Hatteras	B. Shepard
Heatherbel	Dick & Isabel Scott
Henry VIII	Henry & Florence McLaren
Hermosillo	Al & Muriel Simpson
Her Nibs	Cliff & Win Walker
Hi Hopes	Pat & Mel Dahle
Hilary Elaine	George Percy
Ho Hum	William Rathie
Honey Bear	John & Naida Davidson
Honu	Robert Howe
Honu II	Jack & Betty Brown
Hotei	Tom & Doris Douglas
Humming Bird	Andrew Bernard
Idolours I	Maurice Hunt
Idolours II	Jack & Elsie Kovac
I'llaway	Spud & Jeanne Akhurst
Invader	W. Colquhoun
Jasmine	F. O. Whipple
John Antle II	Ralph & Olive Smith
Jucaro	Hugh & Margo Magee
Kalamalka	Syd & Blanche Bowman
Kanga	Dave & Sheila Rolfe
Kim	R. McCarthy
Kittiwake	Bruce & Janet Allan
Kona Kai	Ken & Bernice McRae
Kon-Tiki-Too	John & Mary Phillips
K'Shain	Dr. R. Hicks
Kyanna II	Bob & Audrey Pearson
La Beverie	Jim & Beverley O'Toole
La Donna	Don Johnston
Latin Lady II	John & Joan Belyea
Lazee Gal	J. R. Wilkinson
Leilani II	Dick & Doris Smith
Leprechaun	Tom & Marjorie McClelland
Little Jean	C. H. Corkum
Loafer	A. M. McGavin
Lytescary	Dick & Bea Lewell
Mai Tai	Edith Hackett
Makai	J. O'Brien
Malacandra	Howard & Shirley Bentall
Malampus	B. Curran
Malecite	Bill & Mary Orr
Marillyce	Hew & Marian Brooke
Mark III	Nick & Phillippa Carter
Marlyn IV	Lloyd Parker
Martlet II	Stanley & Myrna Terry
Merri-Lee II	Bruce Harris
Midnight	J. Ouellette
Minotaur	Charles & Ardy Schultz
Miss Emily	E. W. Disher
Miss Melody	Ken & Jean Davidson
Molly Brown	Ernie & Pat Anderson
Moon Winks II	Ted & Darlene Loftus
Mutineer	Alec & Kay Ellett
My Fair Lady II	Hugh & Rose Libby
My Panacea	Alan & Florence Anthony
Neo II	Kenneth Dinham
Nightcap	George & Elizabeth Cumpston
Nimba	Winslow & Betsy Bennett
Niska	Bud & Eileen Garrett
Noreanne	J. Erickson
Norsal	Earson & Dorothy Gibson
Ocean Belle	Bob & Molly Day
Ocean Ooasis	E. E. Arnold
Owaissa	Bob & Grace Orr
Omea	Ed and Mildred Dueck
Pacer	A. J. H. MacDonald
Pamper II	Louis P. Starck
Pamper III	Gunner & Pam Wilson
Pappy San	C. Woodward
Paramount II	Ritchie & Evelyn Nelson
Peppi II	Stan & Peggy King
Pike's Pick	Bill & Ruth Hamilton
Plad. a	Neil Thomson
Polanesia	Rick Hartnell
Prince	Andrew & Helen Robertson
Queen of the "C"	J. B. Costello
ReJoyce	Walter Walsh
Rhinegold	Colin & Patricia Ferrie
Rhodeo	Hugh Rhodes & Paul Delaney

R.V.Y.C. POWER BOATS

Boat	Owners	Boat	Owners
Rhonda L	David Jordan-Knox	Tahini	Wilfred & Ria Buttjes
Riot IV	Jean Runge	Takulli	Doan & Mary Hartnell
Rising Star	G. C. & Sue Murphy	Tangent	Brian McDermott
Robbie Burns	Jim & Isabelle Graham	T Boy Too	Don & Geraldine Cromie
Rockabye II	John & Liesel Maier	Teelee	Ham & Honey Smith
Roma	Fred & Ollie Stow	Tehani	Donald & Amy Baker
Rose Point	Fred & May Fearman	Tempest II	Bob & Adele Sanderson
Rus-Lor	Don & Lee Easton		and Brent & Pauline Brown
San-Dee-No	D. Hnatyszen	Thunderbird	Jack & Doreen Charles
Sandor II	Paul & Joan von Colditz	Tia Maria	Bob & Becky Fraser
Sandpiper V	Cliff & Patricia Billingsley	Tikh Hai	Gerald Hamilton
Sandra G. II	Jack & Nora Steede	Ti Mu	Ted & Betty Cruise
Saronia	Jack & Jean Halse	Tinker Toy	R. J. Cullen
Savory Seas	G. A. Christopher	Tiny Bubbles	W. Emerton
Saxony	Andrew & Joan Saxton	Tlee Ha	C. Elliott
Schatzi	J. Mawhinney	Tom's Folly	T. B. Read
Scimitar	Fred & Peggy Dalgarno	Tovarich	Jack & Elizabeth Gibbs
Sea Breeze	Bob & Dolly Day	Trimaran	L. A. Bates
Sea Home	Fred & Winnifred Warriner	Triton	Dexter & Joan Stockdill
Sea Lark	Doug & Bunty McPherson	Truant	Dana Delaplace
Sea Lure	Ron & Ann Proctor	Tsona	Jack & Shirley Williamson
Seamait	R. R. Maitland		and Dave & Nita Manning
Seaplay II	Robert & Christine Anderson	Tzinquaw	Bill & Joyce McLean
Seashaker	Ken Rooney	Ubique I	Claude & Sue Thicke
Sea Star	Harold & Margaret Gale	Ursa Minor	Emile & Ursula Badre
Seatex	W. H. Mitchell	Valiant V	Bob & Lyda Kerr
Sea Truck	John & Phyllis Dunn	Vandal	Les & Babe Simmers
Seaward	Ralph & Irene McGregor	Vitabella I	Len Boultbee
Senioriva	Frank & Emily Griffiths	Vitabella IV	George & Hesper Glanville
Shaman	Tom & Marjorie Bridge	Wahkeena	Jack & Alice Harrison
Simoon	M. J. Lucas	Wainani	Bill & Edith Hunter
Sky Lark	T. Meagher	Wakala	Gladys & John Murray
Smitty	Tom & Freda Trapp	Wanderer	Douglas & Jean Maitland
Sonora	Bob & Margaret Thatcher	Wardhaven	Bruce & Rae Ward
Spindrift V	Clark & Phyllis Bentall	Water Dancer	Ross & Velma Whiteside
Starquest IV	George & Lillian Fawcett	Wee Chapy	Hugh & Pat Chapman
Summertime	Angus & Joan Kenning	Wild One	Ronald Russell
Sundance	Geoffrey & Elizabeth Tullidge	Yoko Chan	David Nunn & Arnold Nunn
Surprise	P. C. de Beixedon	13K32676	Owen & Jean Wright
Swi-Ve-Lus	Ray & Mary Whittick	13K35900	Glen & Marjorie Olds
Taconite	Mrs. W. E. (Bertha) Boeing		

General Quarters! — all ahead main engine. — a Dale Lawrence photo

CHAPTER 44

The Eight Bells Club

ON CHRISTMAS EVE 1927 a group of businessmen associated with marine industries and members of the Royal Vancouver Yacht Club were gathered at the office of Dale & Company in the Pacific Building, Vancouver, exchanging good wishes and discussing amongst other things the high cost of living, when one of them, Capt. Charles Clarkson, of the Board of Marine Underwriters of San Francisco, made the remark that he was more concerned by the high cost of dying. He enlarged on the unreasonably high charges levied for undertaking services and proposed that a society be formed to perform the ceremony or act of committing the ashes of any deceased members to the sea.

The proposal caught on and prominent men on the waterfront were soon making inquiries, wishing to set up an organization to carry out the object outlined. Notable amongst these were E. R. (Jack) Cribb, Capt. B. L. Johnson, D.S.O., R.N., Lloyd's agent for B.C. and Mr. Sidney Smith, at that time one of our most outstanding marine lawyers (later Hon. Sidney Smith, Judge of the Supreme Court of B.C.), and the Harbour Master, Capt. A. H. Reed.

At a meeting called early in 1928, Mr. Sidney Smith was appointed Secretary and Capt. Reed appointed the Navigator to be in charge of all burials at sea. A bell was presented to the newly formed Eight Bells Club by Mr. William Howey of the B.C. Marine, reputed to be the ship's bell from the C.P.R. *Empress of Japan*, which had been previously scrapped and broken up in Vancouver Harbour. The purpose of this bell was that it be taken to the service with the time arranged that the committal would be as close to 4 p.m. as possible. At the end of the service eight bells were to be sounded to signify the End of the Watch, and later the deceased member's name engraved on the bell.

The first service conducted by the Eight Bells Club took place on English Bay off Point Atkinson in September, 1933, when the ashes of member William F. Beveridge were committed to the sea under the ceremonial rules laid down by the club.

The club only conducted six services in the following fifteen years, and on February 7th, 1947, a revised Constitution and By-Laws was adopted. Captain B. L. Johnson was elected President and H. F. Frederickson Secretary-Treasurer. (The club was incorporated under the Societies Act 1954.) Officers for the succeeding years have been

Year	Chairman	Secretary-Treasurer
1948	Capt. B. L. Johnson	H. F. Frederickson
1949	Capt. B. L. Johnson	H. F. Frederickson
1950	H. F. Frederickson	A. W. Nyblom
1951	H. F. Frederickson	A. W. Nyblom
1952	H. F. Frederickson	A. W. Nyblom
1953	H. F. Frederickson	A. W. Nyblom
1954	H. F. Frederickson	A. W. Nyblom
1955	H. F. Frederickson	A. W. Nyblom
1956	T. W. Ayres	C. J. Dill
1957	T. W. Ayres	C. J. Dill
1958	T. W. Ayres	E. D. Stone
1959	T. W. Ayres	E. D. Stone
1960	T. W. Ayres	E. D. Stone
1961	T. W. Ayres	E. D. Stone
1962	T. W. Ayres	E. D. Stone
1963	C. J. Dill	E. D. Stone
1964	C. J. Dill	E. D. Stone
1965	A. O. Scott	E. D. Stone
1966	A. O. Scott	E. D. Stone
1967	A. O. Scott	E. D. Stone
1968	E. D. Stone	J. S. Skinner
1969	T. F. (Bill) Orr	H. J. Bird
1970	Stan Morton	E. S. Earle
1971	Stan Morton	E. S. Earle

Names of the members for whom the service has been held and whose ashes have been committed to the sea and names engraved on the bell:

William F. Beveridge	Sept. 1933	E. A. Towns	May 1964
Bertram D. Phillips	Nov. 1934	R. E. Strain	May 1964
Ronald R. Maitland	April 1937	Harry Barratt	June 1965
Walter E. Graveley	Aug. 1939	Mrs. Harry Barratt	June 1965
Reginald W. Purves	Oct. 1941	G. G. Fleming	June 1965
H. F. Burton-Brooke	July 1945	T. H. Pakenham	June 1965
Ronald Kenvyn	April 1949	A. W. Nyblom	Aug. 1966
Rev. John Antle	Dec. 1949	Fred L. Townley	Nov. 1966
Alex Marshall	April 1950	Fred O. Mills	May 1967
Harry E. Wylie	Dec. 1951	S. Darnborough	June 1967
George Askew	Sept. 1954	W. S. Day	Aug. 1967
William A. Roedde	June 1955	Mrs. G. A. Cran	Oct. 1967
Harold A. Jones	Jan. 1957	J. Vans MacDonald	Nov. 1968
Mrs. E. Marsden	July 1957	Ron C. Runge	Mar. 1968
Dr. William J. Curry	July 1957	Mrs. C. J. Dill	Mar. 1968
H. St. C. Jellett	July 1957	Capt. B. L. Johnson	Nov. 1968
E. F. (Jack) Cribb	Sept. 1957	Mrs. E. D. Stone	Oct. 1969
George F. Gyles	April 1959	Mrs. B. L. Johnson	Mar. 1969
A. D. Lindsay	Oct. 1960	Temple H. Wright	Feb. 1970
R. R. Mackness	Oct. 1960	Miss Ruth M. Jones	May 1970
H. J. Barkes	Aug. 1961	Bertram R. Tupper	Nov. 1970
D. M. MacDonald	Aug. 1961	F. W. Urry	1971
Douglas P. Urry	Nov. 1961	Mrs. Eulalie Blygh	1971
Mrs. Anna E. Sprott	Nov. 1961	J. A. Longley	1971
		Mrs. Williamson	1971

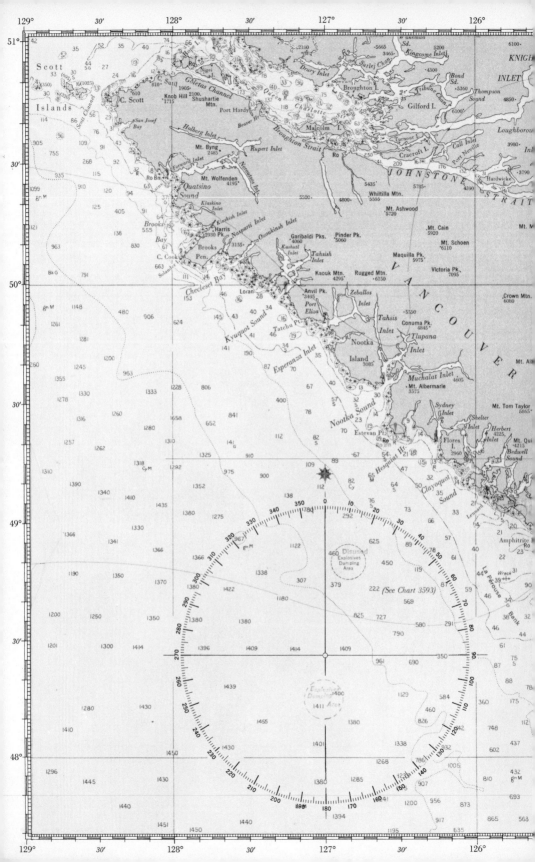